AF605999

The Leonardo Series

I am fully conscious that, not being a man of letters,
certain persons…may…blame me.
…They will say that I, having no literary skill,
cannot properly express that which I desire to treat of;
but they do not know that my subjects
are to be dealt with by experience rather than words;
and experience has been the mistress of those who wrote well.
And so as mistress, I will cite her in all cases.

R 10[1]

The Leonardo Series

Drawings by Anthony Panzera Based on Leonardo da Vinci's Work on Human Proportion

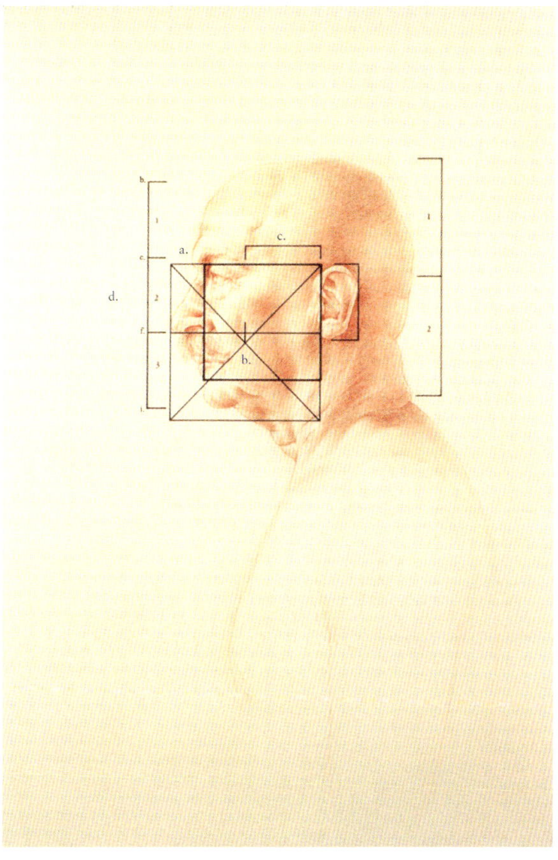

AP 103

Anthony Panzera

State University of New York Press, Albany

Published by State University of New York Press, Albany

Printed in the United States of America

For information, contact
State University of New York Press, Albany, NY
www.sunypress.edu

Production by Jenn Bennett
Marketing by Michael Campochiaro
Book Design by The Mardiney Group, Inc.

Library of Congress Cataloging-in-Publication Data
Panzera, Anthony, artist.
[Drawings. Selections]
The Leonardo series : drawings by Anthony Panzera based on Leonardo da Vinci's work on human proportion / Anthony Panzera.
pages cm
Includes bibliographical references.
ISBN 978-1-4384-5935-6 (hardcover : alk. paper)—ISBN 978-1-4384-5948-6 (e-book)
1. Panzera, Anthony—Themes, motives. 2. Nude in art. 3. Leonardo, da Vinci, 1452-1519—Notebooks, sketchbooks, etc.
I. Title.
NC139.P26A4 2015
741.973—dc23
2015009172

10 9 8 7 6 5 4 3 2 1

IN MEMENTO MORI

The water you touch in a river is the last of that which has passed,
and the first of that which is coming.
Thus it is with time present. Life, if well spent, is long.

R 1174[2]

Mr. Patrick Hamilton
(*An English artist in Florence*)
28 October 1923–8 January 2008

and

Mr. John Harbster
(*A New York model*)
25 April 1922–22 February 2008

Those who take for their standard any one but nature
—the mistress of all masters—
weary themselves in vain.

R 660[3]

To my wife, Marie I. Panzera

CONTENTS

In the Gabinetto dei Disegni e delle Stampe degli Uffizi in Florence there is a beautiful little pen-and-ink drawing in two values of brown, measuring about 7½ x 10½ inches (195 x 286 mm), entitled *Landscape of the Arno River and Valley.* In the catalogue for the 2003 exhibition, *Leonardo da Vinci, Master Draftsman,* at the Metropolitan Museum of Art, Carmen Bambach points out, "Unlike most Italian Renaissance artists, Leonardo inscribed a number of his notebooks and drawings with dates and reminders of places and purposes."[4] He continued this practice throughout his life.

This drawing, done when Leonardo was only twenty-one years old, contains the earliest known recorded date in Leonardo's drawings:

The day of Santa Maria della Neve,
5 August 1473

R 1369[5]

ACKNOWLEDGMENTS

As an artist I have always been somewhat envious of writers who are afforded the opportunity to thank those who contributed to their efforts. We painters and sculptors normally execute our works, sign them, sell them, or put them aside to begin a new project. In this case, however, having completed the drawings and accompanying text which comprise *The Leonardo Series,* and having the good fortune to exhibit and publish that effort, I can now publically thank the many people who helped in the realization of the project.

First and foremost, there were more than twenty professional male models, over a period of more than thirty years, who spent long hours, often in awkward and uncomfortable positions, posing for the drawings in this project. To these men, I offer my sincere gratitude.

Although I had exhibited parts of the Leonardo Series as the project evolved, it was at the Samuel Dorsky Museum at SUNY New Paltz where the completed project finally came together. To Sara Pasti, Director of the Dorsky Museum, and her brilliant staff, for their enthusiastic response to the project, I offer my sincere thanks. I also wish to thank David Lavallee, friend and former Provost at SUNY New Paltz, and the former Dean of the School of Fine and Performing Arts Mary Hafeli, for their support and encouragement. To James Peltz, co-director of SUNY Press, and Sara Pasti for suggesting and shepherding the publication of this catalogue, I offer sincere thanks. To Domenico Laurenza, a true Leonardo scholar, who generously shared his research on Leonardo and graciously agreed to write the preface for the book, I am deeply grateful. To Anne Barthel, my enthusiastic book editor, who envisioned a beautiful publication from the start, and to Megan Mardiney and Kerwin Adduru of the Mardiney Group who designed it, I offer sincere gratitude.

There are many others to thank as well, including my friend and fellow artist, Ephraim Rubenstein, who was a staunch supporter from the beginning, and many friends and colleagues at Hunter College, including former Hunter Art Department Chair Sanford Wurmfeld, Richard Stapleford, Gabrielle Evertz, Robert Huot, Mary Moore, Susan Crile, and Jeff Mongrain, who were supportive and encouraging in many ways. Other friends outside the Hunter family to whom I am indebted for their help and suggestions include William Barcham and Catherine Pugliesi, Lawrence Stryker, Larry Mach, and Gitte Thune-Andersen.

One of the most gratifying experiences during the research process was visiting some of the institutions where Leonardo's Notebooks are housed. My experience at the Royal Library at Windsor Castle, where a majority of Leonardo's work on human proportion is held in the Queen's Collection, was facilitated by Rhia Wong, assistant to Jean Cozens. In Venice, Dottoressa Anna Liza Perissa provided access to the Leonardo drawings at the Accademia including the iconic *Vitruvian Man.* To both of these institutions, and to their courteous, professional curators, I am grateful.

The staffs at the libraries I consulted are also among the most professional and helpful I have ever encountered. I thank the staffs at the Hunter College Library; the Watson Library and the Robert Lehman Collection Library, both at the Metropolitan Museum of Art; the British Library in London; the Frick Collection Library in New York, and the Morris County Library in New Jersey for their assistance.

In the early stages of the project several of my former students helped in many ways. I offer particular thanks to Renee-Laure Moniot and Thomas Tacik for helping to gather information, to Elizabeth Lattanzio and Nina Stojkovic for their magical computer skills, and to Ettore DiSebastiani for occasional Italian translations.

Lastly, I thank my family for their encouragement throughout the project, particularly my daughter Lisa Panzera for her advice and counsel, her husband George Cochrane for his enthusiastic support, and his father Douglas Cochrane for a 1938 edition of Edward MacCurdy's two-volume set on Leonardo's Notebooks, and my son Guido and his wife Joanna Panzera for their much needed legal counsel and moral support. To all of them I am profoundly appreciative, including our beautiful and brilliant granddaughter Fiamma, who is unaware of the inspiration she provides for all of us to do things better and to reach a little higher. Finally, thanks to my wife Marie, who bravely came away with me to Florence in 1975, with two young children in tow, where the seeds of this project were sown, who is the source of stability and continuity in our lives, and is the mother of all editors; it is to her this book is dedicated.

Professor Anthony Panzera
Hunter College, CUNY
August 2014

DIRECTOR'S FOREWORD

I am both pleased and honored to provide an introduction to this publication by artist Anthony Panzera.

My acquaintance with the artist's work began in 2009 when I first became the Director of the Samuel Dorsky Museum of Art at the State University of New York at New Paltz. I knew that Anthony's work would be of great interest to the college—particularly the college's art and art majors—so Anthony, working with the museum's staff, developed an exhibition of his work.

The exhibition *The Leonardo Series: Drawings by Anthony Panzera Based on the Work of Leonardo da Vinci* was on view at the Samuel Dorsky Museum from January 18 to April 15, 2012. The exhibition featured 65 of Anthony's drawings illustrating the relative proportions of the head, torso, whole body, leg and foot, and arm and hand. These drawings, created between the mid-1980s and 2010, contemporized and exemplified the humanistic orientation and intellectual concerns found in the Notebooks of Leonardo da Vinci.

Within the exhibition, a wall panel entitled *Notes to the Viewer* provided an introduction and guide to the works on display. A separate wall panel entitled *Leonardo da Vinci and the Human Body* provided an art historical context for the groundbreaking work accomplished by Leonardo da Vinci. Computers located in the gallery allowed viewers to see several images of the original text and figure drawings from Leonardo's Notebooks.

I am grateful to Anthony Panzera for sharing his drawings with us in both the exhibition at the Dorsky and in this publication. The artist's extensive research and his passion for the human figure have created a body of work that inspires all of us who love the art of the great Leonardo da Vinci.

Sara J. Pasti, The Neil C. Trager Director
The Samuel Dorsky Museum of Art

Why does the eye see a thing more clearly in dreams than with the imagination awake?

R 1144[6]

PREFACE

The Leonardo or Renaissance scholar who examines this work by Anthony Panzera will, no doubt, be as impressed as I am, first of all, by the realism of the drawings, a realism that is obviously different from that of the world of Leonardo and his Renaissance contemporaries; it is, instead, a realism with a contemporary style unique to Panzera, who is an artist and professor of art, and in the realization of this of volume, a Leonardo scholar.

The uniqueness of this work is the manner in which Panzera interweaves its three aspects: his study of Leonardo's notes and drawings on human proportion, his analysis of the information so it is relevant to other artists and scholars, and, for the same purpose, his creation of original illustrations from his artistic point of view. Obviously, these three facets are closely interrelated since the drawings from life of the male nudes in Panzera's contemporary realistic style are conceived to study Leonardo's work on human proportion with the purpose of clarifying the content.

Leonardo's studies devoted to the proportions of the human body were based on empirical investigations directly observed on the bodies of young men, mature men, and older men. The drawings of the human body in which he collected these surveys, however, are subjective drawings of generic human male "types" rather than of specific individual "types" which concisely express, at best, a particular proportional canon of the adolescent, more mature, or older man. Instead, the drawings used by Panzera to verify and demonstrate the proportional theories of Leonardo portray specific individuals with a realism that intentionally enhances their unique features. So, for example, instead of the adolescent or youthful generic "type" drawn by Leonardo on a sheet of Manuscript A (63r), Panzera draws the face of a specific youth with thick hair (AP 105); instead of Leonardo's mature "type" in Leonardo's sheet V. (Inv. 236r), Panzera draws a portrait of an individual who is bald and has a prominent mustache (AP 103).

Scrolling through the studies in the volume, we recognize, one by one, the real models portrayed by Panzera with a style that embodies, in an original and unique way, what is, in my view, the most typical trait of modern and contemporary American art in most of its forms: realism, concreteness. It is precisely through this "artistic" divergence that Panzera approaches his study of Leonardo in his precise attempt to check on the proportional canons fixed by Leonardo; a checking that, case by case, highlights errors or confirms the rules set forth by the Renaissance master, but that, in any case, evokes the empirical study of real bodies that was Leonardo's starting point.

Above these hyper-realistic drawings of real and particular nudes, Panzera has superimposed geometric grids representing the proportional relationships indicated by Leonardo in his drawings and/or written notes. These are not the passive reproduction of Leonardo's grids, but a complex processing of them with a strong didactic purpose: their clarification. In this manner, it goes from the simplification of Leonardo's proportional schematic, which makes it more immediately understood as, for example, in the case of the so-called *Vitruvian Man* (AP 149) to the splitting of Leonardo's original drawings in more complex cases. In the latter case, proportional modules that Leonardo includes in one drawing are split, and if, for example, the original drawing represents a single head, Panzera's reconstruction may have two or three heads, or, in one case (AP 188), four arms connected to the same torso to highlight that number of proportional relationships. Panzera's drawings, while different from Leonardo's, are at the same time based on a method used by Leonardo himself, not only in the *Vitruvian Man* (where four arms and four legs, in various positions, appear in relation to the same body), but also in other studies on the proportions and kinematics of the human body, now lost; however, we are given an idea of them in the late sixteenth-century studies in the Codex Huygens (Morgan Library, New York), studies strongly influenced by Leonardo and, in some cases, based on his original drawings. This "splitting" of vision developed by Panzera, however, starting from a Leonardesque cue, gives the human figure a dynamic aspect, which is shared by another technique used by Panzera, namely, the use of particular and often complex poses in which the nudes illustrate the proportional observations established by Leonardo between different parts of the body (AP 173).

Yet another intervention employed by Panzera is that of real visual reconstruction in relation to concepts expressed by Leonardo only in written notes, relating, for example, to the study of the sturdy male type (AP 147) to that of the emaciated type (AP 148), to the relationship between the height of a three-year-old boy and a fully grown man (AP 151), to the ratio of 1:9 between a body standing and one supine (AP 154). In each of these cases, Panzera freely portrays nudes which evoke Leonardo's concept. It is surprising, and worth mentioning, to find the hyper-realism of the nude in the supine position, cited above, portrayed in a severe foreshortened view, evoking the perspective style of Andrea Mantegna, another great Italian Renaissance painter.

Executed in sanguine pencil, which emulates the red chalk often used by Leonardo after 1500 to portray the human body, Anthony Panzera's "Leonardo Series" provides artists interested in the accurate representation of the human body and Leonardo scholars an unusual form of study, and above all, a reconstruction based on the realistic side of Leonardo's anthropometric work, which certainly will generate further development by other scholars and artists.

Dr. Domenico Laurenza
Museo Galileo-Institute and Museum for the History of Science
Florence, Italy

Notes
Front Matter

[1] J. P. Richter, *The Literary Works of Leonardo da Vinci*, 3rd ed., 2 vols. (New York: Phaidon, 1970), vol. I, R 10, 116.

[2] Richter, *The Literary Works of Leonardo da Vinci*, vol. II, R 1174, 244.

[3] Richter, *The Literary Works of Leonardo da Vinci*, vol I, R 660, 372.

[4] Carmen Bambach, ed., *Leonardo da Vinci, Master Draftsman*, Exhibition Catalogue, Metropolitan Museum of Art (New Haven and London: Yale University Press, 2003), 6.

[5] Richter, *The Literary Works of Leonardo da Vinci*, vol. II, R 1369, 343. "The day of Santa Maria della Neve [Saint Mary of the Snow], August the 2nd 1473," appears in all three of the Richter editions. The date has since been revised to 5 August 1473; see Carlo Pedretti in his *Commentaries*, page 314, and Carmen Bambach in the Exhibition Catalogue, *Leonardo Da Vinci Master Draftsman*, page 6. They, among other scholars, cite it as Leonardo's earliest known dated work.

[6] Richter, *The Literary Works of Leonardo da Vinci*, vol. II, R 1144, 238.

PART ONE
INTRODUCTION

On the 2nd of April 1489, [there is to be a] book entitled "Of the human figure."

R 1370[7]

CHAPTER ONE
A SHORT HISTORY OF THE PROJECT

At the beginning of every semester, at the first meeting of my Advanced Drawing class at Hunter College, I read from a selection of writings by artists and about artists, which are intended to convince students of the importance of drawing. One of my favorite stories for the class was about Leonardo da Vinci and his legacy. Drawing on the remarks of two Leonardo scholars, I explained to the class that if you add up all the known major works by Leonardo there a few dozen that can definitely be attributed to his hand, and if you add in the "school of" it amounts to no more than about twice that many. And of those works, his three most ambitious and important ones, his *capo lavori,* two have been destroyed leaving no trace of them at all, and the third can barely be seen.

The first, his *Battle of Anghiari,* an enormous fresco planned for the walls of the Sala dei Cinquecento of the Palazzo Vecchio in Florence, was left unfinished and eventually painted over by Vasari. His second, the famous gigantic equestrian statue planned for Lodovico Sforza, made it only to the plaster stage; it was abandoned when the French overran Milan, ousted the Sforzas, and used the horse for bow-and-arrow target practice. The last, his most famous *Last Supper,* which began to flake off the wall (due to his experimental methods) within fifty years of its completion, has suffered from repeated restorations and is now, after years of careful rehabilitation, still only barely visible.

Fortunately, what does survive are an enormous number of his drawings and his notebook pages. As Edward MacCurdy, author of *The Notebooks of Leonardo da Vinci,* puts it, "How he disposed of his time would be a complete enigma but for the existence of the vast collection of drawings, and particularly of the notebooks."[8] MacCurdy goes on to say in his 1938 edition that there are countless drawings and more than five thousand notebook pages. That number has since been revised and, with the discovery of two additional notebooks found in Madrid in 1967, is now slightly more than seven thousand pages.

How I became personally engrossed in the Notebooks is another story. During the past forty years I have worked with the human figure as the center of my artistic expression. Because of this, I have long been fascinated with and have held as my heroes the great Renaissance Masters of drawing. The issue of human proportion and an understanding of anatomy is essential to drawing the human figure convincingly and accurately (in essence, *getting it right*); this has been of paramount concern for all artists since the ancient Greeks, as it has been for me as both artist and instructor of figure drawing. Over the centuries, many treatises, formulas, and guides on the subject have been written by countless artists, none more thoroughly and completely than by Leonardo da Vinci.

In 1975 while living in Florence, Italy, I saw for the first time original pages referring to human proportion from Leonardo's Notebooks. Until then, I had seen Leonardo's works only in reproduction, but seeing them firsthand and up close—a few as finished drawings, most as tiny but beautiful pen-and-ink sketches—profoundly impressed me. It led me to begin a critical study of the master's work, in particular his observations on human proportion. Though ultimately rewarding, this was a daunting exercise as his observations, scattered throughout the pages of his Notebooks, are in no particular order; some are simply scribbled notations in Leonardo's hand squeezed in among various other notes of unrelated material. (Please see Part IV for a complete listing of all the Notebooks, and see Appendix III for a listing of Notebooks and pages that contain Leonardo's observations on human proportion.)

My initial purpose in the project was to understand Leonardo's theories of proportion and to discover if there was any order to them. I soon discovered that there was no order and reading the theory was not enough; I had to test the theory by carefully analyzing Leonardo's drawing while at the same time deciphering the text. There were times when even this proved insufficient, because many of the drawings were tiny thumbnail sketches, and there were even times when there was no drawing at all. For instance, the entry AP 146 comes from just such a page. It is found in the large bound volume known as the Codex Atlanticus, made up of 401 folios. On this page Leonardo discusses perspective and light and shadow, both with illustrations, and at the very top of the page, above these entries, he sets forth a rather complex procedure for establishing his theory of a well-proportioned, "most graceful" man, but with no illustration.

This led me finally to an empirical approach much like the one Leonardo used when he created the famous *Vitruvian Man* drawing (see chapter 10 for a more thorough explanation). I began by collecting individual Leonardo notes on human proportion and creating my own drawing of a model. Then I tested the theory by marking out the units of measurement on the drawing of the model, using the same module Leonardo did, to verify their accuracy and effectiveness.

What began as a number of isolated drawings gradually evolved into a decades- long project culminating in the Leonardo Series, a total conceptualization of sixty-five finished drawings based on Leonardo's thoughts and accompanied by my analysis of them. Each drawing in the Leonardo Series is done in sanguine pencil on buff paper, and each is carefully and accurately drawn and measured from life. Over each drawing is a graphic breakdown illustrating Leonardo's particular observation. These vary greatly, from significant to small and specific. For example, he describes the full-length proportion of a mature man as measuring eight heads and elsewhere makes the minor observation that *"the space between the extreme poles inside and outside the foot, called the ancle [ankle] or ancle [ankle] bone a b is equal to the space between the mouth and the corner of the eye."*[9] Leonardo's statements about each observation, followed by my analysis (Was he right? Does it work?), accompany each drawing.

In most cases, the theory works perfectly; in a few others, the measurements, taken directly from the model, do not agree with Leonardo's measurements. The reasons for these differences are varied and difficult to explain. Where I could find an explanation, such as confusion in translation, I have discussed it in my own notes on the drawing, and where there is no evident explanation, I have left it to the reader to decide. All of the drawings were done from life and all of the drawings are of men, using more than a dozen models. In this, I have followed Leonardo's lead, as all of his Notebook entries, with or without drawings, refer, with very few exceptions, to the male proportions, as opposed to the proportions of women. It was certainly not an uncommon view during the Renaissance to believe that "man was the measure of all things." Leonardo was simply following tradition, a tradition one finds clearly stated in Cennino Cennini's advice to the artist: "Take note that, before going any farther, I will give you the exact proportions of a man. Those of a woman I will disregard, for she does not have any set proportions."[10]

Leonardo, who clearly intended to organize his work on human proportion, wrote in 1513: *"And in this treatise, each in its own place, all their peculiarities will be explained—and particularly as to the spaces between the joints of each limb, &."*[11] But he never did get to fulfill his promise to organize his observations. While texts on Leonardo are in no short supply, only a few scholars, such as Jean Paul Richter, Edward MacCurdy, Martin Kemp, and Carlo Pedretti, have attempted the Herculean task of translating and organizing the information by topic. Neither the translating nor the organizing was an easy undertaking. Leonardo wrote in his trademark "mirror writing" from right to left with the letters backward. This was a function of Leonardo being left-handed: he adopted a convenient method for himself of reversing his letters and his writing from right to left. Indeed, he was known during his life as *mancino* (Italian slang for "lefty" or "southpaw"), and G. P. Lomazzo, in his *Trattato,* refers to Leonardo's *Paragone* as being written entirely with the "tired," or lazy, hand (*"egli scrisse di mano stanca"*).[12] This meant that the translator had to turn the page upside down in order to read from the top of the page to the bottom, and to place a mirror along the top edge of the line being read. The mirror reverses the letters, as well as the words, allowing the reader to read from left to right. We can appreciate that translating his notes was quite a feat, not only because of the reversed letters and reversed direction of writing, but because of his unique script and his shorthand spelling. Organizing by topic was equally difficult because the information was spread out in many different manuscripts. My task, as I saw it, was to take Leonardo's work on human proportion and organize it by the individual parts of the body, and to take it one step further by testing his ideas as practical tools for artists and students, myself included.

What profoundly impressed me, at the end of it all, was what I believe to be the key to Leonardo's theory on proportion, which he learns, in part, from Vitruvius. His focus begins with the relationship of the smallest of the parts to a larger part of the body, and then the relationship of the larger part to the whole. For example, Leonardo says that *"4 fingers make 1 palm, and 4 palms make 1 foot, and 6 palms make 1 cubit,"*[13] as examples of smaller parts making up a larger part. He then uses a larger part to form four basic systems, or canons, to define the proportions of the whole man, as in the 4-cubit man, the 6-foot man, the 8-head, and the 10-face (sometimes 9-face) man. What Leonardo provides is a system of measuring human proportions that is both accurate and flexible. The entire concept of his theories is made manifest in Leonardo's drawing the *Vitruvian Man* (see chapter 10 and AP 149).

In an attempt to bring greater clarity and understanding to Leonardo's information, I have organized his conclusions in a systematic manner by: 1) accumulating all of his notes on human proportion, 2) dividing them into specific anatomical groupings, 3) creating a drawing for each significant entry, and 4) devising a new catalogue numbering system to identify the notation with its original source in his Notebooks. Hopefully, it will provide a small window into the world of Leonardo's genius and stature as one of the greatest artists and thinkers of all time.

Some years after I began the Leonardo Series, as I was researching in the process of expanding the project into a book, I found the following quotation by Martin Kemp in his anthology of Leonardo's writings:

> The idea for the present anthology came from observing the difficulties of students and general readers who wanted to read Leonardo's own thoughts on art but found that the existing anthologies did not present a coherent expression of his views. It remains surprising that no one had previously attempted to edit Leonardo's notes on painting into a systematic treatise, which, if not the work that he himself would have produced, would at least be recognizable to him and would respect his intentions.[14]

This, it turns out, is exactly what I hope I have done with his work on proportion.

CHAPTER TWO
NOTES ON USING THE BOOK

The information on human proportion is scattered throughout Leonardo's Notebooks among many pages, some dealing with a variety of subjects, such as Science, Nature, Anatomy, Engineering, Philosophy, and Advice to Artists, to name just a few. The vast body of Notebooks and individual pages is spread throughout more than a dozen cities in Europe and America, and a number of Leonardo scholars have put their hands to translating and organizing the information in those Notebooks. Of those scholars, Jean Paul Richter has provided the most thorough and comprehensive survey of Leonardo's work, and his 1883 two-volume set, *The Literary Works of Leonardo da Vinci,* was at the time, and still is, the most often referred to and respected translation to date. Therefore, I have, for the most part, deferred to Richter's translation throughout *The Leonardo Series,* to the exclusion of other scholars. Occasionally, I have added comments to Richter's translations and referred to other scholars' comments or back to the original Italian, but only where I felt the addition altered Leonardo's meaning or the proof of a theory.

In addition, as the Notebooks have been bought and sold and offered as gifts over and over again, with each new collector's personal catalogue and page numbers attached to the sheet or Notebook, tracking their provenance is difficult. Complicating the issue further are the individual reference numbers given by each of the scholars and experts writing about the Notebooks. This presents an unusual problem, and it required me to add to the confusion by creating my own system of reference numbers.

Focusing on those entries in the Notebooks dealing exclusively with human proportions, I had to create a catalogue system to identify each of my drawings as well as the source and location of the original manuscript pages. Leonardo intended his notes on proportion to be part of a planned book, a painter's guide, as it were, the *Tratatto della Pittura.* (For further information on the *Tratatto,* see chapter 11.) Some of the entries on proportion have drawings to illustrate the text, while others are found without illustration, in the middle of a page having nothing to do with proportion. To catalogue the information and bring order to it, I have separated the entries by the portion of the body they treat. In many cases I have had to divide pages, paragraphs, or even sentences where it seemed appropriate, and in other cases I have added an entry from one source to an entry from another source, sometimes with years separating them. There is some repetition, and for this I refer the reader to the Leonardo quotation at the beginning of Part II, the main section of the book.

My drawings are divided into five groups, all beginning with the catalogue designation AP, for Anthony Panzera. At the head of each entry is an information bar containing the following information:

A. Inventory, Collection, Location	B. AP number
C. Date	D. R number
E. Folio number	

A. The inventory number is the registration number for each drawing or page. These numbers are specific to each institution and were designated at the time the sheet entered the specific collection. The letter following the inventory numbers refer to the side of the sheet, r for recto, sometimes a (front), and v for verso, sometimes b (back).

B. The AP numbers in the upper right-hand corner are divided into five groups of twenty. Twenty spaces were designated for drawings in each section, but no group has all twenty spaces used. The groups are as follows: the head, AP 101–120; the torso and hips, AP 121–140; the whole body, AP 141–160; the leg and the foot, AP 161–180; and the arm and the hand, AP 181–200.

C. Is the approximate date of the page, drawing, or Notebook, except when Leonardo includes a date.

D. The R number designation refers to the catalogue number of Jean Paul Richter. Mr. Richter edited and grouped by subject area almost all of the Notebooks and loose sheets known at the time and translated them from the Italian into English. This massive undertaking was first printed in 1883 and went through three subsequent editions.

E. The folio number designations refer only to the Queen's Collection at Windsor Castle.[15] These folios were collected together and printed as a special bound set of six volumes known as the *Quaderni d'Anatomia*.

All information in italics and the color brown is quoted from Leonardo's text.

All letters and numbers printed in blue are my designations for keying the Leonardo text to the AP drawing. These were added wherever it became necessary to locate the theory on my drawing, especially if the drawing includes more than one theory from different Leonardo texts.

All other numbers and letters, in black, come directly from Leonardo and are found either on his drawings or in his text. In some cases they may have been left out of Richter's translation.

The paragraph following the Leonardo text contains my notes describing the drawing or page where the quote is located. Immediately following is my explanation and analysis of the theories.

What follows is a sample page:

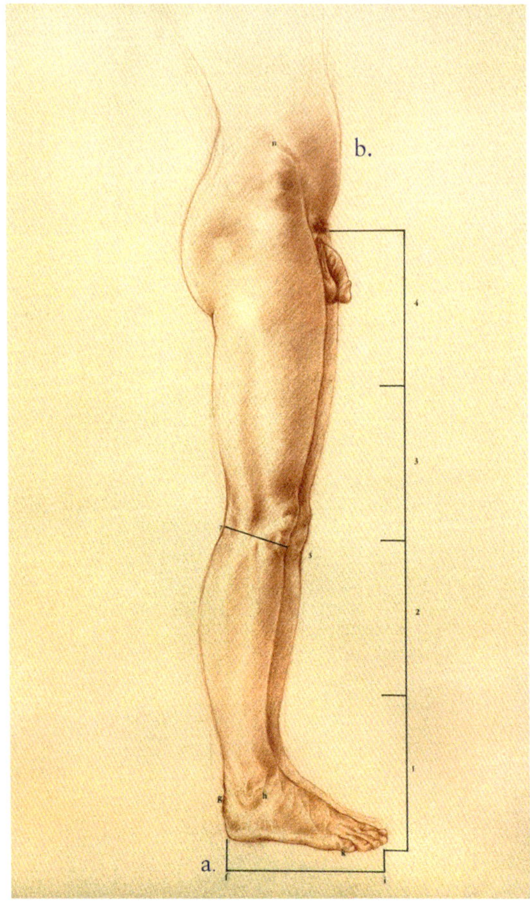

W. 19136–19139b, Royal Library, Windsor — AP 175
c.1490 — R 328
Folio 11 Verso X

a. e [i] f is 4 times in the distance between the genitals and the sole of the foot;

b. 3 7 is 6 times from 3 to 2 and is equal to g h and i k.

This entry, Verso X, comes from the famously informative Windsor sheet folded in four (Plate 29). It is written in the very bottom of the page in the lower left quarter. The text uses the illustration drawn for the text at Verso VIII and treated in AP 166. There are some minor variations. Leonardo obviously wrote *e* when he meant *i*, for there is no *e* on his drawing.

a. i f, the length of the foot in profile, goes four times into the distance from the genitals to the foot perfectly.

b. 3 7, the width of the leg from the knee in front to the back of the leg goes six times from 3 to 2. The enigma here is that there is no 2 on this drawing, as Richter points out when he says in a footnote, "which renders the passage obscure." However, there is the letter n at the top of the pelvis at the iliac crest, and if we measure with Leonardo's module, 3 7, we find it enters exactly six times from 3 to n. As in the case above, where Leonardo wrote *e* instead of *i*, it's a good bet he meant *n* instead of 2. Unfortunately, when we test this idea on Leonardo's drawing, the module 3 7, the width of the leg at the knee, measures only five times into the distance from 3 to n, instead of six times as it does in my drawing.

As for the comparison of similarity of size with the module 3 7, the width of the knee in profile, to g h, the heel of the foot to the front edge of the malleolus of the fibula, and i k, the width of the toes, they do not work at all either in Leonardo's drawing or in mine.

PART TWO

THE LEONARDO SERIES: SIXTY-FIVE DRAWINGS

Begun at Florence, in the house of Piero di Braccio
Martelli, on the 22nd day of March 1508.
And this is to be a collection without order,
taken from many papers
which I have copied here, hoping to arrange them
later each in its place,
according to the subjects of which they may treat.

R 4a[16]

Notes
Part One. Introduction

[7] Richter, *The Literary Works of Leonardo da Vinci*, vol. II, R 1370, 343.

[8] Edward MacCurdy, *The Notebooks of Leonardo da Vinci*, 2 vols. (New York: Reynal and Hitchcock, 1938), 15. The issues addressed here are discussed in the prefaces of the books by both Edward MacCurdy and Jean Paul Richter.

[9] Richter, *The Literary Works of Leonardo da Vinci*, vol. I, R 324, 250.

[10] Cennino Cennini, *The Craftsman's Handbook 'Il Libro dell'Arte,'* trans. Daniel V. Thompson, Jr. (New York: Dover Publications, 1960), 48. There are two instances in the Notebooks where Leonardo refers to the representation of women: "Then describe the fully grown man and woman, with their proportions, and the nature of their complexions, colour, and physiognomy" (R 797) and "Women must be represented in modest attitudes their legs close together, their arms folded, their heads inclined somewhat to one side" (R 583).

[11] Richter, *The Literary Works of Leonardo da Vinci*, vol. I, R 363, 261–262.

[12] Carmen Bambach, ed., *Leonardo da Vinci, Master Draftsman*, 31–32.

[13] Richter, *The Literary Works of Leonardo da Vinci*, vol. I, R 343, 253.

[14] Martin Kemp, *Leonardo on Painting*, trans. Martin Kemp and Margaret Walker (New Haven: Yale University Press, 1989), vii.

[15] Leonardo da Vinci, *Quaderni d'Anatomia*, Twenty-three sheets from the Royal Library at Windsor Castle, compiled by Ove C. L. Vangensten, A. Fonahn, and H. Hopstock, vol. VI (Cristiania: Casa Editrice Jacob Dybwad, 1916).

Notes
Part Two. The Leonardo Series: Sixty-Five Drawings

[16] Richter, *The Literary Works of Leonardo da Vinci*, vol. I, R 4a, 112. It is clear from Leonardo's statement that he started his Notebooks many years before this date, 1508 (the earliest Notebooks date from 1478), and was musing, once again, on how he should bring order to his many subjects.

THE LEONARDO SERIES: SIXTY-FIVE DRAWINGS

THE CATALOGUE (AP) NUMBERS

The catalogue numbers in this publication sequentially follow the AP numbers allotted to the drawings. The AP numbers are divided into five groups of drawings devoted to the five body parts: Proportions of the Head: AP 101–120; Torso: 121–140; Whole Body: 141–160; Leg and Foot: 161–180; Arm and Hand: 181–200. Twenty AP numbers were allotted to each group; not all were used.

All sixty-five of the drawings in the Leonardo Series were completed from the 1980s to 2010. All were executed with the same materials:

- Sanguine pencil on Rives buff paper
- Mylar overlay with ruled India ink lines
- Black and blue Lettraset Press Type

All AP drawing dimensions are frame sizes height followed by width in inches.

Proportions of the Head

Cat. 1. (AP 101) Proportions of Profile Head Using the Rule of Three—27 x 21 inches

Cat. 2. (AP 102) Proportions of Frontal Head—27 x 21 inches

Cat. 3. (AP 103) Proportions of Profile Head—27 x 21 inches

Cat. 4. (AP 104) Proportions of Frontal Face Using the Eyes—27 x 21 inches

Cat. 5. (AP 105) Proportions of Profile and Frontal Face—21 x 27 inches

Cat. 6. (AP 106) Proportions of Profile Face and Torso—21 x 27 inches

Cat. 7. (AP 107) Comparative Measurements of Profile Head—27 x 21 inches

Cat. 8. (AP 108) Comparative Measurements of Profile Face and Whole Body—27 x 21 inches

Cat. 9. (AP 109) Comparative Measurements of Frontal Face—27 x 21 inches

Cat. 10. (AP 110) Proportions of Profile Head—27 x 21 inches

Cat. 11. (AP 111) Proportions of Two Profile Heads—21 x 27 inches

Cat. 12. (AP 112) Proportions of Two Profile Heads—21 x 27 inches

Cat. 13. (AP 113) Proportions of Profile Head and Foot—21 x 27 inches

Cat. 14. (AP 114) Relative Movements of Head—27 x 21 inches

Cat. 15. (AP 115) Proportions of Profile Head—27 x 21 inches

Cat. 16. (AP 116) Proportions of Nose—21 x 27 inches

Proportions of the Torso

Cat. 17. (AP 121) Proportions of Torso—27 x 21 inches

Cat. 18. (AP 122) Proportions of Torso and Hips—27 x 21 inches

Cat. 19. (AP 123) Comparative Measurements of Head and Torso—27 x 21 inches

Cat. 20. (AP 124) Comparative Measurements of Head and Torso—27 x 21 inches

Cat. 21. (AP 125) Comparative Measurements of Head and Torso—27 x 21 inches

Cat. 22. (AP 126) Comparative Measurements of Arm, Leg, and Torso—27 x 21 inches

Cat. 23. (AP 127) Comparative Measurements of Foot and Torso—27 x 21 inches

Proportions of Whole Body

Cat. 24. (AP 141) Proportions of the Body Using the Cubit—21 x 27 inches

Cat. 25. (AP 142) Alignment of Parts the Body of a Standing Figure—27 x 21 inches

Cat. 26. (AP 143) Comparative Measurements of a Standing and Kneeling Figure—35 x 32 inches

Cat. 27. (AP 144) Comparative Measurements of a Seated Figure—27 x 21 inches

Cat. 28. (AP 145) Comparative Proportions of Standing Figure Using the Head and Face—27 x 21 inches

Cat. 29. (AP 146) Proportions of a Standing Figure Using the Face—27 x 21 inches

THE CATALOGUE (AP) NUMBERS (CONTINUED)

Cat. 30. (AP 147) A Robust Body—27 x 21 inches

Cat. 31. (AP 148) A Week Body—21 x 27 inches

Cat. 32. (AP 149) Proportions of a Standing Figure in a Circle and a Square—32 x 32 inches

Cat. 33. (AP 150) Proportions of a Standing Figure Using Various Parts of the Body—32 x 32 inches

Cat. 34. (AP 151) Proportions of a Three-Year-Old—27 x 21 inches

Cat. 35. (AP 152) Comparative Body Landmarks—32 x 32 inches

Cat. 36. (AP 153) Proportions of a Standing Figure Using the Face and Shoulders—27 x 21 inches

Cat. 37. (AP 154) Comparative Height of a Standing and Reclining Figure—27 x 21 inches

Proportions of the Leg and the Foot

Cat. 38. (AP 161) Comparative Measurements of a Standing Figure Using the Leg—27 x 21 inches

Cat. 39. (AP 162) Comparative Measurements of the Leg, Arm, and the Face—27 x 21 inches

Cat. 40. (AP 163) Comparative Measurements of the Leg Using the Foot—27 x 21 inches

Cat. 41. (AP 164) Comparative Measurements of the Leg of a Seated Figure Using the Foot—27 x 21 inches

Cat. 42. (AP 165) Comparative Measurements of a Frontal Leg—27 x 21 inches

Cat. 43. (AP 166) Comparative Measurements of a Profile Leg—27 x 21 inches

Cat. 44. (AP 167) Comparative Measurements of the Foot—21 x 27 inches

Cat. 45. (AP 168) Measurements of the Foot—21 x 27 inches

Cat. 46. (AP 169) Comparative Measurements of the Foot and Hand—21 x 27 inches

Cat. 47. (AP 170) Comparative Measurements of the Foot and Hand—21 x 27 inches

Cat. 48. (AP 171) Comparative Measurements of the Foot, Hand, and Face—21 x 27 inches

Cat. 49. (AP 172) Measurements of the Foot—27 x 21 inches

Cat. 50. (AP 173) Comparative Measurements of the Foot, Arm, and Face—27 x 21 inches

Cat. 51. (AP 174) Comparative Measurements of the Leg and Face—27 x 21 inches

Cat. 52. (AP 175) Measurements of the Leg Using the Foot—27 x 21 inches

Proportions of the Arm and Hand

Cat. 53. (AP 181) Comparative Measurements of the Arm—27 x 21 inches

Cat. 54. (AP 182) Measurements of the Arm Using the Face—27 x 21 inches

Cat. 55. (AP 183) Comparative Measurements of the Arm Using the Hand and Head—21 x 27 inches

Cat. 56. (AP 184) Measurements of the Arm Using the Wrist—21 x 27 inches

Cat. 57. (AP 185) Measurements of a Standing Figure Using the Whole Arm—27 x 21 inches

Cat. 58. (AP 186) Measurements of a Standing Figure Using Half the Arm—31 x 23 inches

Cat. 59. (AP 187) Measurements of the Arm Using Parts of the Arm and Hand—21 x 27 inches

Cat. 60. (AP 188) Comparative Measurements of the Arm, Hand, and Face—21 x 27 inches

Cat. 61. (AP 189) Measurements of the Arm Using the Face—21 x 27 inches

Cat. 62. (AP 190) Movements and Measurements of the Arm—21 x 27 inches

Cat. 63. (AP 191) Comparative Measurements of a Hand to the Face—27 x 21 inches

Cat. 64. (AP 192) Measurements of the Arm Using the Face—27 x 21 inches

Cat. 65. (AP 193) Comparative Measurements of the Arm and Face—21 x 27 inches

CHAPTER THREE

THE HEAD: AP 101–120

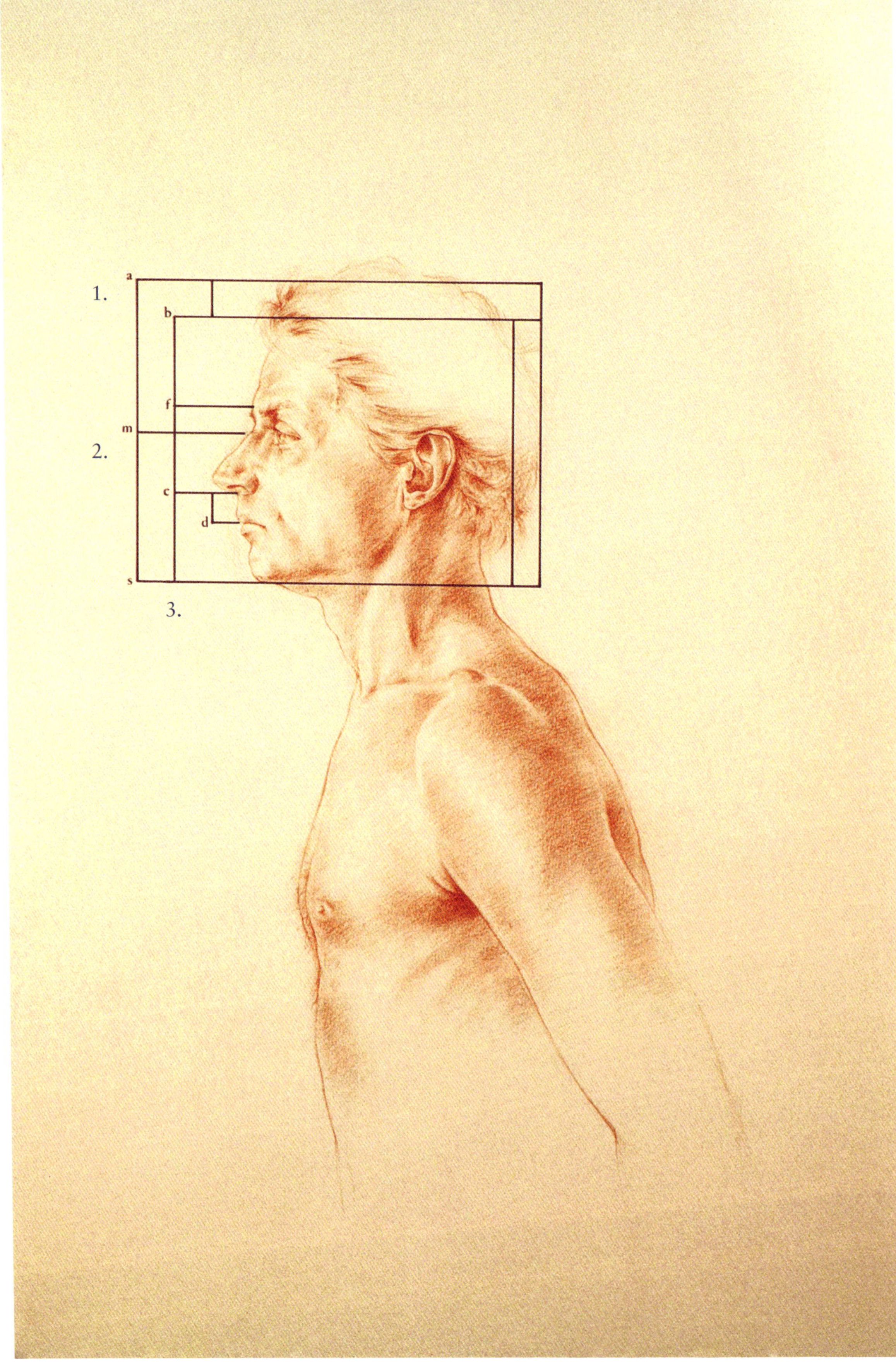

Cat. 1 **AP 101**

W. 12601, Royal Library, Windsor — AP 101
c. 1489–1490 — R 316
Folio 1 Recto

1. ***From a to b...that is to say from the roots of the hair in front to the top of the head...ought to be equal to c d; that is, from the bottom of the nose to the meeting of the lips in the middle of the mouth.***
2. ***From the inner corner of the eye m, to the top of the head a, is as far from m, down to the chin s.***
3. ***s c f b are all at equal distances from each other.***

The original drawing (Plate 14) is one of Leonardo's most exquisite drawings in the series. It is drawn on blue prepared paper and is the image of a nude man seen in profile, facing left, from the head down to below the waist. It was first drawn in silverpoint, then gone over in brown ink, and measures $8^{3}/_{8}$ x 6 inches (213 x 153 mm). Leonardo discusses the proportions of the head using the universal Rule of Three.[17]

1. From a to b, that is from b, the roots of the hair or the beginning of the hairline, to a, the top of the head (*capo*), is equal to c d, from c, the bottom of the nose, to d, the parting of the lips. Leonardo indicates here in his drawing, but does not elaborate in his text, that m, the inner corner of the eye, to f, the eyebrow, is also equal to these two measurements, thus forming the Rule of Three.
2. Leonardo then gives us another classic division of the face: m, the inner corner of the eye, to a, the top of the head, is equal to the distance from m to s, the bottom of the chin, meaning that the eyes are in the center of the head.
3. Leonardo again employs the Rule of Three to establish here the classic divisions of the face. From s, the bottom of the chin, to c, the bottom of the nose, is equal to the distance from c to f, the eyebrow or the superciliary arch, and from f to b, the hairline or the frontal eminence of the skull. These three measurements, s c, c f, f b, are all exactly equal; they form the classic divisions of the face and are a standard measurement for artists.

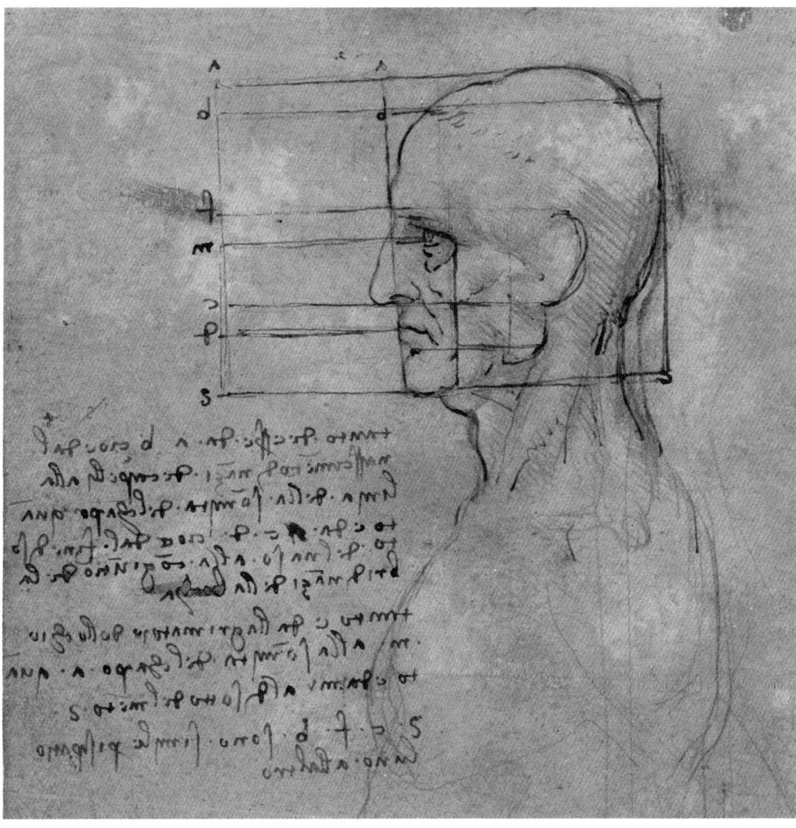

Detail, Plate 14, W. 12601, Royal Collection, Windsor

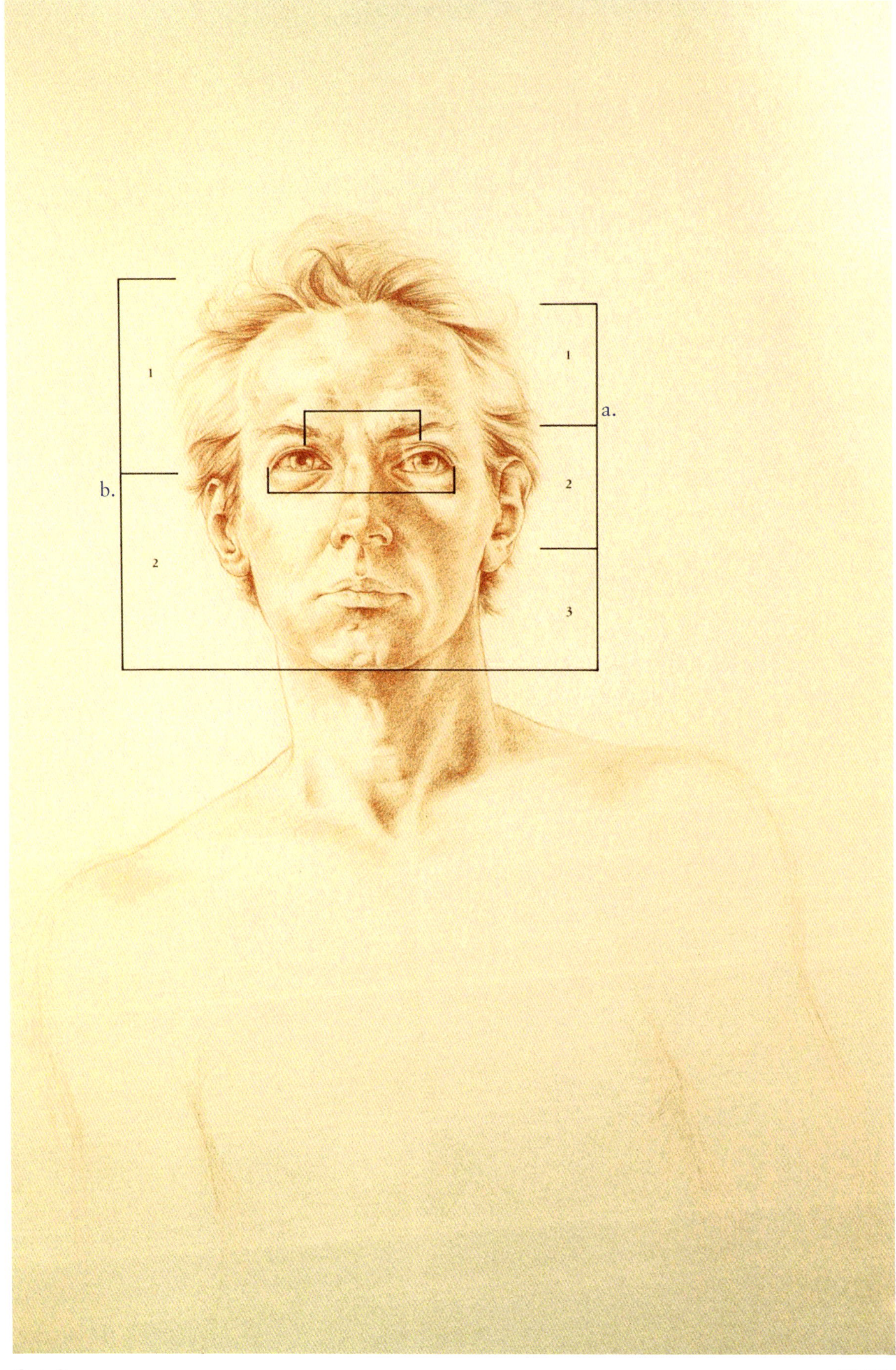

Cat. 2 AP 102

Trn. 15576a, Royal Library, Turin **AP 102**
c. 1489–1490 **R 320**

a. *The distance between the centres of the pupils of the eyes is 1/3 of the face.*

b. *The space between the outer corners of the eyes, that is, where the eye ends in the eye-socket which contains it, thus the outer corners, is one half the face.*

The above quotations (Plate 9) come from one of thirteen folios and one manuscript by Leonardo housed in the Royal Library in Turin. It is a complicated sheet because there are multiple drawings spread over two distinct sections, a full frontal face on the right and eyes and part of a face on the left. Although they were taken apart at some point after Leonardo's death (hence the separate inventory numbers, 15574 on the right, and 15576 on the left), they have since been rejoined. It is clear they were originally one sheet as Leonardo's written observations on the left section sometimes refer to the illustration on the right section, and vice versa. This page deals with the proportions of the head using parts of the face as modules of measurement. I have divided the information into three parts; two treated here as AP 102, the second is discussed in AP 104, and a third has been added to AP 109.

a. This first observation uses a most unusual module, the distance between the pupils of the eyes. While Leonardo refers to the three classic divisions of the face (*volto*), that is: 1. from the eyebrow, or the superciliary arch, to the hairline, or the frontal eminence of the skull, 2. from the bottom of the nose to the eyebrow, and 3. from the bottom of the chin to the bottom of the nose, he uses as a canon of measurement the distance between the centers of the eyes, or from the center of one pupil to the center of the other. (See AP 103 for the same divisions of the face using a different canon of measurement.)

b. The second observation uses the distance from the corner of one eye to the corner of the other eye as a module to measure with, "where the eye ends in the eye socket." Usually, it is the parts themselves that are used to measure with; that is, the distance from the chin to the eyes is equal to the distance from the eyes to the top of the head. This is also an unusual canon of measurement, but it works perfectly well. It is in fact equal to one half of the head (*volto*).[18] The eyes, as the center of the head, are another of the classic divisions of the head, and can be found as such in almost any anatomy book containing a section on proportion. The difficulty here is finding the exact corners of the eyes, or, more specifically, the edge of the zygomatic bone surrounding the orbital cavity of the eye.

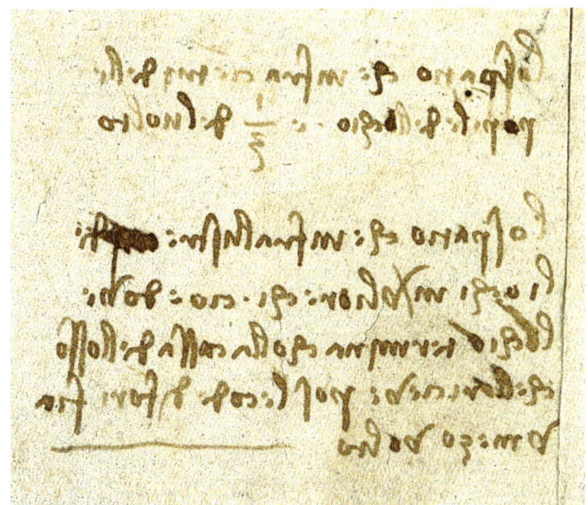

Detail, Plate 9, Trn. Inv. 15574, Biblioteca Reale, Turin

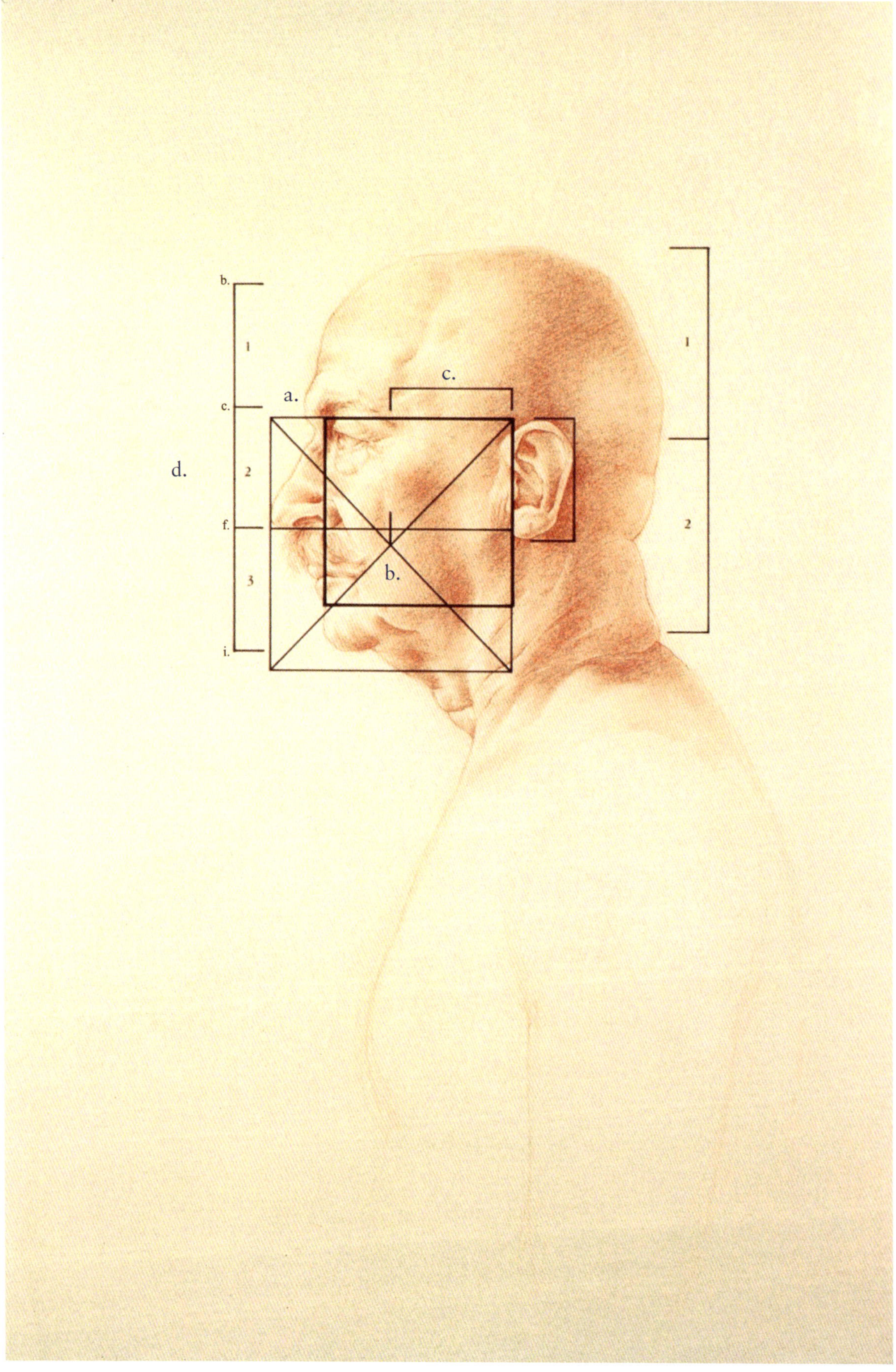

Cat. 3

AP 103

V. Inv. 236 r., 236 v. frame 33, Venice Academy AP 103
c. 1489–1490 and 1503–1504, 236 r. c. 1489–1490, 236 v. c. 1489–1490 R 315

236 r.

a. *From the eyebrow to the junction of the lip with the chin, and the angle of the jaw and the upper angle where the ear joins the temple, will be a perfect square. And each side by itself is one half of the head.*

b. *The hollow of the cheek-bone occurs half way between the tip of the nose and the top of the jaw-bone, which is the lower angle of the setting of the ear, in the frame here represented.*

c. *From the angle of the eye-socket to the ear is as far as the length of the ear, or the third of the face (testa).*[19]

236 v.

d. *f i, is ¹/₃ the face; c f, is ¹/₃ the face; and b c, is ¹/₃ the face.*

This sheet comes from one of five loose sheets housed in the Venice Accademia and measures 8³/₄ x 11 inches (280 x 222 mm). On the verso side of the sheet (Plate 11), there is a profile drawing of an older, bald-headed man facing left, with a grid of geometric lines over much of the face. On the reverse, or recto, side of the sheet (Plate 12), is the same bald-headed man, this time facing right. It is clear that Leonardo traced the original, or first drawing, by turning the sheet over, placing it in front of a source of light, and tracing the corrected lines. Richter does not refer to or include the information on the opposite, or original, side, 236 v.

The newly drawn head, now facing right, is first drawn in metal point, then gone over in brown ink (c. 1490). Below the head and drawn over the man's torso are two nude horsemen done in red chalk (c. 1504). Both animated riders, also facing to the right, are drawn with exquisite assurance, and may have been studies for *The Battle of Anghiari.*[20] There is no mention of the riders in Leonardo's text. The structural geometry imposed on the head, offset by the three orderly paragraphs of text to the left of the head, imparts to the drawing an elegance of design.

Leonardo's text is quite clear and self-explanatory and is written, in the same brown ink, in three distinct paragraphs to the left of the drawing of the head. I have measured countless heads and found that his proportional divisions are consistent and perfect. The classic three divisions of the face are the same as in the previous drawings, AP 101 and AP 102, except that the canons of measurement in this case are the three divisions themselves, each equal to each other and equal to the length of the ear. These divisions are not illustrated on the recto side of Leonardo's drawing, but on the flip or verso side.

236 r.

a. The first entry begins by inscribing a line on the face from the eyebrow (though Leonardo uses in his text the word *ciglio*, which means eyelash) to the junction of the lower lip with the chin, and from the chin to the angle of the jaw, and up to the point where the ear is attached to the temple, and from there back to the eyebrow to form a perfect square on the face. And each side is equal to half a head, that is, from the bottom of the chin to the corner of the eye is equal to the distance from the corner of the eye to the very top of the head (*testa*).

b. The hollow of the cheek, a visual depression below the zygomatic bone, occurs exactly halfway between the tip of the nose and the top of the jawbone, or mandible, and the lower setting of the attachment of the ear, as it is represented both here and in Leonardo's drawing.

c. From the angle of the eye socket, that is, from the upper edge of the zygomatic bone, to the attachment of the ear, is the same as the length of the ear, or a third of the face.

236 v.

d. On the original side, where Leonardo first began this drawing, is the head and torso of the same old, bald-headed man, this time facing left. The drawing is done in pen and two shades of brown ink. The figure is encased in a square and there are several gesture lines inscribed around the back of the head, obviously searching for the correct proportions of the head. Not only did Leonardo make corrections on this original drawing, he then (as mentioned above) flipped it over and traced the original to the other side of the sheet.

To the left of the face are two columns of abbreviated notes and letters that correspond to the geometry inscribed over the face, and underneath the figure is a short paragraph of explanation. I have excerpted from these notes only the three listed above, rearranging their order. From i, the bottom of the chin, to f, the bottom of the nose, is one-third the face, and from f to c, the eyebrow, is one-third the face, and from c to b, the hairline, is one-third the face. Once again, we have the classic three divisions of the face.

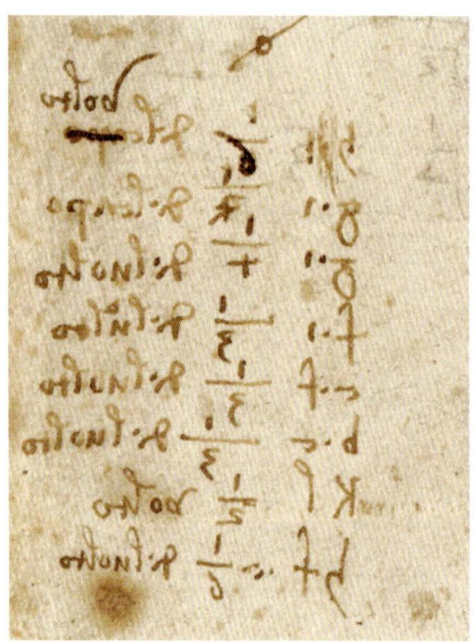

Detail, Plate 11, V. Inv. 236 v. Frame 33, Gallerie dell'Accademia, Venice

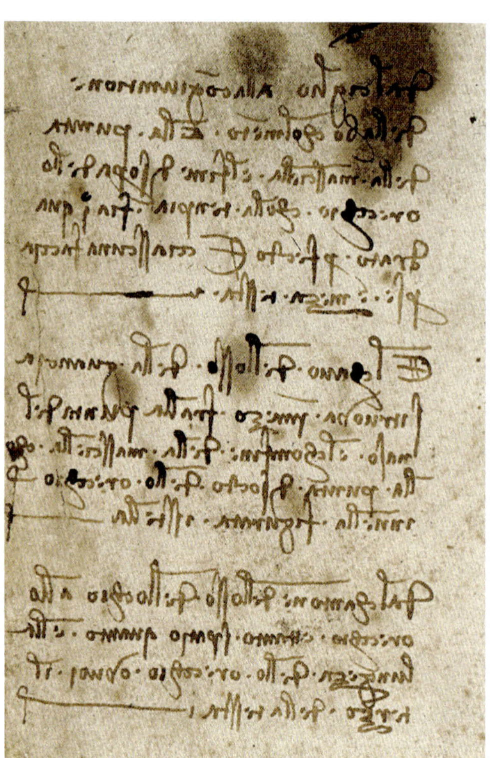

Detail, Plate 12, V. Inv. 236 r., Frame 33, Gallerie dell'Accademia, Venice

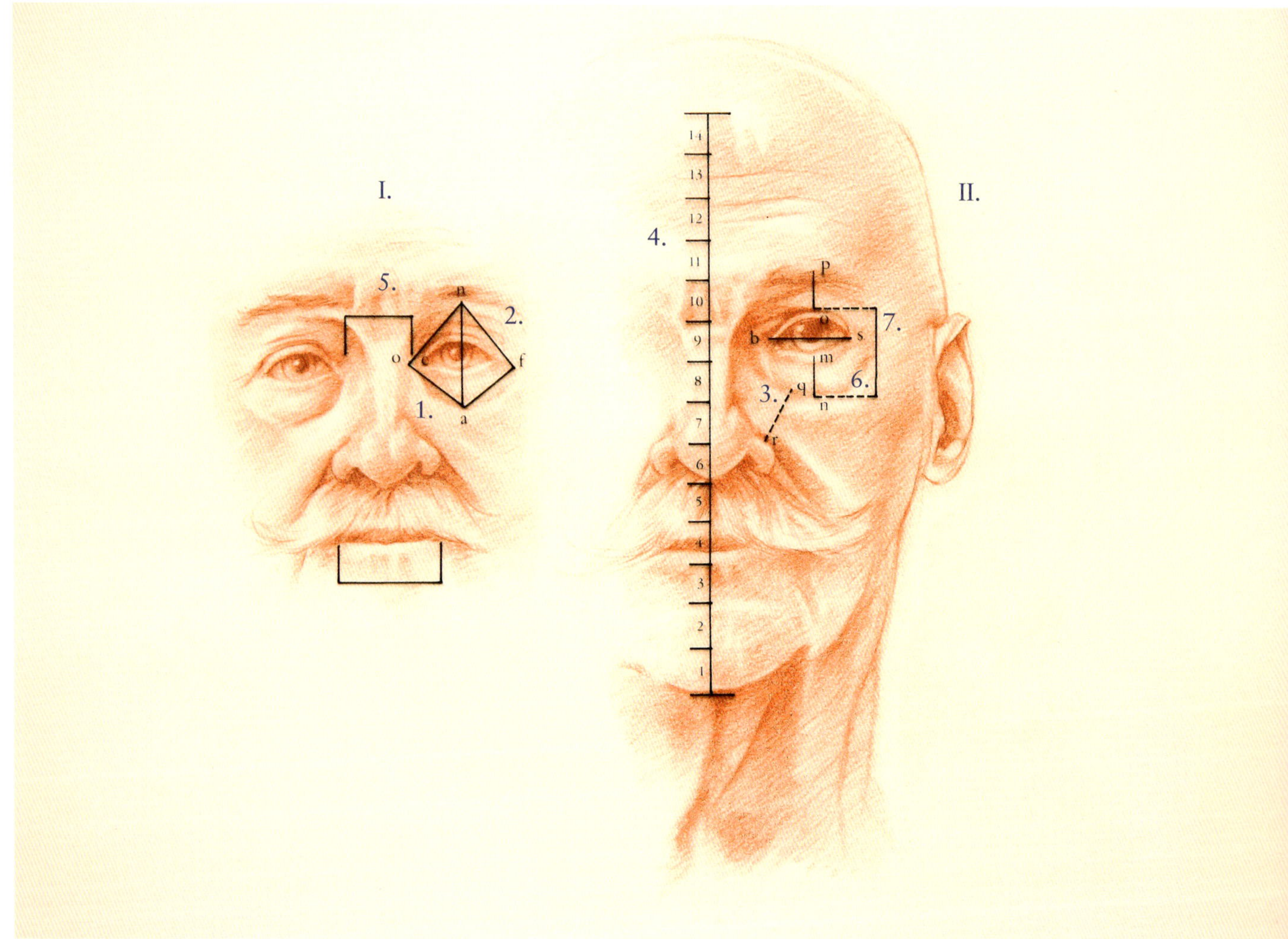

Cat. 4

AP 104

Trn. 15574, Royal Library, Turin
c. 1489–1490

AP 104
R 319

I. 1. *a n o f are equal to the mouth.*

2. *a c and a f are equal to the space between one eye and the other.*

5. *n o is equal to the length of the eye or the space between the eyes.*

II. 3. *n m, o p, q r are equal to half the width of the eyelids, that is from the inner corner (lachrymatory) of the eye to its outer corner; and in like manner the division between the chin and the mouth; and in the same way the narrowest part of the nose between the eyes.*

4. *And these spaces, each in itself, is the 9th [19th] part of the face [head].*

6. *m c is 1/3 of m n measuring from the outer corner of the eyelids to the letter c.*

7. *b s will be equal to the width of the nostril.*

This entry (Plate 9) comes from the same complicated sheet discussed in AP 102. It was drawn in metal point and worked over in brown ink on a yellow-gray prepared paper. It includes several images and partial images of eyes, the frontal full head of a balding older man, and several paragraphs of text all dealing with the proportions of the face and the eye. As was stated earlier, Leonardo's text is spread over the entire sheet and he jumps from one illustration to another. I have followed his lead, as in the case of my illustration II. 7., where he uses the eye as a module to measure the width and height of an eye, as well as the distance between the eyes, I. 5. As a complicated and perhaps obsessive drawing, it is, in fact, quite accurate. One must follow the text and the illustrations quite carefully to keep from getting lost.

I. 1. a n, the vertical distance of the orbital cavity of the eye, and o f, the horizontal cavity of the eye, are similar to the width of the mouth. These are rather small comparisons to make and therefore less precise, so the key word here is *similar.*

2. a to c, the distance from the center of the lower edge of the orbital cavity to the inside corner of the eye, is similar to the distance from a to f, the outer corner of the eye, and each is equal to the space between the eyes.

5. n o, which again is the height of the orbital cavity, is in fact equal to the width of the eye and to the space between the eyes. Here Leonardo refers back to the first, smaller illustration, I., and repeats this theory in an entirely different sheet housed in Paris, which I have illustrated in AP 105, d.

II. 3. The distance from n, the lower edge of the orbital cavity, to m, the edge of the lower lid, is equal to o, the upper edge of the eyelid, to p, the upper edge of the orbital cavity; and q, the lower edge of the orbital cavity, to r, the edge of the nostril (the dilator naris) are all equal to each other and to half the width of the eye, that is, from the corner of the eye to the center of the pupil. These are all fairly accurate comparisons; however, what one does with these very minor measurements is unclear.

4. The next sentence indicates that all of these spaces, m to n, o to p, and q to r, are equal to each other and are approximately one-ninth [one-nineteeth][21] of the face from the chin to the hairline. There is some discrepancy in the translations of this passage as to whether Leonardo meant one-ninth or one-nineteenth; in either case, the theory does not work. Each space only goes thirteen to fourteen times into the length of the face. Even if we measure the whole head, those spaces as modules still do not enter nineteen times.

6. "m c is one third of n m measuring from..." is far too finicky a relationship to be of use to the artist and is therefore not included in my drawing.

7. b s, the width from the corner of the eye to the opposite corner of the eye, is, in fact, approximately equal to the width of the nose.

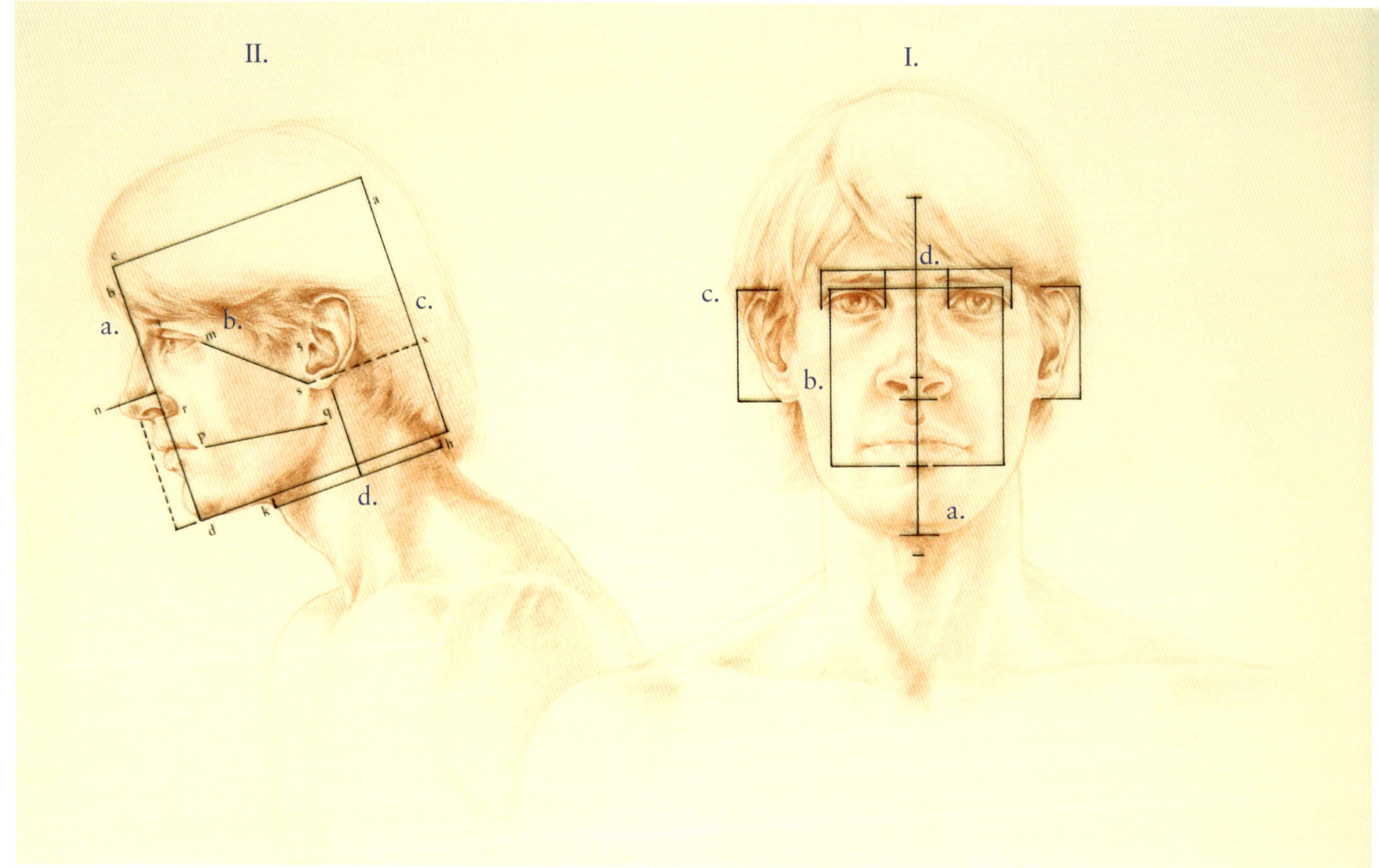

Cat. 5

AP 105

MS A. 63a, Institut de France, Paris AP 105
c. 1490–1492 R 312

I. a. *The cut or depression below the lower lip of the mouth is half-way between the bottom of the nose and the bottom of the chin.*

b. *The face forms a square in itself; that is, with its width from the outer corner of one eye to the other, and its height is from the very top of the nose to the bottom of the lower lip of the mouth; then what remains above and below this square amounts to the height of such another square.*

c. *The ear is exactly as long as the nose. The ear should be as high as from the bottom of the nose to the top of the eyelid.*

d. *The space between the eyes is equal to the width of an eye.*

II. a. *a b is equal to the space between c d; d n in the same way to n c, and likewise s r, q p, h k, are equal to each other.*

b. *It is as far between m and s as from the bottom of the nose to the chin.*

c. *It is as far from x to s as from the nose to the chin. The parting of the mouth seen in profile slopes to the angle of the jaw.*

d. *The ear is over the middle of the neck, when seen in profile. The distance from 4 to 5 is equal to that from 5 to r.*

There are three drawings of faces, two profile and one frontal, on this page (Plate 2), which comes from Notebook A in Paris and measures 8¼ x 6 inches (210 x 145 mm). The page is filled with Leonardo's tiny writing and the letters are very faint. A hand other than Leonardo's has inked over many of the lines. The references jump back and forth between measurements of the frontal face and the profile face. In order to clarify Leonardo's meaning and bring greater uniformity to these entries, I have reordered some of the sentences and placed them into two groups, Section I, the frontal face, and Section II, the profile face. I have also divided each section into four parts from a. to d. Therefore, you will find Leonardo's original statements, as translated by Richter, in a very different order from the order presented here.

I. a. The midway mark between the bottom of the nose and the bottom of the chin is the depression of the lower lip where it meets the beginning of the chin.

b. "The face forms a square…" is quite accurate. From the corner of one eye to the corner of the other eye forms one side of a square, while the distance from the top of the nose to the bottom of the lower lip forms the other side of the square. Then what remains above this square, from the top of the nose to the hairline, is half the square, but what remains below this square, from the depression of the lower lip to the bottom of the chin, is not quite equal to another half square. This last portion of the theory does not quite work.

c. This reference, comparing the length of the ear to the length of the nose, is quite accurate, and is, of course, the second third of the three parts of the face.

d. The space between the eyes is generally the width of one eye. This is yet another measurement often used when making proportional comparisons in the face.

II. a. a b, the width of the head from the back of the head to the forehead when seen in profile, is equal to c d, the length of the face from the hairline to the chin, thus making a perfect square. And d n, or d, the underside of the chin, to n, a point above the tip of the nose, is equal to the distance from n to c, the hairline, which is a very different measurement from the center of the head, the eyes, from the chin to the top of the head.

b. m, the corner of the eye, to s, where the ear attaches to the face, is equal to the distance from the bottom of the nose to the bottom of the chin, d n. This is another unusual measurement, the space between the corner of the eye and the point where the ear is attached to the face, but is an accurate comparison indicated here by the broken line.

c. The distance from s, the attachment of the lower part of the ear, to x, the back of the head (excluding the hair), is exactly equal to the distance again from the bottom of the nose to the chin, d n. The line from the parting of the lips, or the corner of the mouth, p, slopes only slightly to the angle of the jaw at q. This is true in Leonardo's drawing and in mine. Leonardo indicates the letters in his drawing but does not include them in the text. They are included here in my text.

d. The bottom of the ear is positioned over the middle of the neck when seen in profile, and the distance from 4, the inner angle of the eye, to 5, the orifice of the ear, is equal to the distance from s, the attachment of the lower ear, to r, the edge of the nose. Both of these are fairly accurate comparisons but are here only indicated by letters.

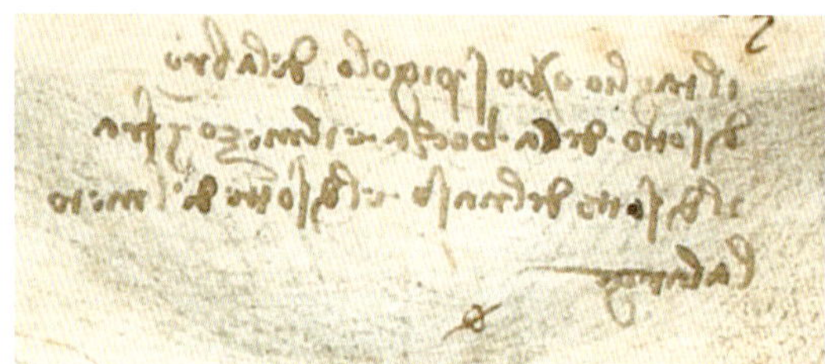

Detail, Plate 2, Ms A, page 63a, Bibliotheque de l'Institut de France, Paris

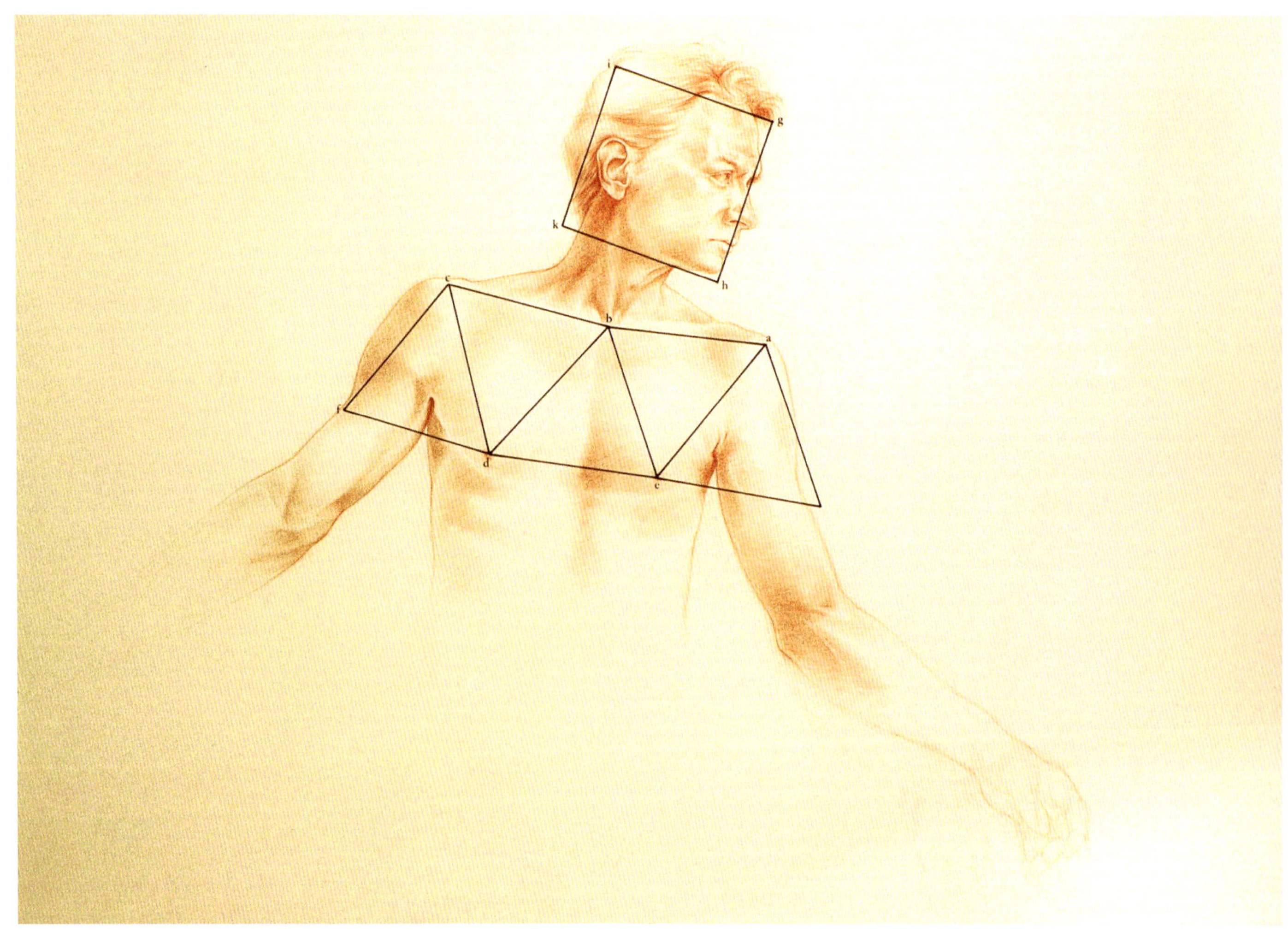

Cat. 6 **AP 106**

W. 12607, Royal Library, Windsor **AP 106**
c. 1487 **R 318**
Folio 2 Recto

a b, c d, e f, g h, i k are similar to each other in size, except d f, which is free [accidental].

One of the most interesting and inventive of Leonardo's compositions (Plate 16), it works quite effectively as long as the model's torso is completely frontal. The measurement d f, from the nipple to the outer edge of the biceps, is free, meaning the distance changes as the position of the arm changes. Richter translates the word *libero* as "accidental," the *Quaderni* as "free"; I think the word *free* is more accurate. It does seem like such an obvious point one has to wonder why Leonardo would even mention it.

Leonardo states that from the letter a, the tip of the left shoulder (where the clavicle meets the scapula), to b, the pit of the throat (the depression created by the sternocleidomastoideus muscles), to c, the left nipple, to d, the right nipple, to e, the tip of the right shoulder, to f, a point somewhere at the edge of the biceps below the deltoid, are all equal to each other, and to the length of the face.

The configuration creating the square imposed on the head starts with the letter g, the hairline of the face to h, the bottom of the chin, and that is similar to the distance from h to k, the lower portion of the back of the head, and from k to i, the back of the head. These are all fixed points and are equal to each other and equal to the measurements of the torso below, all except d to f, which is obviously not a fixed point as the arm can move in different directions, changing the measurement.

Leonardo effectively points out, without actually stating it, that the length of the face and the width of the head are equal to each other and with the other two sides form a square. And any side of that square, just like any of the other measurements, may be used as a module of measurement. (See also AP 105 and AP 146.)

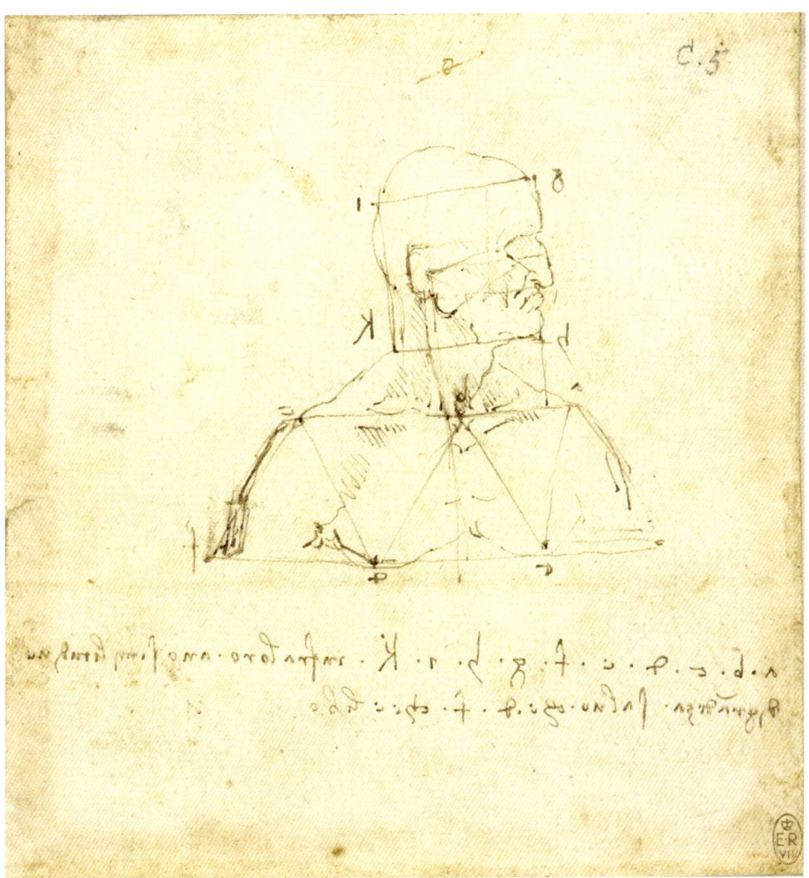

Detail, Plate 16, W. 12607, Royal Collection, Windsor

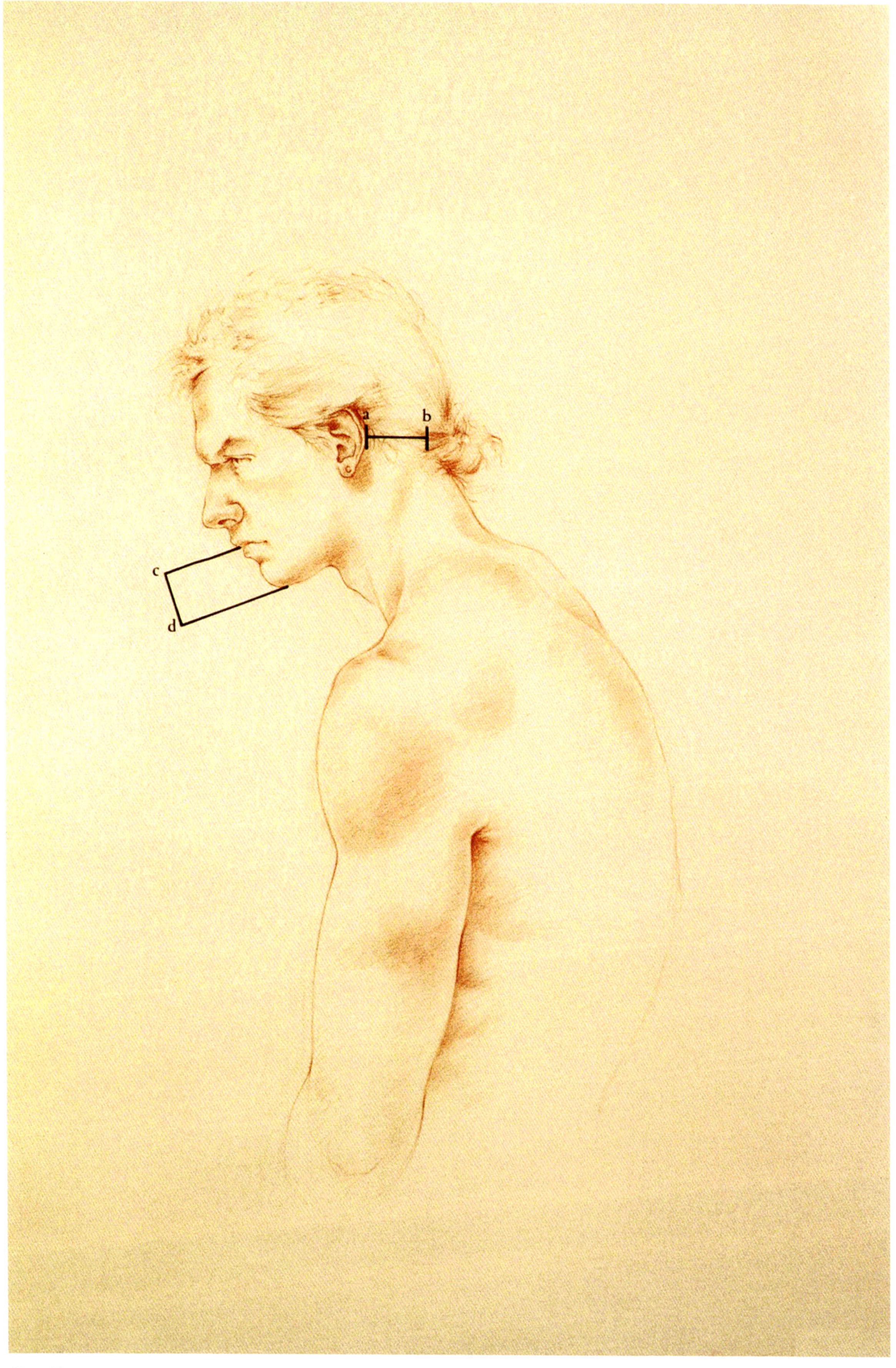

Cat. 7

AP 107

W. 12606, Royal Library, Windsor **AP 107**
c. 1490–1492 **R 313**
Folio 3 Recto

a b is similar to c d.

Leonardo's drawing (Plate 15), a mere 2 x $1^{7}/_{8}$ inches (56 x 47 mm), one of the smallest of his pages, was probably cut out of another page. It is a very fine and delicate portrait, in pen and ink on gray paper, of a middle-aged man with closely cropped hair. Although an obscure proportional relationship, it seems to work quite effectively.

a, the distance from the edge of the ear to b, the back of the head, is equal to c, the parting of the lips, to d, the underside of the chin.

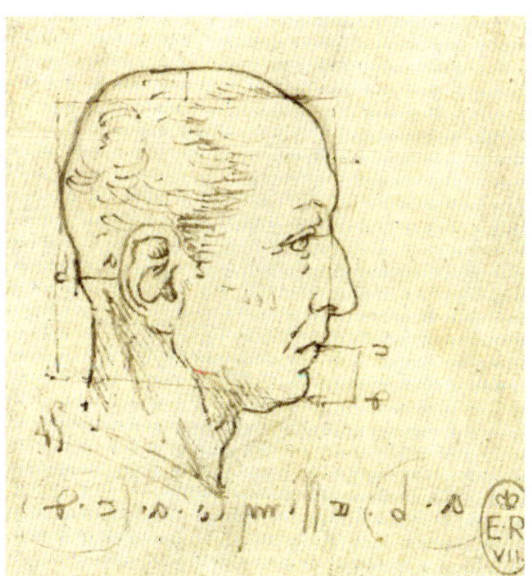

Detail, Plate 15, W. 12606, Royal Collection, Windsor

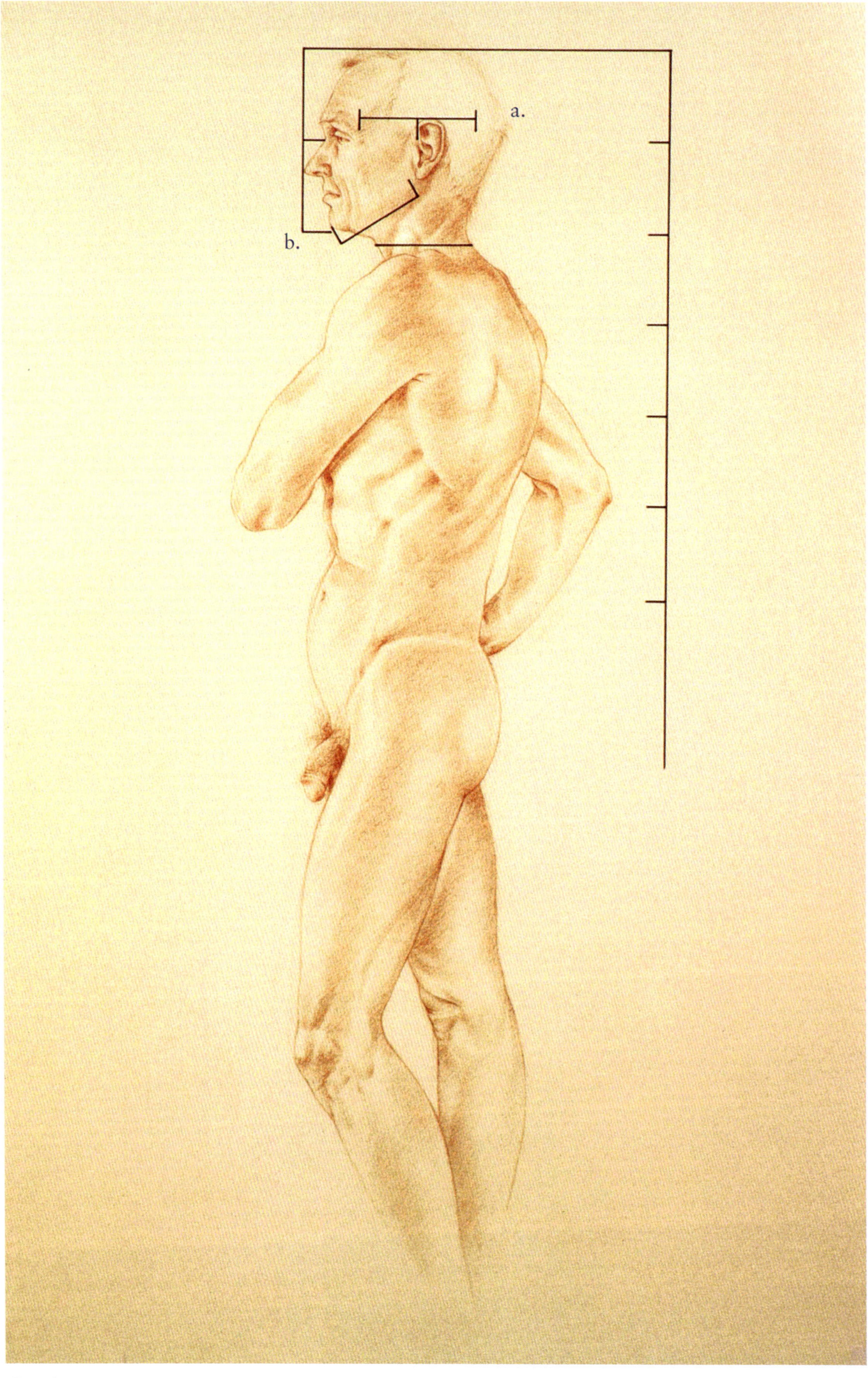

Cat. 8 **AP 108**

W. 19134–19135, Royal Library, Windsor **AP 108**
c. 1490 **R 317**
Folio 10 Recto I, III

I. a. ***The small cartilage which projects over the opening of the ear opposite the nose is half-way between the nape of the neck and the eyebrow.***

III. b. ***The thickness of the neck in profile is equal to the space between the chin and the eyes, and to the space between the chin and the jaw, and it is $^{1}/_{15}$ the height of a man.***

This entry (Plate 27) comes from a double folio page, 17 x $12\frac{1}{2}$ inches (434 x 317 mm), which was folded in half, most likely by Leonardo, because his sentences and drawings are written from every conceivable direction, vertically and horizontally, resulting in no single orientation for the page. It is entirely filled with proportional information from almost every part of the human body, the head, the whole body, the arms and hands, and the legs. It is enormously confusing but has been carefully analyzed by the authors of the *Quaderni,* who numbered the page in outline form. I have isolated parts of the information and, in some cases, combined them with other entries.

I. a. The small cartilage which projects over and protects the orifice of the ear, the tragus (*pincierolo*), is, in fact, halfway between the nape of the neck and the eyebrow; however, we must carefully draw a line upward from the nape of the neck to a line even with the end of the eyebrow to measure its accuracy.

III. b. The thickness of the neck, as seen in profile, is equal to the space between the chin and the eyes, and to the space between the tip of the chin, the mental protuberance, and the angle of the jaw, the mandible. While these distances compare quite accurately, they do not enter into the height of a man fifteen times as Leonardo posits, which is the reason my drawing and the measured units were left unfinished. The unit, from the chin to the eyes, is actually half a whole head and therefore goes at least sixteen times into the height of a man. (See AP 145.)

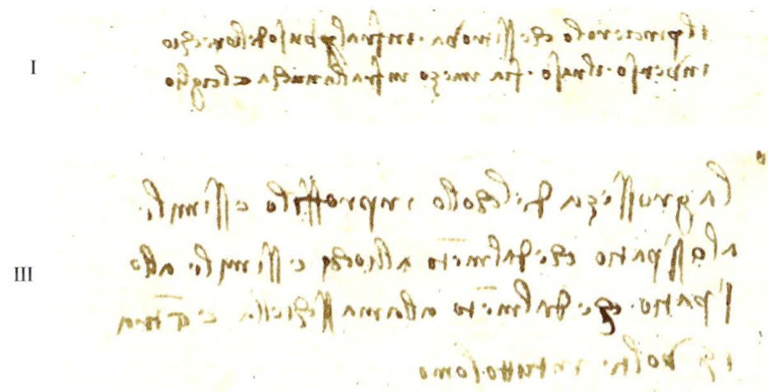

Detail, Plate 27, W. 19134-19135, Royal Collection, Windsor

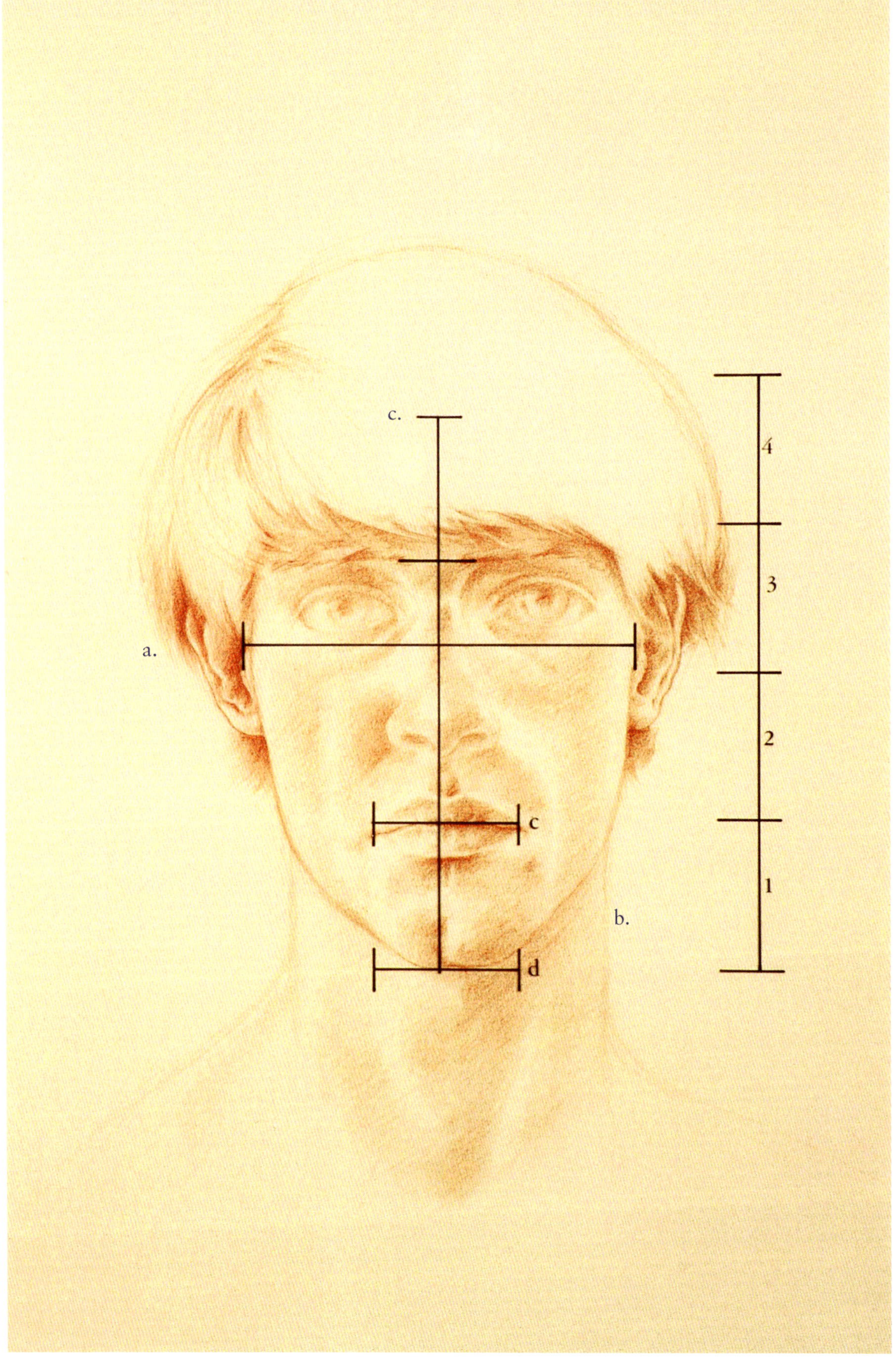

Cat. 9 AP 109

MS A. 62b, Institut de France, Paris — AP 109
c. 1490–1492 — R 311

a. *The distance from the attachment of one ear to the other is equal to that from the meeting of the eyebrows to the chin, and in a fine face the width of the mouth is equal to the length from the parting of the lips to the bottom of the chin.*

W. 12304, Royal Library, Windsor — R 310
c. 1489–1490
Folio 4 Recto 2

b. *The space from the mouth to the bottom of the chin c d is the fourth part of the face and equal to the width of the mouth.*

Trn. 15576, Royal Library, Turin — R 320
c. 1489–1490

c. *The space from the mouth to the bottom of the chin c d is the fourth part of the face and equal to the width of the mouth.*

All three of these entries are from different manuscripts and were written by Leonardo over a period of fifteen years. Each observation deals with the proportions of the face but uses the mouth in each case, particularly the width of the mouth and the distance from the parting of the lips to the chin, as units of measurement. Each of these measurements is accurate and useful.

a. Leonardo gives us two unique modules to work with here (Plate 1). In the first part of this entry Leonardo uses the width of the face at the level of the eyes as a module to measure the length of the face from the meeting of the eyebrows to the bottom of the chin. In the second part of the entry he uses the width of the mouth to determine the distance from the parting of the lips to the bottom of the chin "in a fine face." In this case, I was lucky—I found a fine-faced model—but it does beg the question, does it work if the face is not so fine?

b. In this case (Plate 13), the width of the mouth and its equal, the distance from the parting of the lips to the bottom of the chin, c d, are used as canons to determine the length of the face; each of the modules, in fact, enters into the face, from the chin to the hairline, four times. This is different from the modules established in the Rule of Three, which uses one of the units, the distance from the bottom of the chin to the bottom of the nose.

c. Here (Plate 9), we are asked to use once again the width of the face at the level of the eyes as a module, and to compare that distance to the distance from the hairline to the parting of the lips. A different calculation from the example a. above.

a.

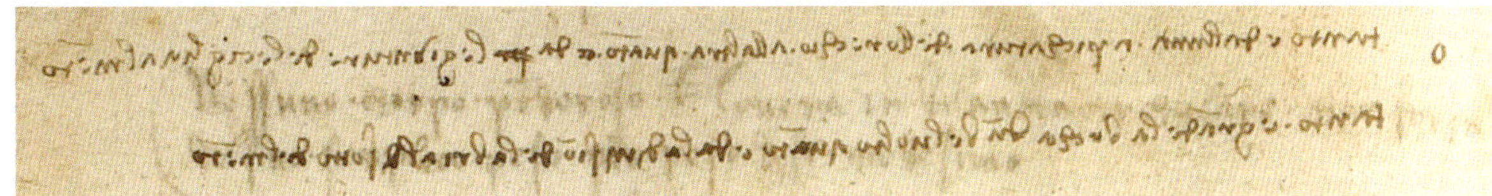

Detail, Plate 1, Ms A, page 62b, Bibliotheque de l'Institut de France, Paris

b.

Detail, Plate 13, W. 12304, Royal Collection, Windsor

c.

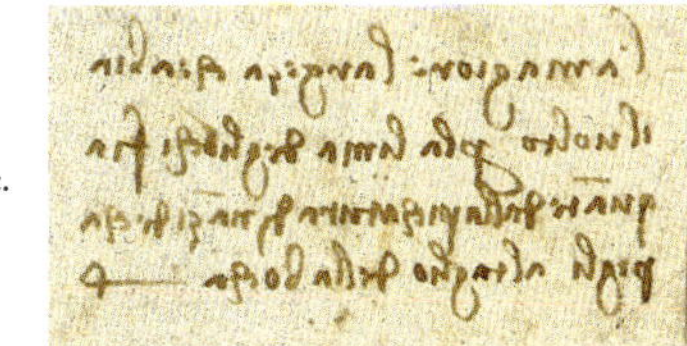

Detail, Plate 9, Trn. Inv. 15576, Bilbioteca Reale, Turin

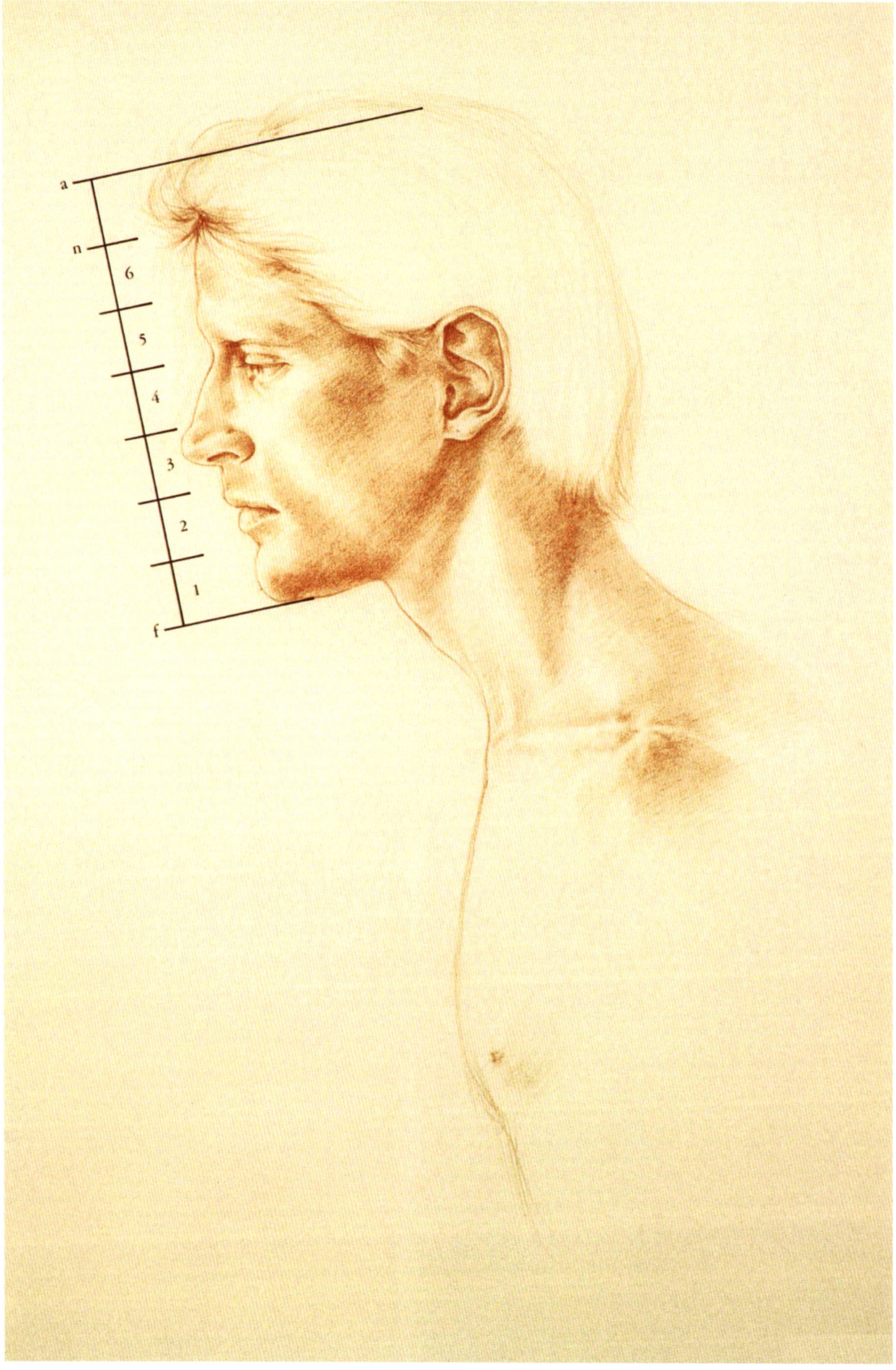

Cat. 10

AP 110

W. 19136–19139b, Royal Library, Windsor **AP 110**
c. 1490 **R 314**
Folio 11 Verso III

The head a f is $^1/_6$ larger than n f.

This entry (Plate 29) is from one of the largest pages at Windsor Castle, measuring 15¾ x 11 inches (405 x 281 mm) and filled with notes and drawings on both sides. Because the sheet was folded into four parts, the Windsor catalogue numbers are from 19136 to 19139, both recto and verso. This particular entry is a tiny drawing at the top left of the verso side of the sheet with a simple, generalized pen-and-ink profile head. The sketch and inscription are placed just below the word *Caravazo*. This is the same sheet, Folio 11, Recto, that contains the word *Trezo*.[22]

a f is the distance from the top of the head, a, to the underside of the chin, f—in other words, the whole head. n f is the distance from the hairline, n, to the bottom of the chin, f. a n, the space between the top of the head and the hairline, is therefore one-sixth larger than the face, n f. n, the hairline, is one of Leonardo's most often-used reference points. Although the term *hairline* sounds elusive, it actually refers to the frontal eminence of the skull, where a slight indentation marks the uppermost area of the forehead.

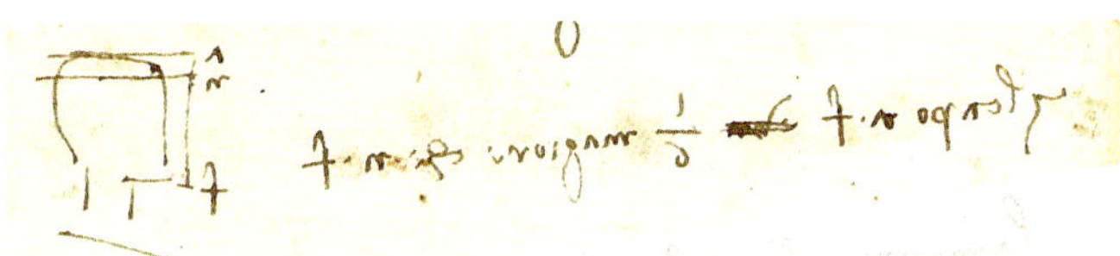

Detail, Plate 29, W. 19136–19139b, Royal Collection, Windsor

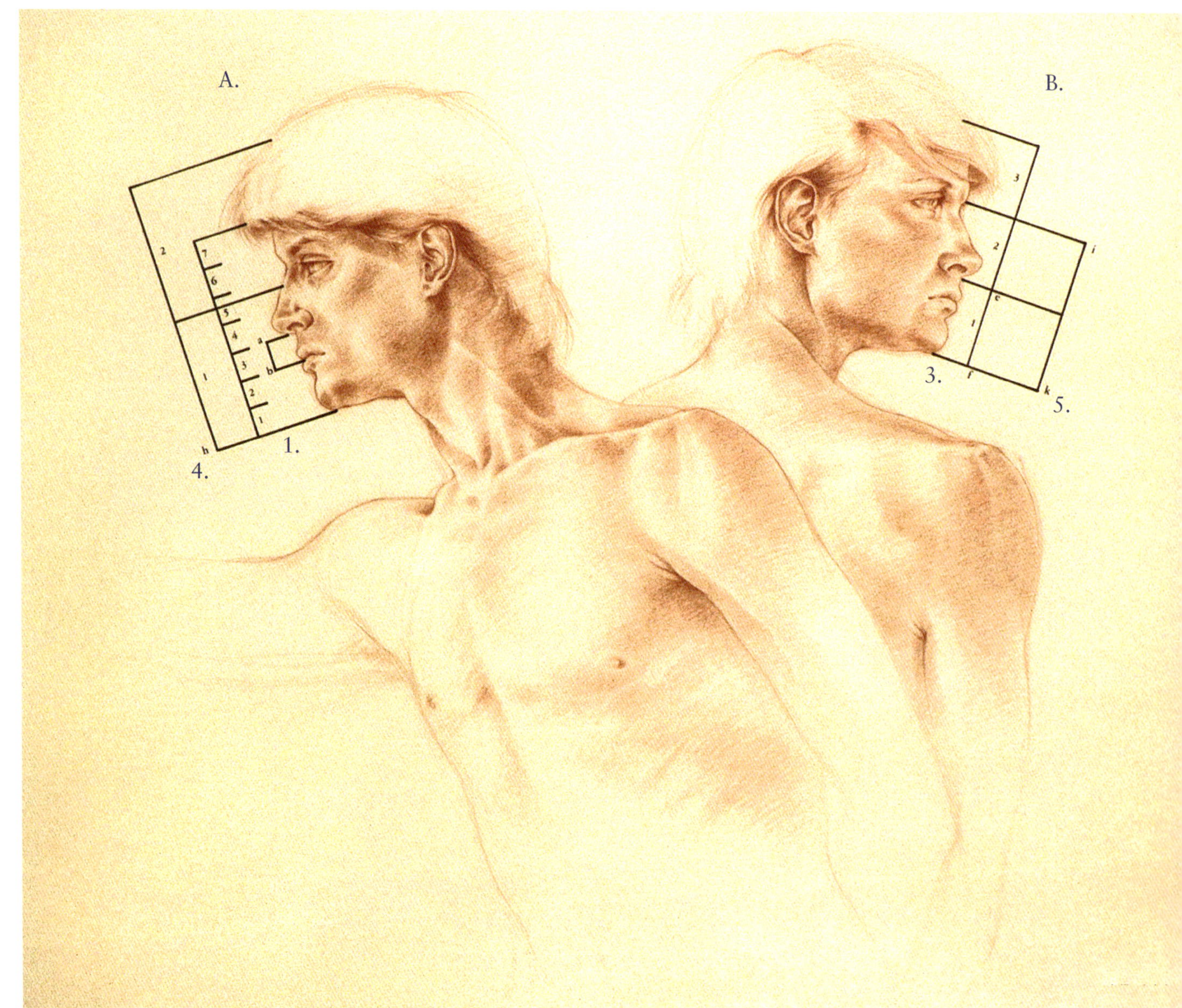

Cat. 11

AP 111

W. 12304, Royal Library, Windsor **AP 111**
c. 1489–1490 **R 310**
Folio 4 Recto 1, 4, 3, 5

A. 1. *[a b] the space between the parting of the lips [the mouth] and the base of the nose is one-seventh of the face.*

4. *The distance from the middle of the nose to bottom of the chin, g h, is half the length of the face.*

B. 3. *The space from the chin to the base of the nose, e f, is the third part of the face and is equal to the length of the nose and the forehead.*

5. *The distance from the top of the nose, where the eyebrows begin, to the bottom of the chin, i k, is two thirds of the face.*

This entire page (Plate 13), Folio 4 Recto, as marked in the *Quaderni,* is devoted almost entirely to the proportions of the face, head, and neck. Leonardo has drawn tiny pen-and-ink sketches in a single column running the length of the page on the right side of the sheet; his theories are listed in a corresponding column on the left side of the sheet. The authors of the *Quaderni* have numbered each entry in sequence. Leonardo's drawings are of individual features, such as a tiny nose, a mouth and chin, a pair of eyes, etc.. To facilitate the reading of this information, I have adopted the numbering system and created two drawings of the same model, designated as A and B. Drawing A, the head facing to our left, treats numbers 1 and 4. Drawing B, the head facing to our right, deals with numbers 3 and 5. See the following drawing, AP 112, for a similar breakdown of the entries. Number 2 in this sequence is an entirely separate drawing, seen in AP 109.

The last entry on this page, however, deals with the proportions of the torso using the foot as a module. That entry has been separated out by Richter as R 337, and by me as AP 127.

A. 1. a, the bottom of the nose, to b, the parting of the lips, is one-seventh the length of the face, from the chin to the hairline.

4. the distance from g, the middle of the nose, to h, the bottom of the chin, is half the length of the face.

B. 3. The space from the chin, f, to the base of the nose, e, is equal to the length of the nose, and is one-third of the face. This is, of course, a retake of the classic divisions of the face from the chin to the hairline using the Rule of Three.

5. The distance from the top of the nose where the eyebrows begin, i, to the bottom of the chin, k, is two-thirds of the face. Again, it's the Rule of Three at work here, but using yet another of one of the three divisions as a module. I find it interesting that Leonardo keeps revisiting the three proportions of the face. (See AP 103.)

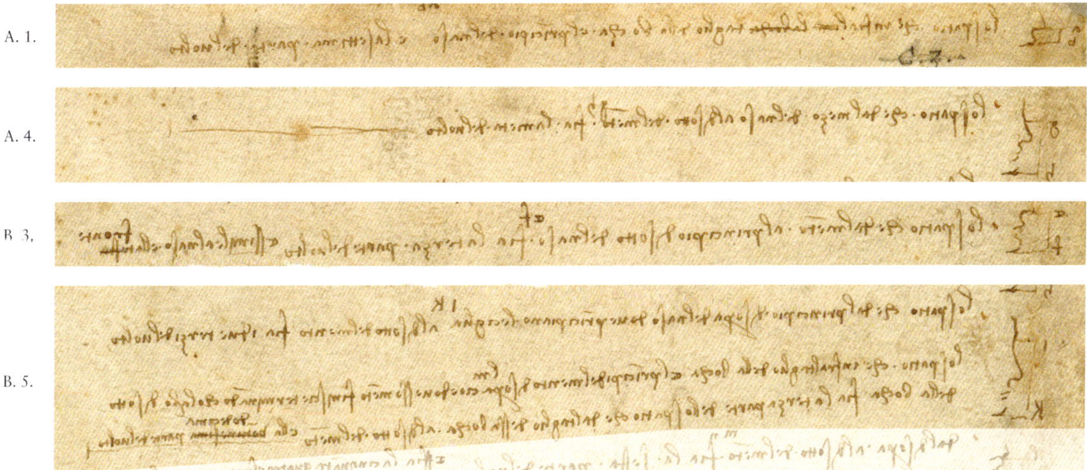

Detail, Plate 13, W. 12304, Royal Collection, Windsor

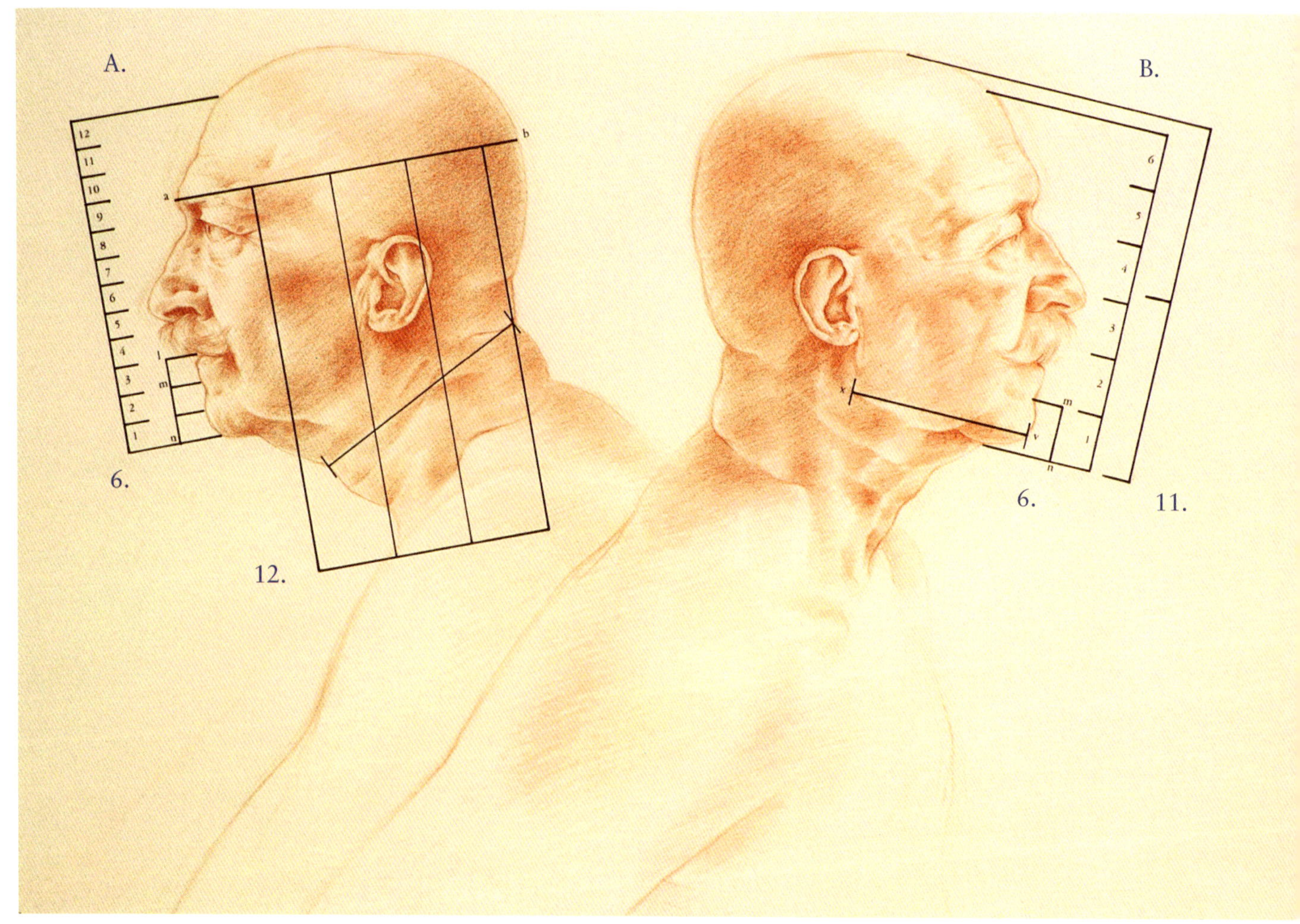

Cat. 12

AP 112

W. 12304, Royal Library, Windsor
c. 1489–1490
Folio 4 Recto 6, 12, 6, 11

AP 112
R 310

A. 6. *The space from the parting of the lips to the top chin l m, that is where the chin ends and passes into the lower lip of the mouth, is the third of the distance from the parting of the lips to the bottom of the chin, and is the twelfth part of the face.*

12. *The thickness of the head [neck] from the brow to the nape [of the neck] is once and 3/4 of that neck [a b].*

B. 6. *From the top to the bottom of the chin m n is the sixth part of the face, and is the fifty-fourth part of a man's height.*

11. *From the chin to the jaw bone v x is half the head, and equal to the thickness of the neck in profile.*

As in the previous drawing, AP 111, I have separated the individual entries into two groups and distinguish them using the *Quaderni* numbers (Plate 13). There are also two heads on this page, with numbers 6 and 12 on the A drawing on the left, and 6 and 11 on the B drawing on the right.

A. 6. From the parting of the lips, l, to the beginning of the chin, m, is in fact one-third the space from l to the bottom of the chin n (the letter n is omitted in Leonardo's and Richter's text but is included on his drawing, and therefore mine as well), and is one-twelfth of the face. This module, l to m, is based on the Rule of Three.

12. This is a strange and confusing comparison, and a case where Leonardo's text conflicts with his drawing and Richter's translation reads differently from the Italian. Leonardo's words read, *"la grossezza del collo entra una volta e 3/4 dal ciglio alla nuca."* The literal translation should read, "the thickness of the neck [not head] enters one time and 3/4 from the eyelash to the nape [of the neck]." Leonardo is saying that the thickness of the neck, the module in this case, goes once and 3/4 (*una volta e 3/4*) from the eyelash [eyebrow] [a] to the nape of the neck [b]. Leonardo's drawing does contain the letters a and b, showing a profile face divided into three parts from the eyebrow at the bridge of the nose, a, to the back of the neck, not the back of the head, b, in effect making the neck two-thirds of the width of a b. I have attempted several variations to solve this problem, and the closest I have come to a solution is that the width of the neck is three-fourths of the width of the head at a b.

B. 6. The first part of this observation, that from the top of the chin, m, to below the chin, n, is one-sixth of the face, works perfectly well. The second part, using the chin as a module fifty-four times to measure the length of a man, seems a difficult measurement to calculate.

11. From the point of the chin in profile, v, to the angle of the jawbone, x, is half the head, and is roughly the thickness of the neck in profile. Compare this to AP 108.

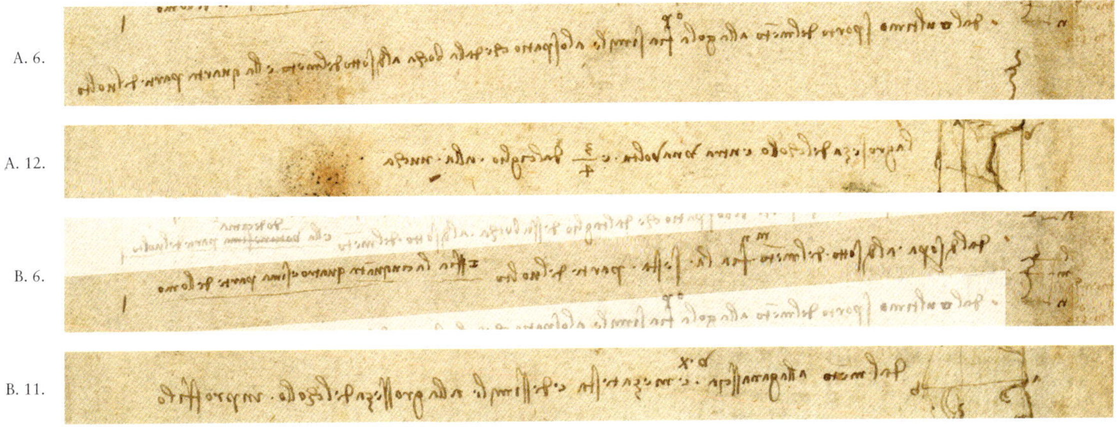

Detail, Plate 13, W. 12304, Royal Collection, Windsor

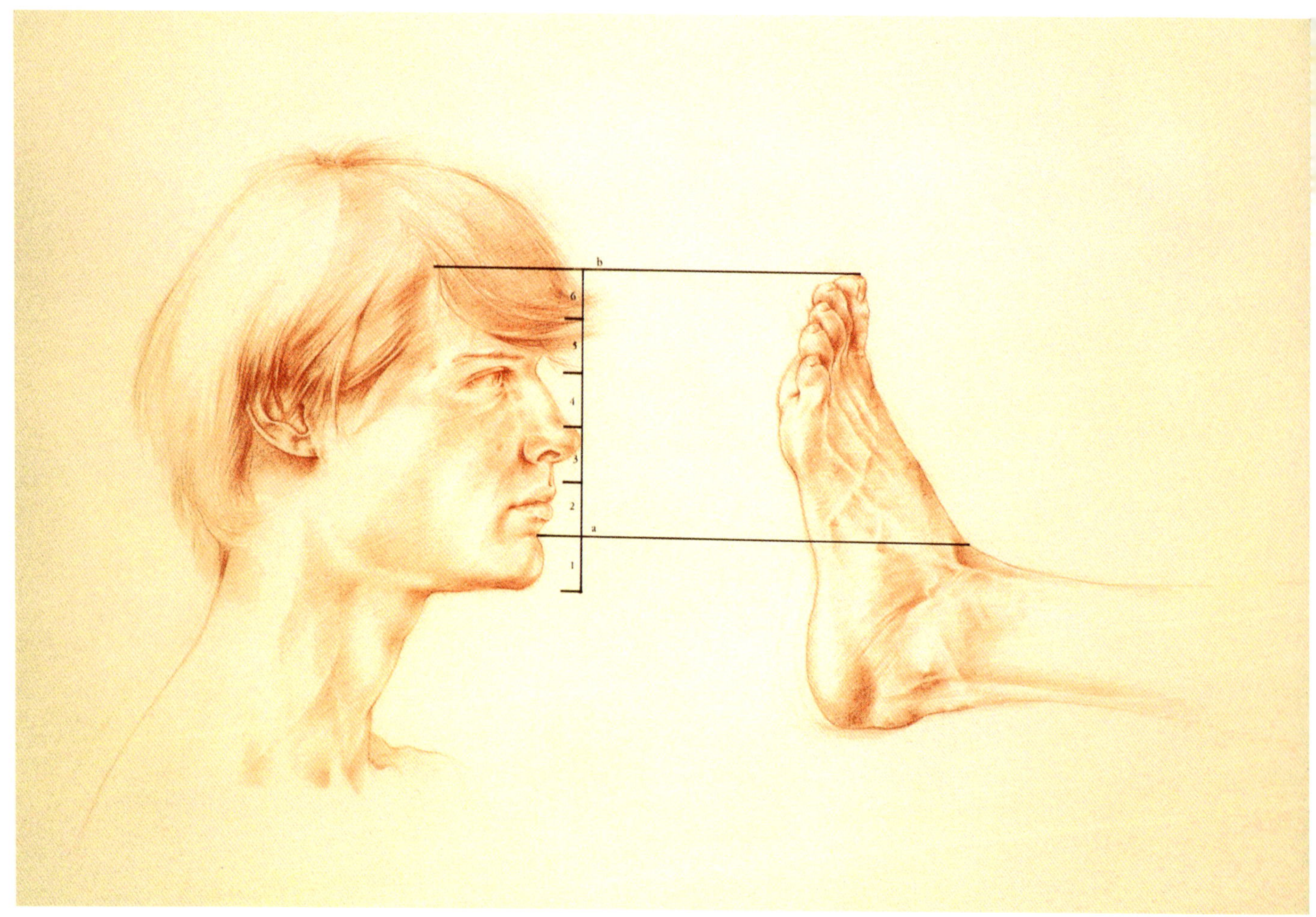

Cat. 13

AP 113

W. 19131b, Royal Library, Windsor **AP 113**
c. 1490 **R 325**
Folio 7 Verso

The foot from where it is attached to the leg, to the tip of the big toe, is as long as the space which is between the upper part of the chin and the roots of the hair, a b; and is equal to five-sixths of the face.

In Leonardo's original drawing of this observation (Plate 22), he compares the length of the foot, from the instep, a, to the tip of the big toe, b, to the length of the entire face, from the bottom of the chin to the hairline. Leonardo then recalculates the measurement and moves the line from the bottom of the chin to a point at the top of the chin and moves the letter b and the big toe as well. It is one of the few times I have found Leonardo to correct himself and change the drawing. (See also the following entry, AP 114.)

Clearly, Leonardo made the drawing first, reconsidered it, changed the drawing, and wrote the entry at the very end. (Compare this entry to AP 172.) It is a unique comparison to make and may not have practical application, but it does give a surprising assessment of the size of the foot in relation to the head.

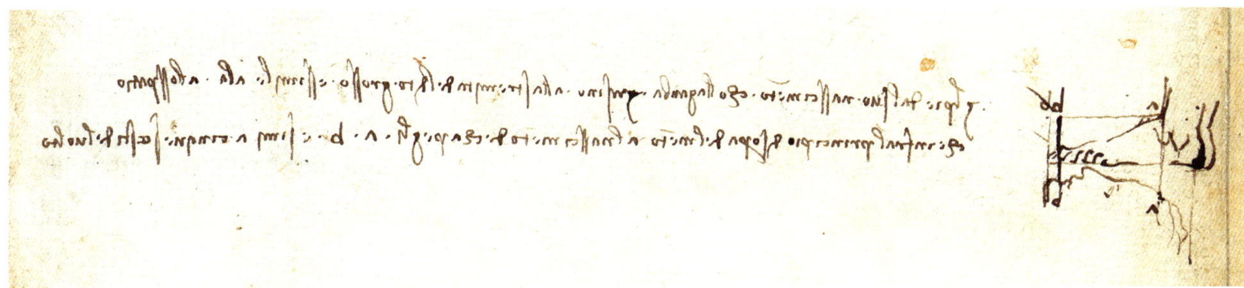

Detail, Plate 22, W. 19131b, Royal Collection, Windsor

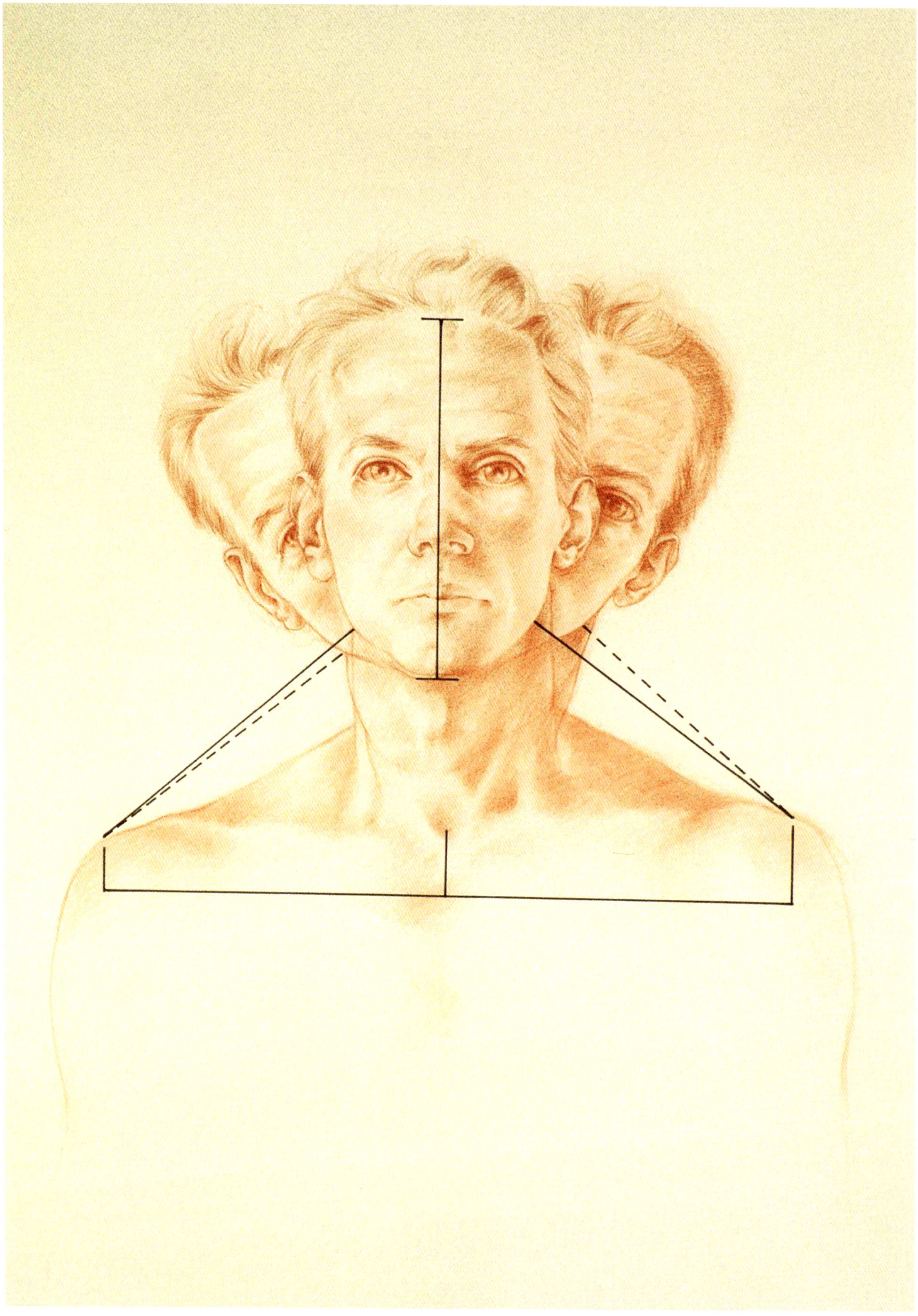

Cat. 14

AP 114

W. 19136–19139a, Royal Library, Windsor
c. 1490
Folio 11 Recto I

AP 114
No R#

I. *From the shoulder joint to the point of the jaw is one head when the face is standing in front.*

And [if] you bend the head in its way over the shoulders, then there will always be in the space which is between these shoulders and the points of the jaws 2 heads, and if one increases the other decreases as much.

This entry (Plate 28) is on the complex Folio 11, which was folded in four. It is one of the larger sheets, measuring 15¾ x 11 inches (405 x 281 mm). Leonardo's notes are on both sides of the page, and this entry was written in the uppermost right-hand quadrant of the Recto side, making it Leonardo's initial statement on this sheet. It is one of three paragraphs on this half of the sheet. This paragraph is not accompanied by a drawing, and Richter does not include this passage in his translation; it is one of the few he has left out,[23] probably because Leonardo himself crossed out this first paragraph with just two quick strokes of the pen. The other two paragraphs, II and III, can be found on AP 122, R 342. The proportional theory here is that the width of the torso from one shoulder to the other measures two faces. (Compare this to AP 123.)

I. If you measure the distance from one shoulder to the pit of the throat, or the center of the sternum, you will find it measures one face, and the same is true from the other shoulder, making the torso two faces wide. In addition, the distance from the shoulder to the point of the jaw is also one face. And, according to Leonardo, if you tilt the head toward the shoulder this distance decreases, as illustrated by the dotted line, while the other increases by the same amount. If you tilt the head in the other direction, the same increase and decrease will occur.

This observation is not particularly important and is, in fact, rather obvious, which leads one to believe that is why Leonardo, and Richter, left it out. The theory does, however, lend itself to an interesting drawing.

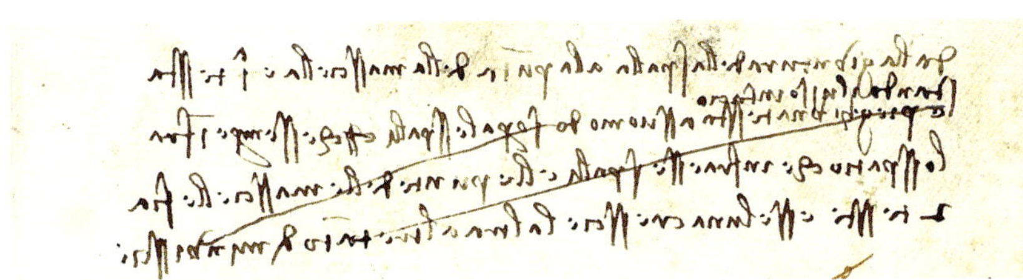

Detail, Plate 28, W. 19136–19139a, Royal Collection, Windsor

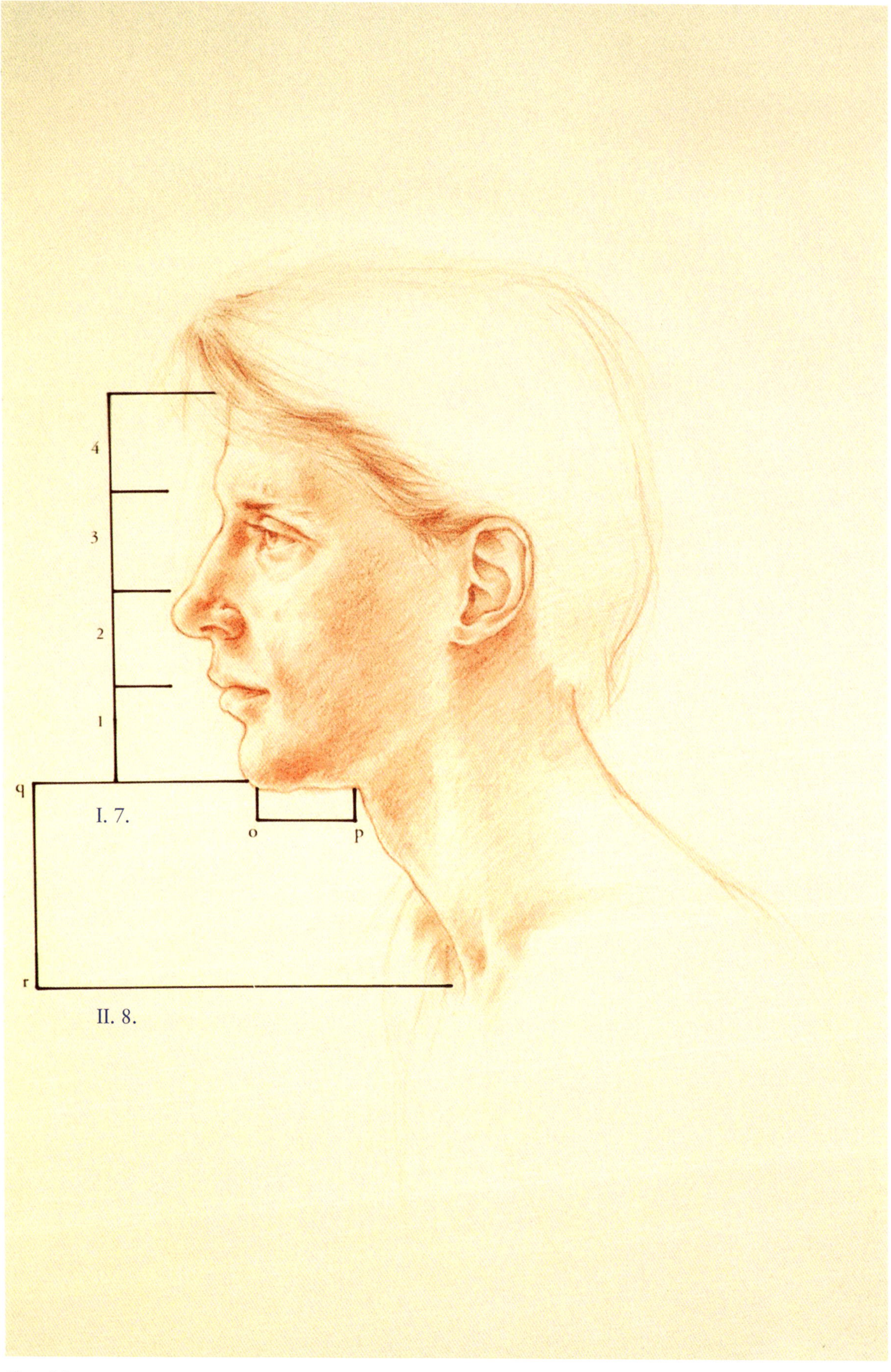

Cat. 15

AP 115

W. 12304, Royal Library, Windsor — AP 115
c. 1489–1490 — R 310
Folio 4 Recto 7, 8

I. 7 ***From the farthest projection of the chin to the throat o p is equal to the space between the mouth and the bottom of the chin, and a fourth part of the face.***

II. 8 ***The distance from the top of the throat to the pit of the throat below q r is half the face and the eighteenth part of a man's height.***

Leonardo is searching for new canons to measure with and new ways to divide the face (Plate 13). Each of these entries is unusual but amazingly accurate.

I. 7. The theory here is that the distance from the tip of the chin, o, to the beginning of the throat, p, is equal to the distance from the mouth, or the parting of the lips, to the tip of the chin. The first part of this comparison, the chin to the throat, is an elusive and unusual measurement and must be made on a man of average weight or less. But as a module with this model, it works quite well and the measurement is a fourth part of the face.

II. 8. The distance from q, the top of the throat, or the underside of the chin where it meets the throat, is equal to the distance from there to the pit of the throat, r, or the top of the manubrium (the first of the three parts of the sternum). And that distance, the length of the throat, is approximately half the length of the face, that is, the distance from the bottom of the chin to a point about the middle of the nose (see AP 111). This module would actually then be one-eighteenth of a man's height, as the full face, from the bottom of the chin to the hairline, measures one-ninth of a man's height. (See AP 146.)

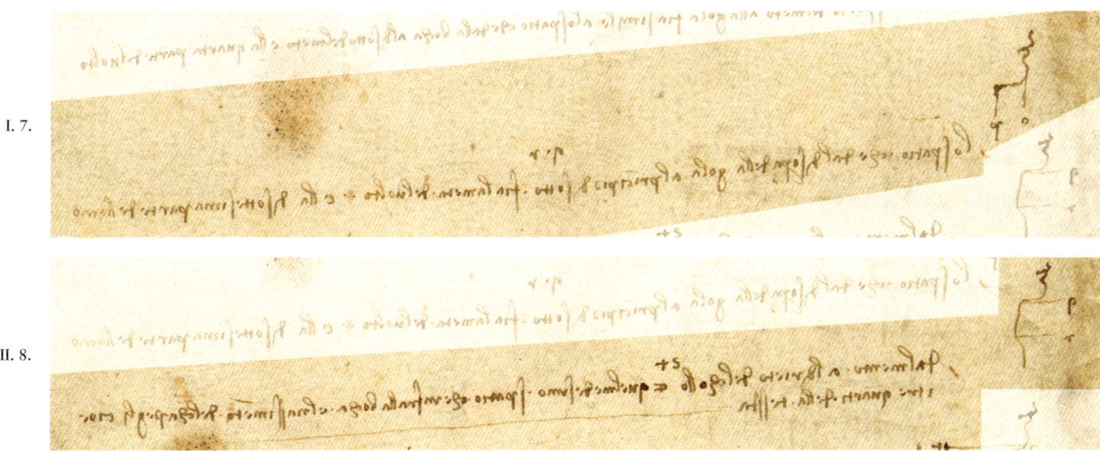

Detail, Plate 13, W. 12304, Royal Collection, Windsor

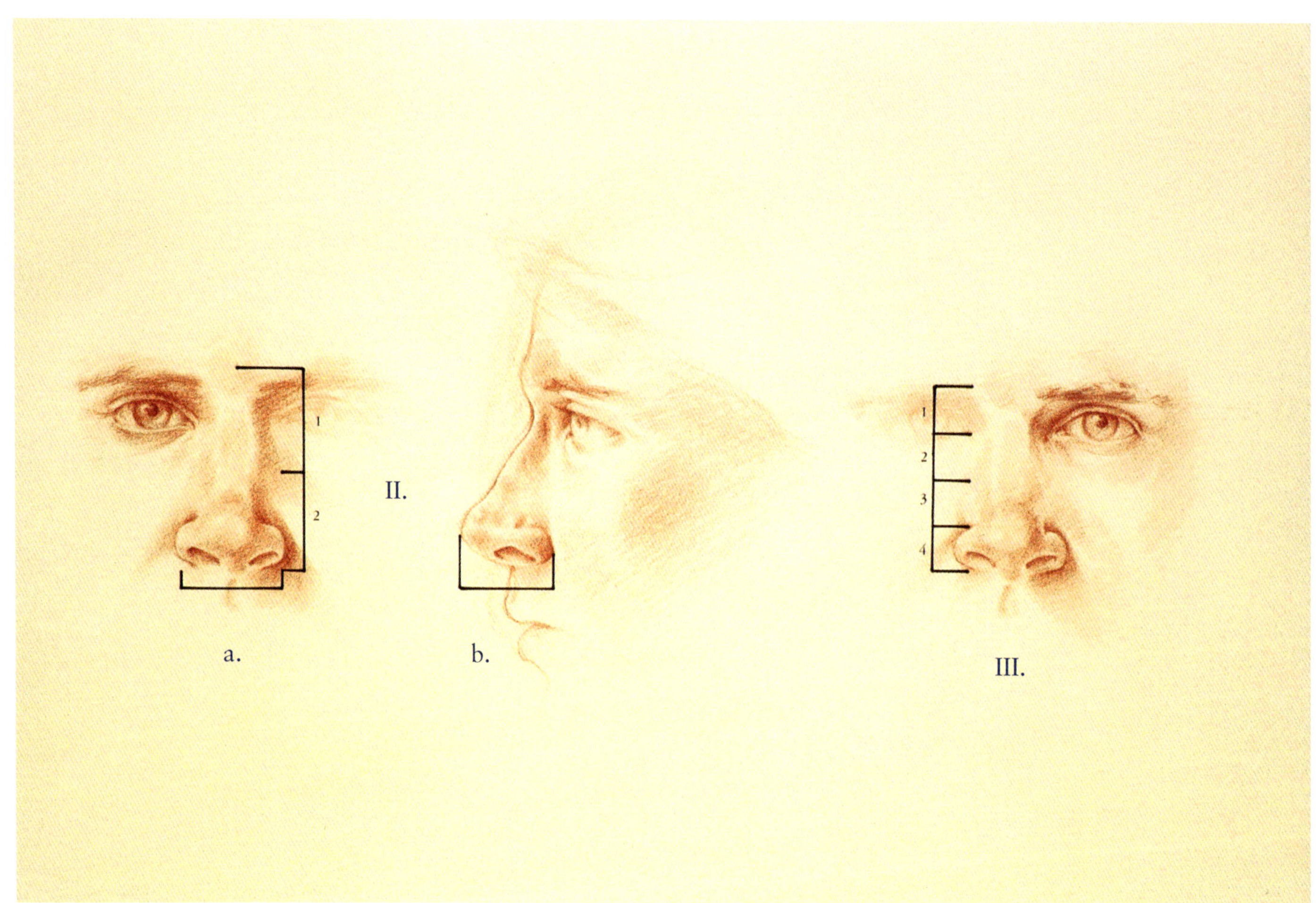

Cat. 16

AP 116

W. 19129, Royal Library, Windsor — AP 116
c. 1489–1490 — R 321
Folio 5 Recto II, III

II. a. *The nose will make a double square; that is, the width of the nose at the nostrils goes twice into the length from the tip of the nose to the eyebrows.*

b. *And, in the same way, in profile the distance from the extreme side of the nostril where it joins the cheek to the tip of the nose is equal to the width of the nose in front from one nostril to the other.*

III. *If you divide the whole length of the nose—that is, from the tip to the insertion of the eyebrows, into 4 equal parts, you will find that one of these parts extends from the tip of the nostrils to the base of the nose, and the upper division lies between the inner corner of the eye and the insertion of the eyebrows; and the two middle parts [together] are equal to the length of the eye from the inner to the outer corner.*

This sheet (Plate 18), measuring $5\frac{7}{8}$ x $6\frac{1}{2}$ inches (150 x 169mm), contains small drawings done in pen and brown ink. The first paragraph, which deals with the foot as a module, is treated by Richter in R 327, and by me in AP 173. Leonardo focuses on the foot as a module to measure other parts of the body, that is, the length of the arm, part of the arm, and the length of the head. However, these theories differ, in some cases dramatically, from other theories Leonardo uses with the foot as a module.

II. a. Leonardo's words are so clear here they hardly need any amplification. In short, the width of the nose, from the edge of one nostril to the other, enters twice into the length of the nose, from the tip of the nose to the eyebrows. These measurements will vary some from individual to individual, but as a general rule they work quite well.

b. In the same way, the width of the nose as seen in profile, from the tip of the nose to edge of the nostril where it meets the cheek, is equal to the width of the nose from one nostril to the other as seen in front. It's a wonderful and compact set of measurements.

III. Here Leonardo uses one of the four divisions of the length of the nose, the nostril, or the wing of the nose (dilator naris), as the canon of measurement. So the distance from the bottom of the nose to the top edge of the nostril goes four times into the length of the nose. And this module, when doubled, is actually the width of the eye from one corner to the other. I have not illustrated this comparison.

II

III

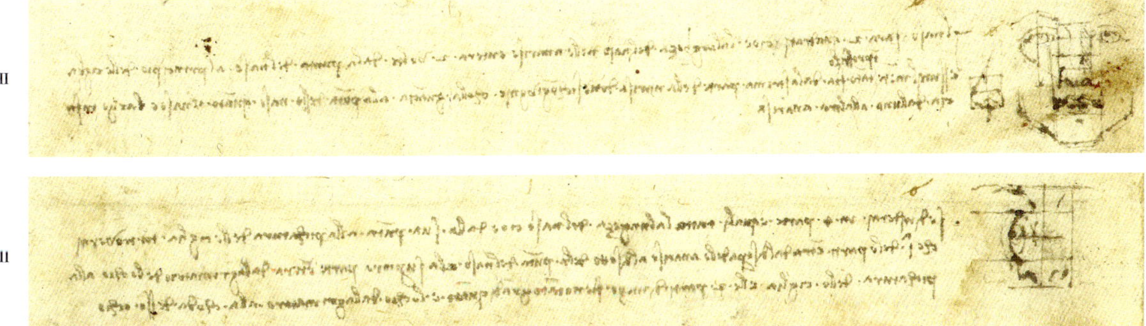

Detail, Plate 18, W. 19129, Royal Collection, Windsor

Notes
Chapter Three. The Head

[17] AP 101: For a most illuminating discussion of the Rule of Three, see Michael Baxandall, *Painting and Experience in Fifteenth- Century Italy*, 2nd ed. (Oxford and New York: Oxford University Press, 1988), 95–102. From page 97: "The Rule of Three was how the Renaissance dealt with problems of proportion." Most artists and merchants during the fifteenth century were familiar with both the practical and the aesthetic value "of geometric proportion: A stands to B as C stands to D. For our purpose, the important thing is the identity of a skill brought both to partnership or exchange problems and to the making of pictures."

[18] AP 102: Here, Leonardo uses the term for face (*volto*) when he actually means the whole head. This is also most unusual, because he continually misuses the term head when in fact he means face, while here he uses the word for face when he means head (capo).

[19] AP 103: Here, Leonardo uses the word head (*testa*) when he clearly means face. Richter rightly transcribes testa as "face."

[20] AP 103: A. E. Popham, *The Drawings of Leonardo da Vinci*, Compiled, Introduced, and Edited by A. E. Popham, Deputy Keeper of Prints and Drawings, British Museum (London and New York: Reynal and Hitchcock, 1945), LXVII, commentary to drawing marked #191: "The horsemen are probably studies for *The Battle of Anghiari*, 1503–1504."

[21] AP 104: Frank Zollner, *Leonardo da Vinci 1452–1519: The Complete Paintings and Drawings* (London: Taschen, 2005), fig. 226, 386. See also Carlo Pedretti, *The Literary Works of Leonardo da Vinci*, Compiled and Edited from the Original Manuscripts by Jean Paul Richter, Commentary by Carlo Pedretti (Berkeley and Los Angeles: University of California Press, 1977), vol. I, R 319, 236: "The abbreviation 'no' in line [number] 19 is interpreted by Richter to mean '19th'. If Leonardo meant 'nona,' that is, the ninth part of the head, then one should read 'faccia' instead of 'testa.'" Hereafter, cited as *Commentaries*.

[22] AP 110: See note 52 in chapter 7, "The Arm and Hand," AP 192. See also Pedretti, *Commentaries*, vol. I, R 349, 254,: The words *Caravazo* and *Trezo* are references by Leonardo suggesting "… Carravaggio and Trezzo are the names of two towns in Lombardy, so that the two models used by Leonardo must have been designated with the names of their hometowns, just as Francesco Melzi is once referred to as 'il melzo.'"

[23] AP 114: The authors of the *Quaderni* divided the entire page into eight parts or paragraphs. Only the first paragraph is left out by Richter, and I have been perplexed for some time by Richter's decision to omit it. Recently, I found in the authors' notes on the condition of the individual pages the following sentence: "The last [first] three lines of passage [I] are cancelled." The paragraph written by Leonardo is composed of five lines, and upon more careful inspection I found two delicate diagonal pen strokes drawn through the last three lines. As I have pointed out at other times, seldom does Leonardo cross anything out, so I was surprised to find the above statement. But in this case the answer may be found in his proposed theory.

CHAPTER FOUR

THE TORSO: AP 121–140

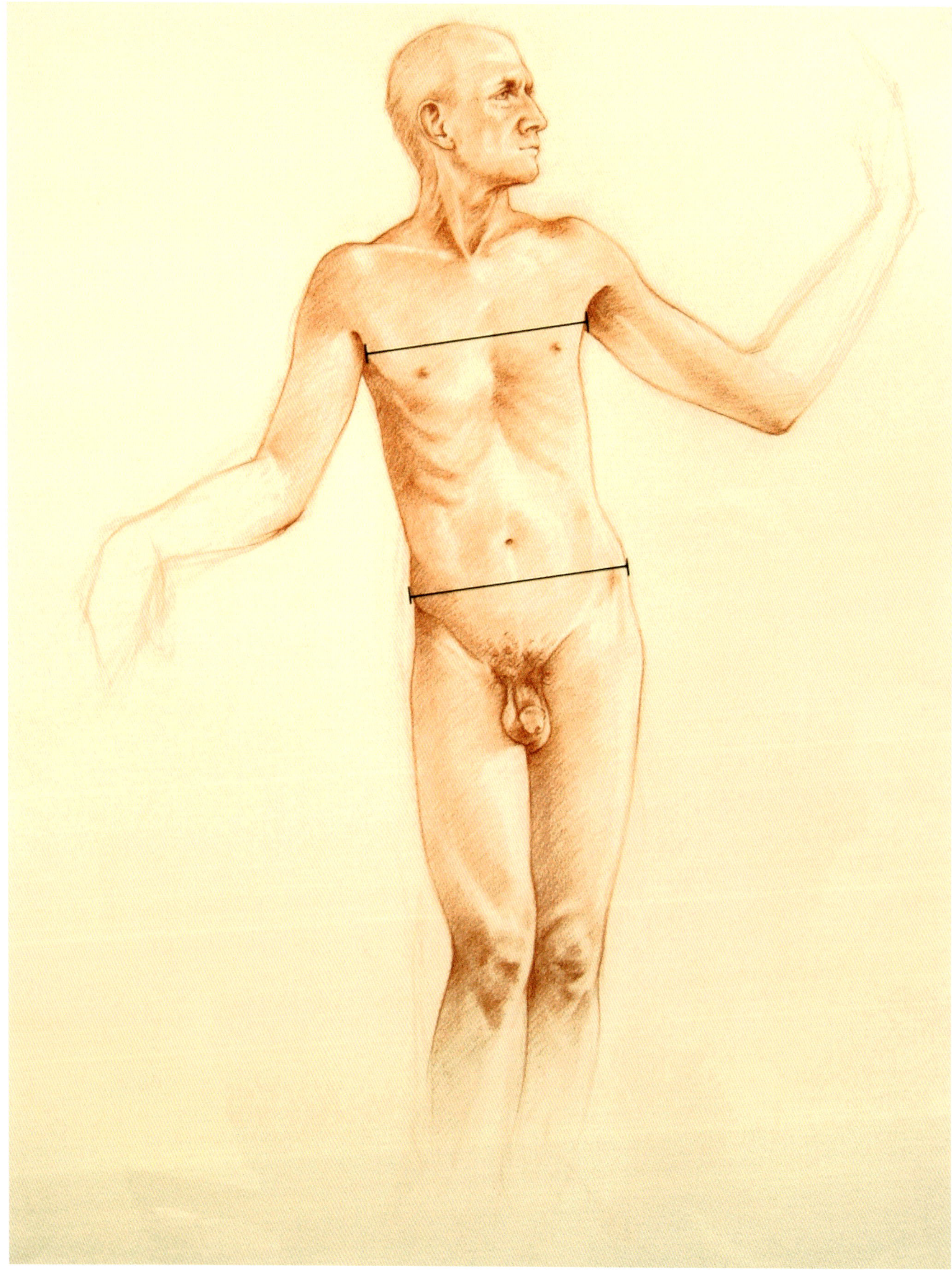

Cat. 17

AP 121

W. 19136–19139a, Royal Library, Windsor **AP 121**
c. 1490 **R 342**
Folio 11 Recto VIII

The width of a man under the arms is the same as at the hips.

This statement, one of those beautifully simple but carefully conceived observations, comes from the very large sheet, $15^{3}/_{4}$ x 11 inches (405 x 231 mm), marked Folio 11 (Plate 28), which was folded in four and, therefore, has four Windsor catalogue numbers. This statement is the last in the lower left-hand corner of the page and has a fine little pen-and-ink drawing of a frontal male torso from the shoulders to below the hips. However, unlike my drawing, Leonardo's drawing suggests the width of a man under the arms as the same as the hips by drawing two perfectly straight, vertical lines projecting downward from under the armpits to the pelvis. They line up perfectly, one above the other, and confirm the comparison.

The rest of this side of the page deals mainly with the proportions of the arm and hand, with three entries that deal with the whole figure and the torso.

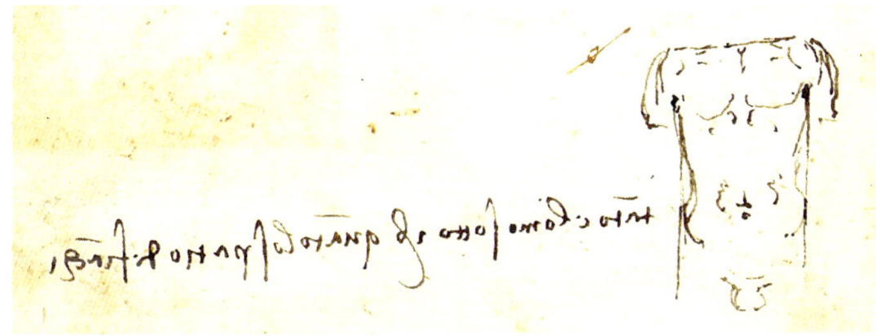

Detail, Plate 28, W. 19136–19139a, Royal Collection, Windsor

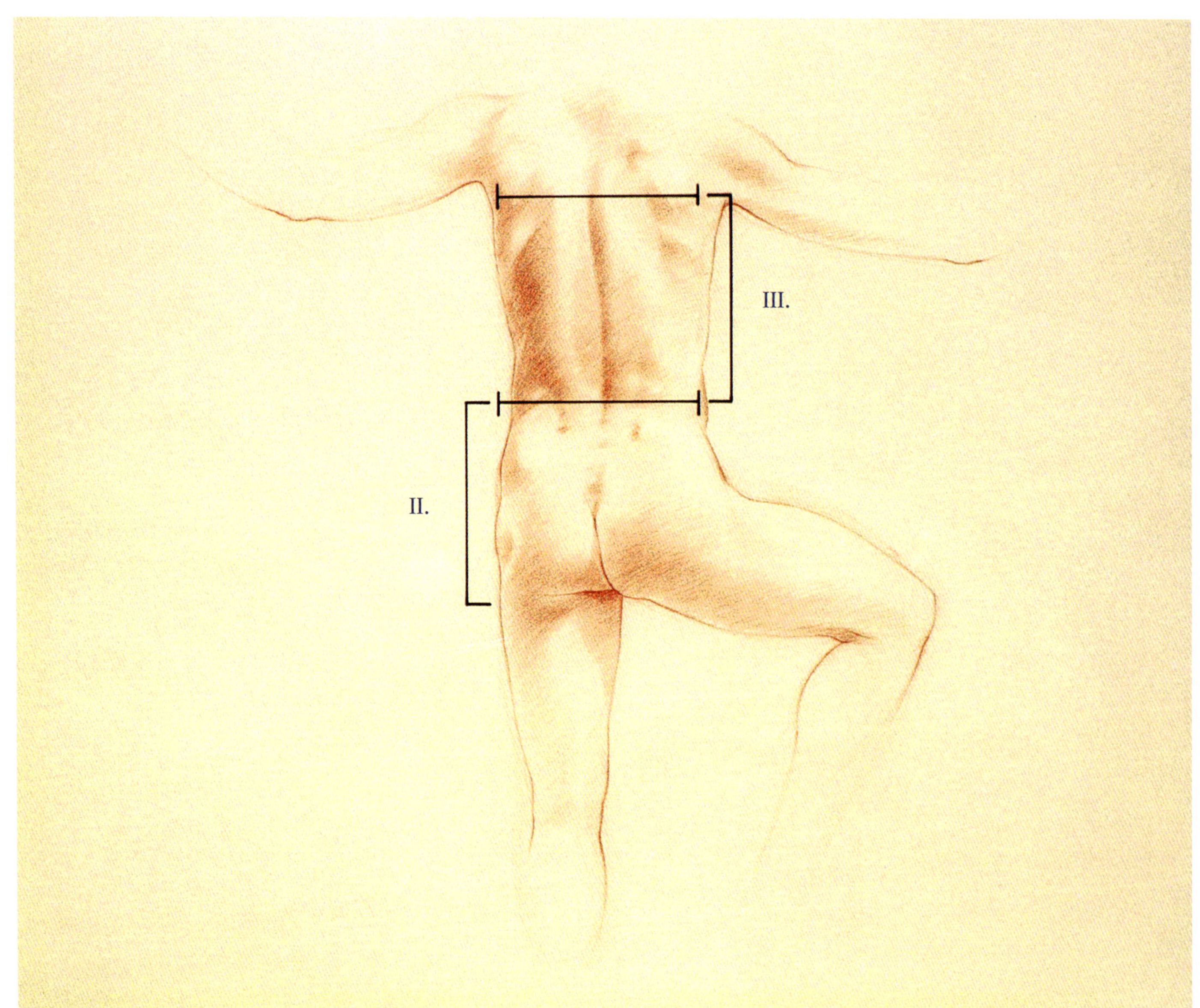

Cat. 18 AP 122

W. 19136–19139a, Royal Library, Windsor **AP 122**
c. 1490 **R 342**
Folio 11 Recto II, III

II. ***A man's width across the hips is equal to the distance from the top of the hips to the bottom of the buttocks, when a man stands equally balanced on both feet; and there is the same distance from the top of the hips to the armpit.***

III. ***The waist, or narrower part above the hips will be half-way between the armpits and the bottom of the buttocks.***

This entry also comes from the large Folio 11 (Plate 28), this time from the upper right-hand corner or quadrant. There are three paragraphs done in the same pen and brown ink. The first paragraph is one which was crossed out by Leonardo, discussed in AP 114, and was omitted by Richter. The third paragraph has another beautiful, small pen-and-ink drawing like the one noted in AP 121, again of a male torso from the shoulders to below the buttocks, but this time as seen from the back and enclosed in a square. The measurements and comparisons are perfect.

The first entry is an elaboration and extension of AP 121. A man's width across the hips is equal to the distance from the top of the hips to the bottom of the buttocks, thus forming a square. At this point Leonardo says the width of the hips is equal to the distance from the hips to the armpits, thus forming another square. The waist, or the area just above the hips, the iliac crest of the pelvis, is the center of this double square.

The theory works just as well when a man is perfectly balanced on both feet or on one foot as seen here. The important thing is that the hips and shoulders must be perfectly parallel to the ground.

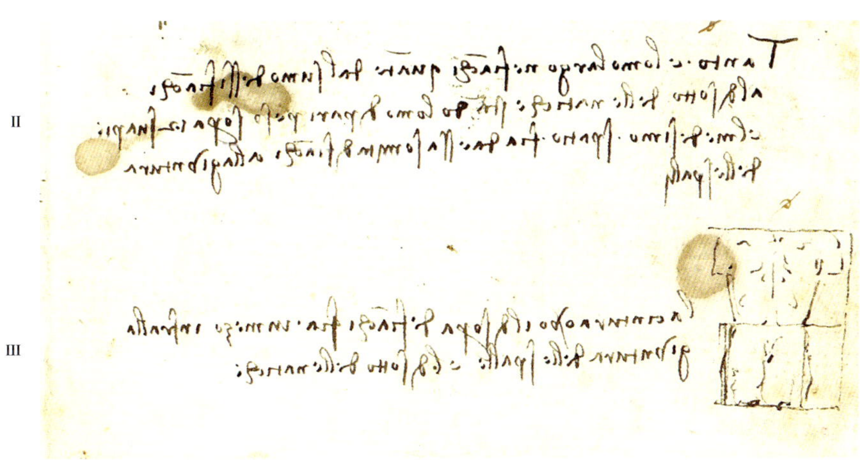

Detail, Plate 28, W. 19136–19139a, Royal Collection, Windsor

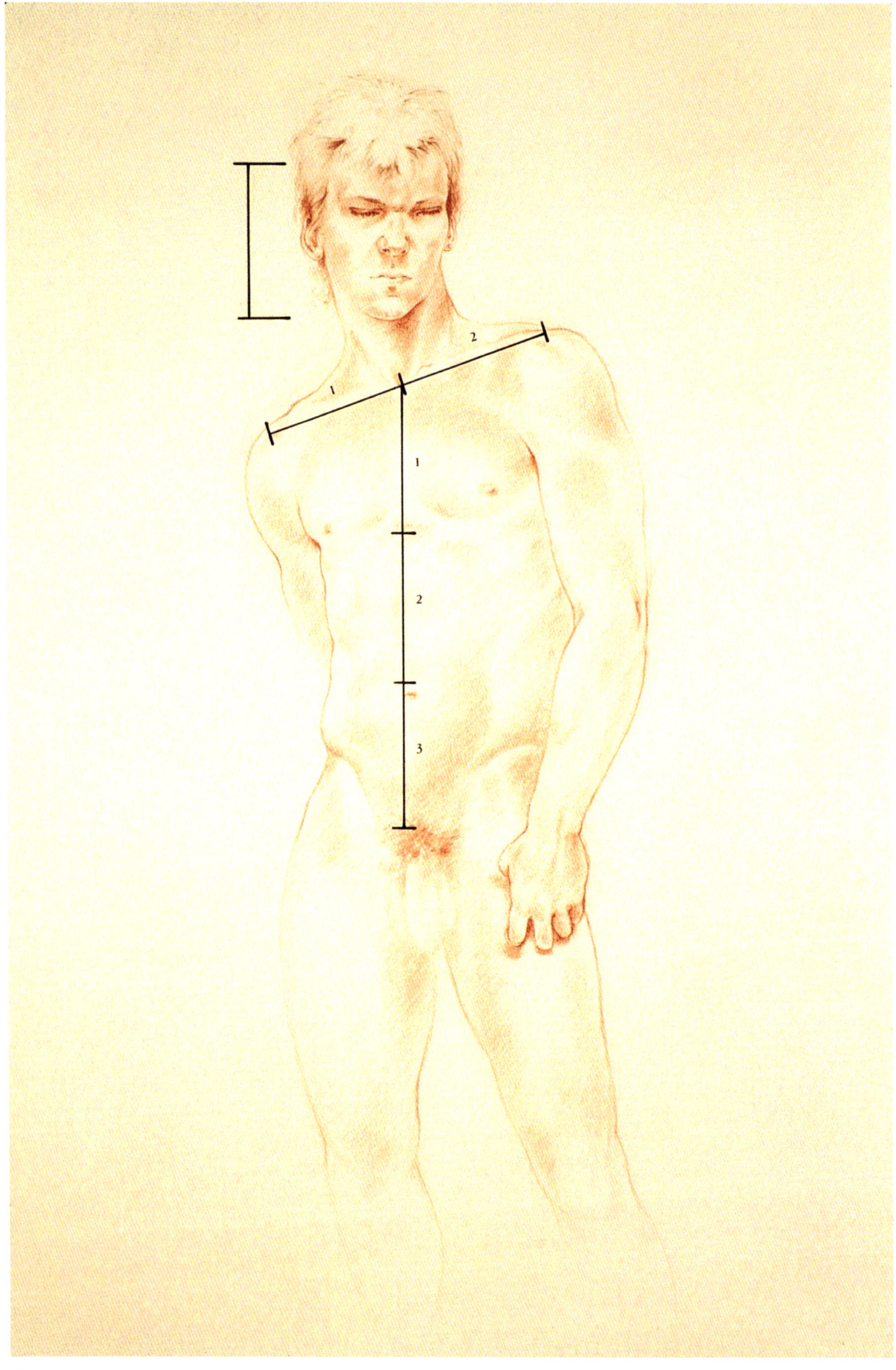

Cat. 19 AP 123

W. 19132b, Royal Library, Windsor **AP 123**
c. 1490 **R 333**
Folio 8 Verso II

From the joint of one shoulder to the other is two faces [heads] and is equal to the distance from the top of the breast to the navel. From this point to the genitals is a face's length.

Here (Plate 24), Leonardo uses the word head (*testa*) for face. Richter translates it as "face," and rightly so. The use of the head as a canon of measurement is standard practice, but using the face to divide up the torso horizontally as well as vertically is unusual but very effective here. (See AP 146.)

The face as a module, from the chin to the hairline, will enter two times into the distance between the shoulders. (See also AP 114.) But then Leonardo says that using that distance, two faces or the distance between the shoulders, as a module, is equal to the distance from the top of the breast to the navel, and then one more face to the genitals.

When we break down the theory using the face as our canon, we find that: the face goes twice into the distance from one shoulder to the other, once from the top of the breast to the bottom of the sternum, below the nipple, once from the bottom of the sternum to the navel, and once from the navel to the beginning of the genitals (*il nascimeto [nascimento] al mebro [membro]*), literally, "the birth of the male member." This is an important distinction, because in using the head and not the face to measure the height of a man, the center of a standing figure from the top of the head to the feet is the pubis symphasis, the lowest part of the pelvis, or four heads down from the top and four heads up from the bottom.

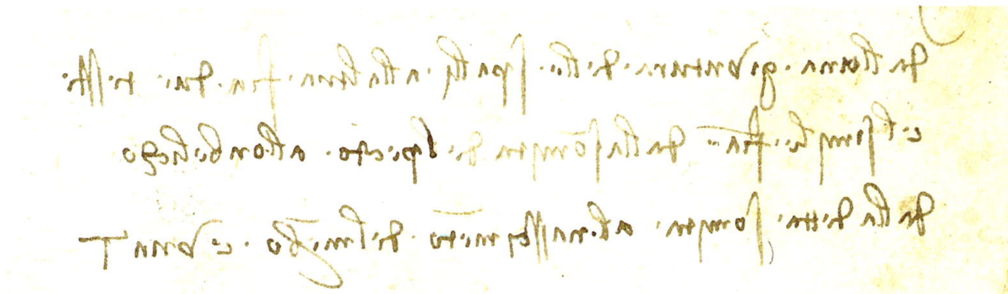

Detail, Plate 24, W. 19132b, Royal Collection, Windsor

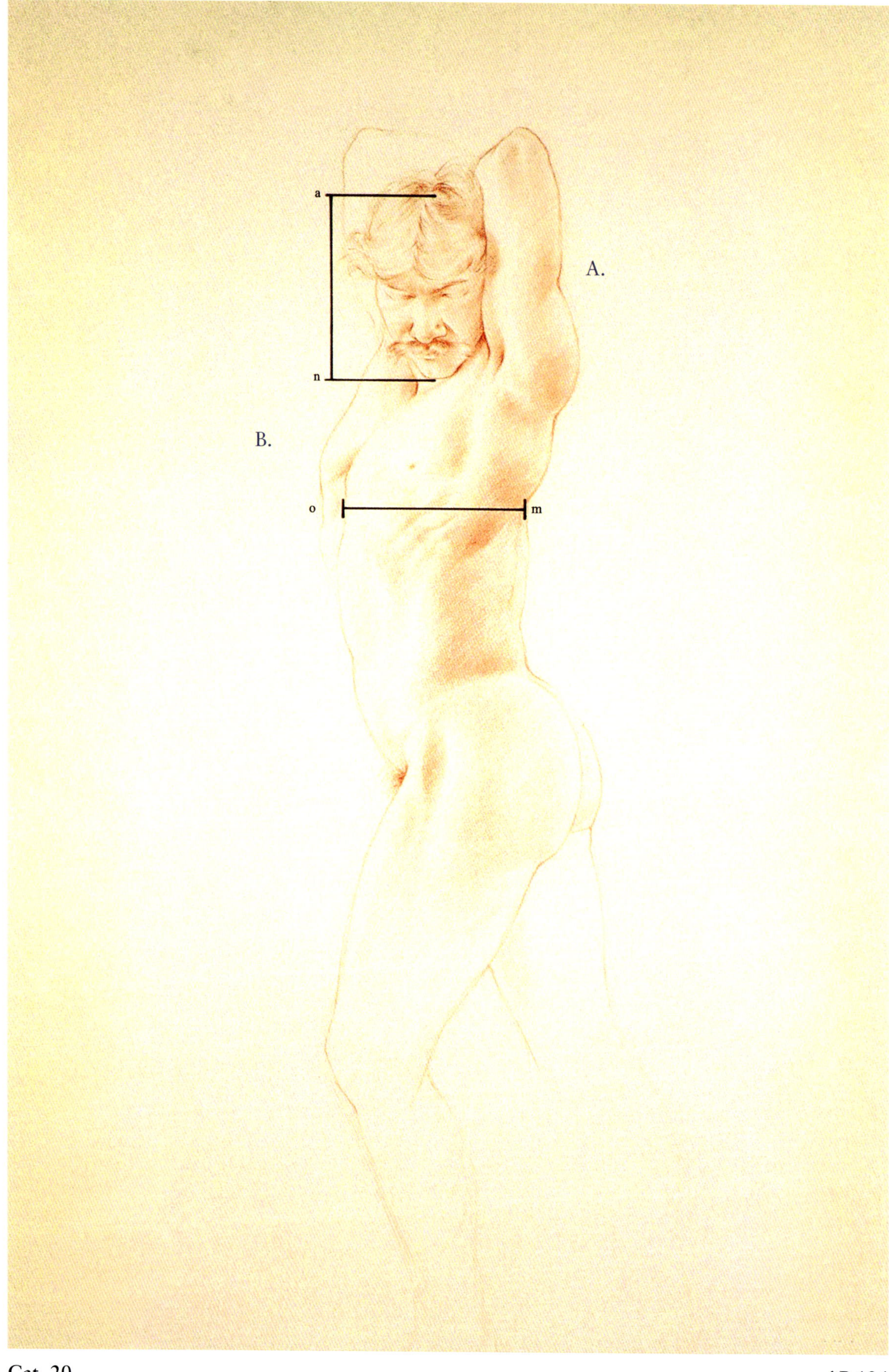

Cat. 20

AP 124

W. 19134–19135, Royal Library, Windsor **AP 124**
c. 1490 **R 341**
Folio 10 Recto II

A. *The greatest thickness of a man from the breast to the spine is one-eighth of his height and is equal to the space between the bottom of the chin to the top of the head.*

W. 19136–19139a, Royal Library, Windsor **R 339**
c. 1490
Folio 11 Recto VII

B. *a n is similar to m o.*

The model must be seen in profile and this measurement taken at the thickest section of the torso from the breast through to the spinal column. This measurement seems to work best in well-developed men, whereas underdeveloped men might measure less.

There is no drawing for the first entry, Folio 10 Recto II (Plate 27), but there is a small, beautiful pen-and-ink drawing, on Folio 11 Recto VII, R 339, of a full, standing male in profile, facing right, slightly more than three inches high (Plate 28). This drawing contains two horizontal construction lines, one at the top of the head marked a, and one at the bottom of the chin marked n. There are two more letters, m and o, marked at the thickest part of the chest. The comparison is clear: the length of the head is equal to the thickness of the chest from the sternum in front to the spinal column in the back.

I have separated these entries from their original paragraphs and combined the two entries because they each use the same module, the length of the head, and there is no doubt here that it is the whole head. Leonardo confirms his use of the whole head by emphasizing that it is one-eighth the height of a man. (See AP 142 for the first part of R 339.)

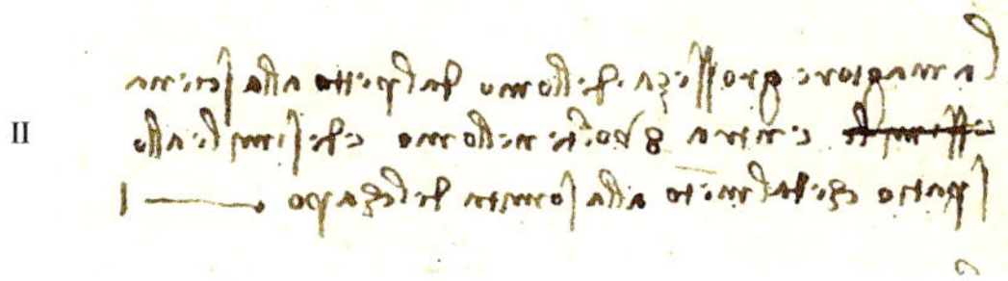

Detail, Plate 27, W. 19134–19135, Royal Collection, Windsor

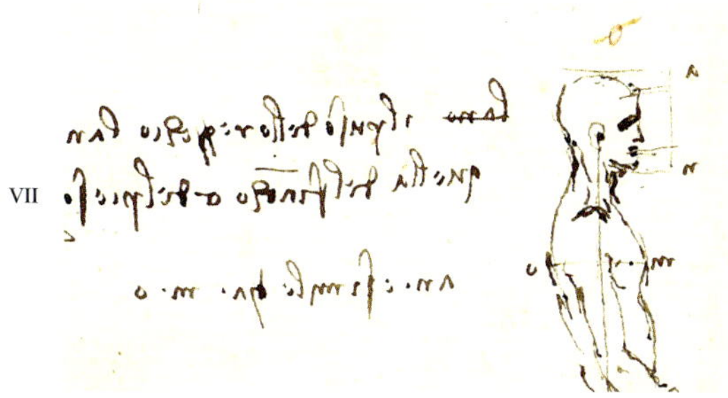

Detail, Plate 28, W. 19136–19139a, Royal Collection, Windsor

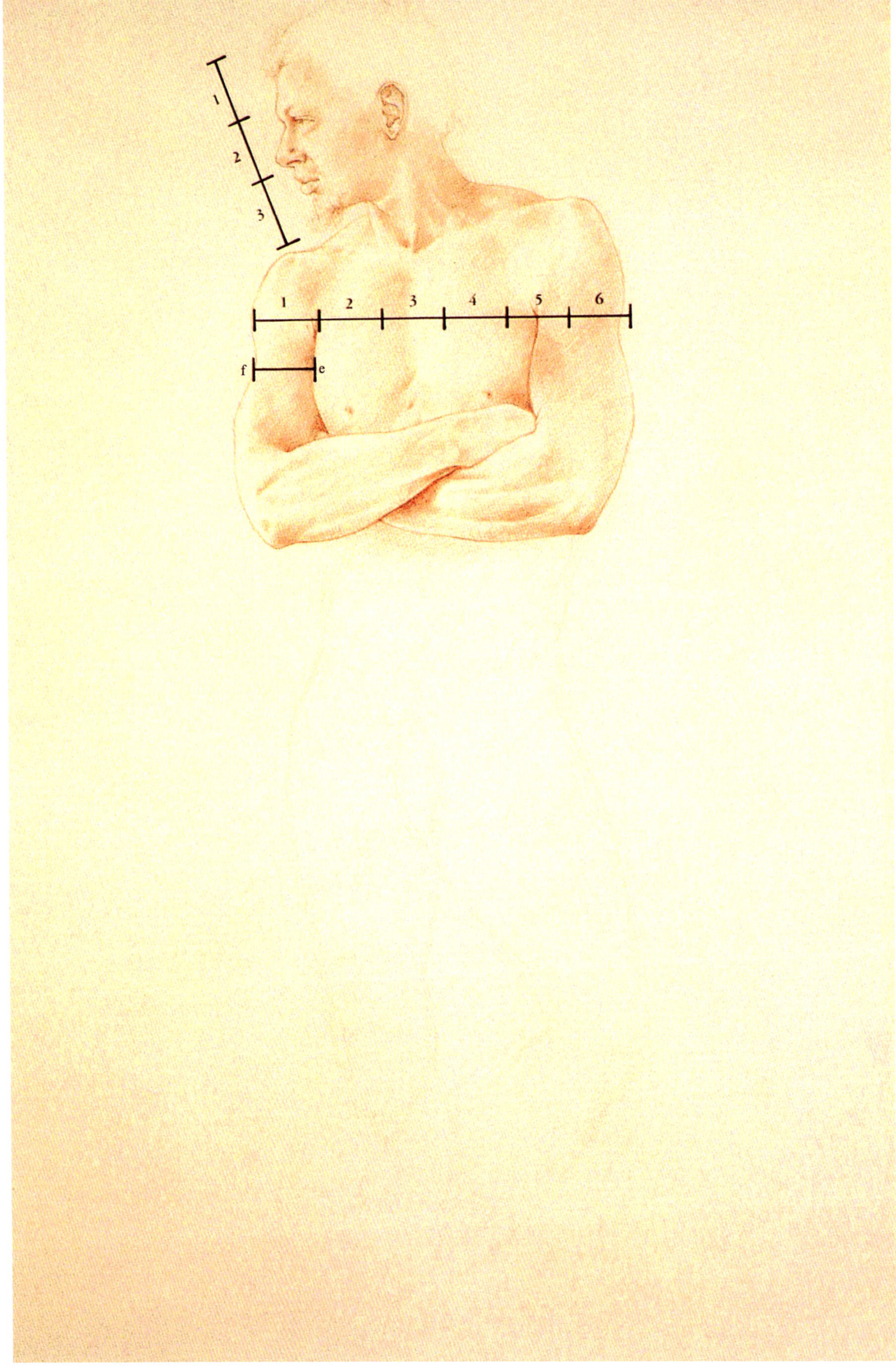

Cat. 21 **AP 125**

W. 19130a, Royal Library, Windsor **AP 125**
c. 1490 **R 334**
Folio 6 Recto III

The [thickness of] the arm where it springs from the shoulder in front goes 6 times into the space between the two outside edges of the shoulders, and 3 times into the face, and four times into the length of the foot, and three times into the hand inside and out.

The verb Leonardo uses here (Plate 19), *spiccare,* means to jump, to leap, or to spring forward. Richter translates it as "springs," but the *Quaderni* translation is "...where it detaches itself...". Leonardo's words and Richter's translation are far more poetic. They refer to that section of the arm where the deltoid meets the biceps, the conjuncture of which forms an indentation, and it is the thickness of this indentation that Leonardo uses as a module. It is not a unit of measurement used often, if ever, but Leonardo's drawing is quite clear. The drawing is of a male torso from the shoulders to just below the pectoral muscles. On the model's right arm is a horizontal line, from the outer edge of the arm to the inner edge, just below the deltoid muscle, with the letters e f; obviously it is meant to define that portion of the arm as the module. Leonardo excludes the letters from his text, and so does Richter, but they are clearly marked on his drawing and I have included them in my drawing. Why he chose this module is unclear, but his use of language to characterize this section of the arm is a creatively poetic description of a non-anatomical function.

In addition, Leonardo uses the word head (*testa*), but Richter translates it as "face." In this case head is correct and not face. After many measurements on multiple models, I have found that the odd little space (e f) goes three times into the whole head.

The additional notations in his entry on the foot and hand are not treated here, nor does Leonardo treat them in his little drawing of only a male torso. Neither of these observations is accurate or useful, based on my experience, and I have left them out of my drawing as well. It leads one to speculate why Leonardo would have made these very specific measurements without a drawing to prove the theory. He may have made the measurements on a figure, found them inconclusive, and left them out of his drawing. He did not, however, remove or strike them from the text, which is something I have rarely seen him do.

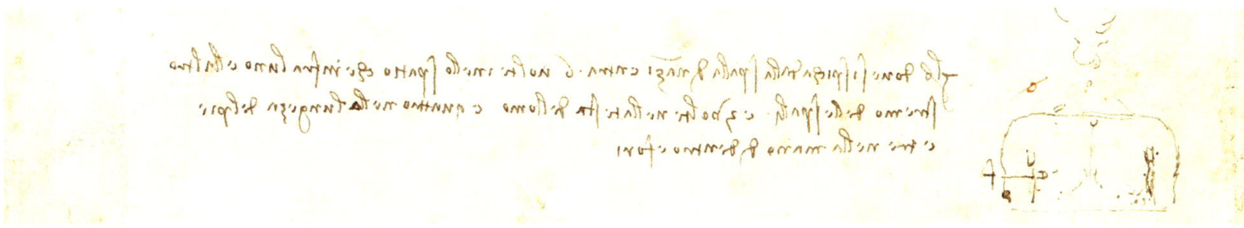

Detail, Plate 19, W. 19130a, Royal Collection, Windsor

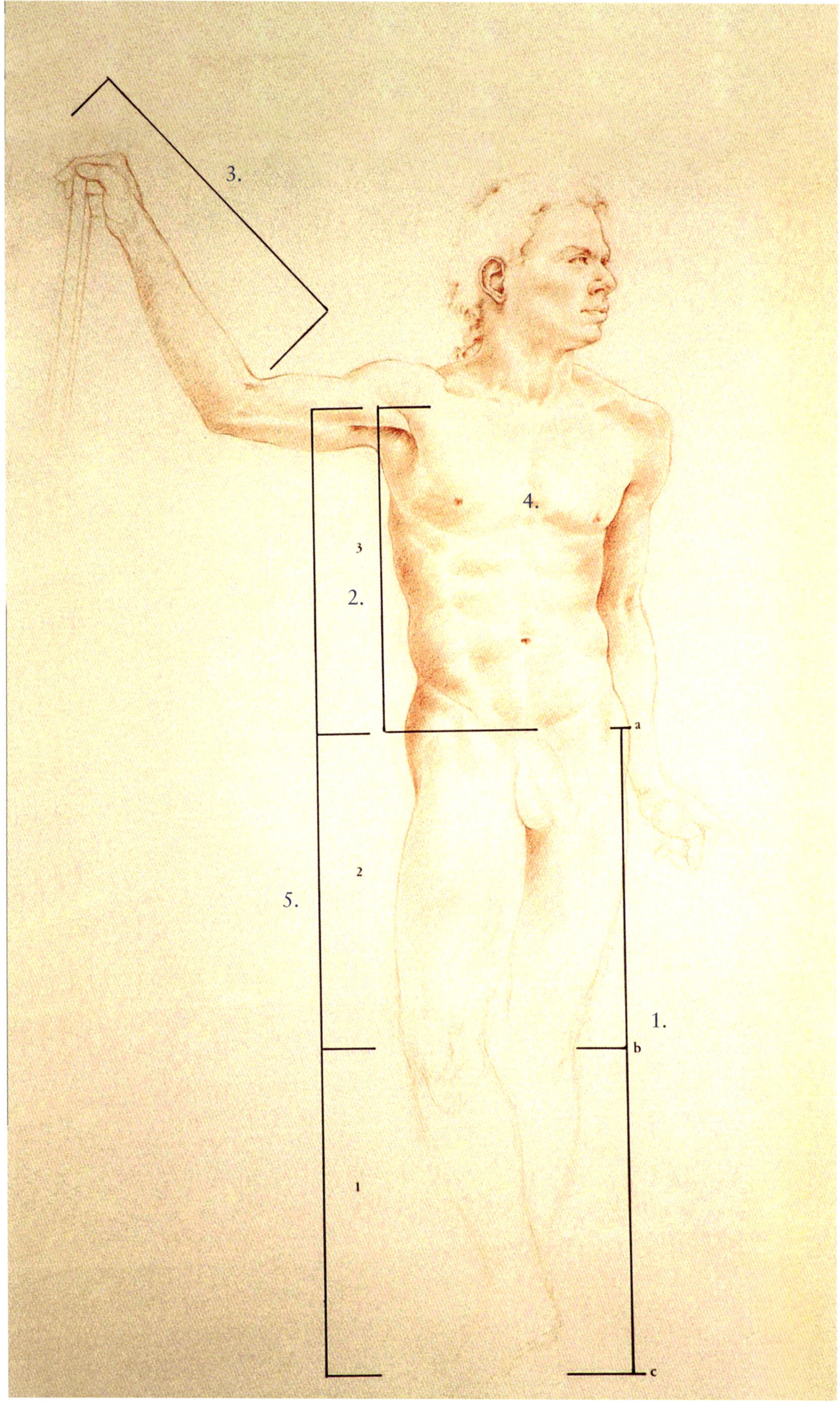

Cat. 22

AP 126

W. 19130b, Royal Library, Windsor **AP 126**
c. 1490 **R 335**
Folio 6 Verso I

(1) ***a b c are equal to each other and to the space from*** (2) ***the armpit of the shoulders to the genitals, and*** (3) ***to the distance from the tip of the fingers of the hand to the joint arm, and*** (4) ***to the half of the breast; and you must know that*** (5) ***c b is the third part of the height of a man from the shoulders to the ground.***

This drawing is on a modest-size sheet, $5^3/_4$ x $8^9/_{16}$ inches (146 x 218 mm), and starts on the right side, showing a right leg and then a left leg, both using the construction lines and letters to clarify the comparisons (Plate 20). There are also three torsos drawn, one indicating a line from the armpit to the genitals, the second showing the distance from the pit of the throat to the navel, the third turned on its side to equal the other two, and all three equaling the modules a b, or b c, at the very beginning of the above entry.

As pointed out in chapter 2, "Notes on Using This Book," I have quoted Richter's translations consistently throughout and have added comments about his translations only where it altered Leonardo's meaning or theory. The very first line in this entry is one in need of such clarification. Leonardo says, *"a b c sono equali (uguale) e son simili (simile) allo spatio..."* (a b c are equal to each other and are similar to the space...). Richter consistently translates the word *similar* as "equal," and most of the time the comparisons are exactly equal. This is one of the few times Leonardo uses both *equal* and *similar,* and the word *similar* in this case clearly means "almost but not exactly the same."

1. a, from the top of the femur, to b, the center of the patella, to c, the very bottom of the foot are equal to each other and are similar to
2. the distance from the armpit to the beginning of the genitals, or the pubis symphysis, and
3. from the tip of the fingers to the joint of the arm, which must be understood as the elbow, and
4. to the half of the breast, which makes absolutely no proportional sense no matter how it is interpreted;
5. and is a third part of the height of a man only from the shoulder, not the top of the head, to the ground.

The last portion of the entry is discussed in AP 161.

Detail, Plate 20, W. 19130b, Royal Collection, Windsor

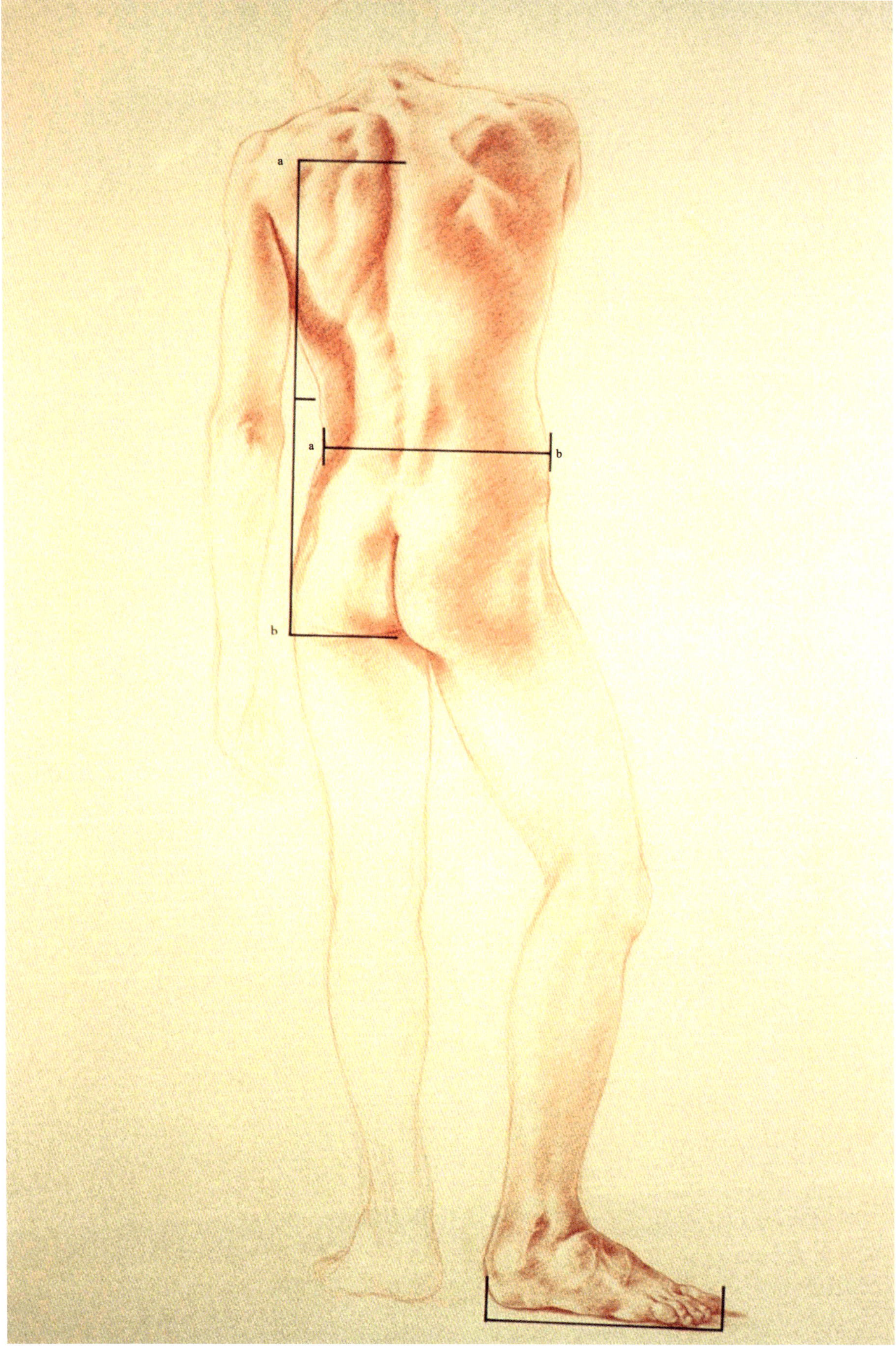

Cat. 23 AP 127

W. 12304, Royal Library, Windsor **AP 127**
c. 1489–1490 **R 337**
Folio 4 Recto 13

The torso a b in its thinnest part will measure one foot; and from a to b is two feet which makes two squares [to the seat.] [And the horse] — the thinnest part goes three times into the length, thus making three squares.

This entry, at the end of the long and famous sheet (Plate 13), devoted almost exclusively to the proportions of the face and head, Folio 4 (see: AP 111, 112, 115), measures 10$^3/_8$ x 8$^1/_2$ inches (264 x 215 mm) and is done in brown ink with some silverpoint. This sheet, separated out by Richter as R 337, is accompanied by a precise little drawing of the back view of a standing male figure without the head, measuring less than 2$^1/_2$ inches high.

There are several discrepancies in Richter's entry. The first, the initial set of letters a b, indicating the thinnest part of the torso, the waist, does not exist in Leonardo's drawing but does exist in his text, and Richter therefore rightly includes the letters in his text. The words are quite clear: the torso is the reference and the foot is the canon. The second discrepancy is in the last part of Richter's translation of Leonardo's sentence, "...and from a to b is 2 feet which makes two squares." The sentence should end there because Leonardo then writes, on the next line in a new sentence, "In the horse, the thinnest part goes 3 times into the length, thus making 3 squares." This reading makes much more sense, particularly as an example of Leonardo's use of comparative anatomy. Carlo Pedretti, in his commentary to Jean Paul Richter's edition, *The Literary Works of Leonardo da Vinci,* not only explains the discrepancy but discusses the 1:2 proportions of a man as well as the 1:3 proportions of a horse.[24] See the full text in the note.

The comparison of the foot to the waist is quite accurate and useful, particularly in the trim young man shown here, but as a canon of measurement it enters into the length of the torso, from a, the top of the shoulders, to b, the bottom of the buttocks, more than two times. In fact, the measurement enters into that distance more than two times, and it is more like two and one-quarter times in both Leonardo's drawing and my drawing. The use of the foot as a canon of measurement determining the length of the entire figure goes back to ancient times.

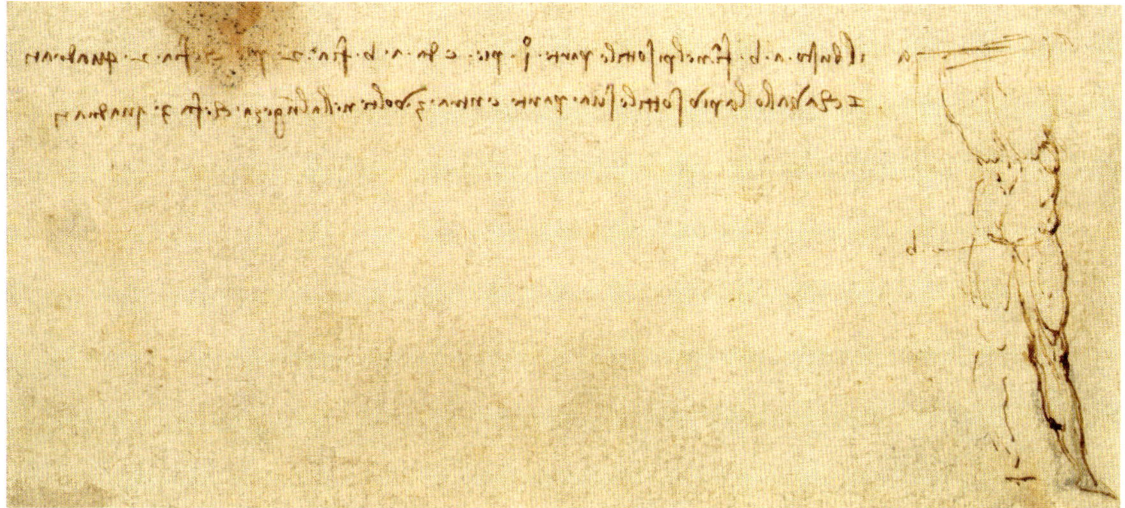

Detail, Plate 13, W. 12304, Royal Collection, Windsor

Notes
Chapter Four: The Torso

[24] AP 127: Pedretti, *Commentaries*, vol. I, R 337, 243. "The text is on comparative proportions and makes sense when revised as follows (transcription in modern Italian): *'The torso a b in its thinnest part measures a foot: and from a to b is two feet, which makes two squares. In the horse, the thinnest part goes three times into the length, thus making three squares.'* The two square system of proportion does not quite work in the Venice drawing of the Vitruvian proportions (although the foot there does correspond to the 'piu sottile parte' of the torso). The proportion 1:3 referred to the horse can be checked in W.12321 and other drawings of the Sforza horse."

CHAPTER FIVE

THE WHOLE BODY: AP 141–160

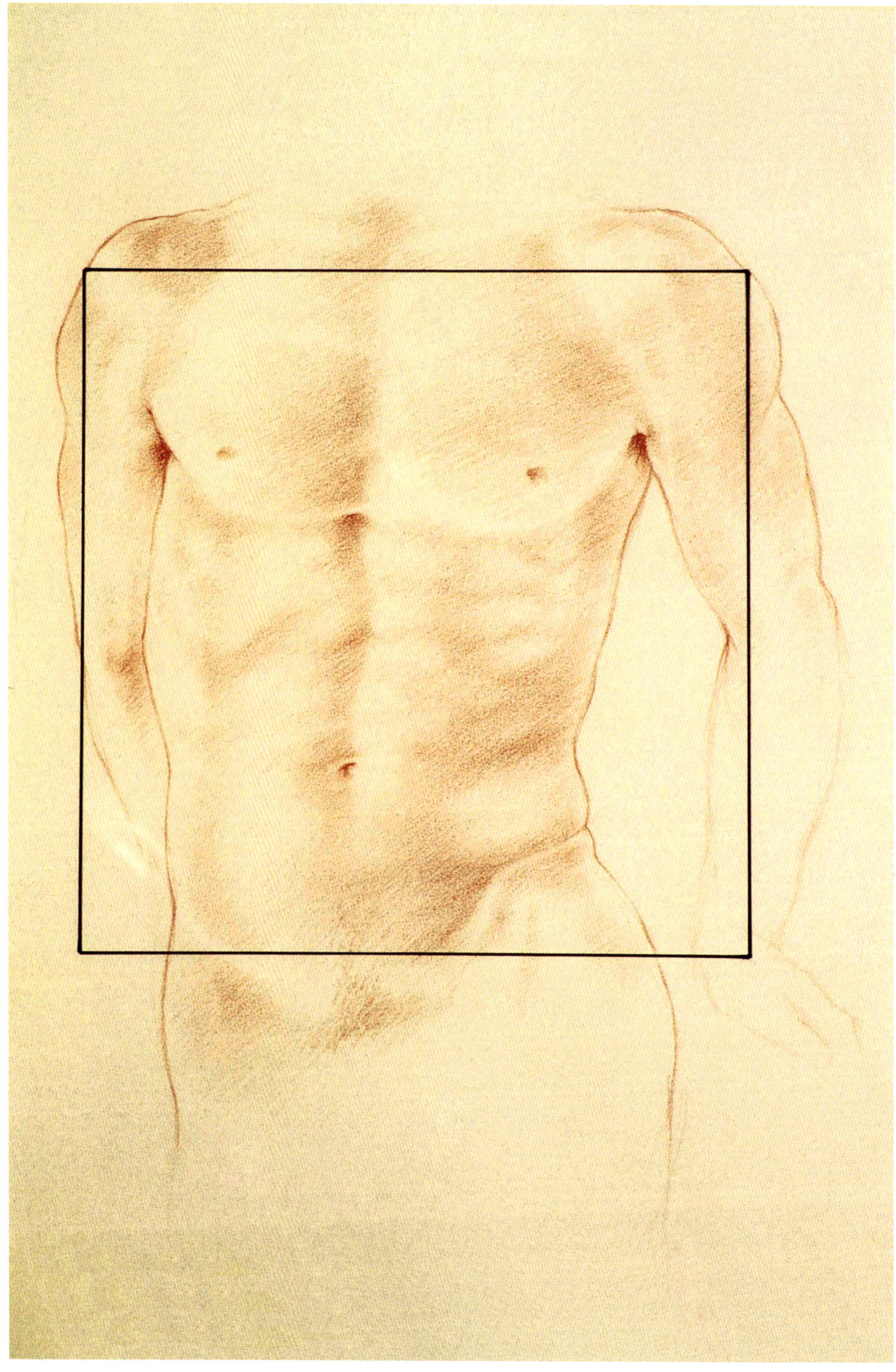

Cat. 24

AP 141

W. 19132b, Royal Library, Windsor **AP 141**
c. 1490 **R 333**
Folio 8 Verso I

The cubit is one-fourth of the height of a man and is equal to the greatest width of the shoulders.

The entry is on the verso side (Plate 24) of a modest sheet measuring $6\frac{1}{4}$ x $8\frac{1}{2}$ inches (160 x 218 mm). There is no drawing, only text with one paragraph consisting of two sentences. The first sentence is treated here, while the second is explained in AP 123.

As there is no drawing and thus no visual information with this entry, the theory needs to be proven by defining the meaning of the word *cubit*. The cubit was "…an ancient measure of length, about 18-22 inches; originally, the length of the arm from the end of the middle finger to the elbow."[25]

If we take the measurement of a man's shoulders approximately edge to edge, and compare it to the length of his arm from the tip of the middle finger to the elbow, we find that they are equal. So the cubit, as a module, is the breadth of a man's shoulders as well as the length of a man's arm, from the elbow to the tip of the fingers.

The cubit, like the *braccio* (see note to AP 146), was used as a standard canon of measurement from ancient times through the Renaissance. The term originally comes from the Greek word *kybos*, meaning cube, which in geometry is a solid with six equal square sides. As Vitruvius explains in great detail in his book on architecture, the Greeks developed their concept of ratio and proportion by measuring the members of the body, that is, "the finger, the palm, the foot and the cubit."[26] In any case, Leonardo's measurement does work.

Detail, Plate 24, W. 19132b, Royal Collection, Windsor

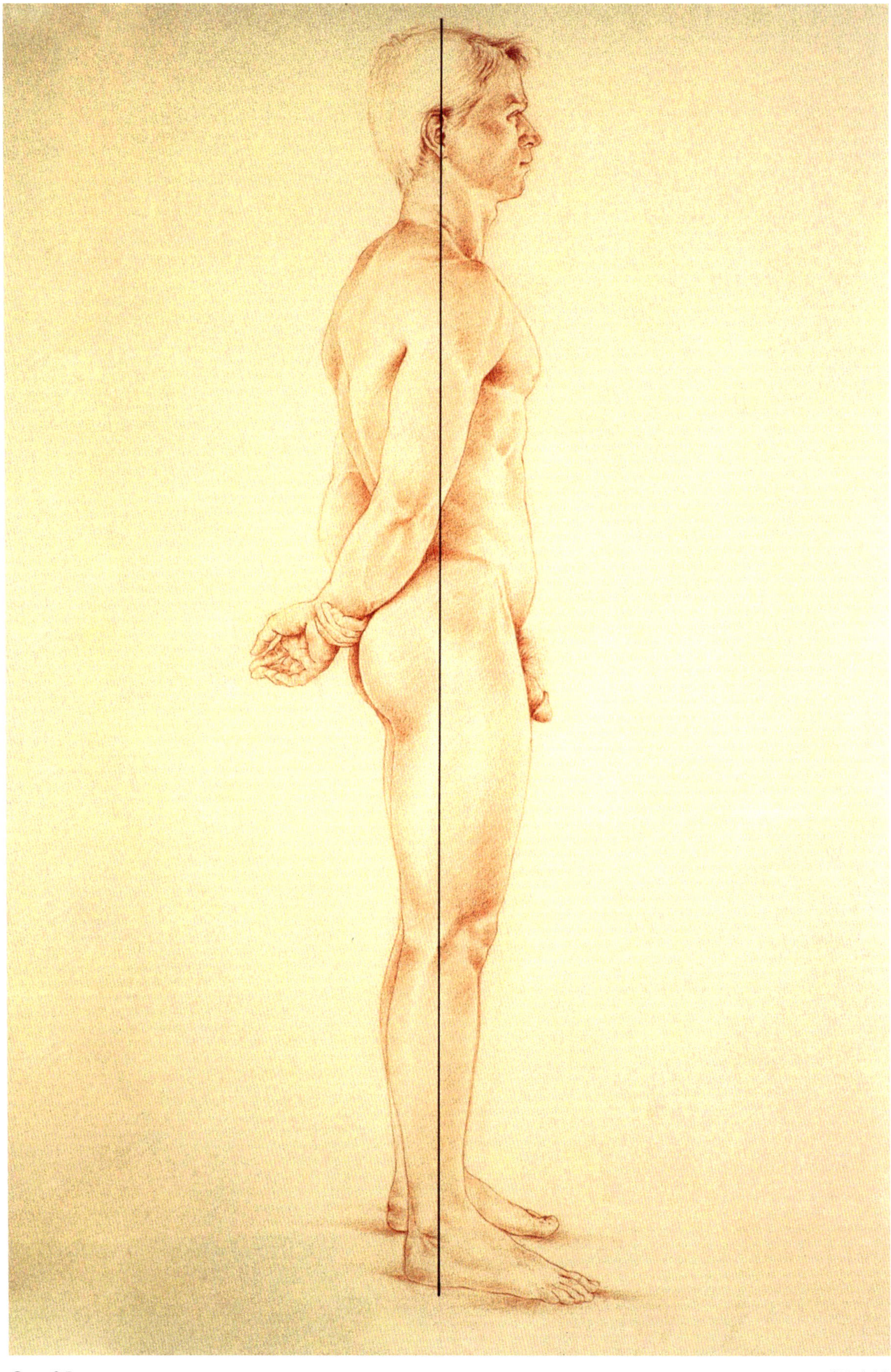

Cat. 25 AP 142

W. 19136–19139a, Royal Library, Windsor **AP 142**
c. 1490 **R 339**
Folio 11 Recto VII

The opening of the ear, the joint of the shoulder ("la nascita della spalla"), that of the hip and of the ankle [foot] form a perpendicular line.

The drawing for this observation comes from the famous Folio 11, W. 19136–19139r, folded in four (Plate 28).[27] The entry is composed of two succinct sentences; this drawing is based on the first, while the second is explained in AP 124. Leonardo uses the same beautifully drawn little figure of a man in profile to illustrate both.

While I have attempted to quote Richter's translations verbatim throughout, I have found it necessary in this case to interpret Leonardo's words differently. Instead of reading, as in Richter, "... are in perpendicular lines," they should read "... are in, or form, a perpendicular line." Richter's translation makes Leonardo's words seem vague, while both the meaning and the drawing are crystal clear. Also, Leonardo uses the word *pie* (*piede*), foot, but *ankle* would be more precise.

Leonardo suggests that with a man standing straight and in full profile, one could draw a perfectly perpendicular line starting through the opening of the ear, through the beginning of the shoulder at the head of the humerus, literally, "the birth of the shoulder," through the center of the great trochanter and ending through the center of the ankle, the lower extremity of the lateral malleolus of the fibula. The fact that all of these parts of the body line up so perfectly is truly a marvel of Nature's construction.

We should point out here that in my drawing the model's torso is rotated just slightly to his left, pushing the shoulders a bit forward. But one can clearly see that with a slight rotation to his right the model would be in perfect alignment with the theory.

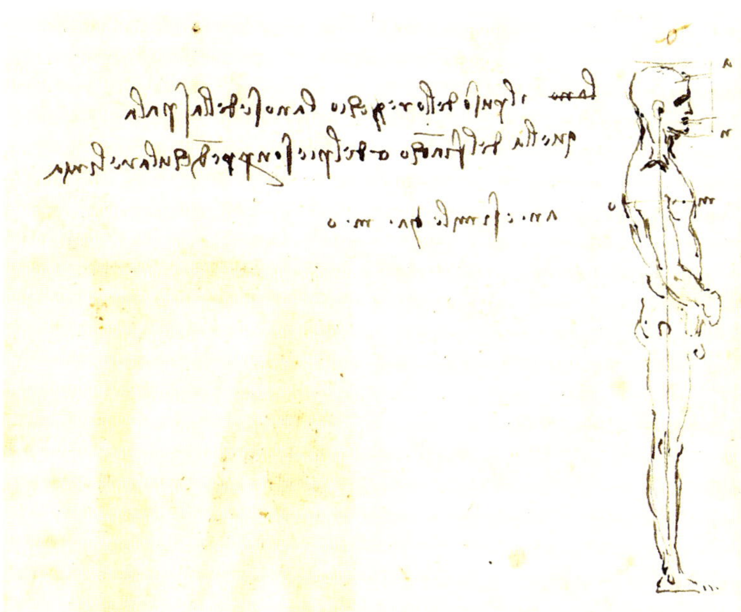

Detail, Plate 28, W. 19136–19139a, Royal Collection, Windsor

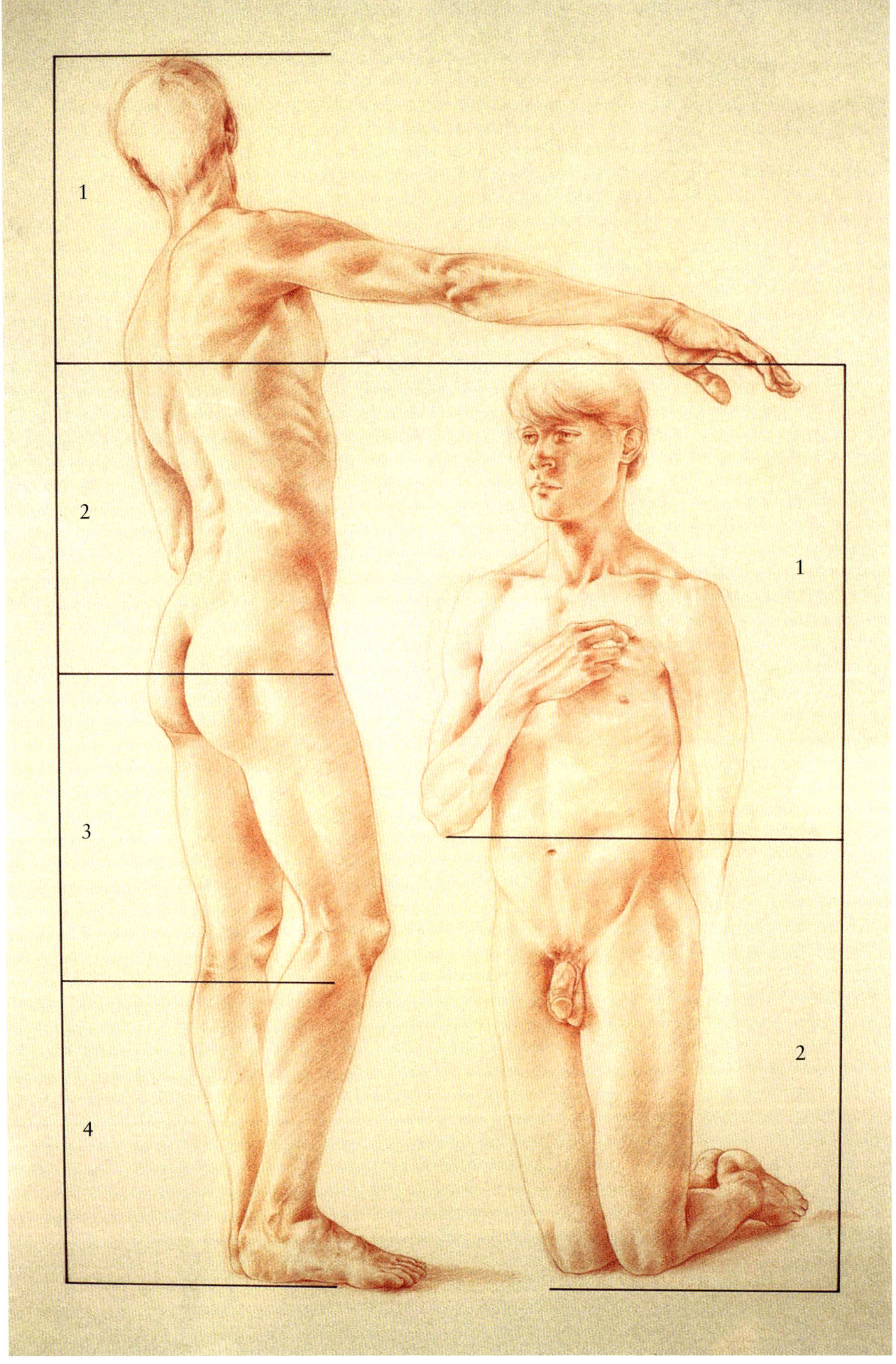

Cat. 26 AP 143

W. 19132a, Royal Library, Windsor
c. 1490
Folio 8 Recto I

AP 143
R 332

In kneeling down a man will lose the fourth part of his height. When a man kneels down with his hands folded on his breast, the navel will mark half his height, and likewise the points of his elbows.

Along with this text is Leonardo's wonderful drawing illustrating not only this entry but the following entry, AP 144, as well (Plate 23). His drawing, on the $6^{1}/_{4}$ x $8^{5}/_{8}$ inch (160 x 218 mm) sheet, is done in pen and brown ink.

The theory here is brilliant in its simplicity. A kneeling man will lose a fourth part of his height, another way of saying that the distance from the knee to the bottom of the foot is one-fourth the height of a standing male figure.

Leonardo then invigorates the theory by finding that not only does the navel become the center, or halfway point, of this kneeling figure, but the halfway mark also corresponds to the tip of the elbow folded across his chest. One wonders how Leonardo came upon such an obscure addition (the folding of the arm) to this comparison, particularly since it is such a perfectly formed theory by itself.

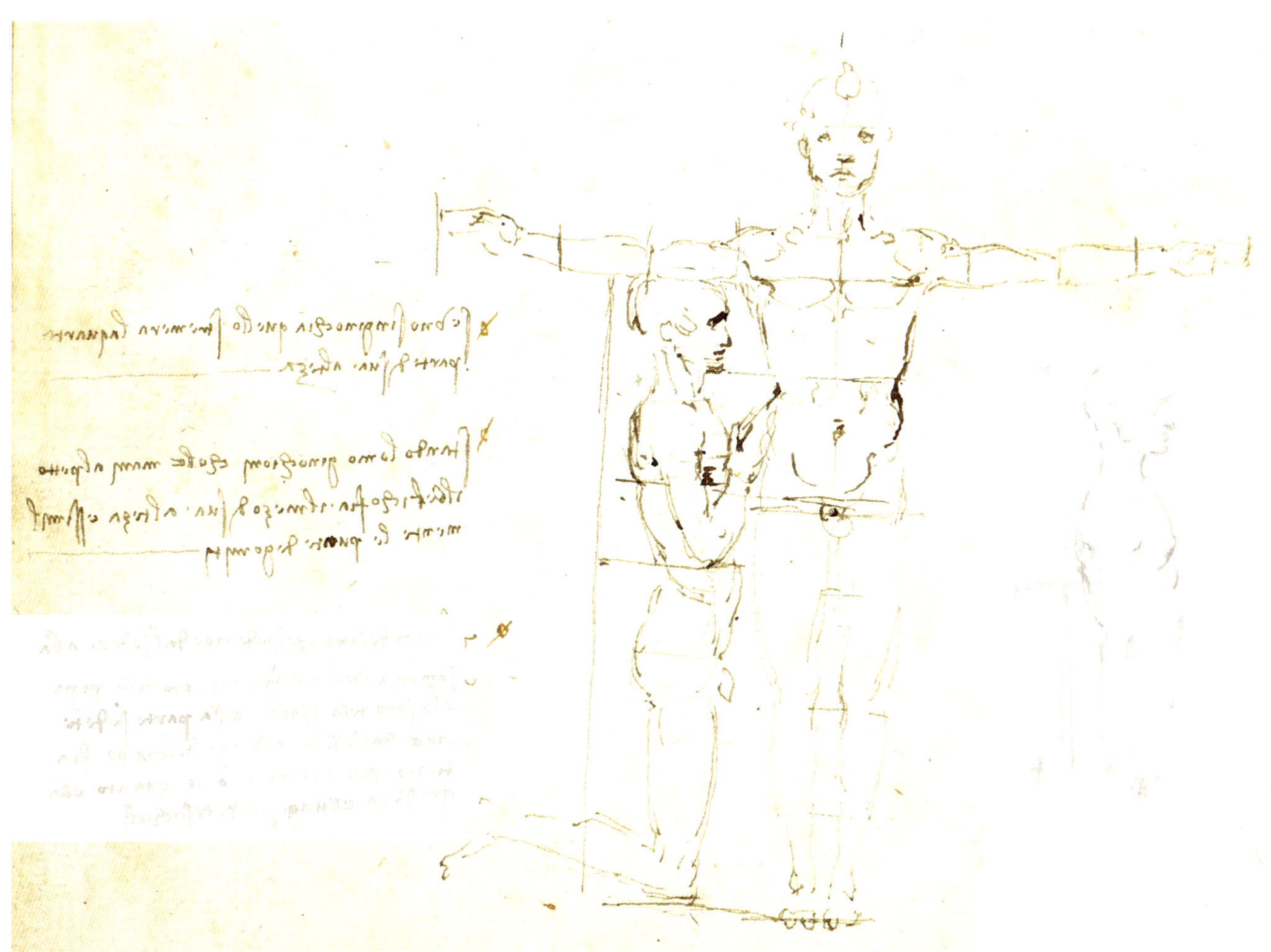

Detail, Plate 23, W. 19132a, Royal Collection, Windsor

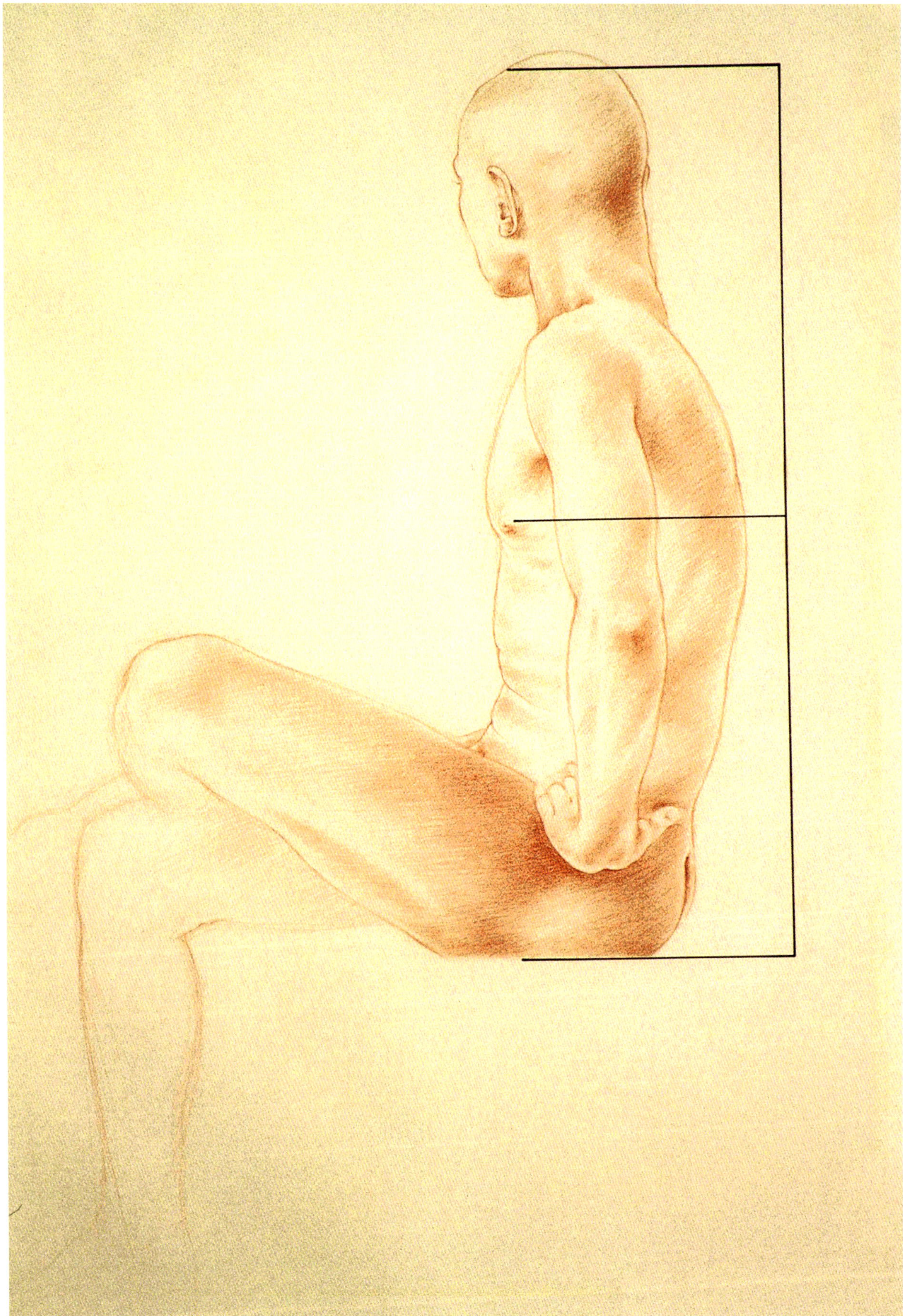

Cat. 27 AP 144

W. 19132a, Royal Library, Windsor — **AP 144**
c. 1490 — **R 332**
Folio 8 Recto II

Half the height of a man who sits—that is, from the seat to the top of the head—will be where the arms fold below the breast, and below the shoulders. The seated portion, that is from the seat to the top of the head, will be more than half the man's [whole height] by the length of the scrotum [the thickness and length of his testicles].

This is one of Leonardo's more bizarre entries, and it is perhaps one of the most difficult theories to prove (Plate 23). It becomes all the more difficult to comprehend because the halfway point he chooses, "…where the arms fold below the breast and below the shoulders," is not an exact reference point, nor is it a strategic bony landmark. Also, Leonardo uses the words "the thickness and length of the testicles." It is unclear why Richter may have changed the wording. We can only proceed with what Leonardo offers us as a visual clue.

In his beautiful little drawing, just to the right of the standing and kneeling figures, used to illustrate the theory in AP 143, is a small, seated figure facing right. A vertical line runs perfectly parallel along his perfectly straightened back, from his buttocks, marked by a horizontal line, to the top of his head, marked by another horizontal line. In the approximate center is a third horizontal line marked *mezzo*, half, crossing the torso at an anonymous point below the scapula and near the bottom edge of the pectoral muscle. However, if you measure the distance with a pair of calipers or a compass from the buttocks to that halfway mark and compare it to the distance from there to the top of the head, it measures just slightly less by about "the thickness and length of a testicle."

While I must confess that I have never actually taken a pair of calipers to the model to measure and test this theory, it does seem approximately to work in this drawing.

Some years ago, Professor Leo Steinberg, a Renaissance scholar and author of the book *Leonardo's Incessant Last Supper,* kindly agreed to review a portfolio of these drawings and offer his comments. When we came to this one and I expressed my confusion over its meaning, he suggested that it might simply be an example of Leonardo's humor, an idea I found very appealing.

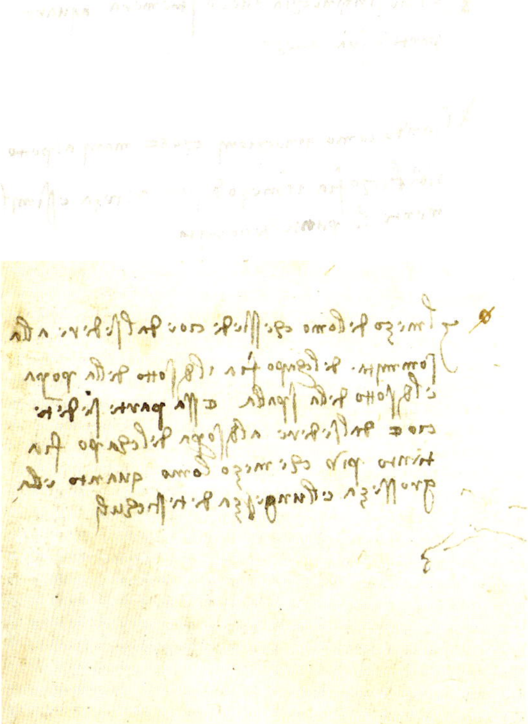

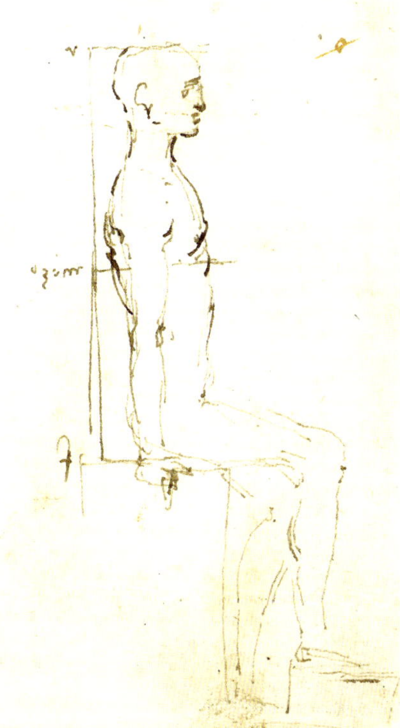

Detail, Plate 23, W. 19132a, Royal Collection, Windsor

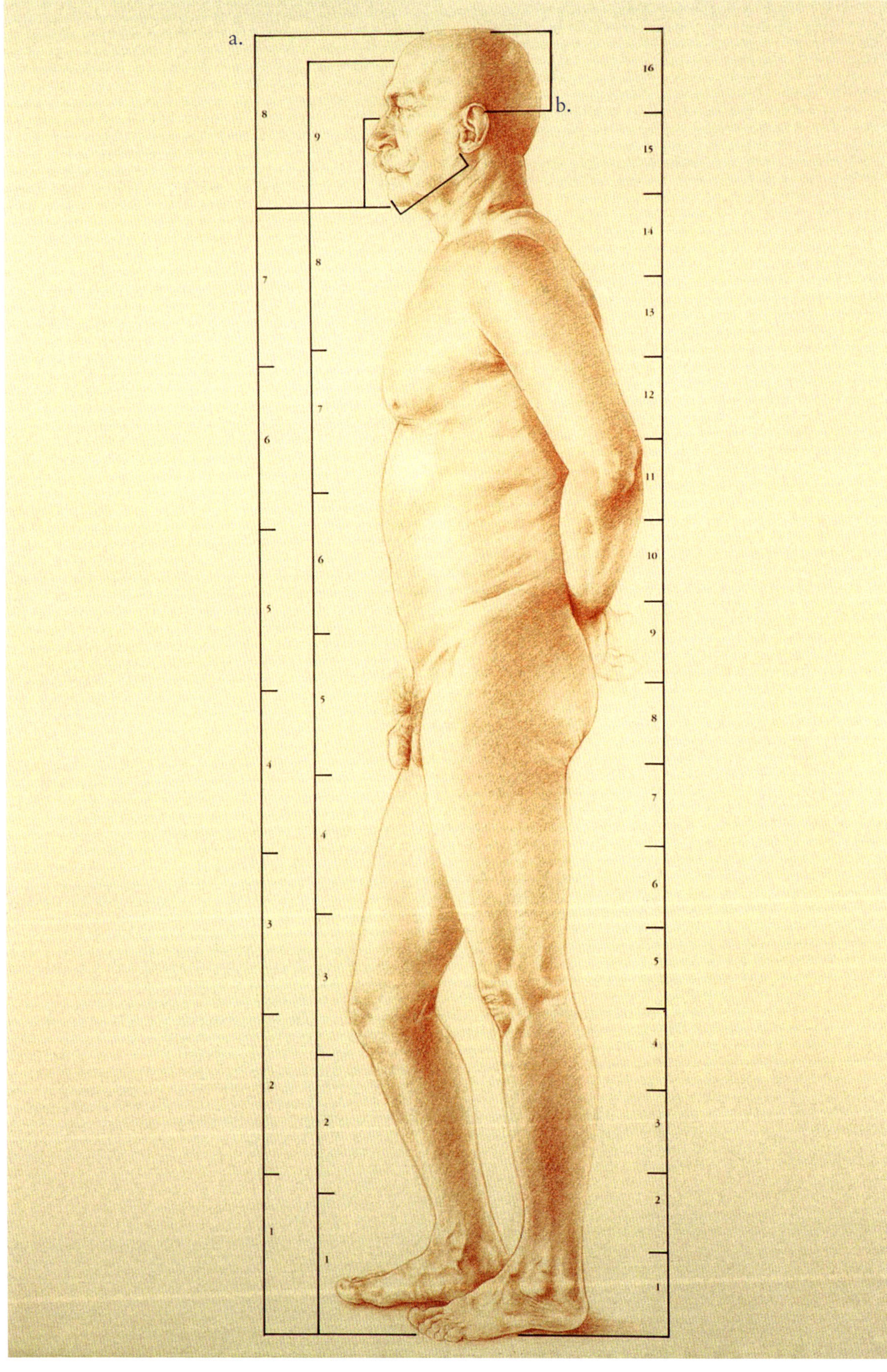

Cat. 28 **AP 145**

W. 19134–19135, Royal Library, Windsor **AP 145**
c. 1490 **R 317**
Folio 10 Recto I

"il Treco" [Trezo]

I. a. *From the top of the head to the bottom of the chin is 1/8 [of the whole man], and from the roots of the hair [the hairline—*"dal nascimento de'capelli,"* literally, the birth or beginning of the hair] to the chin is 1/9 of the distance from the roots of the hair [hairline] to the ground.*

b. *From the top of the ear to the top of the head is equal to the distance from the bottom of the chin to the lachrymatory [tear] duct of the eye; and also equal to the distance from the angle of the chin to that of the jaw; that is 1/16th of the whole.*

This is part of the first observation on Folio 10, Recto I (Plate 27), which is initially described at AP 108, the first use of the information from that folio. There is no drawing with this entry, and the information is contained in the first paragraph.

I. a. Leonardo uses the standard canon of measurement, the head, to define the height of an adult male as eight heads, and he clearly defines the length of the head as measured "from the top of the head to the bottom of the chin." He then distinguishes the face, from the hairline to the chin, as a secondary unit of measurement as one-ninth the height of a man, from the hairline to the ground.

b. The next three units of measurement, from the top of the ear to the top of the head, from the chin to the tear duct of the eye, and from the angle of the chin to the jaw, are all equal and go sixteen times into the height of a man. These are unusual canons to measure with, but they do clearly establish the eyes as the very center of the head. This is, therefore, another way of saying that if a man's head is one-eighth of the whole figure, then half a head is one-sixteenth of a whole figure.

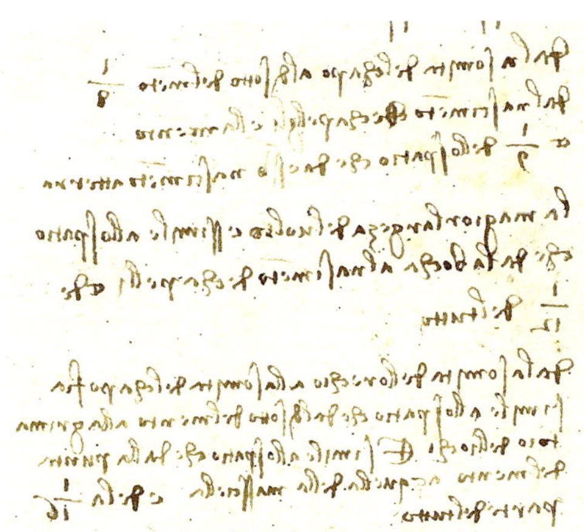

Detail, Plate 27, W. 19134–19135, Royal Collection, Windsor

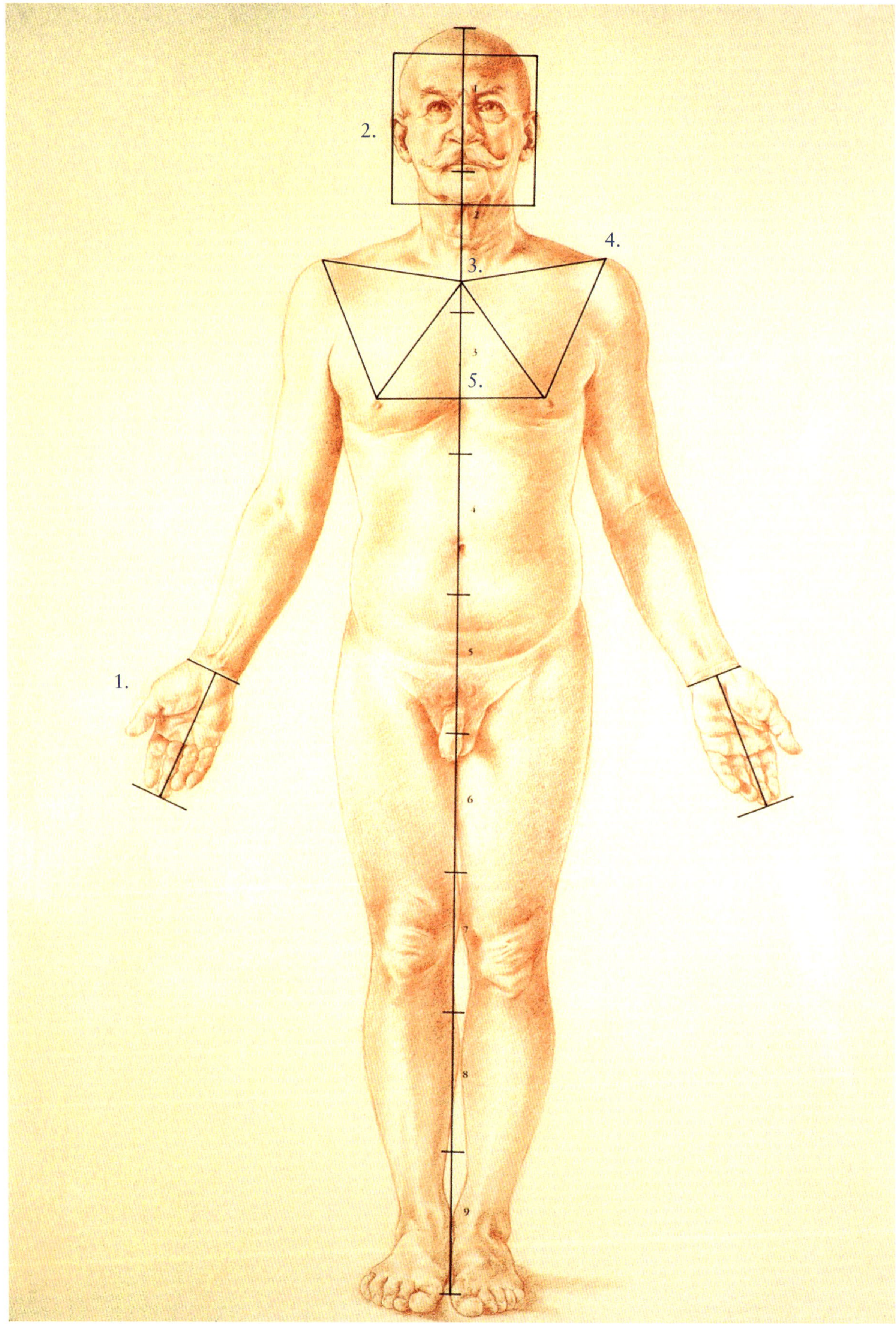

Cat. 29

AP 146

C.A. 160a (430a) AP 146
Codex Atlanticus, Ambrosiana Library, Milan R 309
c. 1490–1492

If a man 2 braccia high is too small, one of four is too tall, the medium being what is admirable. Between 2 and 4 come 3; therefore take a man of 3 braccia in height and measure him by the rule I will give you. If you tell me that I may be mistaken, and judge a man to be well proportioned who does not conform to this division, I answer that you must look at many men of 3 braccia, and out of the larger number who are alike in their limbs choose one of those who are most graceful and take your measurements.

1. *The length of the hand is $^1/_3$ of a braccio [c. 8 inches] and this is found 9 times in a man.* 2. *And the face [Leonardo uses* testa, *head, but Richter rightly translates "face"] is the same,* 3. *and from the pit of the throat to the shoulder,* 4. *and from the shoulder to the nipple,* 5. *and from one nipple to the other, and from each nipple to the pit of the throat.*

Only the first paragraph on this complicated sheet (Plate 5) deals with human proportion. The rest of the sheet deals with light and shade and perspective. To begin, a *braccio,*[28] the Italian word for arm, is also a standard unit of measurement equal to 0.5836 meters, or 22.9768 inches, slightly less than 23 inches. (See also Appendix I.) This is one of the rare cases where Leonardo uses a standard unit of measurement as a module to measure the human figure. (See also AP 141.) In all other cases he uses either a body part, such as the length of a hand, or the space between body parts, such as the distance between the chin and the bottom of the nose. So, if we take Leonardo's advice and find many men of three *braccia* in height, or about 66 inches, or five feet six inches, tall, and choose the most graceful among them, he will conform to the following measurements:

1. The length of the hand is one-third of a *braccio*. If we round the *braccio* out to 23 inches and divide it by 3, we get $7^1/_2$ to 8 inches in length. And if we say that this measurement is equal to the face, from the chin to the hairline, it then enters into the height of a man nine times.
2. The face, therefore, as a ninth part of the whole figure, is the same as seen in Vasari and Guaricus.[29] It is another example of the Rule of Three, 1, 3, 9, 27 (the root of this system of numbers is 3): 1 divided into 3 = 3, and 3 divided into 9 = 3, and 9 divided into 27 = 3. The height of a man is three *braccia,* or nine faces, or twenty-seven parts of one division of the face.
3. Leonardo continues: and from the pit of the throat (*la fontanella,* the little fountain) to the shoulder,
4. and from the shoulder to the nipple,
5. and from one nipple to the other, and from each nipple back to the pit of the throat, all of these are equal to the length of the face. (See also AP 106.)

This passage is a wonderful description of how to define a "well-proportioned" man[30] with a set of accurate measurements based on the face as a canon. The harmonic geometry created by Nature, recognized and described by Leonardo, forms in this passage an image every bit as iconic and graceful as the *Vitruvian Man*.

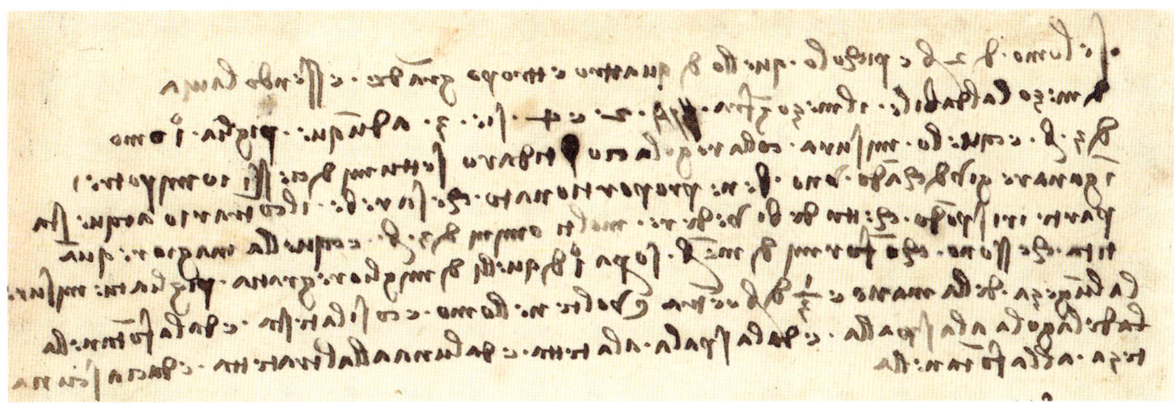

Detail, Plate 5, Ms C.A. Inv. 160a (430a), Biblioteca Ambrosiana, Milan

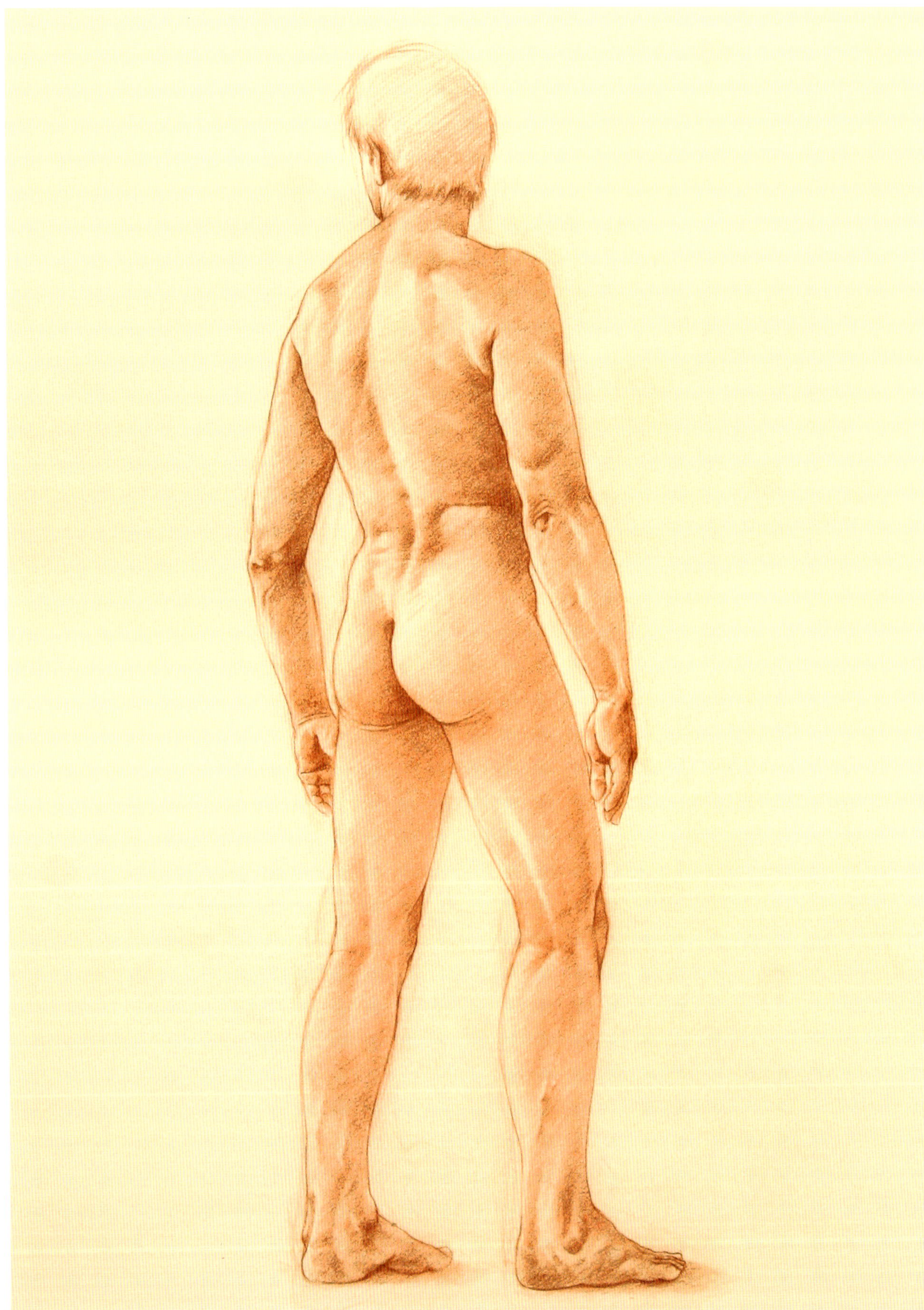

Cat. 30 AP 147

W. 12632, Royal Library, Windsor **AP 147**
c. 1490 **No R #**
Folio 14 Recto

The robust nudes will be muscular and thick.

This entry and the following entry, AP 148, come from a modest-size sheet, 7 1/2 x 5 3/8 inches (191 x 144 mm). The paper has a brownish tint, and the ink is rather light and runs from diluted brown to dark sepia (Plate 17).

There is a drawing of a nude male figure standing fully erect in left profile from the rib cage to the feet. The muscles in his leg and torso are taut and well defined, and this image was obviously the first thing drawn on the page, because the written entries (this one and the one used in AP 148) are inscribed over the upper torso. There is also a drawing of a mechanical gear and sprocket and a very faint triangular configuration, which may be a watermark.

Leonardo's suggestion that a robust nude will be muscular and thick does not imply an ideal or universal body type or image. Rather, I think he is suggesting that the human form in all its harmonic glory must be healthy and physically fit. And indeed the robust, muscular nude he offers as an example is the picture of health and power; it is only one of a dozen or more of such exquisite drawings scattered throughout his pages on anatomy and proportion of fully defined and partially drawn male figures—without text—that are well articulated, finely toned and endowed, exuding health and well-being.

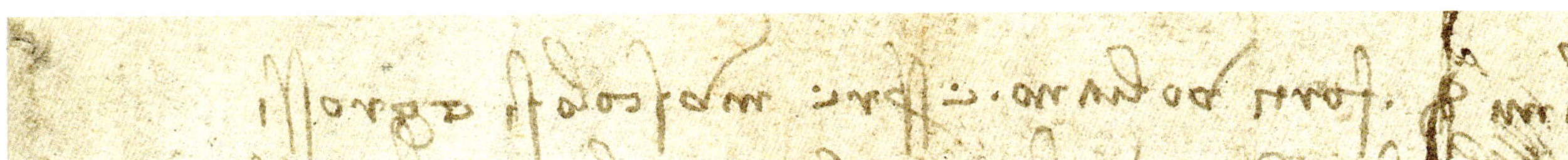

Detail, Plate 17, W. 12632, Royal Collection, Windsor

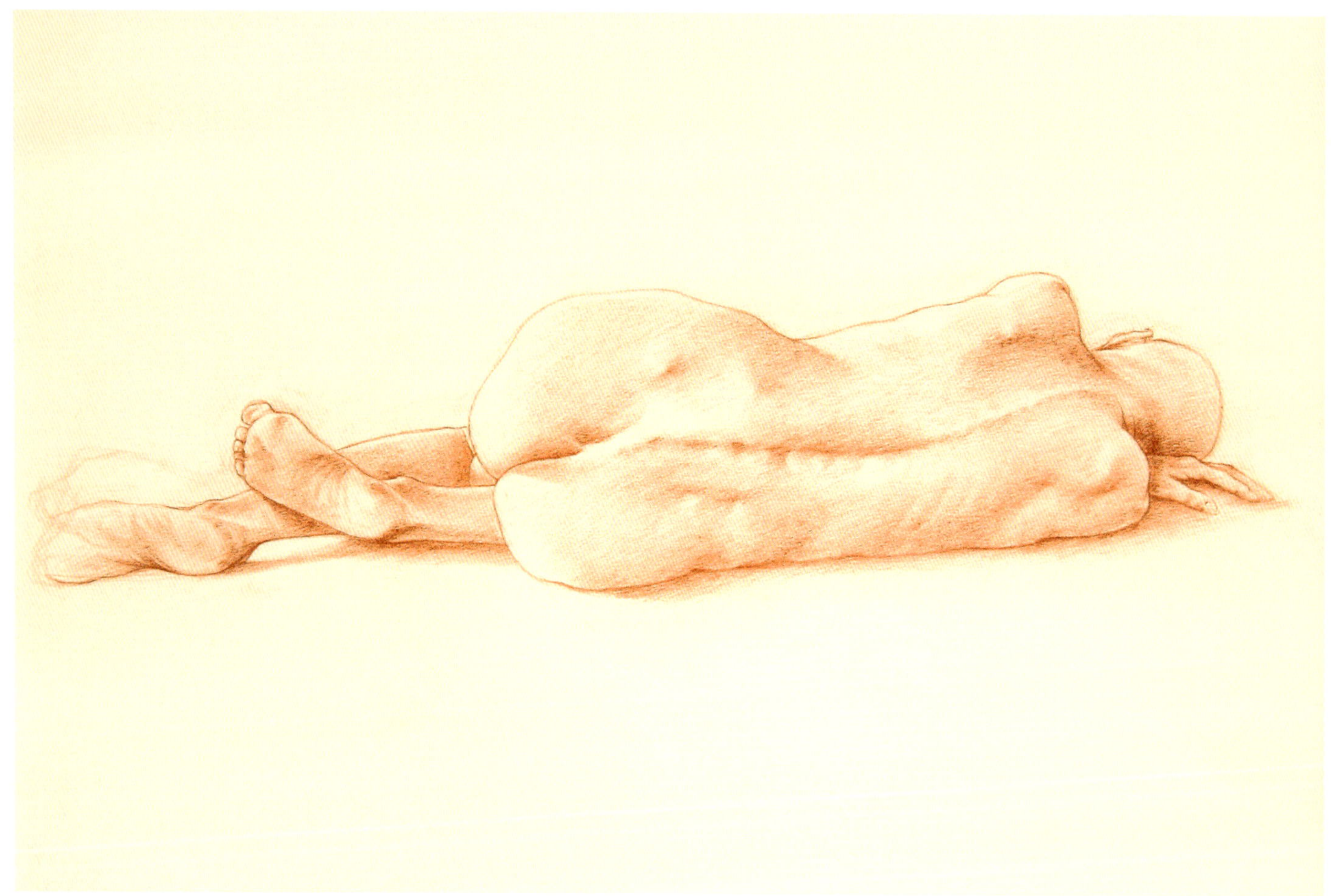

Cat. 31 AP 148

W. 12632, Royal Library, Windsor **AP 148**
c. 1490 **No R #**
Folio 14 Recto

Those who are of less strength will be lacertous and thin.

In the previous entry Leonardo makes the case for what the well-formed, healthy male figure should look like and provides us with a partial drawing of a standing nude. In this case, he describes the opposite, in other words, what a man should not look like (Plate 17).

It seems that Leonardo is proposing a visual theory for a sound psychological and emotional state of being based on a healthy, physically fit appearance. A thin, puny man, one "of less strength," will have ill-defined muscles, will look weak and have a paltry constitution, and will project nothing of strength and power. These are my personal opinions and are guided by the implied, as well as clearly stated, qualitative descriptions Leonardo suggests in both of his statements. Richter did not deal with either of these entries but omitted them from his text.

An entirely different explanation is offered by O'Malley and Saunders in their book *Leonardo da Vinci on the Human Body.*[31] They point out that medieval anatomists used different terms to describe certain muscle shapes. In fact, the authors cite a note by Leonardo in the Queen's Collection at Windsor, Folio 19014r, in the lower-right margin, "The muscles are of two shapes with two different names, of which the shorter is called *'musculus'* and the longer is called *'lacertus.'*" Saunders and O'Malley write, "It should be remembered that the terms at this period still contained the imagery of their derivation so that *musculus* meant 'little mouse' (from the Greek) and was reserved for a short muscle, while *lacertus,* a lizard, was used for long muscles."

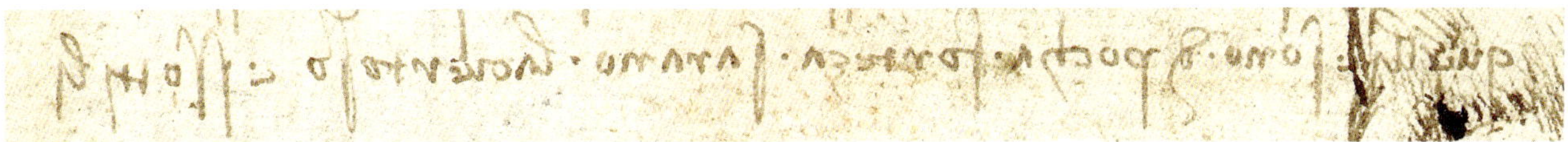

Detail, Plate 17, W. 12632, Royal Collection, Windsor

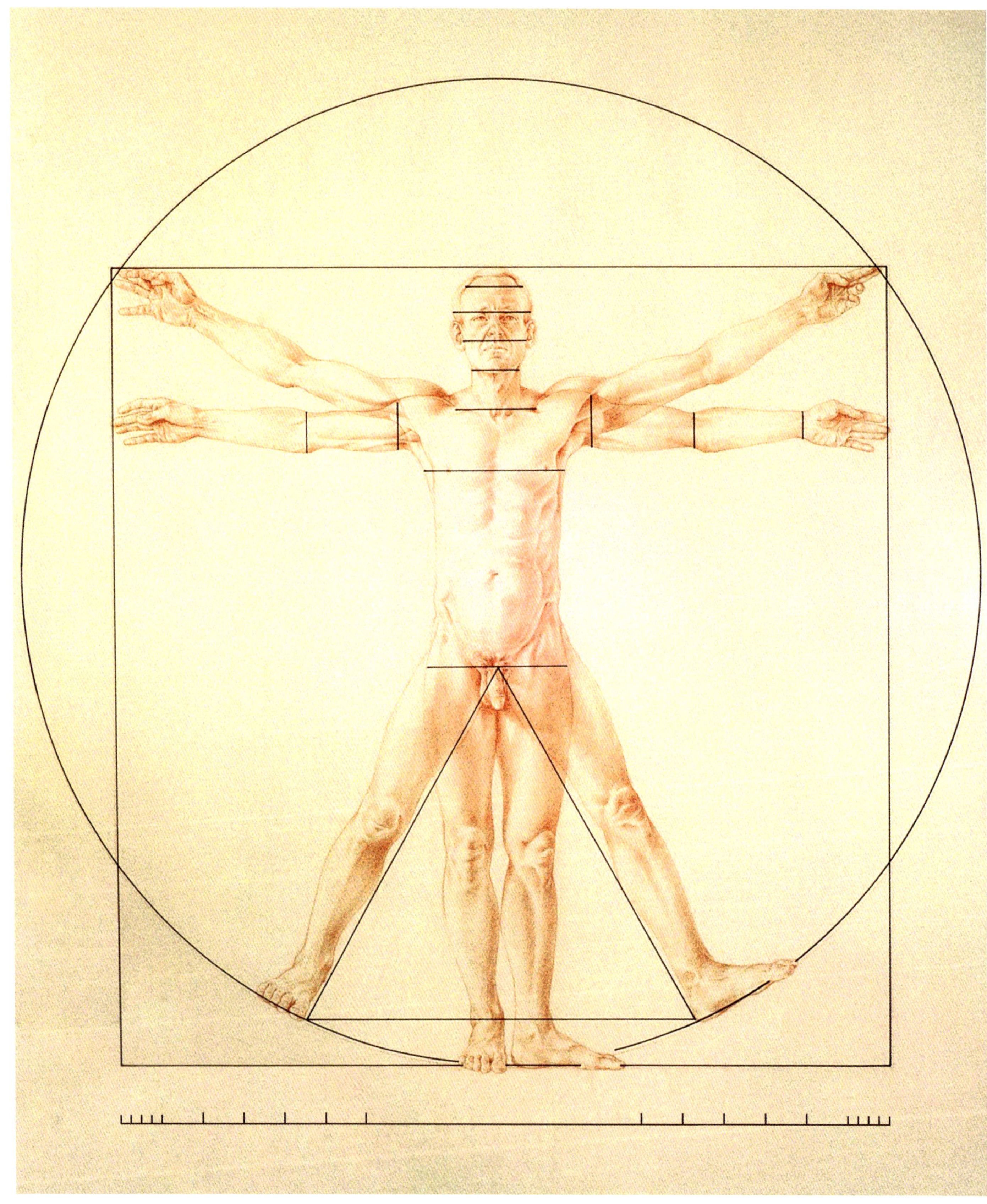

Cat. 32 AP 149

V. Inv. 228 Frame 29, Venice Academy AP 149
c. 1490 R 343

I. *Vitruvius, the architect, says in his work on architecture that the measurements of the human body are distributed by Nature as follows: that is,* 1. *that 4 fingers make one palm,* 2. *and 4 palms make one foot,* 3. *6 palms make one cubit,* 4. *4 cubits make a man's height.* 5. *And 4 cubits make one pace,* 6. *and 24 palms make a man; and these measurements are used in his buildings. If you open your legs so much as to decrease your height $^{1}/_{14}$ and spread and raise your arms till your middle fingers touch the level of the top of your head you must know that the center of the outspread limbs will be in the navel and the space between the legs will be an equilateral triangle.*

II. 7. *The length of a man's outspread arms is equal to his height.*

III. 8. *From the roots of the hair to the bottom of the chin is the tenth of a man's height;* 9. *from the bottom of the chin to the top of his head is one-eighth of his height;* 10. *from the top of the breast to the top of his head will be one-sixth of a man.* 11. *From the top of the breast to the roots of the hair will be the seventh part of a whole man.* 12. *From the nipples to the top of the head will be the fourth part of a man.* 13. *The greatest width of the shoulders contains in itself the fourth part of a man.* 14. *From the elbow to the tip of the hand will be the fifth part of a man;* 15. *and from the elbow to the angle of the armpit will be the eighth part of a man.* 16. *The whole hand will be the tenth part of a man;* 17. *the beginning of the genitals marks the middle of the man.* 18. *The foot is the seventh part of a man.* 19. *From the sole of the foot to below the knee will be the fourth part of a man.* 20. *From below the knee to the beginning of the genitals will be the fourth part of a man.* 21. *The distance from the bottom of the chin to the nose and from the roots of the hair to the eyebrows is, in each case the same, and like the ear, a third of a face.*

Leonardo's drawing of the *Vitruvian Man* (Plate 10) is an icon of such stature that Dr. Martin Kemp referred to it as "probably the most famous drawing in the world."[32] The drawing was meant to illustrate the essential theories of human proportion as set forth by the first century BC Roman architect and engineer Marcus Vitruvius Pollio in his *Ten Books on Architecture.* The importance of Vitruvius's history of architecture, the only such history to have survived ancient times, and its relevant dependence on human proportion was profound. It aided in defining the core of the Italian Renaissance and its emphasis on the classical motif in both architecture and art. I have therefore devoted an entire chapter to the *Vitruvian Man*, so here we will focus only on the theories of proportion proposed by Vitruvius as understood and elaborated on by Leonardo.

Leonardo's drawing measures about 13$^{1}/_{2}$ x 9$^{3}/_{4}$ inches (344 x 245 mm) and is executed in light brown watered ink on a soft, warm-gray paper. It is one of the earliest of his drawings on human proportion and was done during Leonardo's first Milanese period. His text divides Vitruvius's information into three paragraphs, and not entirely in the order established by Vitruvius. (See Appendix II for the entire Vitruvian text.) In the first part he describes how Nature has determined the measurements of the human body by using smaller parts of the body as modules to define larger parts of the body as modules. He ends the first part of the text by inscribing his famous male figure in a circle, using the navel as the center of the compass.

The second paragraph, a single sentence, establishes the height of the figure, from the soles of the feet to the top of the head, as equal to the outstretched arms and defined by the sides of a perfect square.

The third section defines the height of the whole figure using various parts of the body as modules. In the first paragraph the smaller modules are used incrementally to establish larger modules and eventually arrive at the height of a whole man. In this last paragraph each module is used as a canon to discover the proportion of the part to the height of a whole man.

What follows here is an assessment, line by line, of the accuracy of Vitruvius's theories as interpreted and illustrated by Leonardo, using both his drawing and mine. In order to clarify Leonardo's transcription of Vitruvius, I have separated and enumerated each of the theories with blue numbers in the text, as done throughout these pages, but I have not added the numbers to the drawing itself. To do so would have cluttered the drawing.

Leonardo begins his interpretation of Vitruvius with "the measurements of the human body are distributed by Nature as follows":

I. 1. *4 fingers make one palm.* Perfect; a simple measurement with a caliper or compass will confirm this. Just below the figure inscribed in the circle and the square, there is a horizontal line with markings at both ends. The word *diti* (fingers) is written directly under four spaces, defined by five small lines, indicating the width of the fingers. And next to that the word *palmi* (palms) is written directly under the larger five spaces, defined by six lines, the width of each measuring exactly four fingers.[33]

2. *4 palms make one foot.* Not quite; the length of the foot in both Leonardo's drawing and mine is less than three palms.

3. *6 palms make one cubit.* Correct; I have found that in verifying Leonardo's theories one should trust in the ratio of the module to the part being measured. However, in this case, as the cubit is not part of the body but an ancient form of measurement, 18 to 22 inches (see AP 141, note 1), we must rely on the accepted measurement of the cubit. So, if the width of a man's palm is approximately 3.25 inches, then six palms would measure 19 inches, which fits into the width of a cubit. And if we measured this same man of average height at his shoulders, we would find that the width of his shoulders, between 18 and 20 inches, would enter into the height of a man four times, proving the theory in AP 141, here, and in numbers 4 and 13.

4. *4 cubits make a man's height.* Usually correct.

5. *And 4 cubits make one pace*[34] *and 24 palms make one man.* Variable; one cubit at 18 inches x 4 = 72 inches or 6 feet, but a pace, according to *Webster's* definition, is smaller, at 58 inches, less than 5 feet. The conclusion here is to stick to the anatomical modules to establish a canon, and as for the second part, the measurement is slightly less than 24 palms in a whole man.

6. *If you open your legs so much as to decrease your height by* $^1/_{14}$*...the space between the legs will be an equilateral triangle.* Variable; in Leonardo's drawing, the decrease, the distance from the feet which rest on the bottom of the equilateral triangle to the feet resting on the bottom of the square, measures slightly more than one-fourteenth, but in my drawing the decrease measures more than one-seventeenth of the total height of the figure. However, in both drawings the equilateral triangles are perfect.

II. 7. Once again, in order to bring further clarity to the text, I have rearranged Leonardo's text by combining a portion of the last sentence in the first paragraph with the single sentence of the second paragraph.

...and spread and raise your arms till your middle fingers touch the level of the top of your head you must know that the center of the outstretched limbs will be in the navel. ... The length of a man's outspread arms is equal to his height. Perfect. A man standing perfectly erect in a square, stretching his arms upward, will find that his middle fingers touch the top of the square, level with his head, at the exact point where the circle intersects the square. And his navel will be at the compass point of this perfect circle. In addition, we will find that the length of a second set of his horizontally outstretched arms is equal to his whole height.

Leonardo was the first (after Vitruvius) to comprehend and combine these theories together, and the first to combine the circle and the square together in a single drawing, not by trying to square the circle, but by projecting it outside the square. In so doing he surpassed others before him and those who followed. (See chapter 10, "Leonardo's Vitruvian Man.")

Continuing with the third paragraph, Leonardo says:

III. 8. *From the roots of the hair to the bottom of the chin is the tenth of a man's height.* In this Leonardo quotes Vitruvius's words verbatim, but contradicts them to measure nine faces in several other examples, most notably in AP 146. But even here, in both Leonardo's and my drawings, the full figure measures only slightly larger than nine faces.

9. *From the bottom of the chin to the top of his head is one-eighth of his height.* Correct. This is the standard, acceptable, and reliable measurement, which works perfectly in Leonardo's and my drawings.

10. *From the top of the breast to the top of his head will be one-sixth of a man.* Correct. The measurement must be taken at the pit of the throat formed by the manubrium, the top of the sternum. It is perfect in Leonardo's drawing and mine.
11. *From the top of the breast to the roots of the hair will be the seventh part of the whole man.* This forms an unusual module, and it measures slightly more in Leonardo's drawing and slightly less in mine.
12. *From the nipples to the top of the head will be the fourth part of a man.* Correct. Perfect in both Leonardo's and my drawings.
13. *The greatest width of the shoulders contains in itself the fourth part of a man.* Correct. Perfect in both Leonardo's and my drawings and proven in several other examples.
14. *From the elbow to the tip of the hand will be a fifth part of a man.* In both Leonardo's and my drawings, it measures no more than one-fourth of a man, and this measurement agrees with AP 186 and several other drawings.
15. *...and from the elbow to the angle of the armpit will be the eighth part of a man.* Correct. This should mean that the module is roughly equal to the size of the head; I find it slightly more in both Leonardo's drawing and mine.
16. *The whole hand will be the tenth part of a man.* We already have established that the hand is equal to the face and is closer to one-ninth of the whole man.
17. *The beginning of the genitals marks the middle of the man.* Perfect. This point is the pubis symphasis, where the two halves of the pelvis come together in front. This bony landmark is a standard, reliable reference point and is proven several times over in these pages.
18. *The foot will be the seventh part of a man.* Here Leonardo parts from Vitruvius, for Vitruvius states unequivocally on several occasions that the foot is one-sixth of the whole height of a man. In both Leonardo's and my drawings the measurement is closer to seven than to six.
19. *From the sole of the foot to below the knee will be the fourth part of a man.* Perfect in both Leonardo's drawing and mine. (See AP 186.)
20. *From below the knee to the beginning of the genitals will be a fourth part of a man.* If we take 19 and 20 together, they will equal two-fourths, and make half a man.
21. *The distance from the bottom of the chin to the nose, and from the roots of the hair to the eyebrows is, in each case the same, and like the ear, a third of the face.* Perfect. (See AP 103.)

In this third and last paragraph, Leonardo sums up for us all of the major variables of anatomical modules used to measure the whole figure.

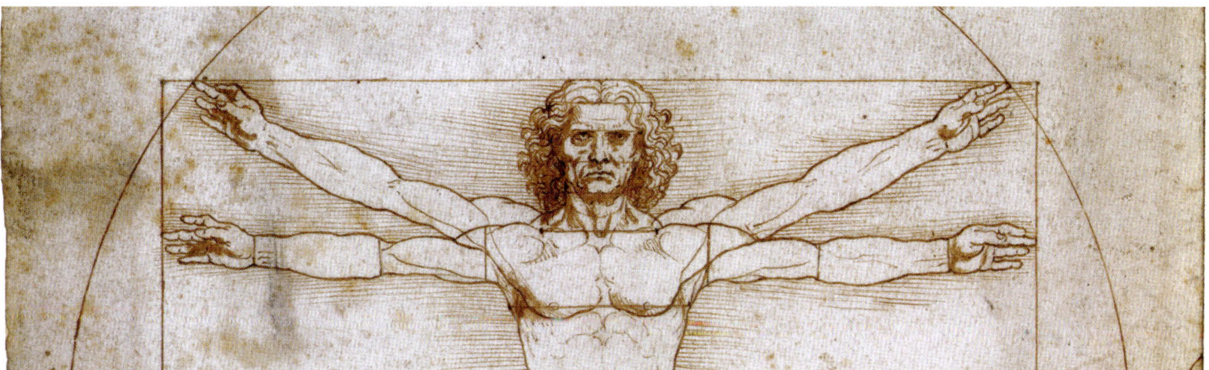

Detail, Plate 10, V. Inv. 228 Frame 29, Gallerie dell'Accademia, Venice

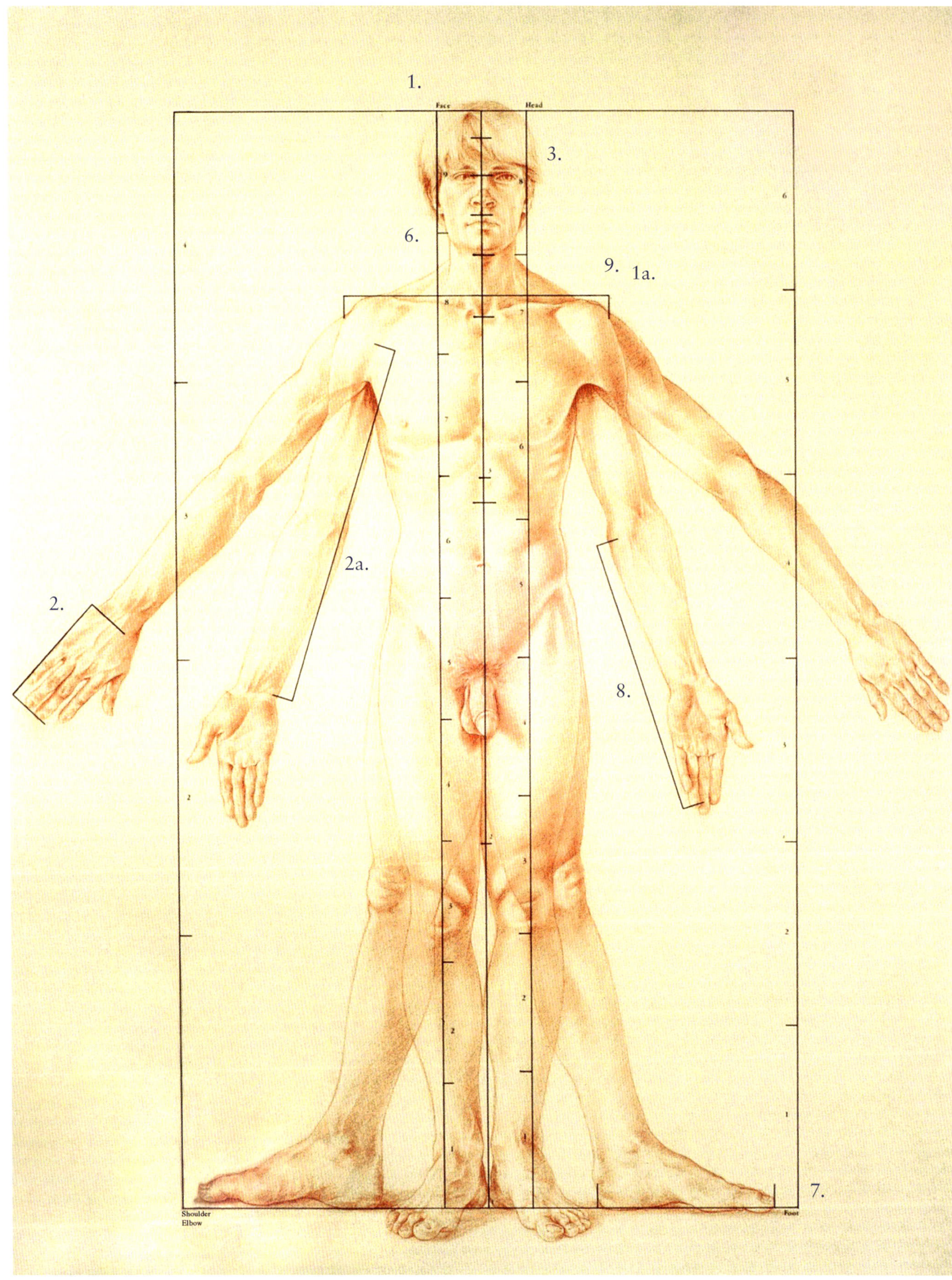

Cat. 33

AP 150

C.A. 358a (994a) AP 150
Codex Atlanticus, Ambrosiana Library, Milan R 340
c. 1487

1. *From the chin to the roots of the hair is 1/10 of the whole figure.* 2. *From the joint of the palm of the hand to the tip of the longest finger is 1/10.* 3. *From the chin to the top of the head 1/8;* 4. *and from the pit of the stomach to the top of the breast is 1/6,* 5. *and from the pit below the breastbone to the top of the head 1/4.* 6. *From the chin to the nostrils 1/3 part of the face, the same from the nostrils to the brow and from the brow to the roots of the hair,* 7. *and the foot is 1/6,* 8. *the elbow 1/4,* 9. *the width of the shoulders 1/4.*

W. 19134–19135, Royal Library, Windsor R 341
c. 1490
Folio 10 Recto I

1a. *The width of the shoulders is 1/4 of the whole.* 2a. *From the joint of the shoulder to the hand is 1/3,* 3a. *from the parting of the lips to below the shoulder blade is one foot.*

The dating of this page (Plate 6) in the Codex Atlanticus is suggested by Pedretti as being stylistically related to the drawings in the Paris MS B, dated between 1487–1490, but it is then mitigated by additional text on the page in the form of a draft for a joke found on another page in the Codex Atlanticus, dated 1490–1493.[35] While the dating of the drawings and texts has not been a priority in these pages, it is a significant factor in this case because of the bearing it may have on the *Vitruvian Man* drawing done in 1490. In either case, whether it came before or after the iconic drawing, much of the same information is repeated here, but in a much less comprehensive and elegant way. In addition to some of the vague and confusing language in these entries, neither this sheet in the Codex Atlanticus nor the complicated Folio 10 (Plate 27) at Windsor Castle is supported by an illustration.

1. *From the chin to the roots of the hair is 1/10 of the whole figure.* Nine faces is the more accurate measurement.
2. *From the joint of the palm of the hand to the tip of the longest finger is 1/10.* Variable. Again, the hand equals the length of the face, so nine is a more accurate number.
3. *From the chin to the top of the head is 1/8.* Perfect.
4. *...and from the pit of the stomach to the top of the breastbone is 1/6,*
5. *...and from the pit below the breastbone to the top of the head 1/4.* There is some discrepancy about both the meaning of the term and the exact position of the "pit of the stomach."[36] If we define the pit of the stomach as a point above the navel and below the sternum, an amorphous section of neither bone nor joint, neither theory works in our illustration. If we force the issue by using the bottom of the sternum, we find two different reference points. It is a concrete reminder of the importance of using reliable and standard parts of the body as modules to measure with.
6. *From the chin to the nostrils 1/3 part of the face, the same from the nostrils to the brow, and from the brow to the roots of the hair.* Perfect—our familiar, standard Rule of Three, first established in AP 103.
7. *...and the foot is 1/6...* In this case Leonardo chooses to follow Vitruvius's model of six feet in the total height of a man.

8. *...the elbow is 1/4, and*

9. *the width of the shoulders 1/4.* Correct in both cases. The elbow, meaning the distance from the elbow to the tips of the fingers, is the same as the width of the shoulders, and both are one-fourth of the whole man.

Similar comparisons are also found on the Windsor sheet, Folio 10 (Plate 27):

1a. *The width of the shoulders is 1/4 of the whole.* Perfect.

2a. *From the joint of the shoulder to the hand is 1/3.* Perfect.

3a. *...from the parting of the lips to below the shoulder blade is one foot.* This statement is incorrect and is therefore not marked in the drawing. As explained above, there are no drawings with these entries, and my drawing is a frontal figure. However, with the use of other drawings, anatomical charts, and measurements of other models, I have determined that the distance from the parting of the lips to below the shoulder blade (scapular), as seen in profile, is longer than one foot.

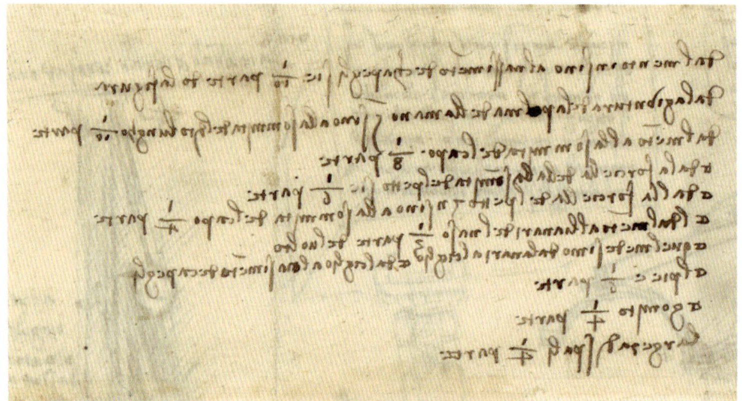

Detail, Plate 6, Ms C.A. Inv. 358a (994a), Biblioteca Ambrosiana, Milan

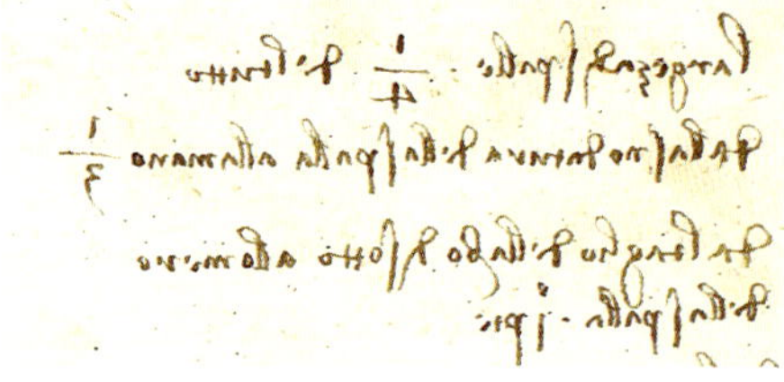

Detail, Plate 27, W. 19134–19135, Royal Collection, Windsor

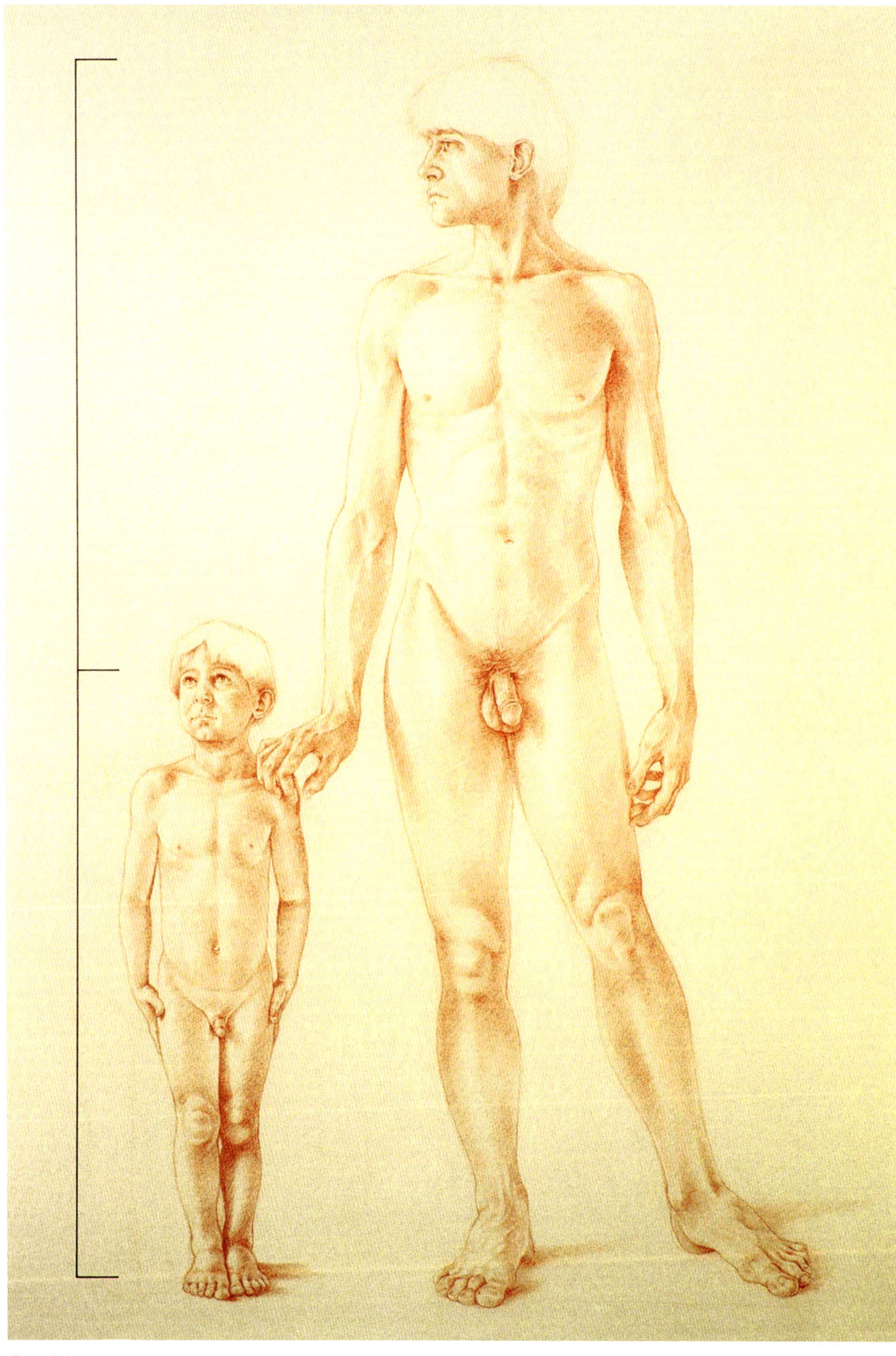

Cat. 34 AP 151

MS. H1 31b, Institut de France, Paris **AP 151**
c. 1494 **R 308**

I. ***Every man in his third year is half the full height he will grow to ultimately.***

Richter chooses this entry (Plate 8) as the first selection to start the section on "The Proportions and the Movements of the Human Figure." It was to me a surprising and moving statement when I first read it—to think that a child reaching the tender age of three years old has already attained half his ultimate height. Even more surprising is Leonardo's source for this statement. It comes from a passage in the comprehensive study *Natural History* by Gaius Plinus Secundus (Pliny),[37] written in the first century AD. I have since learned that this is a commonly accepted fact that can be verified in almost any contemporary book on pediatrics.[38]

In addition, Leonardo's choice of words is surprising to modern ears. He says *ciascuno uomo nel terzo anno…,* literally, every man, or each man, in his third year…using the word *uomo* (man) instead of *bambino* (male child), or *ragazzo* (young boy), or *fanciullo* (young lad). It suggests a very different view of young Renaissance boys compared to how we see today's children. In Leonardo's era, young children functioned on a footing much closer to adulthood than children of our own times. And if we consider the apprenticeship system of the Renaissance we find a very different understanding of the role of children as well.

My nephew Matthew was three years and four months when this drawing was made and he measured 3 feet 2½ inches tall. He was 6 feet 2 inches tall at age 20. Clearly, the principle works now as it did during Leonardo's time.

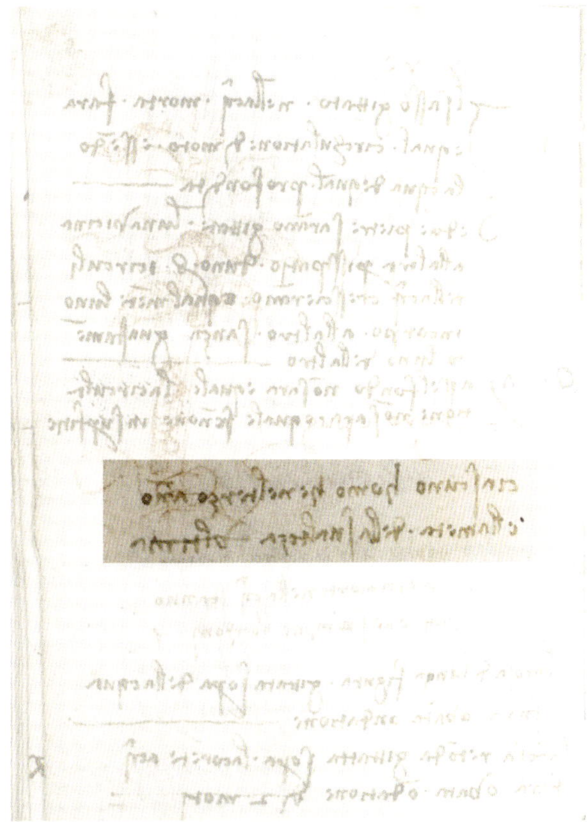

Detail, Plate 8, Ms H1, page 31b, Bibliothéque de l'Institut de France, Paris

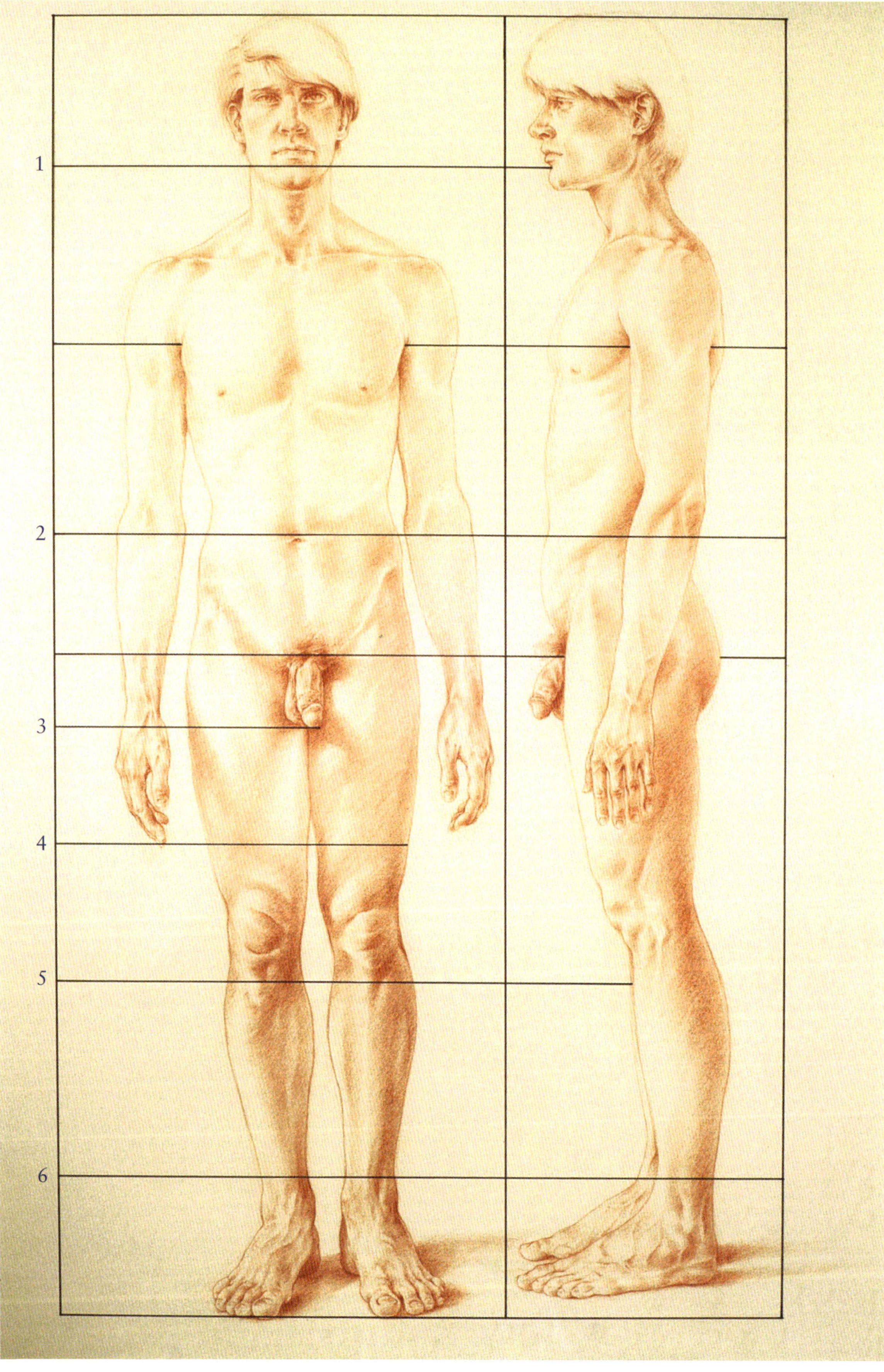

Cat. 35 AP 152

W. 19134–19135, Royal Library, Windsor AP 152
c. 1490 R 336
Folio 10 Recto XI

1. *Top of the chin*
2. *Hip*
3. *The insertion of the big finger*
4. *The end of the calf of the leg*
5. *The end of the swelling of the shin-bone of the leg*
6. *The smallest thickness of the leg goes 3 times into the thigh, seen in front.*

Once again we turn to the large sheet housed at Windsor Castle, the famous Folio 10 (Plate 27). The page is filled with proportional notes and comparisons of every part of the body; it is written on from every direction and includes drawings of various sizes. In the center of the sheet is an exquisite little drawing of two figures, one fully frontal and one fully profile facing left, measuring no more than 2³/₈ inches high. The page is folded in half at the juncture where the heads of the two figures meet with the shoulders. Flanking both figures is a series of vertical and horizontal construction lines with text.

Leonardo's text, in a most unusual list-like fashion, inscribed to the left of the figure, corresponds to the construction lines running from the frontal figure to the profile figure. In most cases there is no description or explanation, just identifying words. We have followed Leonardo's example throughout except in the case of 3, explained below.

1. *Top of the chin.* The word Leonardo used, *fopel* or *sopel,* is not found in Italian dictionaries. It must be assumed to be the groove or top of the chin at the angle of the mandible, as the construction line quite clearly points to that place in Leonardo's drawing.
2. *Hip.* The word *fianco,* flank, is used, meaning the external oblique muscle above the pelvis.
3. *The insertion of the middle finger* (*al nascimento del grosso ditto*). Literally, "the birth of the big finger." Leonardo does not say the middle finger, nor the longest finger, but "the big finger," which could mean the thumb. In his tiny drawing there are two horizontal construction lines that extend from the right arm to different points on the body. The first runs from the insertion of the thumb, where the hand meets the wrist, to the beginning of the penis (at the pubis symphasis), the line in my drawing with no number. And the second line, numbered 3, which runs from the insertion of the middle finger into knuckles of the hand, through the middle of the thumb to the tip of the penis. To construct the arm according to the formula in Leonardo's drawing would render the arm far too short, and end the fingers of the hand, as is the case in Leonardo's drawing, just slightly longer than the penis. While the penis is a less than reliable landmark, we do know that in an extended adult male's arm, with the hand, the tip of the longest finger ends at about the midway mark of the upper leg. I have, therefore, decided to rely not on Leonardo's illustration in this case but on his text.
4. *The end of the calf...*(*"fin del pescie di detro della coscia"*). Calf is incorrect; it is really the end of the inner muscle of the thigh, the vastus medialis.
5. *The end of the swelling of the shinbone of the leg.* Leonardo is simply pointing to the end of the shank, or more precisely the beginning of the anterior tuberosity of the tibia.
6. *The smallest thickness of the leg goes 3 times into the thigh in front.* The smallest thickness of the leg is the width of the ankle, and it enters into the length, not the width, of the thigh, more than three times—closer to four and a half or five times.

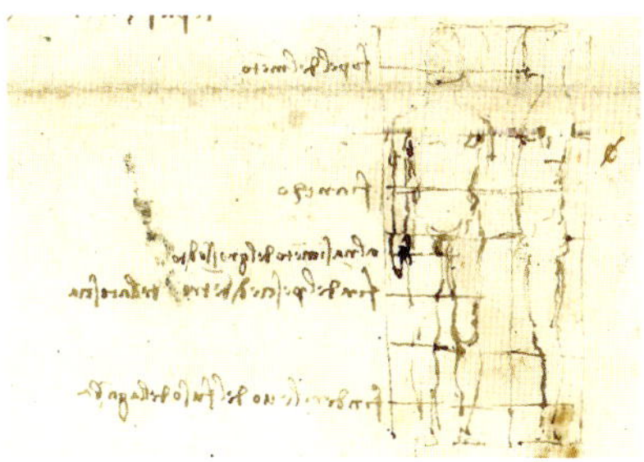

Detail, Plate 27, W. 19134–19135, Royal Collection, Windsor

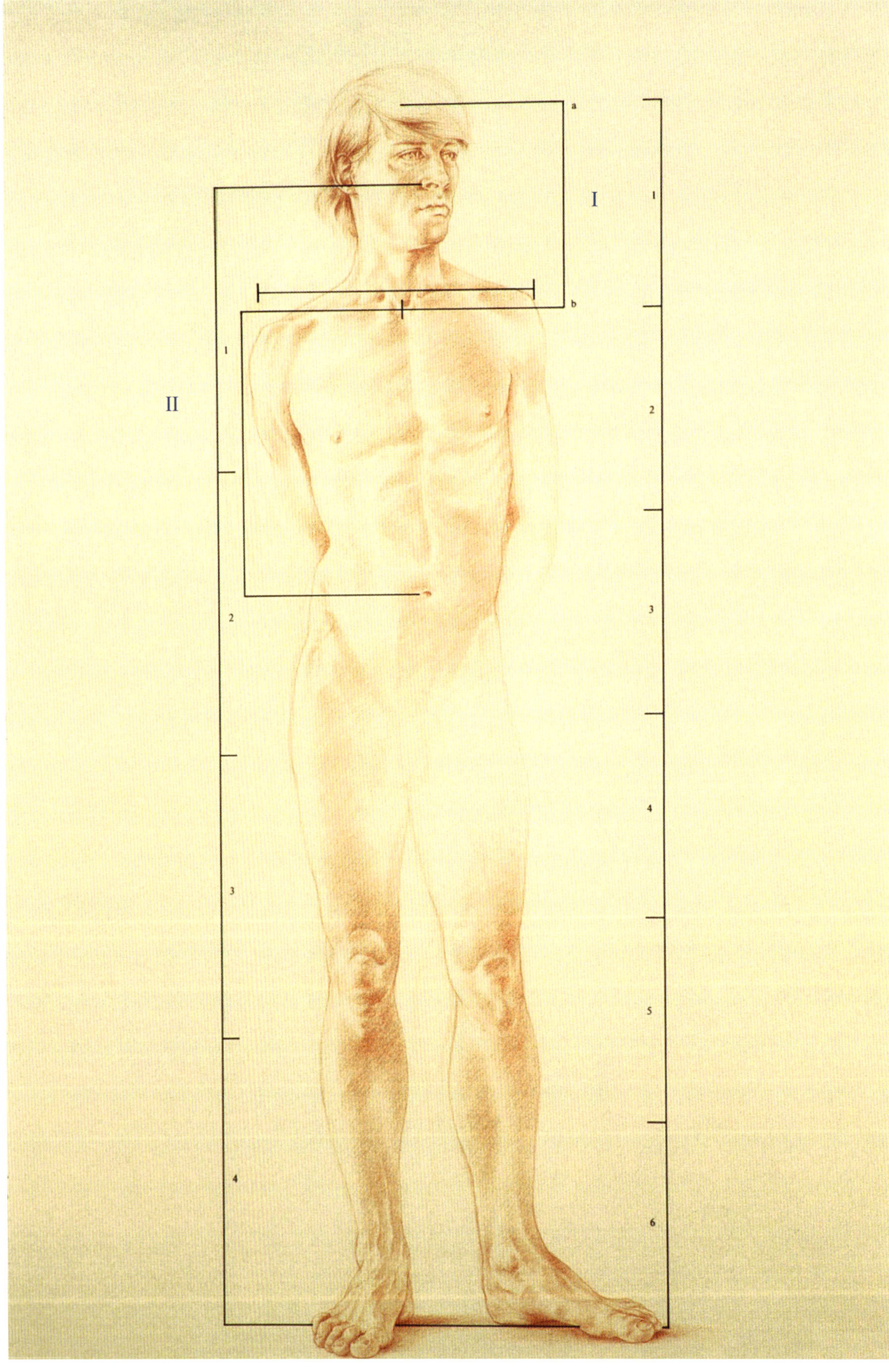

Cat. 36 AP 153

W. 19130a, Royal Library, Windsor **AP 153**
c. 1490 **R 334**
Folio 6 Recto I, II

I. *From the roots of the hair to the top of the breast, a b, is the sixth part of the height of a man and this measure is equal...*

II. *From the outside part of one shoulder to the other is the same distance as from the top of the breast to the navel, and this measure goes four times from the sole of the foot to the lower end of the nose.*

This page (Plate 19) measures 5¾ x 8⅜ inches (146 x 218 mm) and contains only three entries, each one accompanied by a small pen-and-ink drawing of the head and/or the upper torso of the figure. The first two paragraphs are treated here, while the third is represented in AP 125. All three employ different modules used to measure the entire figure, but none of the drawings illustrates the entire figure, only that portion of the body representing the module.

I. While the module, from a, the roots of the hair, to b, the top of the breast, is unusual as a module, it works perfectly well in this illustration and has been used by Leonardo elsewhere. In his precise little drawing, we see a profile head and bust of a man with construction lines carefully marking the module, from the hairline to the pit of the throat. The last part of Leonardo's sentence is translated by Richter as "...and this measure is equal." The *Quaderni* translates it as "...and this measure is similar to." Whether we translate it as equal, or similar to, it is accurate to say that the module from the hairline to the top of the breast is, in fact, a sixth part of the height of a man.

II. The width of the shoulders is equal to the distance from the top of the breast to the navel: this is correct and can be verified in several other entries, the standard canon being the width of the shoulders. However, Leonardo runs counter to his own observations and to those of Vitruvius when he says that the module "goes four times into the figure from the sole of the foot to the lower end of the nose" instead of to the top of the head. (See AP 186.) So, why the change? And how do we verify the change without the aid of a visual example from Leonardo?

The theory works well in the present illustration, and it works equally well in AP 186. But it only works well if we adopt as the operating canon the distance from the pit of the throat to the navel, and not the more standard width of the shoulders. In fact, if I measure the width of the shoulders "from the outside part of one to the other," I have a slightly larger module that then measures four times to the top of the head. How to explain this? There is only one conclusion here, and it is one we have avoided until now. Throughout Leonardo's writings he often uses the words *e simile,* "is similar to." Richter constantly translates this phrase as "is equal to," creating a rule, and I have followed that example in most cases. But I have come to believe that Leonardo's thrust in all of his proportional writings is not to create an iron-clad universal principle from his findings but to come to an understanding of the theories based primarily on the observation of Nature. In the end only Nature can be our true guide.

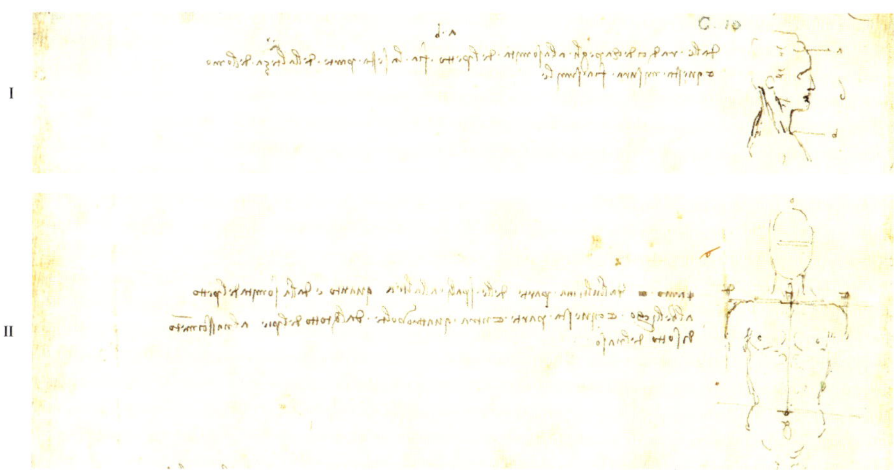

Detail, Plate 19, W. 19130a, Royal Collection, Windsor

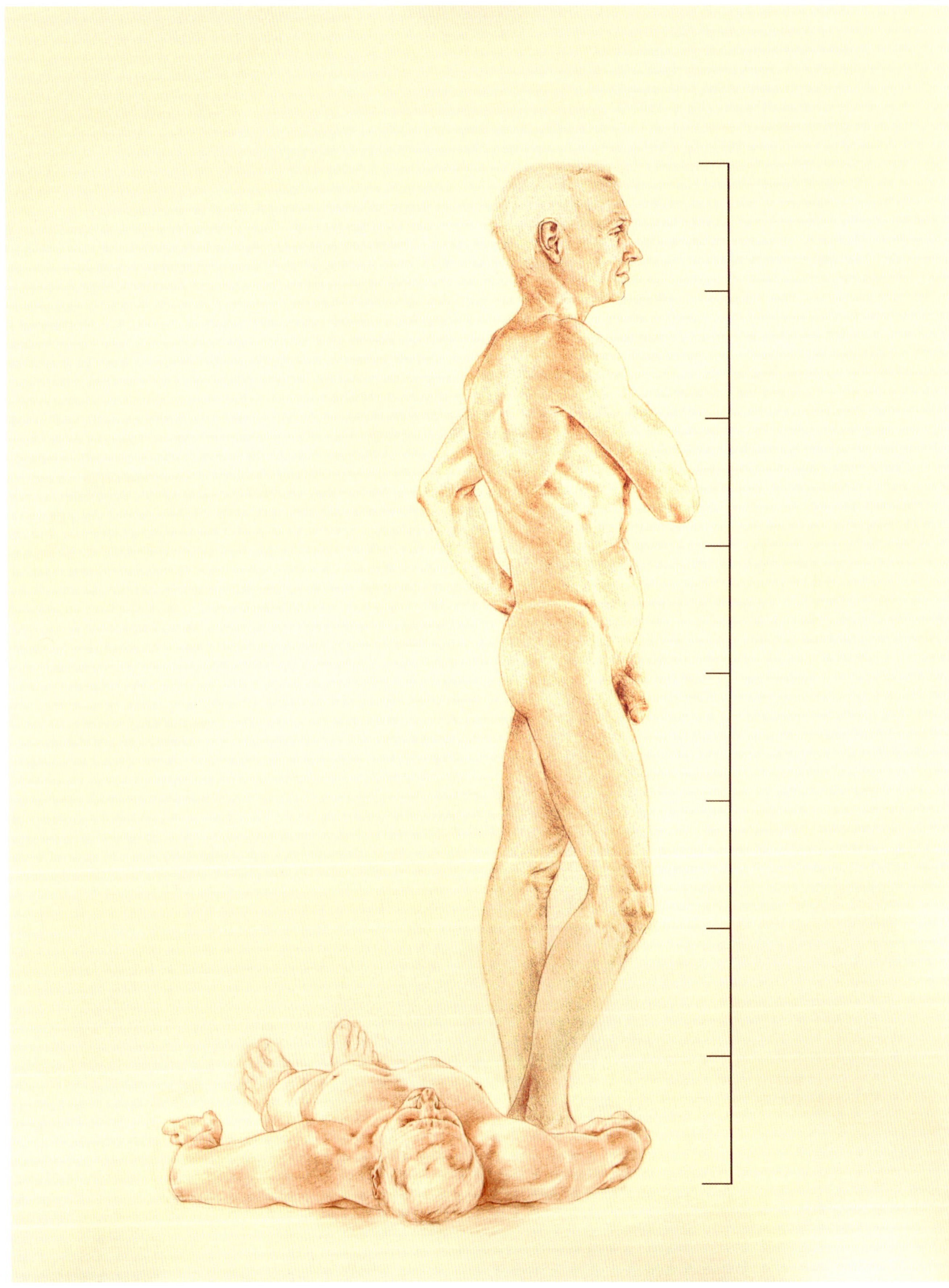

Cat. 37 AP 154

W. 19136–19139b, Royal Library, Windsor **AP 154**
c. 1490 **R 338**
Folio 11 Verso V

A man when he lies down is reduced to 1/9 of his height.

This entry is squeezed in between several other longer, illustrated texts from the famous Windsor sheet (Plate 29) folded in four. There is no illustration for this theory. It is interesting that Richter chooses to change the Italian translation while maintaining the essence of its meaning. Leonardo says, *...giacere arriva' a 1/9 di sua altezza,* meaning, a man "...lying down arrives at 1/9 of his height," as opposed to the above, "...is reduced to 1/9..." Richter's translation is more logical and makes more sense than Leonardo's poetic version of the theory; however, no matter how it is expressed, the theory is not perfect.

In fact, using the head as a module, when a man lies down flat he is reduced to approximately one-eighth of his height, because the distance from the back of the head to the tip of the nose is equal to the distance from the top of the head to the bottom of the chin. This assessment agrees with the proportions in AP 124, where Leonardo uses the torso of the figure as a module, and also in AP 106, where he uses the head. Again, it is hard to be exactly sure of what Leonardo meant, particularly without an illustration by him.

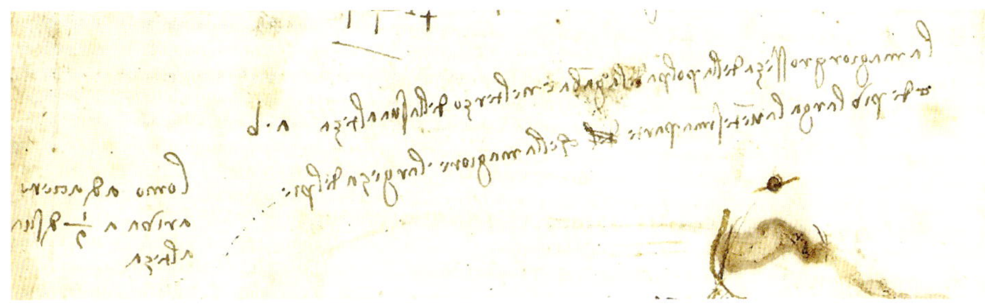

Detail, Plate 29, W. 19136–19139b, Royal Collection, Windsor

Notes
Chapter Five. The Whole Body

[25] AP 141: *Webster's New World Dictionary* (New York: World Publishing Company, 1959), 357. "Cubit n. [L. cubitum, the elbow, cubit; akin to Latin cubare; see CUBE], an ancient measure of length, about 18–22 inches; originally, the length of the arm from the end of the middle finger to the elbow."

[26] AP 141: Marcus Vitruvius Pollio, *The Ten Books on Architecture*, trans. Morris Hicky Morgan, Ph.D., LI.D. (New York: Dover Publications, 1960), 73.

[27] AP 142: See note 52 in chapter 7, AP 192, for a complete description of this page.

[28] AP 146: Richter, *The Literary Works of Leonardo da Vinci*, vol. I, R 309, 245. A discussion of the word *braccio* appears in the Phaidon 1970 edition. "The Florentine standard of measure is equal to metre 0.5836 = 22.9768 inches. It has been used until only recently. Its size varied in all Italian cities. In the canon cited by Pomponius Guaricus (*De Sculptura*, 1504) the length of the face is 1/9 of the total length and constitutes a module."

[29] AP 146: Pedretti, *Commentaries*, vol. I, R 309, 233.

[30] AP 146: It needs to be pointed out here that in discussing human proportions throughout these pages Leonardo refers only to the proportions of a man. In this he follows the traditional and prevailing thinking as set forth in the mid-fourteenth-century treatise by Cennino Cennini, *The Craftsman's Handbook*, 48. "Take note that, before going any further, I will give you the exact proportions of a man. Those of a woman I will disregard, for she does not have any set proportion."

[31] AP 147 and AP 148: O'Malley and Saunders, eds., *Leonardo da Vinci on the Human Body* (New York: Crown Publishers, 1982), plate 61, 162; plate 64, 168.

[32] During the lecture delivered at the Victoria & Albert Museum, London, on the occasion of the exhibition organized by Dr. Martin Kemp, "Leonardo da Vinci, Experience, Experiment, and Design," October 4, 2006.

[33] AP 149: Some clarification is needed here. Vitruvius says in Section 5, of Chapter 1, page 87 (See Appendix III), "...that they [the ancient Greeks] derived ratios of measurement that seemed to be necessary in all works, namely the finger, palm, foot, and cubit. They apportioned these to form the perfect number,...ten. The palm is found from the number of fingers of the hand (five) and the foot from the palm." Vitruvius goes on to point out that the mathematicians held a different point of view than the ancient Greeks and found that six was the perfect number. He then explains the logic of fixing six as the perfect integer, or whole number, and therefore the perfect base. Adding further clarification in Section 7 he says, "Further, as the foot is one-sixth of a man's height, the height of the body being limited to six, the ancients held that this was the perfect number. They observed that the cubit consisted of six palms, or twenty-four fingers." Obviously, Leonardo fixed upon the width of the palm as four fingers and established it as his own module as well.

[34] AP 149: *Webster's New World Dictionary*, 1960, page 1048, "Pace: from the Latin Passus, a stretching out of the leg in walking. 1. a step in walking, running, etc., 2. a conventional measure of length, approximately the distance covered in a step or stride: estimated at 2 1/2 feet, 3 feet or 3.3 feet. The regulation pace of the U.S. Army is 30 inches, 36 inches for double time. The ancient Roman pace, measured from the heel of one foot to the heel of the same foot in the next stride was 5 Roman feet, or about 58.1 inches; it is now known as a geometric pace, about 5 feet."

[35] AP 150: Pedretti, *Commentaries*, vol. I, R 340, 243–244.

[36] AP 150: Pedretti, *Commentaries*, vol. I, R 340, 244.

[37] AP 151: Pedretti, *Commentaries*, vol. I, R 308, 230. Pliny (Gaius Plinius Secundus), *Natural History*, Book VII, Chapter 16.

[38] AP 151: T. Berry Brazelton, M.D., *The Children's Hospital (Boston) Guide to Your Child's Health and Development* (Cambridge: Perseus Press, 2001), 216, 734.

CHAPTER SIX

THE LEG AND FOOT: AP 161–180

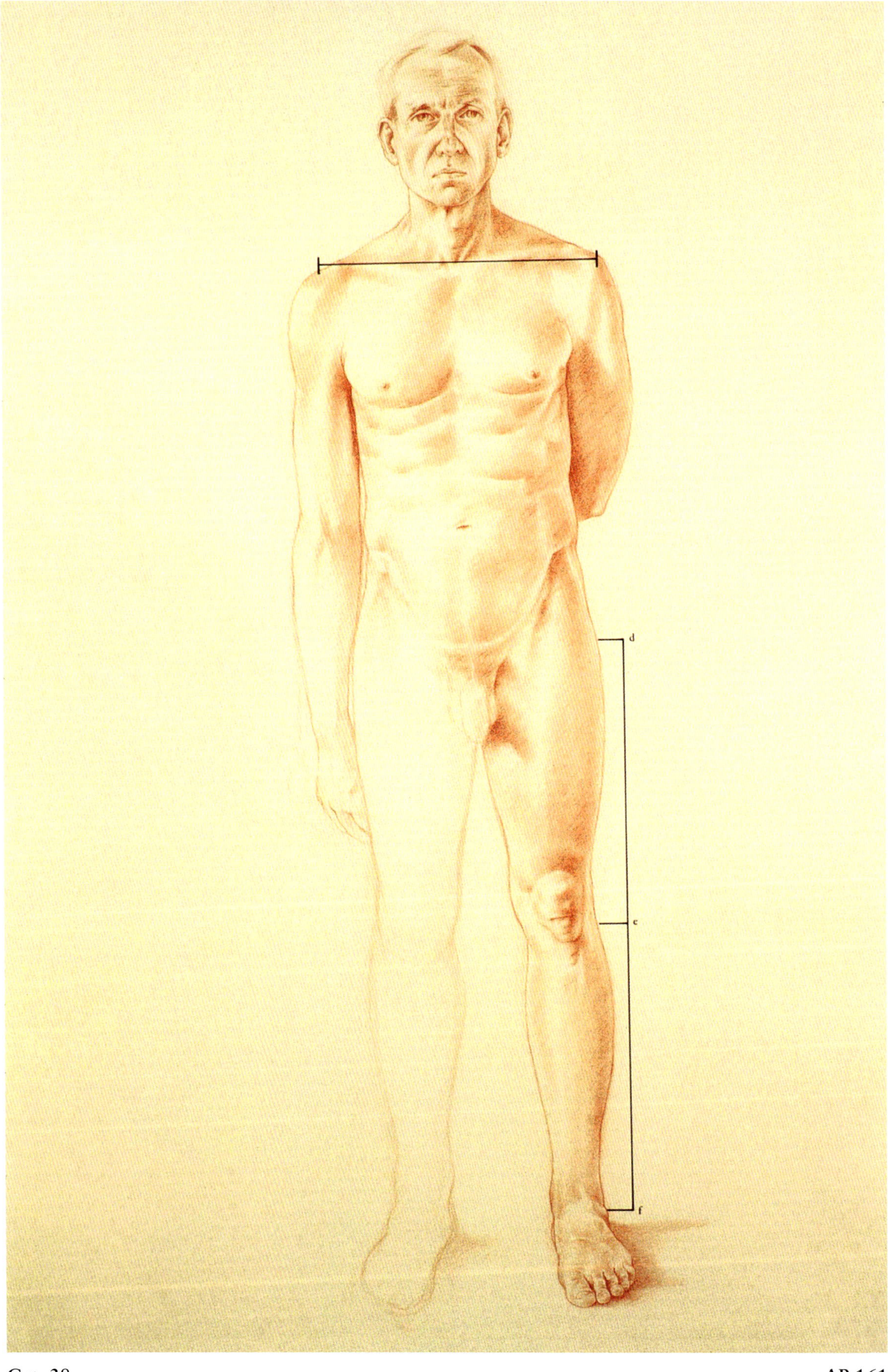

Cat. 38 AP 161

W. 19130b, Royal Library, Windsor **AP 161**
c. 1490 **R 335**
Folio 6 Verso II

d e f are equal to each other and equal to the greatest width of the shoulders.

As the first part of this entry, Folio 6 Verso I (Plate 20), deals more directly with the torso, it has been included as AP 126, even though the drawing accompanying Leonardo's text is no more than a drawing of the right leg. As noted earlier, Leonardo's drawings do not always illustrate the complete text of his theory.

On the original sheet there is not only the sketch of the right leg mentioned above but also a sketch of the left leg next to it. Both of Leonardo's drawings make a very careful distinction of where the measurements begin and end, and the comparison is supported by the indicatory letters used; it begins on the right side with the left leg, using a b c to mark the top, middle and bottom, and continues with the leg on the left side, the right leg, and marked d e f.

In this case, Leonardo says that the distance from d, the great trochanter, to e, the center of the knee (that is, the center of the patella), is equal to the distance from there to f, the ankle joint, the lateral malleolus of the fibula. And this distance is equal to the width of the shoulders.

It is an accurate comparison. Compare this entry to AP 126. You will find that the center of the leg remains the same while the beginning and ending points differ. Here, Leonardo uses the distance from the great trochanter (not the top of the femur) and ends at the ankle joint (not the sole of the foot); he then makes the comparison to the width of the shoulders, but it is the bony structure of the shoulders where the acronium process of the scapular meets the humerus (not the outer edges of the shoulders) that allows this comparison to work.

Detail, Plate 20, W. 19130b, Royal Collection, Windsor

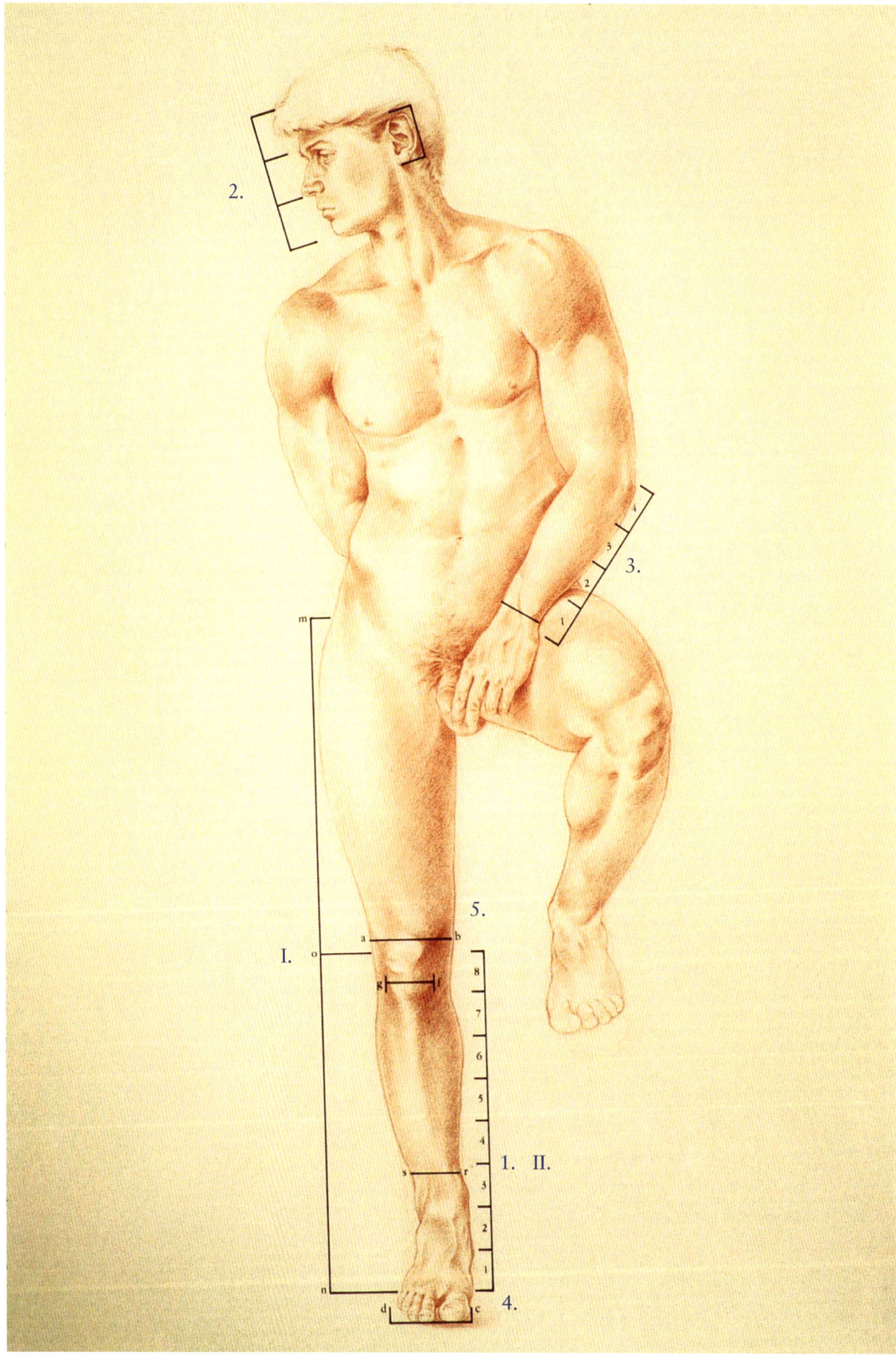

Cat. 39

AP 162

W. 19140, Royal Library, Windsor **AP 162**
c. 1490 **R 331**
Folio 12 Recto I, II

I. *m n o are equal.*

II. 1. ***The narrowest width of the leg seen in front goes 8 times from the sole of the foot to the joint of the knee, and is the same width as the arm, seen in front at the wrist, and*** 2. ***as the longest measure of the ear, and as the 3 chief divisions into which we divide the face;*** 3. ***and this measurement goes 4 times from the wrist joint of the hand to the point of the elbow.*** 4. ***The foot [d c, included in the drawing but not in the text] is as long as the space from the knee between a and b; and*** 5. ***the patella of the knee [g f] is as long as the leg between r and s.***

This entry comes from one of Leonardo's most confusing pages (Plate 30) at Windsor and is marked as Folio 12. (See AP 182 for a more detailed description of the sheet.) On the far right of this page is a small but perfect drawing of a right leg, marked with letters and construction lines illustrating the text. What follows is a series of rather finicky comparisons, but all carefully measured and verified to be correct.

I. This measurement is the same as that in AP 126. 1. The knee joint is the center of the leg; the lower measurement, n o, is from the sole of the foot, and the upper measurement, m o, is from the very top of the femur where the head of the femur inserts into the pelvis. Leonardo's drawing makes this very clear, and it is the placement of the starting measuring points at m and n that create the distinction between this measurement and the measurements used in AP 161.

II. 1. The narrowest width of the leg seen in front, the ankle, marked s r in the drawing, goes eight times into the lower leg from the sole of the foot to the knee; it works perfectly.

2. The width of the wrist is the same as the length of the ear, which is the same as the three major divisions of the face;

3. and this module may be used to measure the length of the arm from the wrist to the elbow. As a canon it is unusual, but linked to the divisions of the face it becomes part of the acceptable mainstream modules of measurement.

4. The foot, d c, again marked in the drawing but not in the text, is the width of the toes from end to end, and is equal to the knee, a b, just above the patella;

5. and the patella of the knee, g f, is as wide as the leg between r and s, that is, the width of the ankle. This comparison works perfectly well.

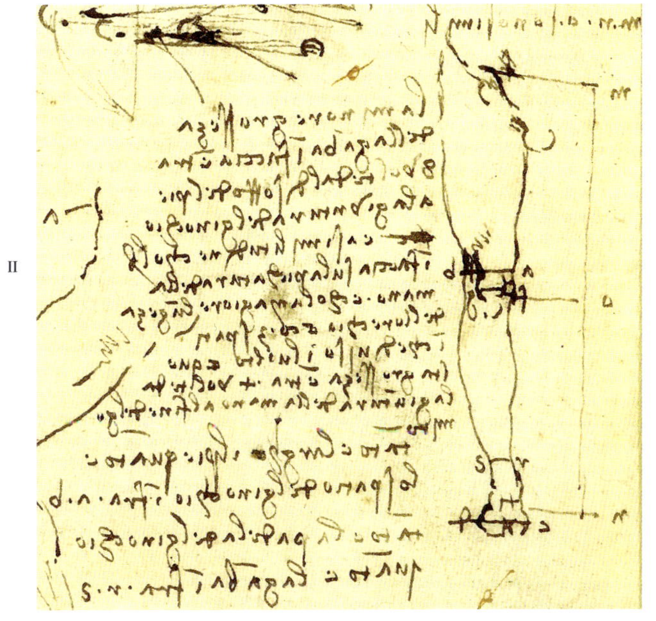

Detail, Plate 30, W. 19140, Royal Collection, Windsor

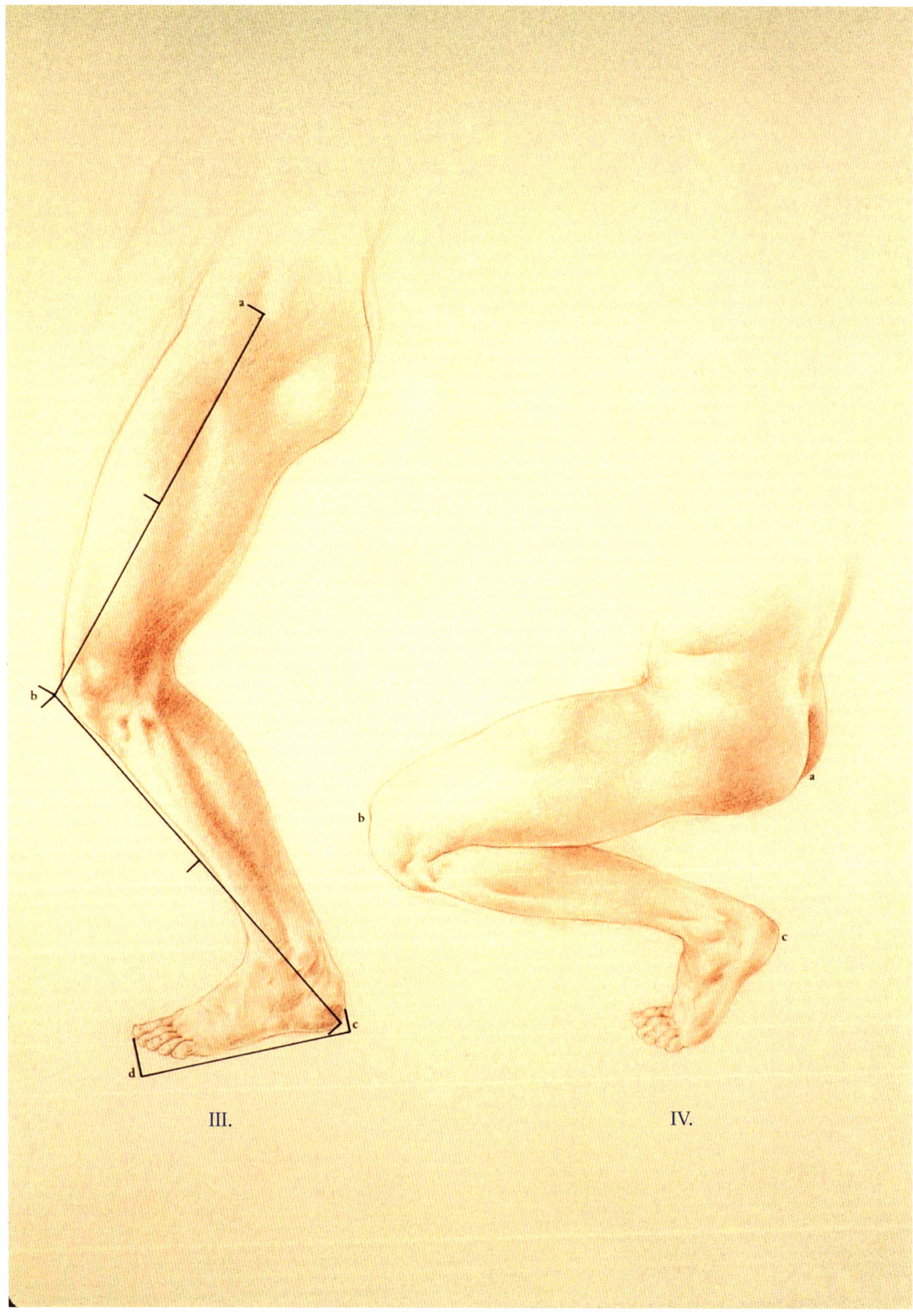

Cat. 40

AP 163

W. 19140, Royal Library, Windsor **AP 163**
c. 1490 **R 331**
Folio 12 Recto III, IV

III. *a b c are all relatively equal in length. c d goes twice from the sole of the foot to the center of the knee and the same from the knee to the hip.*

IV. *a b c are equal; a to b is 2 feet—that is to say, measuring from the heel to the tip of the great toe.*

In both of these entries, and in entry AP 164, Leonardo uses the foot as a module to measure the length of the leg (Plate 30). It is interesting to note that in this entry, on the same page and only inches apart from each other, there are two small drawings, both making the same comparisons using the same module. On many occasions we have found duplicate comparisons on different pages done at different times, but the same comparison on the same page is unusual. To simplify matters, part of III (above) is treated separately in AP 174.

III. a, the head of the femur, to b, the center of the knee, to c, the heel of the foot, are equal to each other. And c d, the length of the foot, from the heel to the tip of the toe, does indeed go twice from the sole of the foot to the knee and twice from the knee to the head of the femur.

IV. a b c are equal. In the second drawing, probably done after the first drawing, Leonardo places the letter a on the outside of the figure near the buttocks, the letter b at the center of the leg, the knee, and the letter c at the heel of the foot. Because of the unusual crouching position (as illustrated in Leonardo's drawing and in mine), the leg is stretched out a bit, but the principle remains the same: two feet make up the lower leg and two make up the upper leg.

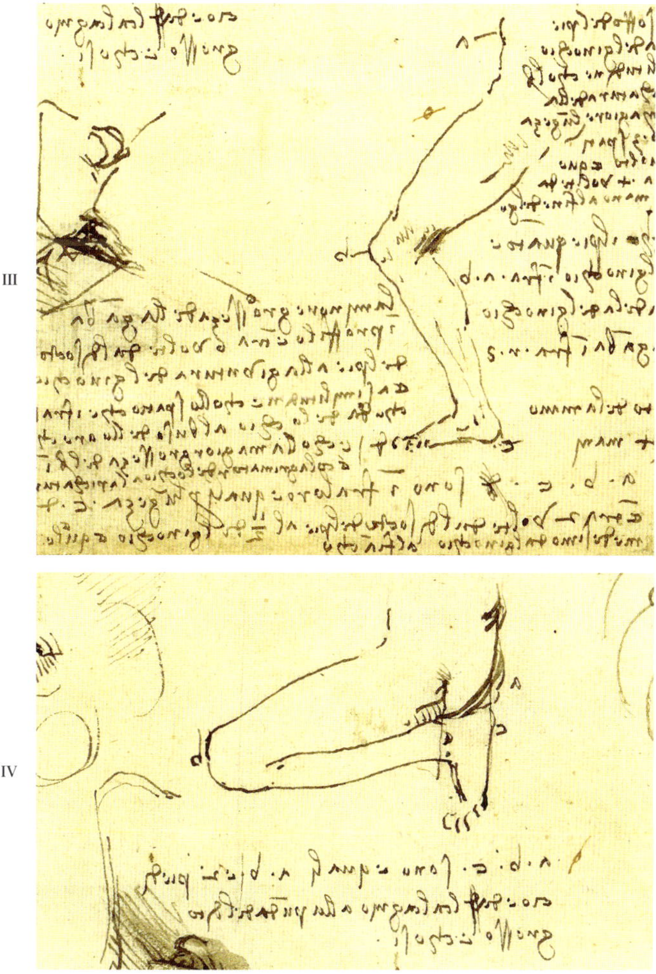

Detail, Plate 30, W. 19140, Royal Collection, Windsor

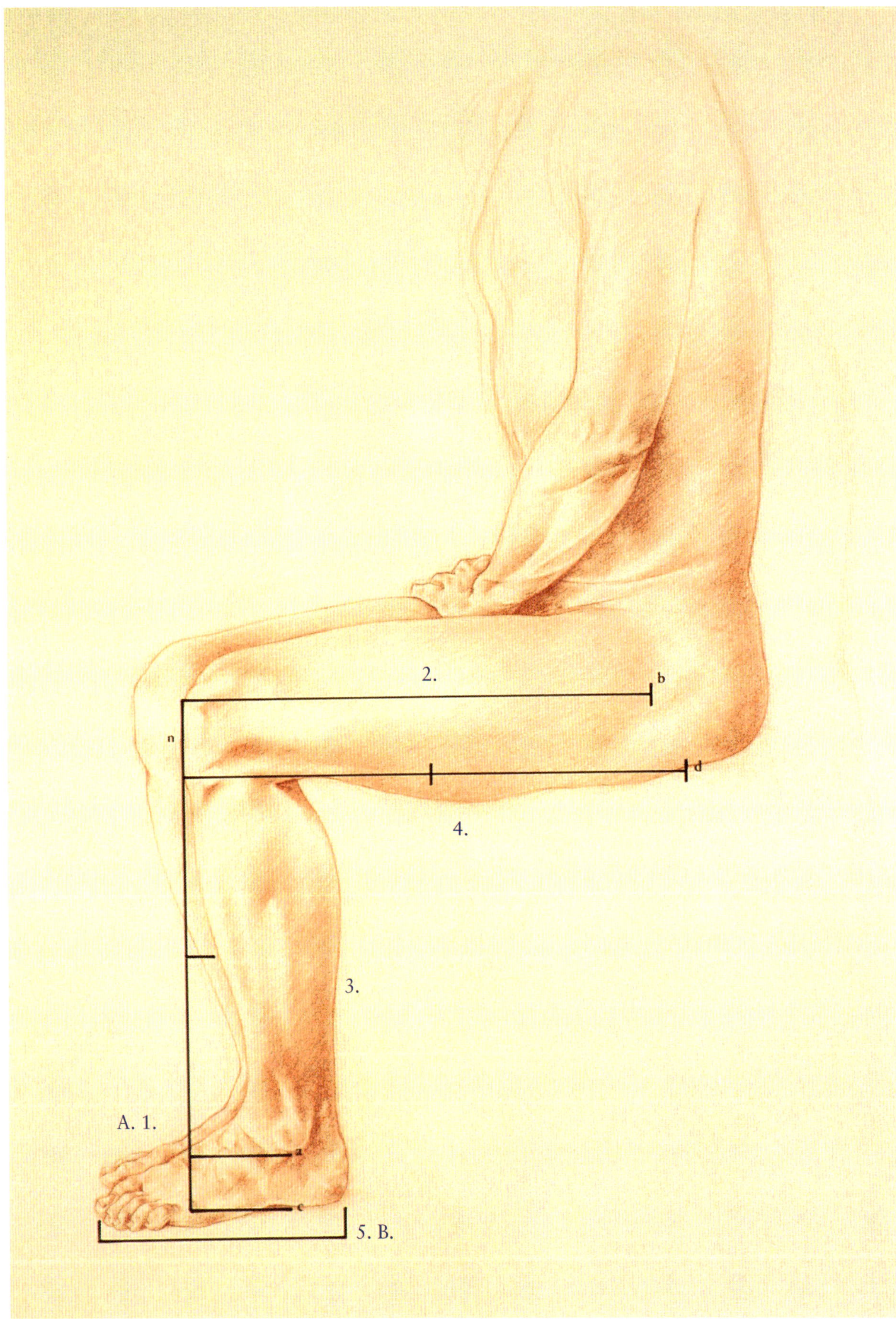

Cat. 41

AP 164

W. 19136–19139b, Royal Library, Windsor AP 164
c. 1490 R 330
Folio 11 Verso II

A. 1. *a n b are equal*
2. *c n d are equal*
3. *n c makes two feet*
4. *n d makes two feet.*

Volume marked B, Institut de France, Paris R 329
c. 1490–1492
MS. B. 3b

B. 5. *The length of the foot from the end of the toes to the heel goes twice into that from the heel to the knee, that is, where the leg bone [fibula] joins the thigh bone [femur].*

These two entries, Folio 11, housed at Windsor, and MS B, in Paris, both deal with the same comparisons, using the foot as a module. The observation from Windsor (Plate 29) is from the large Folio 11, folded into four parts numbered 19136–19139, measuring 16 x 11 inches (405 x 281 mm). The text has been divided in the *Quaderni* edition into ten major parts or paragraphs designated by ten Roman numerals. I have separated the many parts of the text and created entries for the drawings in AP 164, 165, 166, 172, and 175, all of which deal with the proportions of the feet and legs. The information on the original page is illustrated by Leonardo's three drawings emphasizing a man's leg and one drawing of a foot. There is also a drawing of weights and measures with its own separate explanatory text on the page. This specific entry is taken from the upper-right quarter of the page, which depicts only the torso and leg of a seated man in profile facing our right.

The entry from Paris (Plate 3) is found in MS B, a beautiful modest-size notebook, or pocket book, as they were known, measuring 9½ x 7 inches (242 x 173 mm.) The notebook is crammed with a variety of information on war machines, architectural plans, models, and instruments. Leonardo's drawing, at the very beginning of the book, page 3, side b, is a tiny, very faint pen-and-ink sketch of a leg, R 329, with the explanatory text next to it, and an arm, R 346, with its own text.

A. 1. The distance from a, the lateral malleolus of the fibula, to n, the top of the patella, is equal to the distance from n to b, the head of the great trochanter.

2. The distance from c, the bottom of the foot, to n, the patella, is equal to the distance from n to d, the insertion of the head of the femur. One must picture the femur and distinguish between the uppermost part, or the head of the femur, where it actually inserts into the pelvis, and the great trochanter, that part of the femur closest to the surface of the skin and a few centimeters lower than the inserted head of the femur. (Notice the difference in the placement of b to d.)

3. Leonardo continues, saying, rather cryptically, that n c makes two feet, and

4. that n d also makes two feet, both of which are correct.

B. 5. And lastly, on the verso side, at the very top of the third page of MS B, we find the little sketch of a leg bent at the knee. Leonardo uses the foot again as a module, but only to measure the lower leg. While this drawing is not diagrammed with letters detailing the measurement as minutely as the Windsor sheet, he does carefully spell out that the foot, from the heel to the toes, goes twice into the distance from the heel to the knee, where the fibula joins the femur. Although he calculates them differently, Leonardo arrives at the same conclusion in both cases.

A

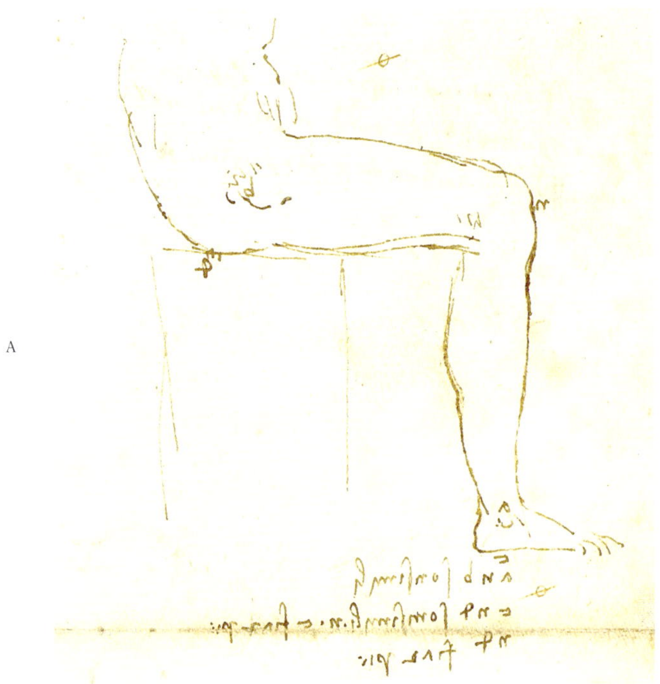

Detail, Plate 29, W. 19136–19139b, Royal Collection, Windsor

B. 5

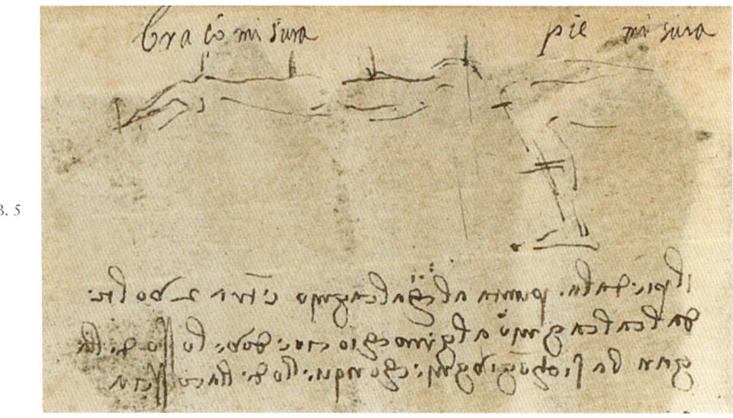

Detail, Plate 3, Ms B, page 3b, Bibliothéque de l'Institut de France, Paris

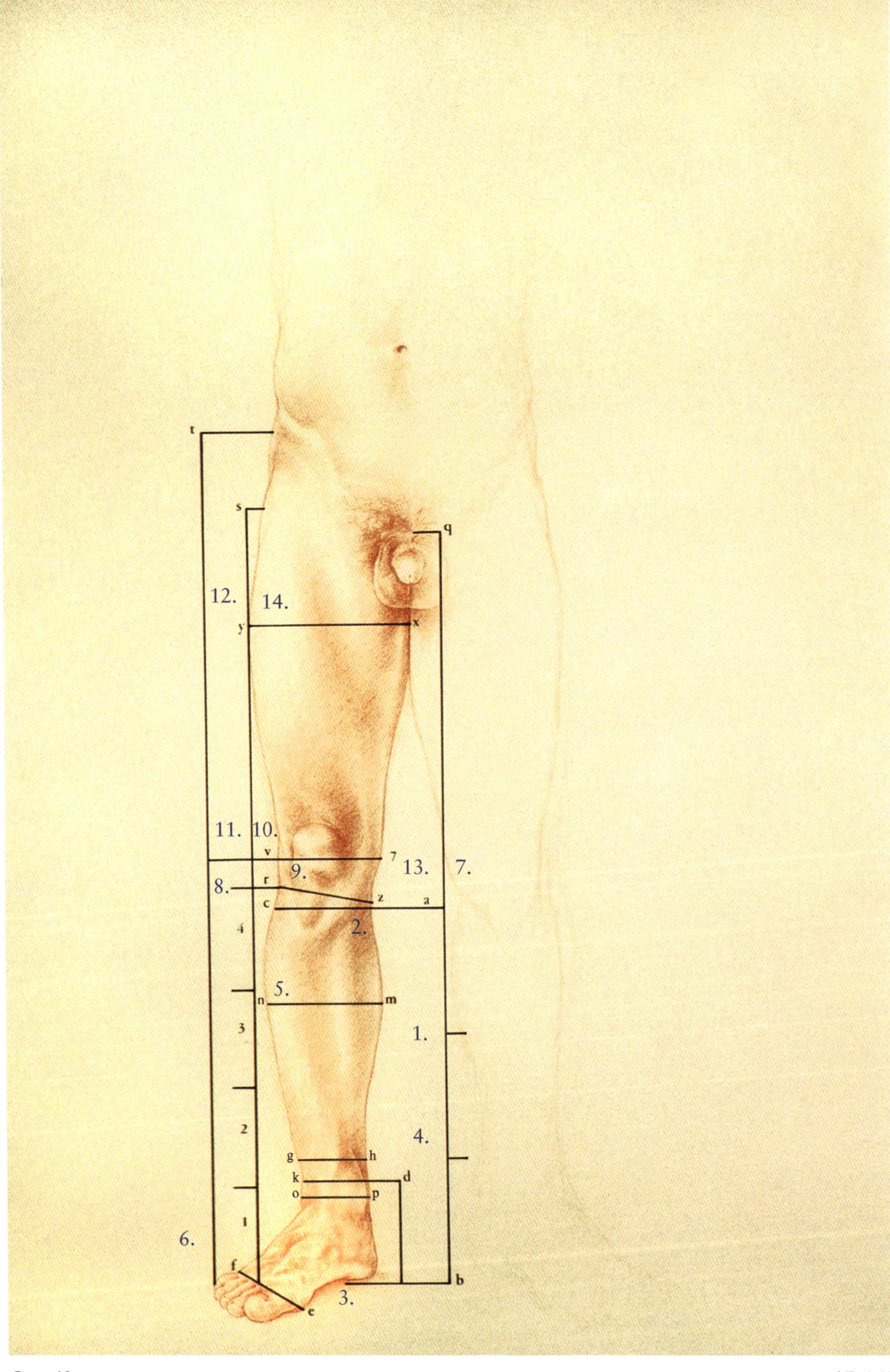

Cat. 42 AP 165

W. 19136–19139b, Royal Library, Windsor AP 165
c. 1490 R 328
Folio 11 Verso IV, VI

IV. 1. *The greatest thickness of the calf of the leg [m n] is at a third of its height a b, and is a twentieth part thicker than the greatest thickness of the foot.*

VI. 2. *a c is half of the head, and* 3. *equal to d b, and to the insertion of the five toes e f.* 4. *d k diminishes one-sixth in the leg in g h. g h is* $^1/_3$ *of the head [face];* 5. *m n increases one sixth from a e[c] and is* $^7/_{12}$ *of the head.* 6. *o p is* $^1/_{10}$ *less than d k and is* $^6/_{17}$ *of the head.* 7. *a is at half the distance between b q, and is* $^1/_4$ *of the man.* 8. *r is half-way between s and b.* 9. *The concavity of the knee outside r is higher than that inside a.* 10. *The half of the whole height of the leg from the foot r, is half-way between the prominence s and the ground b.* 11. *v is half-way between t and b.* 12. *The thickness of the thigh seen in front is equal to the greatest width of the face, that is,* $^2/_3$ *of the length from the chin to the top of the head.* 13. *z r is* $^5/_6$ *of 7 to v; m n is equal to 7 v and is* $^1/_4$ *of r b,* 14. *x y goes 3 times into r b and into r s.*

The observations included here are found on the large Windsor folio sheet (Plate 29) folded in four and measuring 15$^3/_4$ x 11 inches (405 x 281 mm). In the *Quaderni* edition the entries on this page have been divided into ten major parts designated by Roman numerals. As explained in AP 164, I have divided the entire text into several parts and used them as supplemental texts along with the drawings in AP 164, 165, 166, 172, and 175. Most of the information relates to three drawings emphasizing a man's leg and one drawing of a foot. There is also a drawing of weights and measures with its own explanatory text.

I have transcribed here, in AP 165, only sections IV and VI, the explanatory text relating to the exquisite drawing by Leonardo of a fully frontal standing male figure from the top of his pelvis to the bottom of his foot.

IV. 1. The greatest thickness of the calf of the leg [m n] is at a third of the distance between a, the knee, to b, the bottom of the foot (for an entirely different reading of this text, see note 39). m n is included in Leonardo's drawing but not in his text, whereas a b is in both the drawing and the text. The ratio Leonardo suggests, that the thickest part of the calf is equal to one-third of the height of the lower leg, works quite well. The last part of the entry is too obscure to be of use.

VI. 2. a c, the width of the leg at the knee, is half of the head. This proportion is not illustrated here or in Leonardo's drawing, but it is quite accurate.

3. a c is equal to the distance from d, the medial malleolus of the tibia, to b, the bottom of the foot but is only slightly similar to f, the width of the insertion of the toes.

4. Observing that d k, the width of the leg just above the medial malleolus of the tibia, is one-sixth larger than g h, the thinnest part of the ankle, is a very minor distinction. g h is, in fact, also one-third of the face, not the head; it is not shown here.

5. That m n, the widest part of the calf, increases by one-sixth of a c, the width of the knee, is probably correct, but it is inconsequential as a comparison, just as seven-twelfths of the head is. Both have been left out of the illustration.

6. Knowing that o p, the width of the ankle below the malleolus, is one-tenth less than d k and is six-seventeenths of the head is another comparison of little value.

7. a, the knee, is at the center between b, the bottom of the foot, and q, the pubis symphasis, and is one-fourth of a man. Leonardo means here that a to b and a to q are each one-fourth of a man's height; this is quite a reliable comparison, which has been verified several times.

8. r, also the knee, is halfway between s, the head of the great trochanter of the femur, and b, the sole of the foot; this has also been proven by Leonardo previously.

9. The concavity of the knee at r, at the outside of the leg (or the lateral side), is higher than the inside of the leg (or the medial side) at a. Every beginning art student fails to see this subtle but essential offset of alignment in muscular structure, which pinches the body's appendages at the joints.

10. Half of the whole leg at r, the knee, is halfway between s, the great trochanter, and b, the ground or the sole of the foot. This is the same observation as in 8 above.

11. v, the top of the patella, is halfway between t, the top portion of the pelvis, the iliac crest, and b, the sole of the foot. Notice the slight distinction here, the center of the leg up to v, the top of the patella, which changes the relationship of the upper leg to the lower leg.

12. The thickness of the thigh seen in front, in this case x y, is equal to the width of the face and two-thirds of the head, from the chin to the top of the head, in other words, the face. This observation is surprisingly correct. Try using this theory in AP 149.

13. z r, the diagonal width of the knee, is five-sixths of the width from 7 to v, the widest part of the knee, and is meant to emphasize the observation in 9 above. Visually and anatomically, this beautiful, but subtle, distinction can be explained as the lower part of the sartoris (the longest muscle in the body) descends and inserts into the medial surface of the tibia, a point lower than the gentle curve of the biceps femoris where it inserts into the lateral side of the head of the fibula. And m n, the width of the calf, is similar to 7 v, the width of the knee; using that as a module, it enters into the distance from r, the center of the knee, to b, the sole of the foot, four times.

14. And lastly, x y, the width of the thigh, does not go three times into r b or r s, either in Leonardo's drawing or in mine. It only measures slightly more than two times in both.

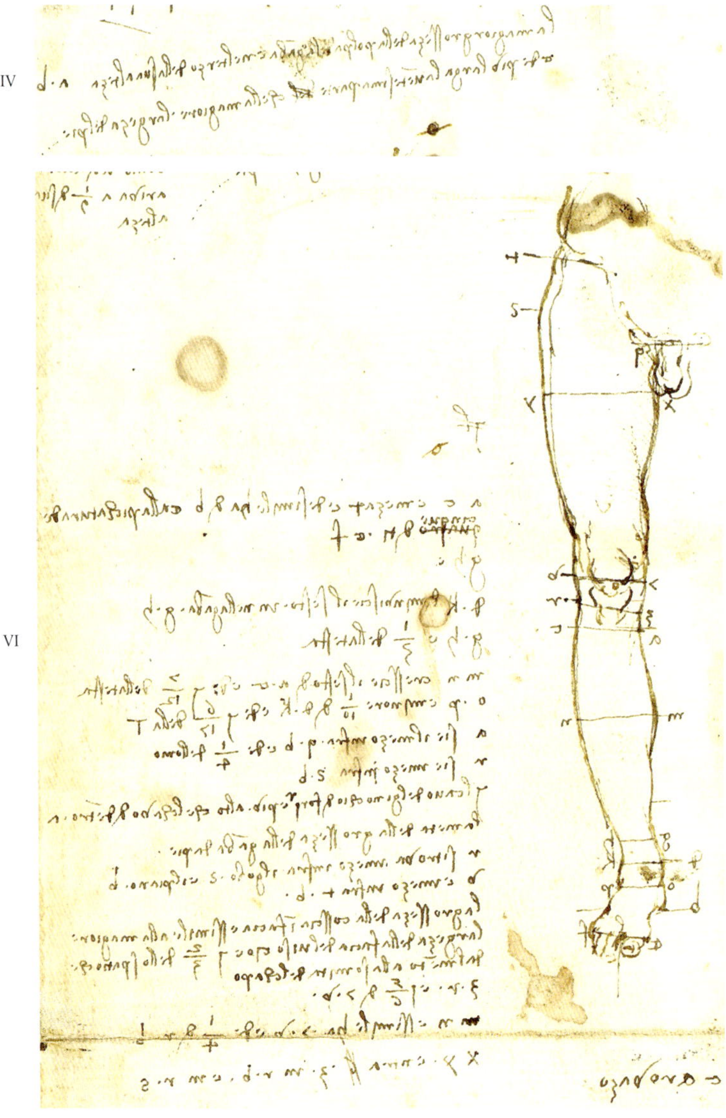

Detail, Plate 29, W. 19136–19139b, Royal Collection, Windsor

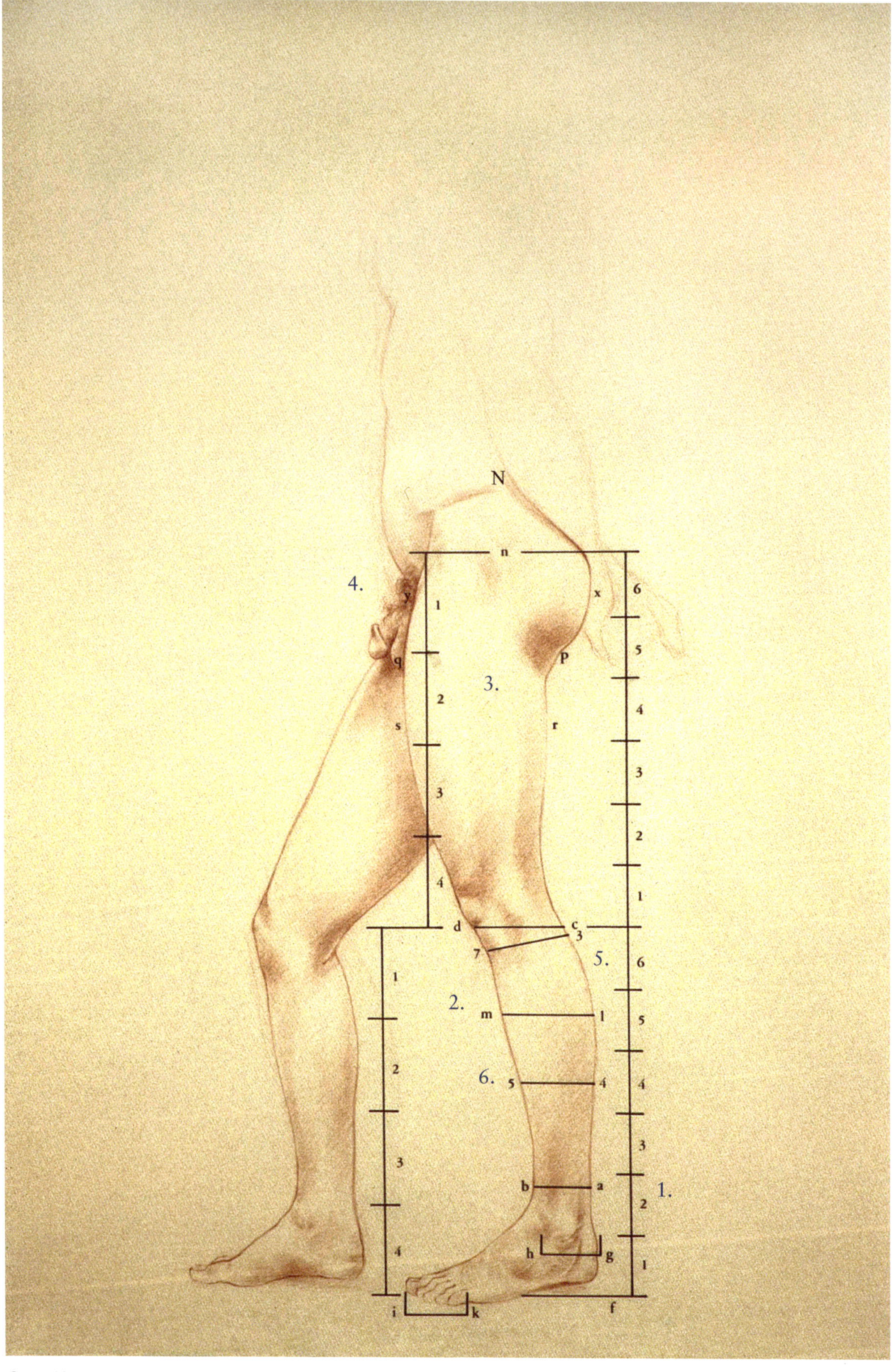

Cat. 43 AP 166

W. 19136–19139b, Royal Library, Windsor **AP 166**
c. 1490 **R 328**
Folio 11 Verso VIII

1. *a b goes 6 times into c f and 6 times into c n, and is equal to g h [and] i k;*
2. *l m goes 4 times into d f, and 4 times into d n, and is 3/7 of the foot;*
3. *p q r s goes 3 times into d f, and 3 times into b [d] n;*
4. *x y is 1/8 of x f and is equal to n q.*
5. *3 7 is 1/9 of n f.*
6. *4 5 is 1/10 of n f.*

As in the previous entry (AP 165), these observations are also from the large Windsor sheet folded in four (Plate 29). The authors of the *Quaderni,* in an effort to clarify some of Leonardo's words, assigned Roman numerals to his statements, whether single sentences or entire paragraphs. In AP 165, Richter jumps from IV to VI, discussing V in R 338. We have included it as AP 154. Roman numeral VII, as marked in the *Quaderni,* is simply three words, "e a rovaco [e ha rotato]" (and is reversed or rotated), and is written between the drawing of the frontal leg in AP 165 and the profile leg dealt with here in AP 166. Leonardo continues with the same highly detailed measurements of the leg, this time rotated in profile, using some of the same letters and numbers found in AP 165.

1. a b, the width of the ankle in profile, does go six times into c, the center of the knee, to f, the sole of the foot, and six times into c, again the center of the knee, to n, the top of the femur; and this measurement is equal to g h, the distance from the heel to the frontal side of the lateral malleolus of the fibula, and to i k, the width of the foot at the insertions of the toes.
2. l m, the width of the leg in profile, at the thickness of the calf, does go four times into d, the center of the knee, to f, the sole of the foot, and also four times into d to n, the head of the great trochanter; and that measure, l m, is close to being three-sevenths (almost half) the length of the foot.
3. p q, the thickness of the thigh at the bottom of the buttocks, and r s, the thigh further down the leg, are similar in width, *similar* being the operative word. This measurement, unique and variable at best, does not go three times into the distance d f, the center of the knee to the sole of the foot, and three times into d n, the knee to the head of the great trochanter. At best it measures only two and a half times in both the upper and lower legs.
4. x y, the width of the pelvic area from the beginning of the genitals, or the pubis symphasis, to the back of the buttocks, is not one-eighth of x f, the distance from the buttocks to the sole of the foot, but more like one-fourth in both Leonardo's drawing and mine. In addition, x y is not equal to n q but equals the distance from q to the top of the pelvis, marked here on my drawing as N. We know that the width of the pelvis is loosely the same as its height, making a square, with p q the bottom of the pelvis and N q the height of the pelvis. I think that Leonardo intended to make a distinction here between the top of the great trochanter and the top of the pelvis, as he did in AP 165 and marked on his drawing as t.

5. 3 7, the width of the knee at the base of the patella, is one-ninth of the distance from n, the head of the great trochanter, to f, the bottom of the foot: this seems to work perfectly well in Leonardo's drawing and mine if n[40] remains at the top of the femur. But, if we take the measurement from the top of the pelvis, that distance measures over ten times. I have not provided a proportional schema for this observation nor for the one below on my drawing. Neither did Leonardo.
6. 4 5, the width of the leg just below the bottom of the calf muscle (the lateral and medial heads of the gastrocnemius), does go ten times into n, the head of the great trochanter, to f, the bottom of the foot.

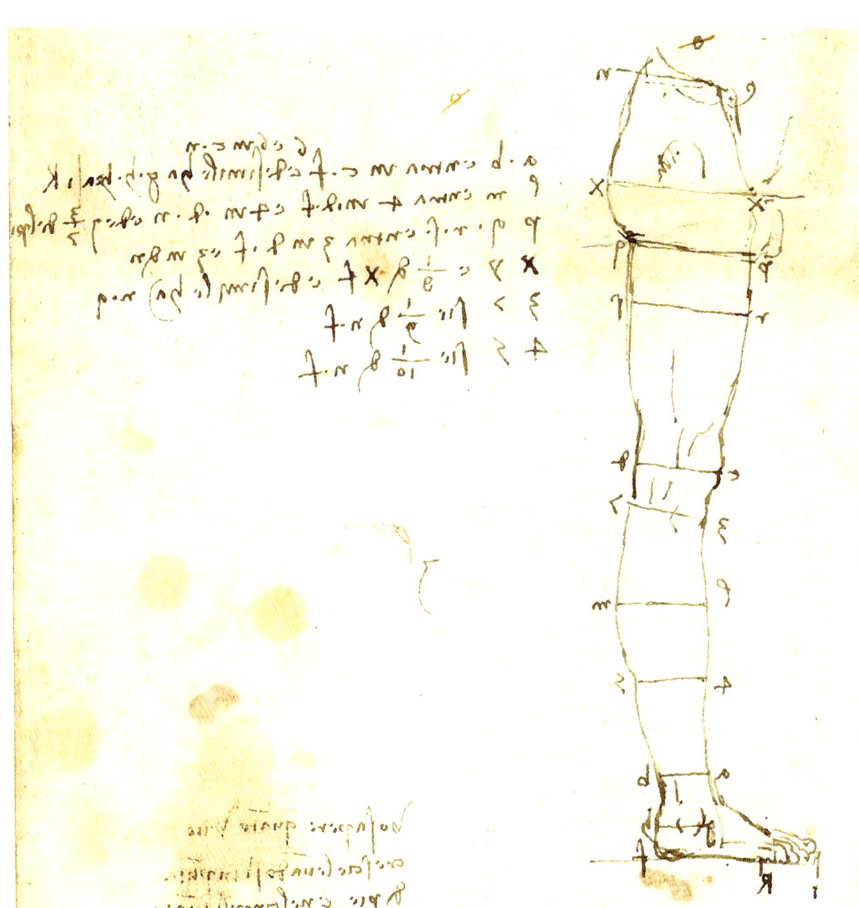

Detail, Plate 29, W. 19136–19139b, Royal Collection, Windsor

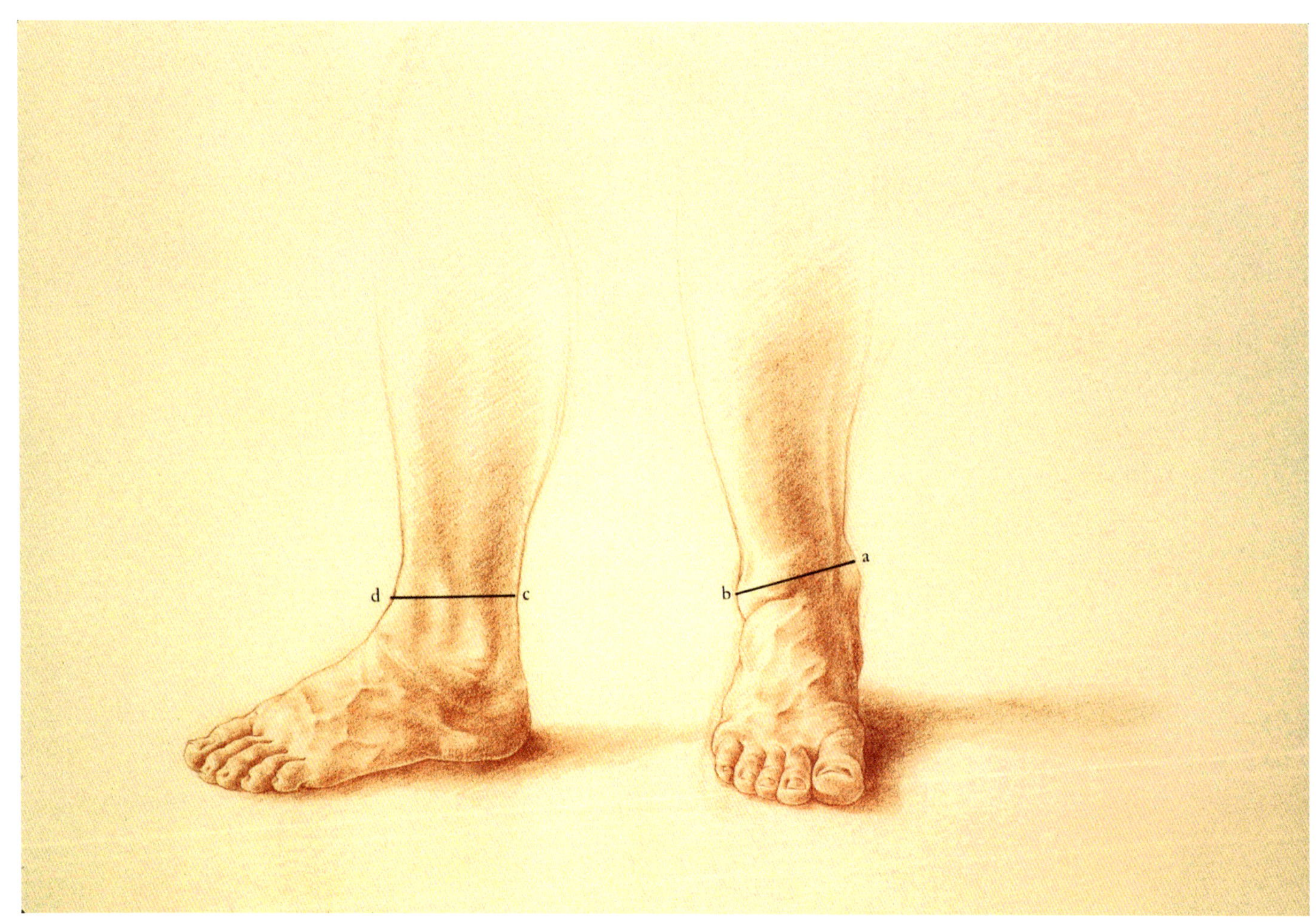

Cat. 44 AP 167

W. 19140a, Royal Library, Windsor **AP 167**
c. 1490 **R 323**
Folio 12 Recto VI

For each man respectively the distance between a and b is equal to c d.

This is the last entry in the bottom left corner of the complex Windsor page, Folio 12 (Plate 30). Leonardo's statement is simple and straightforward. I have found the measurement to be close but not exact. Many dancers and athletes have highly developed muscles, particularly at the joints of the legs, so this comparison can vary wildly. There is one essential issue I am compelled to point out: Leonardo's drawing lines up the two malleoli condyles, the bulbous parts of the lower extremity of the leg bones, on the same level. This is an odd mistake for one with such keen powers of observation, but he repeats the mistake in AP 171. The medial malleolus of the tibia is higher than the lateral malleolus of the fibula. Professor Leo Steinberg pointed to this small anatomical fact as an essential piece of information every beginning art student should learn early on.

In essence, Leonardo says that for each man the distance from a, the medial malleolus of the tibia, to b, the lateral malleolus of the fibula, as seen in a frontal view, is equal to the width of the ankle, above the malleoli bones of the tibia and the fibula, as seen from the side. Also that is equal to the distance from c, the back of the foot (location of the tendo calcaneus, the tendon connecting the muscles of the lower leg, the soleus and gastrocnemisis, to the calcaneus bone of the foot), to d, the point where the lower leg meets the instep of the foot, or the superior extensor retinaculum, a tendon-like band covering the malleoli bones across the front of the foot.

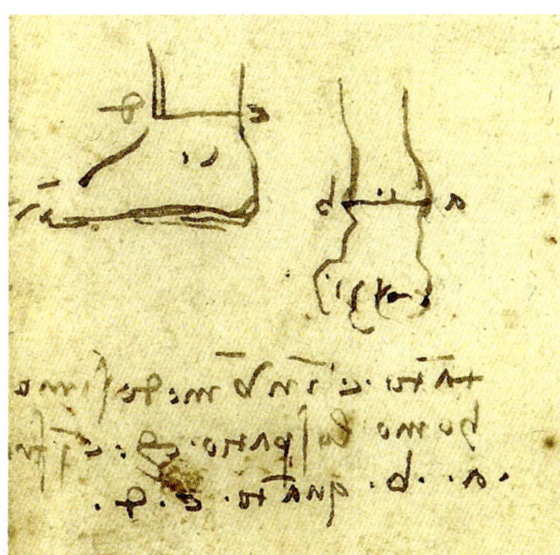

Detail, Plate 30, W. 19140, Royal Collection, Windsor

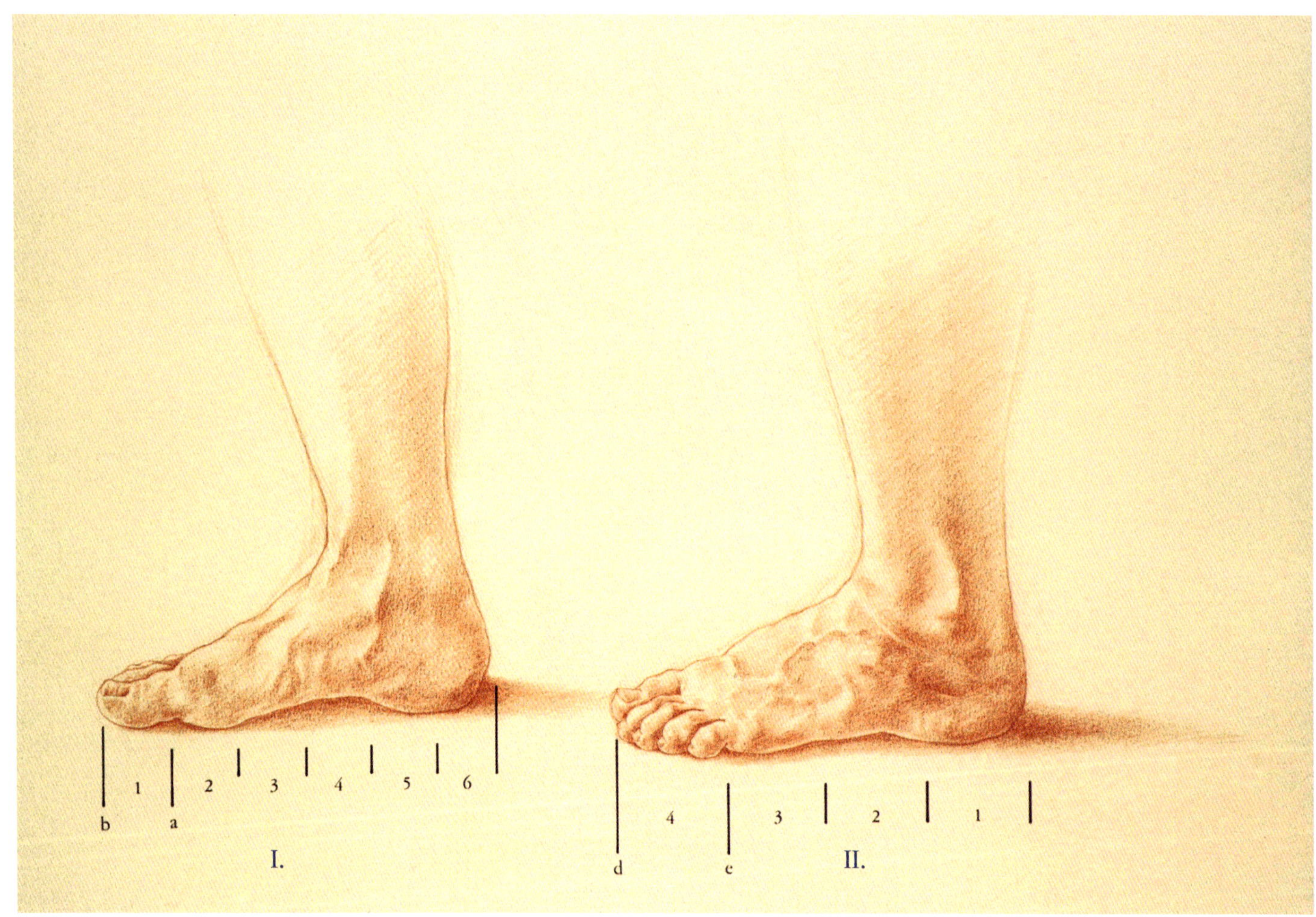

Cat. 45

AP 168

W. 19133b, Royal Library, Windsor **AP 168**
c. 1490 **R 322**
Folio 9 Verso I, II

I. ***The great toe is the sixth part of the foot, taking the measurement in profile on the inside of the foot, where this toe springs from the ball of the sole of the foot to its tip a b; and it is similar to the distance from the mouth to the bottom of the chin.***

II. ***If you draw the foot in profile from the outside, make the little toe begin at three-quarters of the length of this foot, and you will find the same distance from the insertion of this toe as to the farthest prominence of the great toe.***

These entries come from the Windsor sheet, 19133b (Plate 26). It measures 12 x $8\frac{1}{4}$ inches (303 x 206 mm) and deals exclusively with proportions and comparisons of the hand and foot. On the a, or recto, side of the page, Leonardo follows form by stating the theory, then adding an illustration below it. Each theory is a line or two written from right to left in a vertical page with the illustration drawn under the sentence. On the b, or verso, side, he follows the same form, but there are only two entries on that side and both are treated here. One wonders whether Leonardo writes the theory, then does the drawing, or does the drawing and then writes the theory. There are but a few instances where he corrects the drawing, suggesting that the theory may have come first. (See AP 113.)

I. The great toe from "where this toe springs" from the ball of the foot, a, to the very tip of the toe, b, is the module in this comparison. It measures one-sixth of the length of the foot perfectly. Oddly enough, the second part of the comparison, the distance from the mouth to the chin as equal to the great toe, also works perfectly well. Using the toe as a module to measure parts of the face is a bit unusual at best and is not illustrated here.

II. One of the few times that Leonardo talks about the act of drawing while explaining a proportional theory. Simply put, if you divide the foot, as seen from the outside profile, or lateral view, into four parts, you will find that the distance from the insertion of the small toe, e, to the tip of the large toe, d, will be equal to one-fourth of the length of the foot. Leonardo includes the letters e and d in his drawing but not in his text. I have included them here, and it is a sound proportional observation when drawing the foot.

I

II

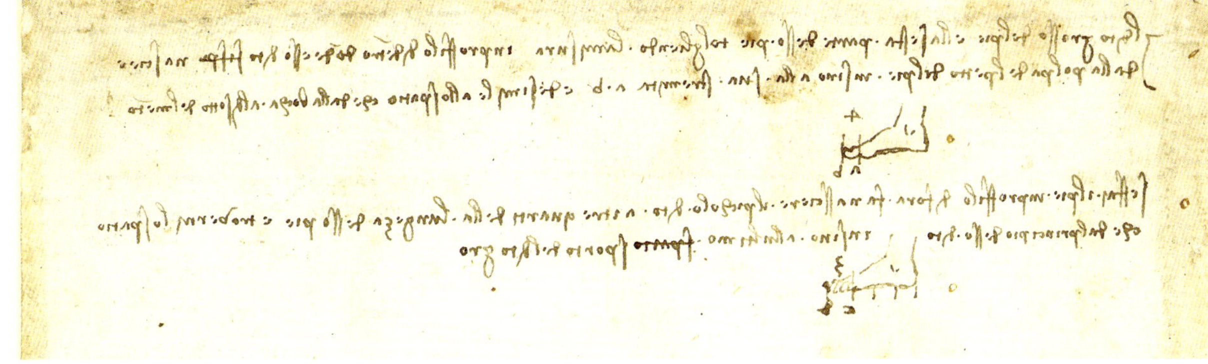

Detail, Plate 26, W. 19133b, Royal Collection, Windsor

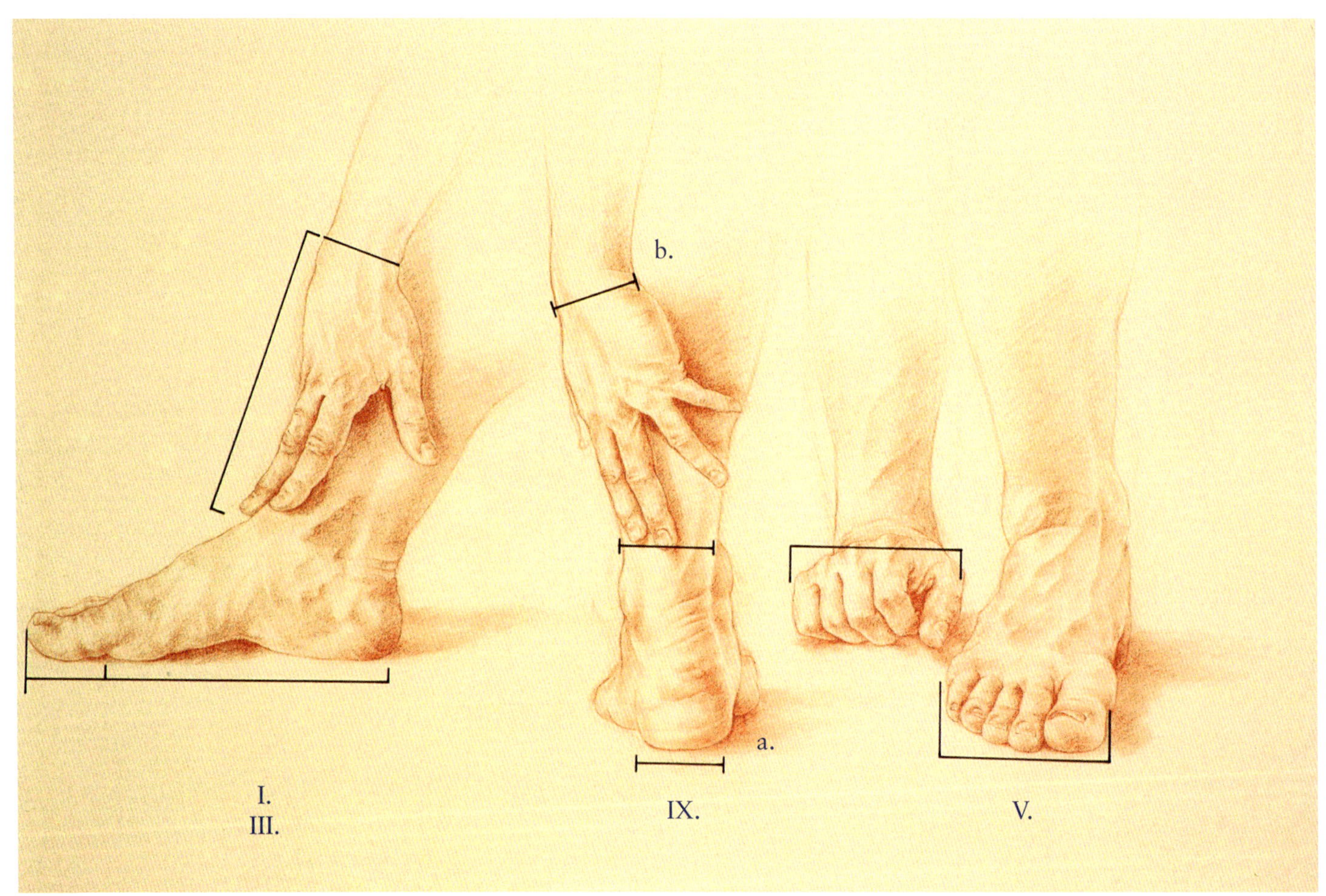

Cat. 46 AP 169

W. 19133a, Royal Library, Windsor **AP 169**
c. 1490 **R 324**
Folio 9 Recto I, III, IX, V.

I. ***The foot is as much longer than the hand as the thickness of the arm at the wrist where it is thinnest seen facing.***

III. ***Again, you will find that the foot is as much longer than the hand as the space between the inner angle of the little toe to last projection of the big toe, if you measure along the length of the foot.***

IX. ***The width of the heel at the lower part is equal to that of the arm where it joins the hand; and also to the leg where it is thinnest when viewed in front.***

V. ***If you hold your hand with the 5 fingers straight and close together you will find it to be of the same width as the widest part of the foot, that is, where it is joined onto the toes.***

The four theories listed here come from the recto side of the Windsor sheet, 19133a (Plate 25), described in AP 168. As explained, all of the entries, both recto and verso, and there are over a dozen, are devoted to comparisons of the hands and feet. Leonardo's drawings are tiny fragments of hands and feet, ankles and wrists. Entry II (from the *Quaderni*) has been omitted by Richter, as it is simply the word *braccio* (arm) with no explanation.

I. To state the first principle as simply as possible, the foot is as long as the hand plus the width of the wrist. This is another one of those unexpected revelations that works perfectly well.

III. The foot is longer than the hand by the amount of space between the inner angle of the little toe and the tip of the big toe. This is another way of stating the same principle as in number I, so I have combined numbers I and III in the same drawing. Further verification is illustrated in AP 168.

IX. a, the width of the leg at the lower end of the heel, or ground level, is equal to the arm where it joins the hand, b, or the wrist, and is also equal to the thinnest part of the leg, the ankle, as viewed from either the back or the front of the foot.

V. If you hold your hand with all five fingers straight out, or even with the fingers closed together in a fist, as seen here, you will find it to be the same width as the widest part of the foot, again as pictured here.

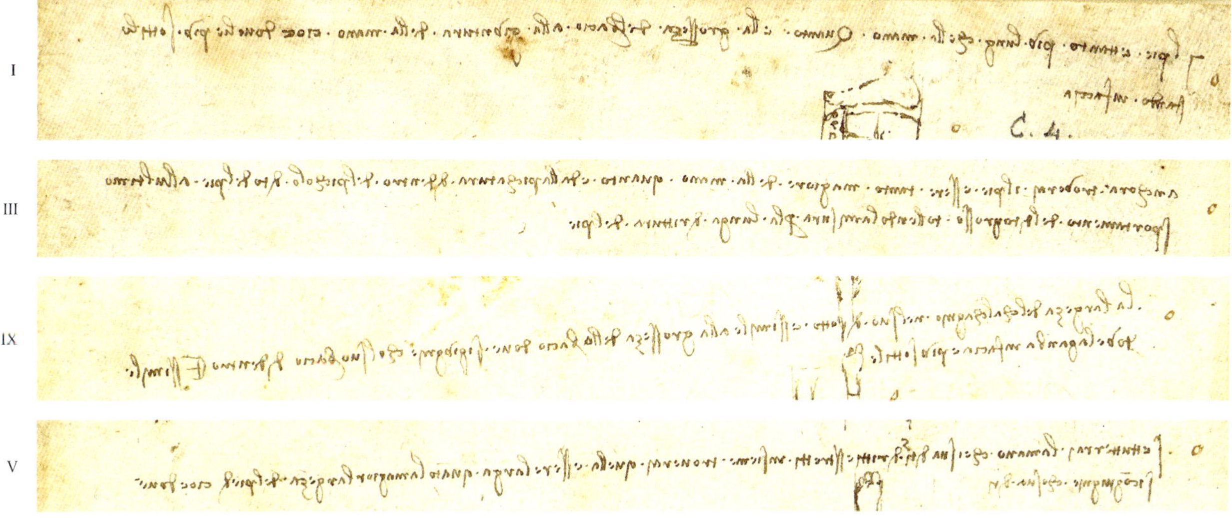

Detail, Plate 25, W. 19133a, Royal Collection, Windsor

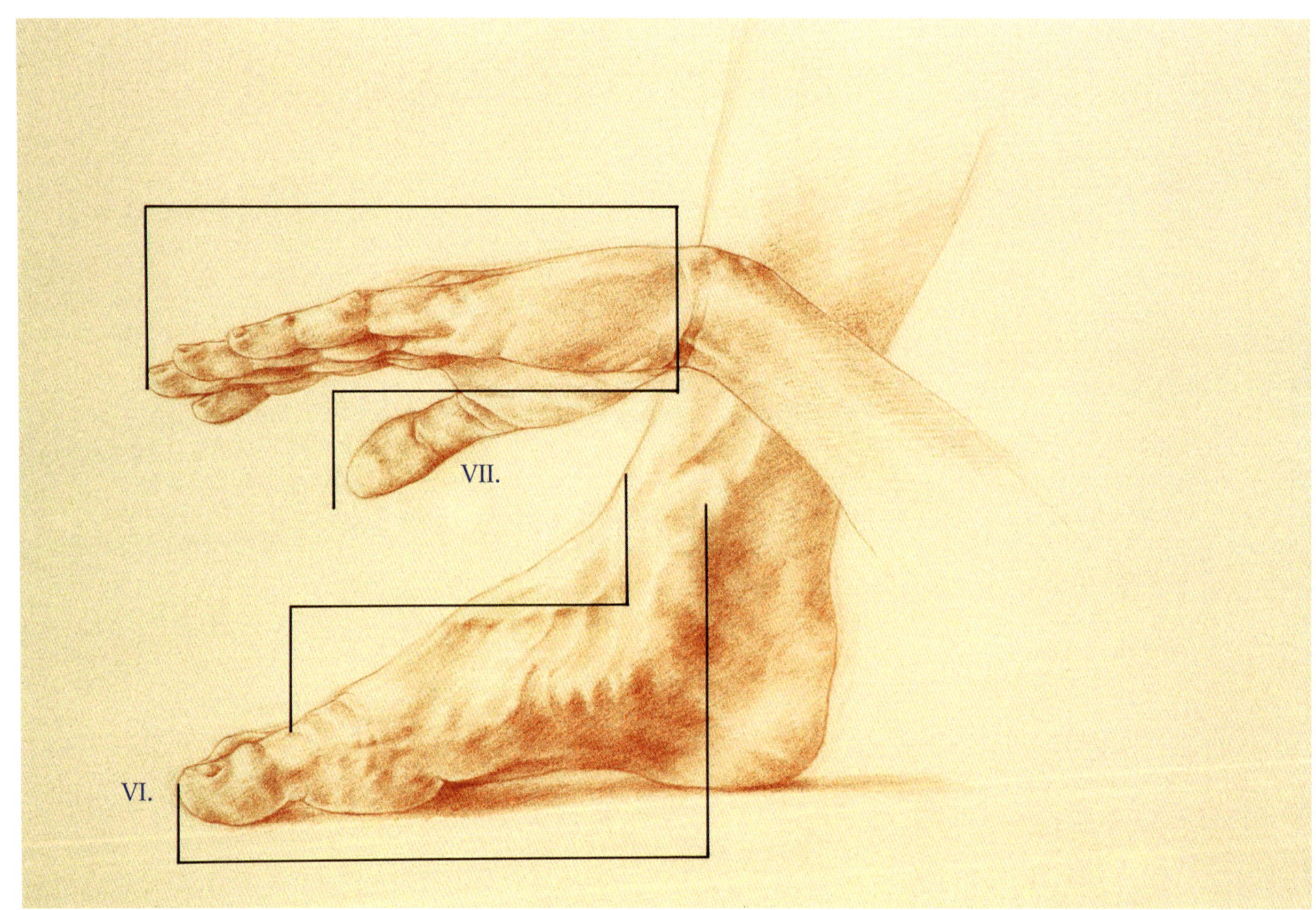

Cat. 47 AP 170

W. 19133a, Royal Library, Windsor — **AP 170**
c. 1490 — **R 324**
Folio 9 Recto VI, VII

VI. ***And if you measure from the prominence of the inner ankle to the end of the great toe you will find this measure to be as long as the whole hand.***

VII. ***From the top of the angle of the foot to the insertion of the toes is equal to the hand from the wrist joint to the tip of the thumb.***

Some of Leonardo's comparisons on this page (Plate 25) are a little too obscure to be of much practical use, such as using for a module the hand without the fingers (IV) or the hand without the thumb (VIII). Therefore, I have omitted these entries.

VI. If you measure from the center of the "prominence of the inner ankle," or the medial malleolus of the tibia, to the tip of the big toe, you will indeed find it to be equal to the length of the whole hand, from the wrist to the tip of the longest finger.

VII. From the top angle of the foot, that is, where the tibia rests on the first bone of the foot, the talus, to the insertion of the toes, will be the same as the length of the thumb from the wrist to the tip.

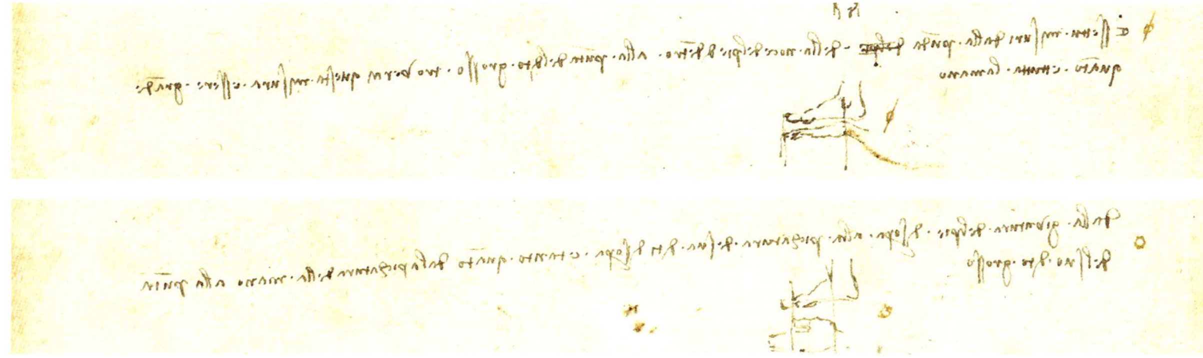

Detail, Plate 25, W. 19133a, Royal Collection, Windsor

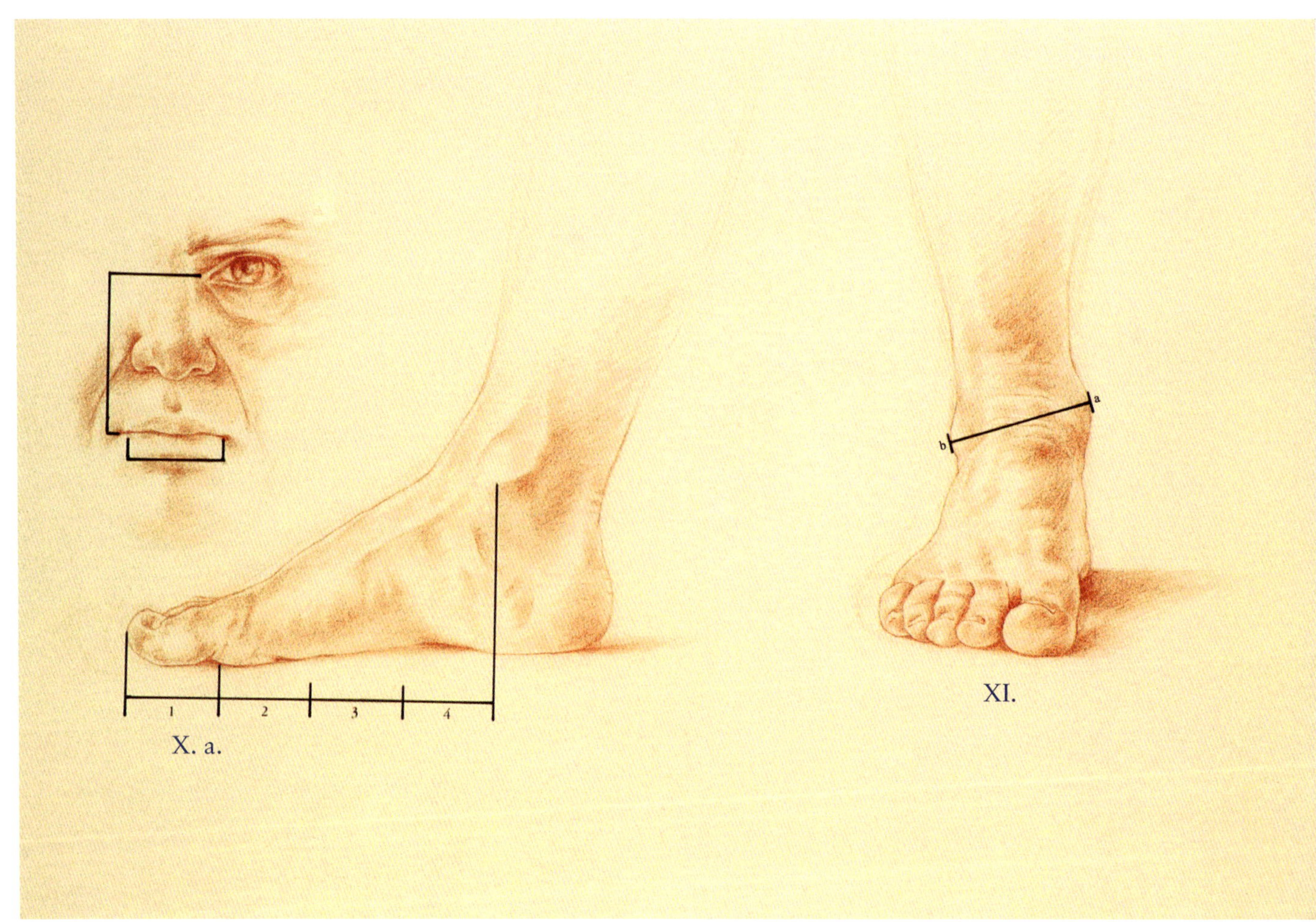

Cat. 48 AP 171

W. 19133a, Royal Library, Windsor **AP 171**
c. 1490 **R 324**
Folio 9 Recto X, XI

X. a. *The length of the longest toe, from its first division from the great toe to its tip, is the fourth part of the foot, from the center of the ankle-bone to the tip, and it is equal to the width of the mouth.*

XI. *The space between the extreme poles inside and outside the foot called the ankle or ankle-bone a b is equal to the space between the mouth and the inner corner of the eye.*

On this page (Plate 25), mainly devoted to numerous comparisons of the hand to the foot, and parts of the foot to the whole foot, Leonardo inserts a few comparisons of the foot to parts of the face. It may seem inconvenient and impractical while working with the model to jump from the foot to the face to establish comparable proportions, but there is some value in understanding the relative ratio of proportions in diverse parts of the body.

X. a. Leonardo uses the length of the longest toe, actually from the neck, or the center of its second division, the proximal phalanx, to its tip, as a module. This module enters four times into the distance from the center of the ankle, the medial malleolus of the tibia, to the tip of the big toe and is indeed equal to the width of the mouth.

At this point on the page, Leonardo begins a set of proportional comparisons dealing with the face and the hand. These I have treated in another category. (See chapter 7, AP 191.)

XI. The space which is between the extreme poles, inside and outside the foot, a b, from the medial malleolus of the tibia on the inside of the foot, to the lateral malleolus of the fibula on the outside of the foot, is equal to the space between the mouth and the inner corner of the eye. This is a surprisingly accurate measurement.

One has to wonder at such an odd comparison and how Leonardo would have come to compare the two sections of anatomy distanced so far from each other. However, we have seen him do this often.

I must point out here that in his drawing, Leonardo again lines up the malleoli of the bones in the lower extremities of the legs in a horizontal line, as he also incorrectly did in Plate 30, treated in AP 167.

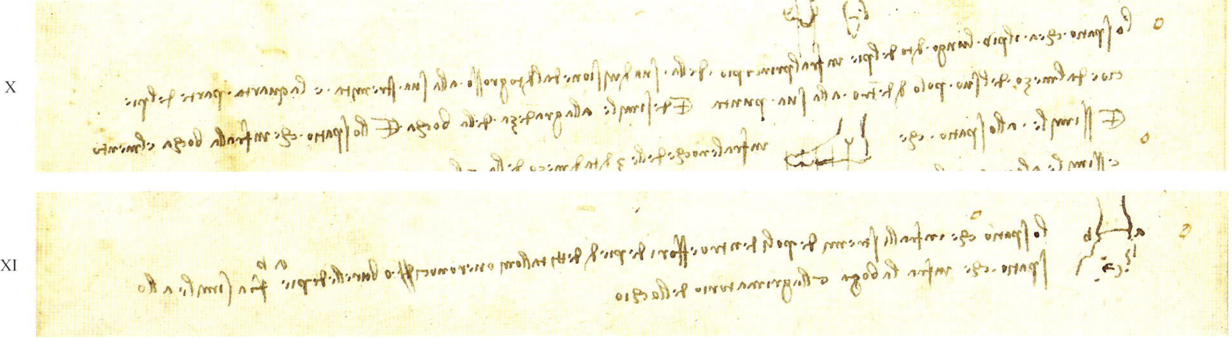

Detail, Plate 25, W. 19133a, Royal Collection, Windsor

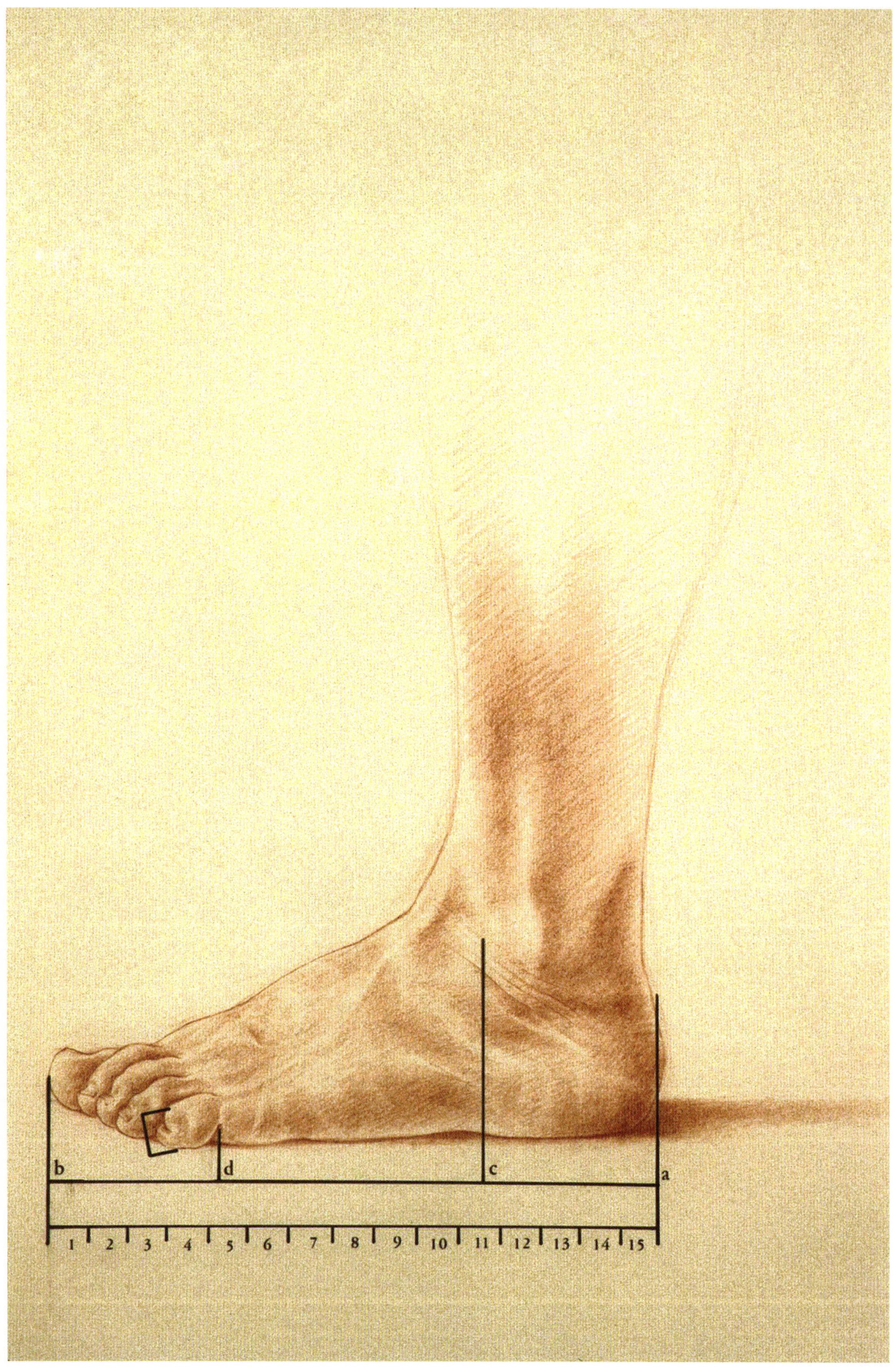

Cat. 49 **AP 172**

W. 19136–19139b, Royal Library, Windsor **AP 172**
c. 1490 **R 326**
Folio 11 Verso I

a d is a head's [face] length, c b is a head's [face] length. The four minor toes are all equally thick from the nail at the top to the bottom, and are $^{1}/_{13}$ [$^{1}/_{15}$] of the foot.

From the complicatedly elegant page (Plate 29) folded in four, this entry is located in the top right-hand quarter. Leonardo has drawn a beautifully executed left foot, seen in profile, in its lateral aspect. It is quite large in relation to the other illustrations on the page, particularly the seated figure he has drawn just below the foot, which is discussed in AP 164.

a, the heel of the foot, to d, the joint of the smallest toe, is equal to the length of the face, not the head,[41] and from c, the forward edge of the lateral malleolus of the fibula, to b, the tip of the great toe, is equal to a b and also to the length of the face. There is a slight discrepancy between this comparison and the one formulated in AP 113. While the module in AP 113 used the foot from the tip of the large toe to its instep (see AP 113 for an explanation of "instep"), the module here uses the distance from the tip of the big toe to the forward edge of the inferior extremity of the lateral malleolus of the fibula. There is just enough of a difference to cut off the height of the chin.

Lastly, Richter mistakenly transcribes $^{1}/_{13}$ instead of $^{1}/_{15}$. The original drawing clearly shows $^{1}/_{15}$ and is transcribed correctly in the *Quaderni,* Folio 11, Verso I.

In Leonardo's statement in AP 153, Recto I, he uses the distance from the roots of the hair to the top of the sternum as a module to measure the length of the figure. He finds that the module goes six times into the whole figure, just as the foot does in AP 149. At the very end that sentence trails off, "...and is similar to...," and he never finishes the thought. Could he have been thinking of the foot?

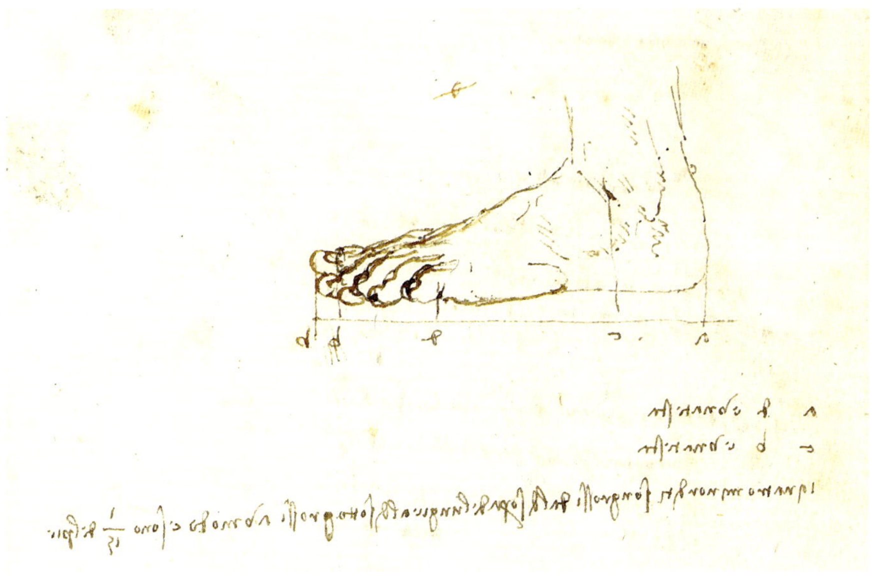

Detail, Plate 29, W. 19136–19139b, Royal Collection, Windsor

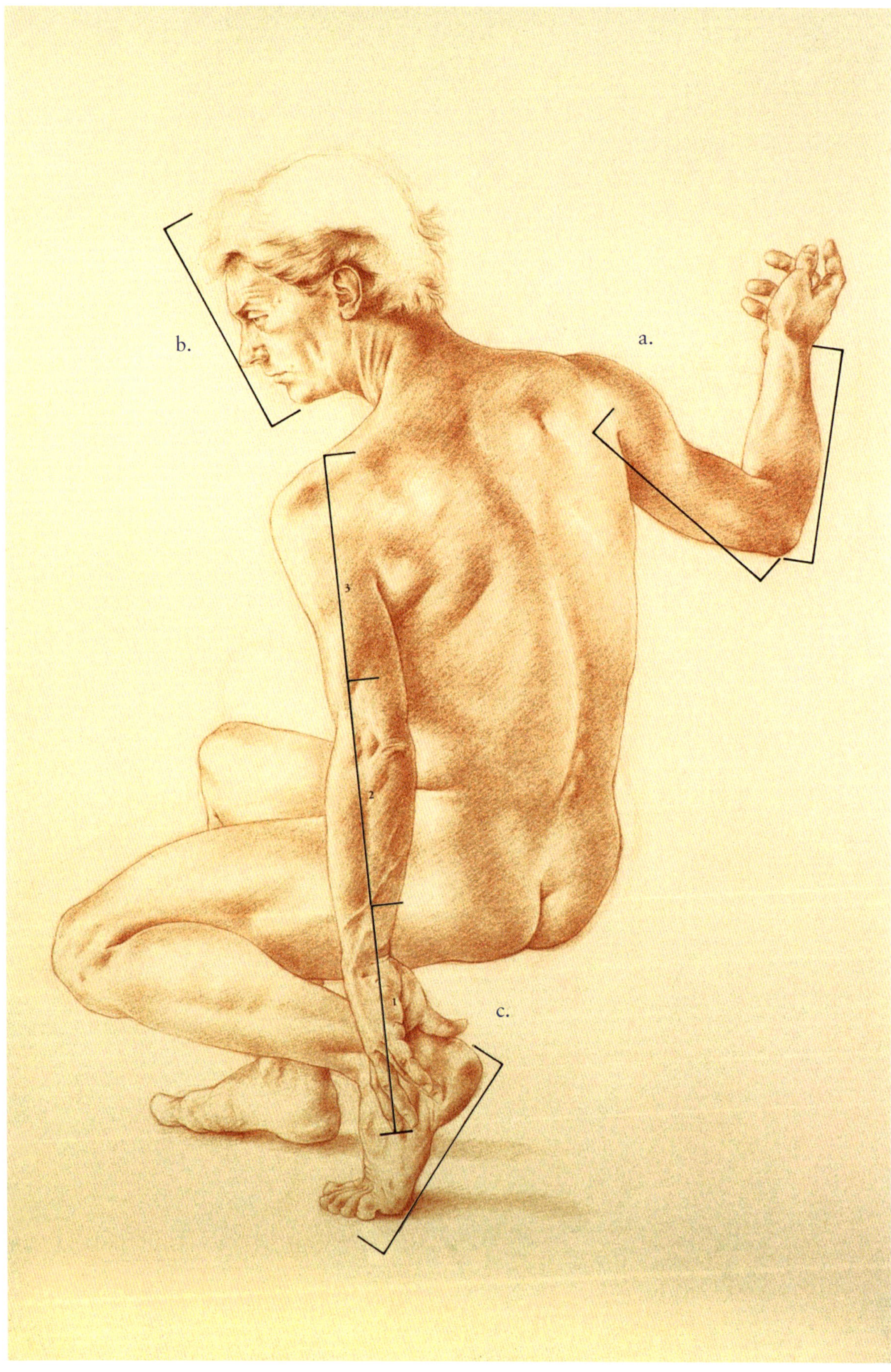

Cat. 50

AP 173

W. 19129, Royal Library, Windsor | **AP 173**
c. 1489–1490 | **R 327**
Folio 5 Recto I

a. ***The whole length of the foot will lie between the elbow and the wrist and between the elbow and the inner angle of the arm towards the breast when the arm is folded.***

b. ***The foot is as long as the whole head of a man, that is, from under the chin to the topmost part of the head in the way here figured.***

c. ***The foot goes three times from the tip of the long finger to the shoulder, that is, to its joint.***

This rather small sheet (Plate 18), housed at Windsor, measures only $5\frac{7}{8}$ by $6\frac{3}{4}$ inches (150 x169 mm). The text is divided into three neat paragraphs, each with its own illustration. Here in Recto I only the first paragraph is dealt with; it is divided into three sentences. For some unexplained reason, Richter leaves off the third line, but it is included in both the *Quaderni* and the MacCurdy editions.[42] Paragraphs II and III are dealt with in AP 116.

There is only one tiny drawing accompanying this text, a small head facing the sole of a foot. There are three other small drawings of frontal heads on this sheet as well, each with its own appropriate text. Illustrations of how Leonardo might have made his measurements comparing the foot to other parts of the body are nowhere to be found on this entry.

The proportions of the foot in relation to other parts of the body are perhaps the most elusive of all proportional relationships. In general, the foot is a bit larger than the head, and Leonardo seems to confirm this in AP 113. In the measurements of this drawing, as in the measurements of other drawings I have done, it is clear that the foot is only loosely similar to the size of the head.

a. The whole length of the foot does lie between the elbow and the wrist, while the distance from the elbow to "the inner angle of the arm towards the breast" is a bit shorter than the length of the foot.

b. "The foot is as long as the whole head of a man...in the way figured here" refers to Leonardo's tiny illustration, which agrees perfectly with his text. The foot, however, is considerably larger than the head, as measured in this drawing and countless other of his drawings. It totally disagrees with Leonardo's theories in AP 113, AP 171, and AP 172. Even in other examples of Leonardo's illustrations, most notably the *Vitruvian Man,* AP 149, the foot is clearly much larger than the head.

c. The foot goes three times from the tip of the longest finger to the shoulder joint, that is, where the humerus joins the scapular and the clavicle. This is a perfect measurement and can also be verified in other drawings, such as AP 150.

I

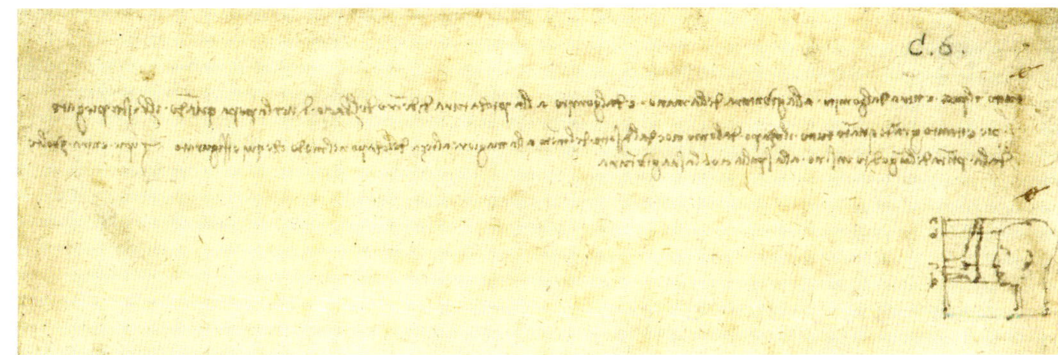

Detail, Plate 18, W. 19129, Royal Collection, Windsor

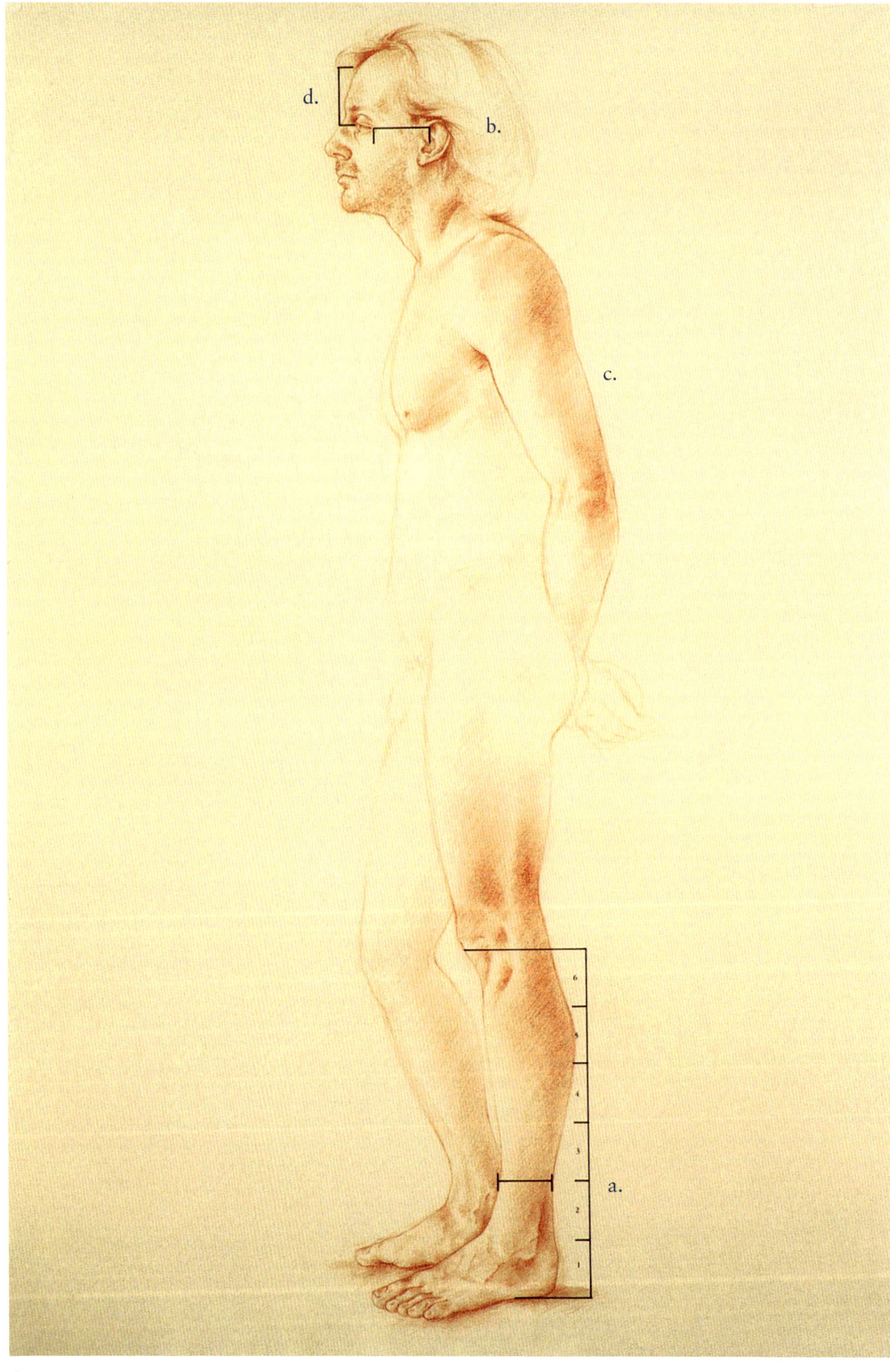

Cat. 51 AP 174

W. 19140, Royal Library, Windsor **AP 174**
c. 1490 **R 331**
Folio 12 Recto III

a. *The least thickness of the leg in profile goes 6 times from the sole of the foot to the knee joint and is the same width as*

b. *the space between the outer corner of the eye and the opening of the ear, and*

c. *as the thickest part of the arm seen in profile and*

d. *between the inner corner of the eye and the insertion of the hair.*

This is another entry from the jumbled and confusing Windsor sheet, Folio 12, which contains several written observations and ten drawings (Plate 30). This paragraph, AP 174, marked in the *Quaderni* as III, is squeezed in among the text and illustrations. There is, however, no drawing connected to this particular observation.

a. The least, or smallest, thickness of the leg in profile is the ankle, and it does go into the length of the leg from the sole of the foot to the joint of the knee six times. See the same comparison in AP 166, and compare these with the theory in AP 162 where he uses the frontal leg.

b. Using this same module, the width of the ankle in profile, Leonardo says that it is equal to the space between the corner of the eye and the opening of the ear. This works perfectly.

c. He then compares the module, the ankle in profile, to the thickest part of the arm, the biceps just below the shoulder. The ankle as a module enters almost two times into the width of the arm. The theory does not work at all.

d. And lastly, the same module is equal to the distance between the corner of the eye to the hairline, a perfect comparison.

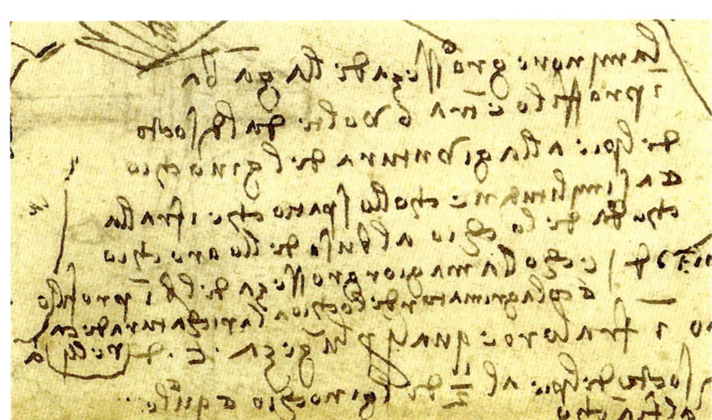

Detail, Plate 30, W. 19140, Royal Collection, Windsor

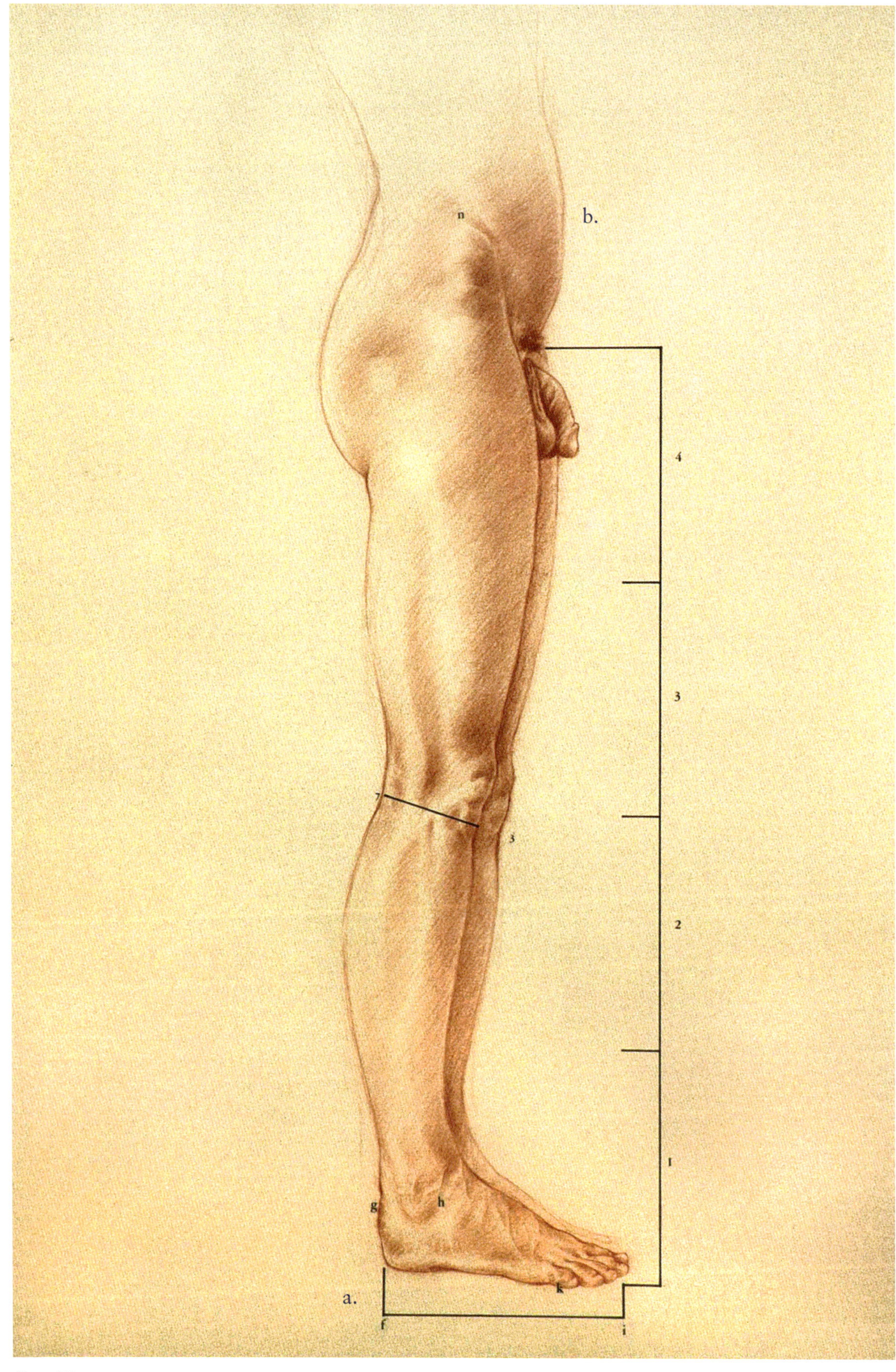

Cat. 52 **AP 175**

W. 19136–19139b, Royal Library, Windsor **AP 175**
c. 1490 **R 328**
Folio 11 Verso X

a. ***e [i] f is 4 times in the distance between the genitals and the sole of the foot;***

b. ***3 7 is 6 times from 3 to 2 and is equal to g h and i k.***

This entry, Verso X, comes from the famously informative Windsor sheet folded in four (Plate 29). It is written in the very bottom of the page in the lower-left quarter. The text uses the illustration drawn for the text at Verso VIII and treated in AP 166. There are some minor variations. Leonardo obviously wrote e when he meant i,[43] for there is no e on his drawing.

a. i f, the length of the foot in profile, goes four times into the distance from the genitals[44] to the foot perfectly.

b. 3 7, the width of the leg from the knee in front to the back of the leg, goes six times from 3 to 2. The enigma here is that there is no 2 on this drawing, as Richter points out when he says in a footnote, "which renders the passage obscure."[45] However, there is the letter n at the top of the pelvis at the iliac crest, and if we measure with Leonardo's module, 3 7, we find it enters exactly six times from 3 to n.[46] As in the case above, where Leonardo wrote *e* instead of *i,* it's a good bet he meant *n* instead of 2. Unfortunately, when we test this idea on Leonardo's drawing, the module 3 7, the width of the leg at the knee, measures only five times into the distance from 3 to n, instead of six times as it does in my drawing.

As for the comparison of similarity of size with the module 3 7, the width of the knee in profile, to g h, the heel of the foot to the front edge of the malleolus of the fibula, and i k, the width of the toes, they do not work at all either in Leonardo's drawing or in mine.

Detail, Plate 29, W. 19136–19139b, Royal Collection, Windsor

Notes
Chapter Six. The Leg and Foot

[39] AP 165: An understanding of this entry hinges on the interpretation of Leonardo's word *polpa*, meaning fleshy or meaty. Richter interprets it as *polpaccio*, the calf, where others have interpreted the word as thigh. I have sided with Richter on this one, but please see Pedretti, *Commentaries*, vol. I, 239.

[40] AP 166: Pedretti, *Commentaries*, vol. I, 239. There is much disagreement among the authors' translations of this passage. I have followed Leonardo's drawings as closely as possible, but in this case I have followed the empirical method he so often uses to prove his theories. This accounts for the different placement of the letter n at the head of the great trochanter and also for the introduction of the letter N at the top of the pelvis.

[41] AP 172: Leonardo writes *head* instead of *face*. For a fuller explanation, see Pedretti, *Commentaries*, vol. I, 237.

[42] AP 173: *Quaderni*, Folio 5, Recto I, Edward MacCurdy, *The Notebooks of Leonardo*, vol. I, 221. See also Pedretti, *Commentaries*, vol. I, 238.

[43] AP 175: See notes to R 328, line 34, Richter, *The Literary Works of Leonardo da Vinci*, vol. I, 178. This note appears only in the 1970 Dover reprint of the 1883 edition: "By reading i for e the sense of this passage is made clear."

[44] AP 175: Richter translates the word *cazzo* as "genitals," and the authors of the *Quaderni* translate it as "membrum." Both avoid the more colloquial and vulgar words.

[45] AP 175: Richter, *The Literary Works of Leonardo da Vinci*, vol. I, 178, line 35, "2 is not to be found in the sketch which renders the passage obscure."

[46] AP 175: Pedretti, *Commentaries*, vol. I, 239. Pedretti says, "line 35: *'da 3 a 2'* (from 3 to 2) should be *'da 3 a 9'* (from 3 to 9) in fact there is no '2.'" There is on Leonardo's drawing a small 9 written just opposite the letter n at the top of the pelvis. The problem is that the 9 is not written backwards like the n next to it (and like all of Leonardo's letters and numbers throughout his notebooks), but like a perfectly written number 9. What Leonardo meant by this configuration and why Pedretti read it as a number 9 is totally unclear. However, the principle only works by measuring from the knee to the top of the pelvis at n.

CHAPTER SEVEN

THE ARM AND HAND: AP 181–200

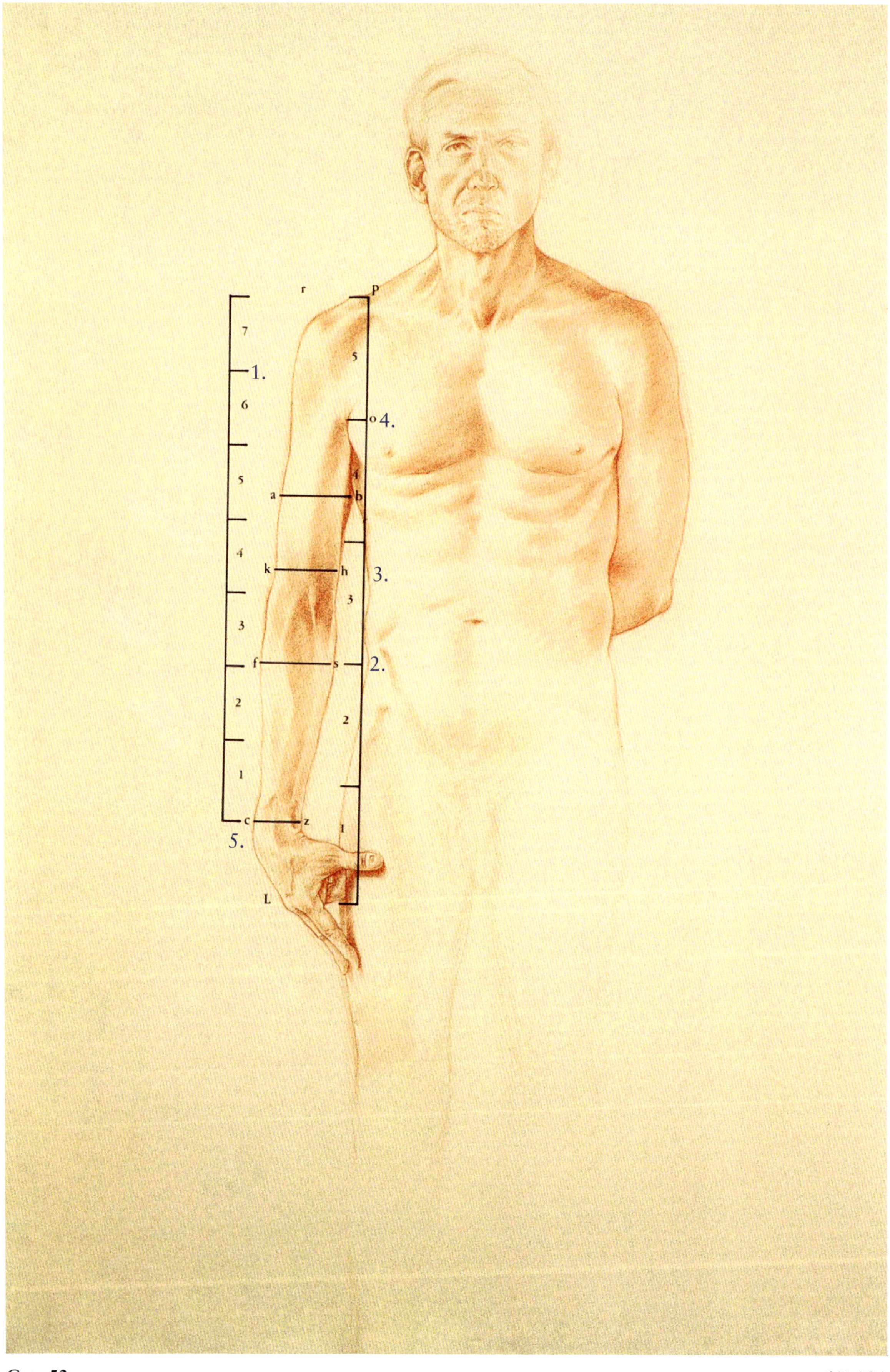

Cat. 53 AP 181

W. 19136–19139a, Royal Library, Windsor — AP 181
c. 1490 — R 349
Folio 11 Recto VI

1. *a b is* $^{1}/_{7}$ *of r c.*
2. *f s is* $^{1}/_{8}$ *of r c; and each of these 2 measurements is the thickest of the arm.*
3. *k h is the narrowest part which is between the shoulder and the elbow, and is* $^{1}/_{8}$ *of the whole arm r c.*
4. *o p is* $^{1}/_{5}$ *of r l.*
5. *c z goes 13 times into r c.*

This is from the large drawing, $15^{3}/_{4}$ x 11 inches (405 x 281 mm), folded in four, which has been numbered at Windsor in four parts from 19136a to 19139a (Plate 28). The same is true for the verso, 19136v-19139v (Plate 29). Leonardo's notes on both the recto and verso sides deal with the proportions of the arm, torso, and leg. The ratios in this entry are about the proportions of the arm using different parts of the arm, hand, and wrist as modules of measurement. (See AP 184.)

1. a b, the thickness of the upper arm between the shoulder to the elbow, is one-seventh of the length r c, from the very top of the shoulder, r to the wrist, c.
2. f s, the thickness of the lower arm, at the center of the forearm between the elbow and the wrist, is not one-eighth as Leonardo says, but is approximately one-seventh, as in the first measurement.
3. k h, the thinnest part between the shoulder and the elbow, is clearly not one-eighth of the whole arm, r c, and does not measure so even in Leonardo's drawing. Like the previous notations, it is closer to one-seventh of r c. How Leonardo could have made these errors in proportion is a mystery, but his drawing, the placement of his indicatory letters marked on the drawing, and his words are crystal clear.
4. o p, the distance from the beginning of the armpit, o, to the top of the shoulder, p, is one-fifth of the distance from the top of the shoulder, r, to the inception of the fingers, marked with the letter l in Leonardo's drawing and in mine.
5. c z, the width of the wrist, does not go thirteen times into r c, from the wrist to the top of shoulder, even in Leonardo's beautiful little drawing of the arm. At most it goes only ten and a half to eleven times in his drawing, and eleven and a half to twelve times in my drawing. I have not included this measurement in my drawing, because of the differing calculations. Please compare this entry to AP 188 and the important note attached.

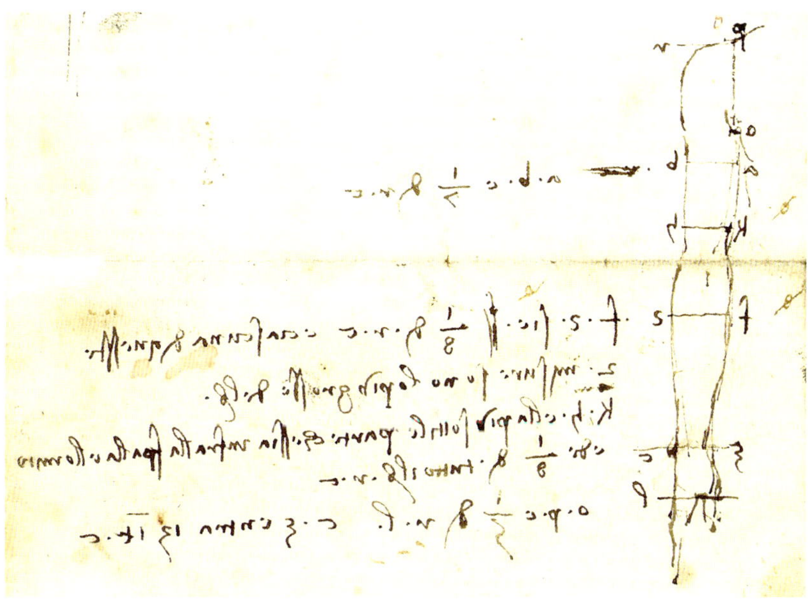

Detail, Plate 28, W. 19136–19139a, Royal Collection, Windsor

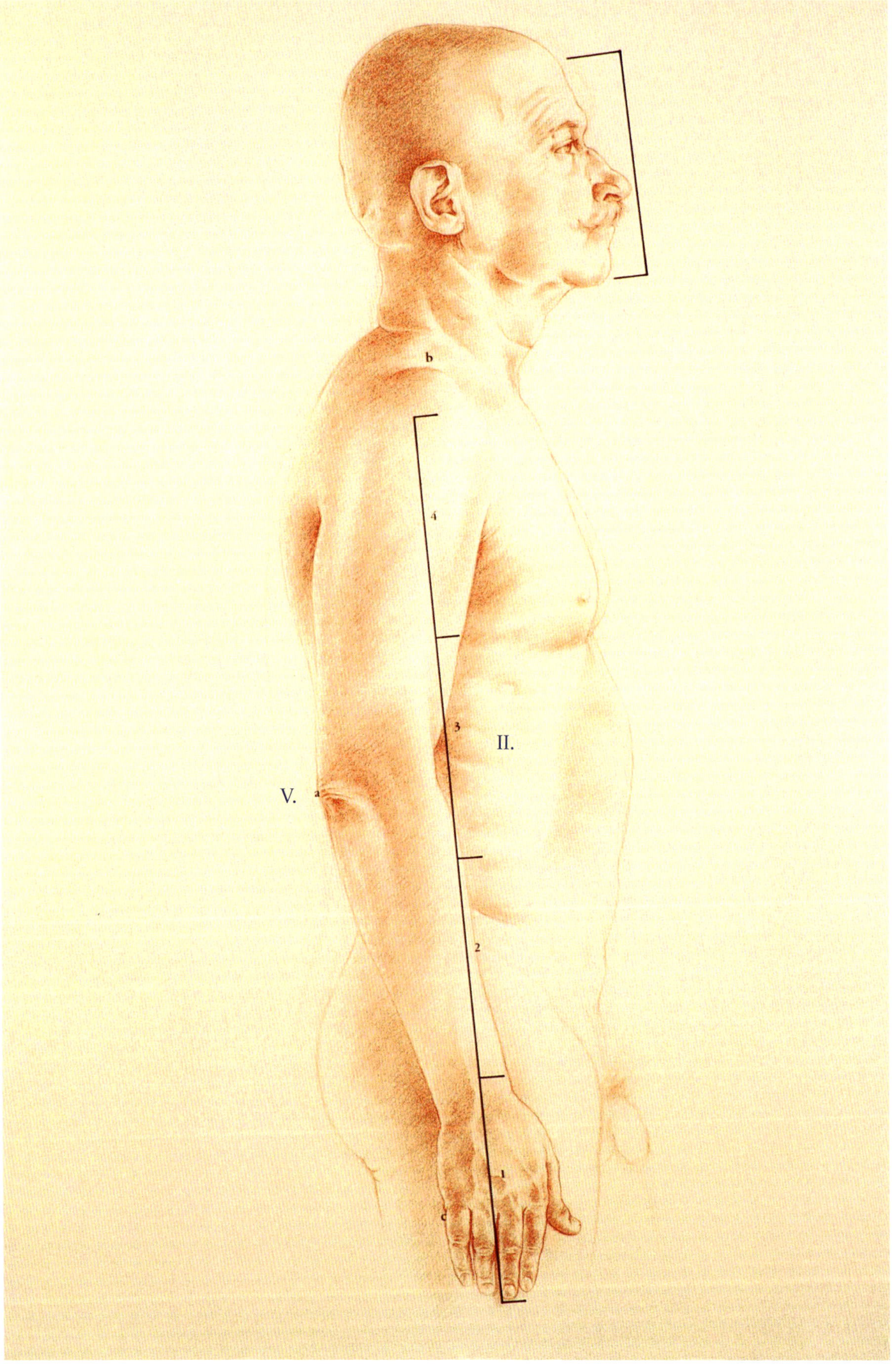

Cat. 54 AP 182

W. 19140, Royal Library, Windsor **AP 182**
c. 1490 **R 345**
Folio 12 Recto II, V

II. *From the tip of the longest finger of the hand to the joint of the shoulder is 4 hands, or if you will, 4 heads [faces].*

V. *a b c are equal, and each interval is 2 heads [faces].*

I find this (Plate 30) to be one of Leonardo's most confusing pages. He seems to have started his notes in the center of the page with a profile eye and nose facing right. He repeats that image once, and then again with a full profile from the hair to the chin. To the left of these profiles is a circle, its diameter composed of smaller circles with whip-like tails swirling and turning to the right. Their meaning is unclear.[47] The page, apparently at some other time, was turned upside-down, and Leonardo began a series of notations on the proportions of the leg, arm, and foot, crammed into the space below the above-mentioned circle and profiles.

II. From the tip of the longest finger of the hand to the shoulder joint, that is, at the insertion of the humerus, is four hands, or four faces.[48] Leonardo clearly means faces even though he uses the word heads (*teste*). Richter rightly transcribes the meaning as "faces."

V. a b c are equal, meaning that the distance from a, the elbow, to b, the top of the shoulder, is equal to the distance from a, the elbow, to c, the inception of the fingers. We have to rely on Leonardo's words rather than his drawing, as it is very small and unclear. I find each interval, a to b and a to c, indeed to be approximately two faces.

Compare this to AP 183, AP 189, and AP 192.

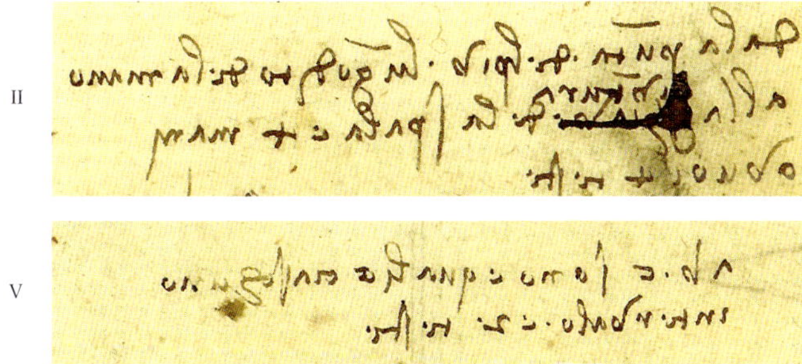

Detail, Plate 30, W. 19140, Royal Collection, Windsor

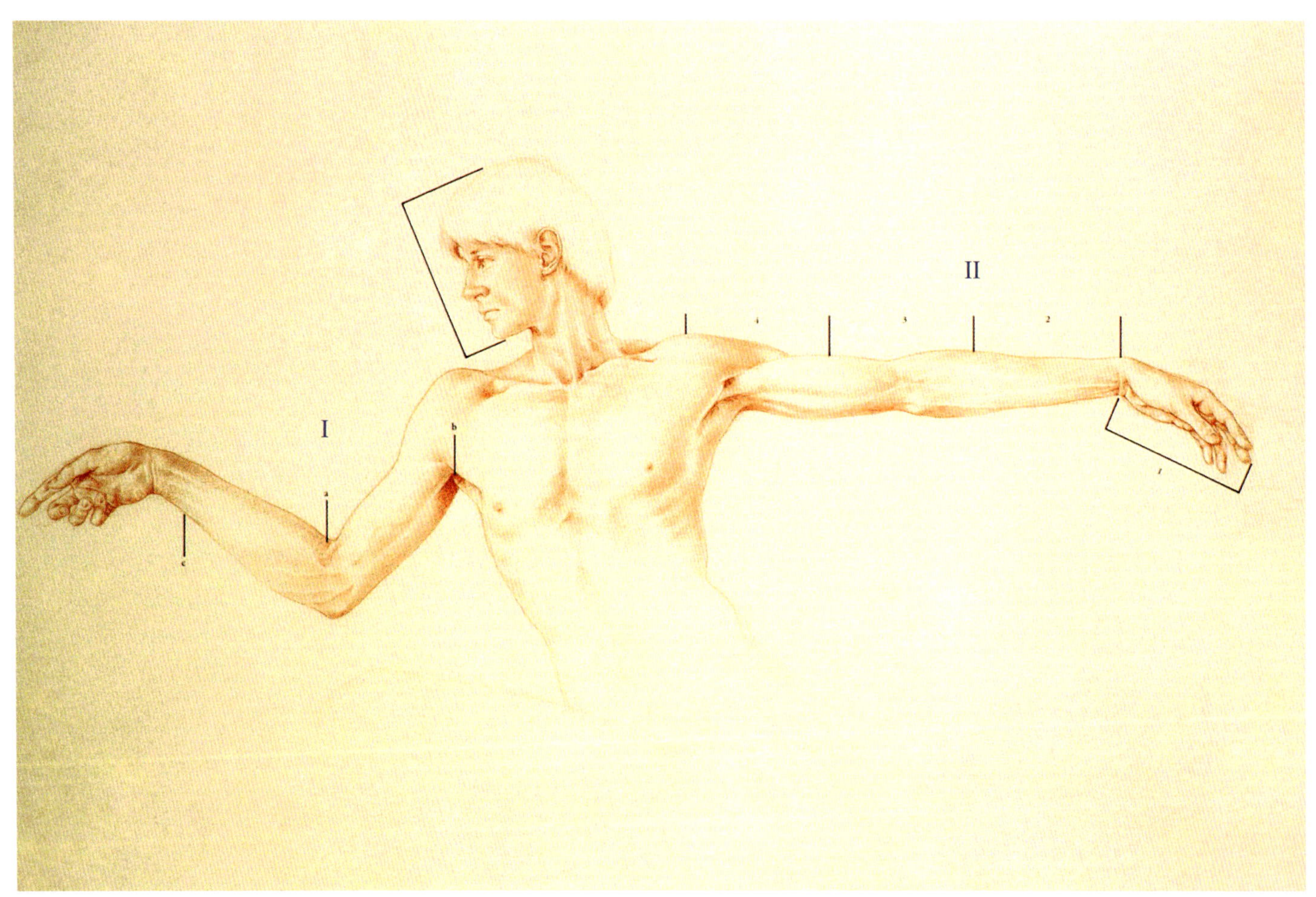

Cat. 55 AP 183

BN 2038. 23b, MS. Ashburnham II 1875/2,[49] Institut de France, Paris **AP 183**
c. 1490–1492 **R 344**

I. *From b to a is one head, as well as from c to a and this happens when the elbow forms a right angle.*

MS. B. 3b, Bound Volume marked B, Institut de France, Paris **R 346**
c.1490–1492

II. *The hand from the longest finger to the wrist joint goes 4 times from the tip of the longest finger to the shoulder joint.*

Leonardo completed these two entries at least two years apart.

The first entry (Plate 4), R 344, on the left side of my drawing, uses the whole head, from the chin to the top of the head, as a module, while the second (Plate 3), R 346, on the right side of my drawing, uses the length of the hand, or the face, as a module of measurement. Using both the head and the face as modules to measure the arm seemed an interesting contrast, and it made for such a creative composition, I decided to combine the two into a single drawing. I have indicated only the length of the head and not that of the face.

I. From b, the armpit, to a, the crook or the point of the elbow, is one head, just as the distance from c, that point somewhere near but not at the wrist, to a, the elbow, is another head, *testa* (here Leonardo does mean the head), and this happens when the arm at the elbow forms a right angle. The strange notion of forming a right angle with the arm and then using the length of the head to measure is impractical at best. One must be careful in measuring to calculate from the letters indicated on the drawing to the very tip of the elbow. (Compare this entry to AP 188.)

II. The length of the hand from the tip of the longest finger to the wrist, or the length of the face, goes four times from the longest finger to the shoulder joint. This time Leonardo is using the hand, which is the length of the face from the chin to the hairline, as a canon of measurement. Using the hand to measure the length of the arm works perfectly.

I

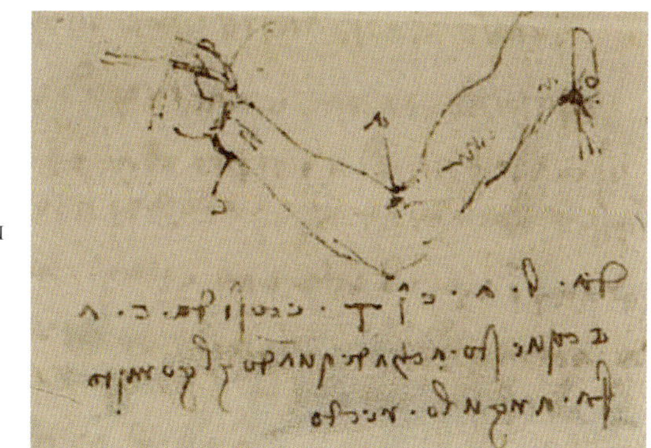

Detail, Plate 4, Ms BN 2038 Ash II, page 23b, Bibliothéque de l'Institut de France, Paris

II

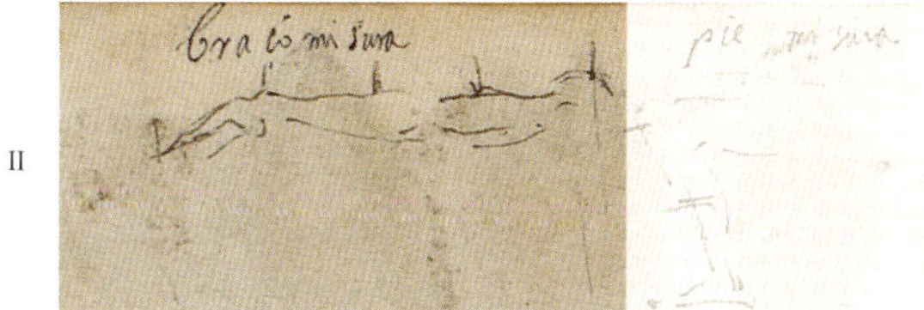

Detail, Plate 3, Ms B, page 3b, Bibliothéque de l'Institut de France, Paris

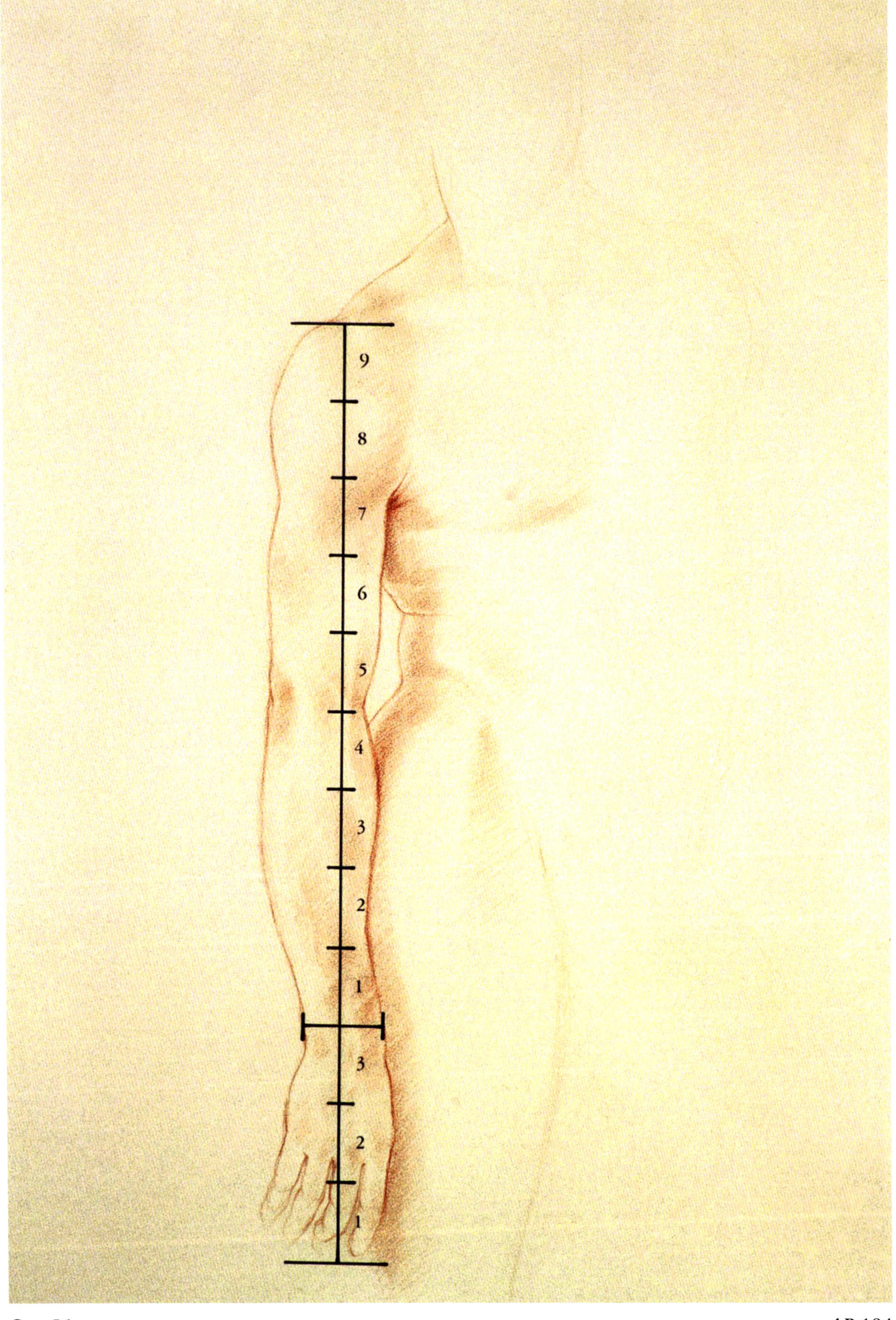

Cat. 56 AP 184

W. 19134–19135, Royal Library, Windsor **AP 184**
c. 1490 **R 348**
Folio 10 Recto XIII

The width of the wrist goes 12 times into the whole arm; that is, from the tip of the fingers to the shoulder joint; that is, 3 times into the hand, and 9 into the arm.

This page (Plate 27), which is folded in two, is one of Leonardo's largest drawings, measuring $12\frac{3}{8}$ x $17\frac{3}{8}$ inches (317 x 433 mm), and is another complicated page in his notebooks. It contains numerous drawings with over twenty-four separate entries, and some of these contain multiple theories. (See also AP 181.)

This entry is written underneath an extended right arm with the palm side facing the viewer. It is only one of a half-dozen observations sprinkled about this drawing, all using this same arm as a common illustration. I have turned the arm so that we see the back view.

The measurement is quite accurate and has proven correct on many different models. Here the arm is pronated to provide the full width of the posterior view of the back of the wrist and hand. Compare it to AP 181 and note the difference. In this drawing (AP 181) we see the lateral, or side, view of the wrist and the hand, which is considerably smaller than the posterior, or back, view of the hand and wrist.

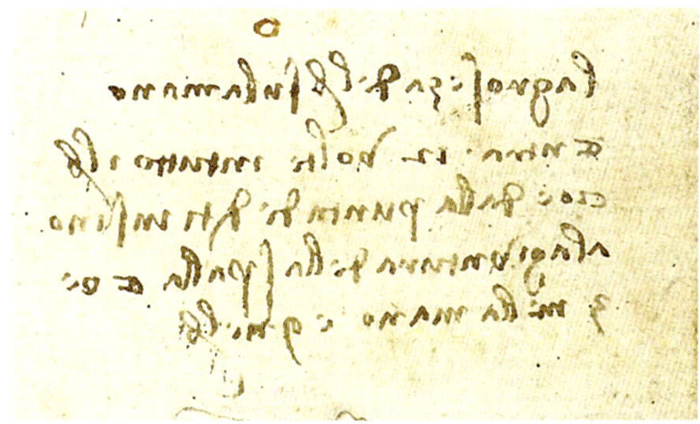

Detail, Plate 27, W. 19134–19135, Royal Collection, Windsor

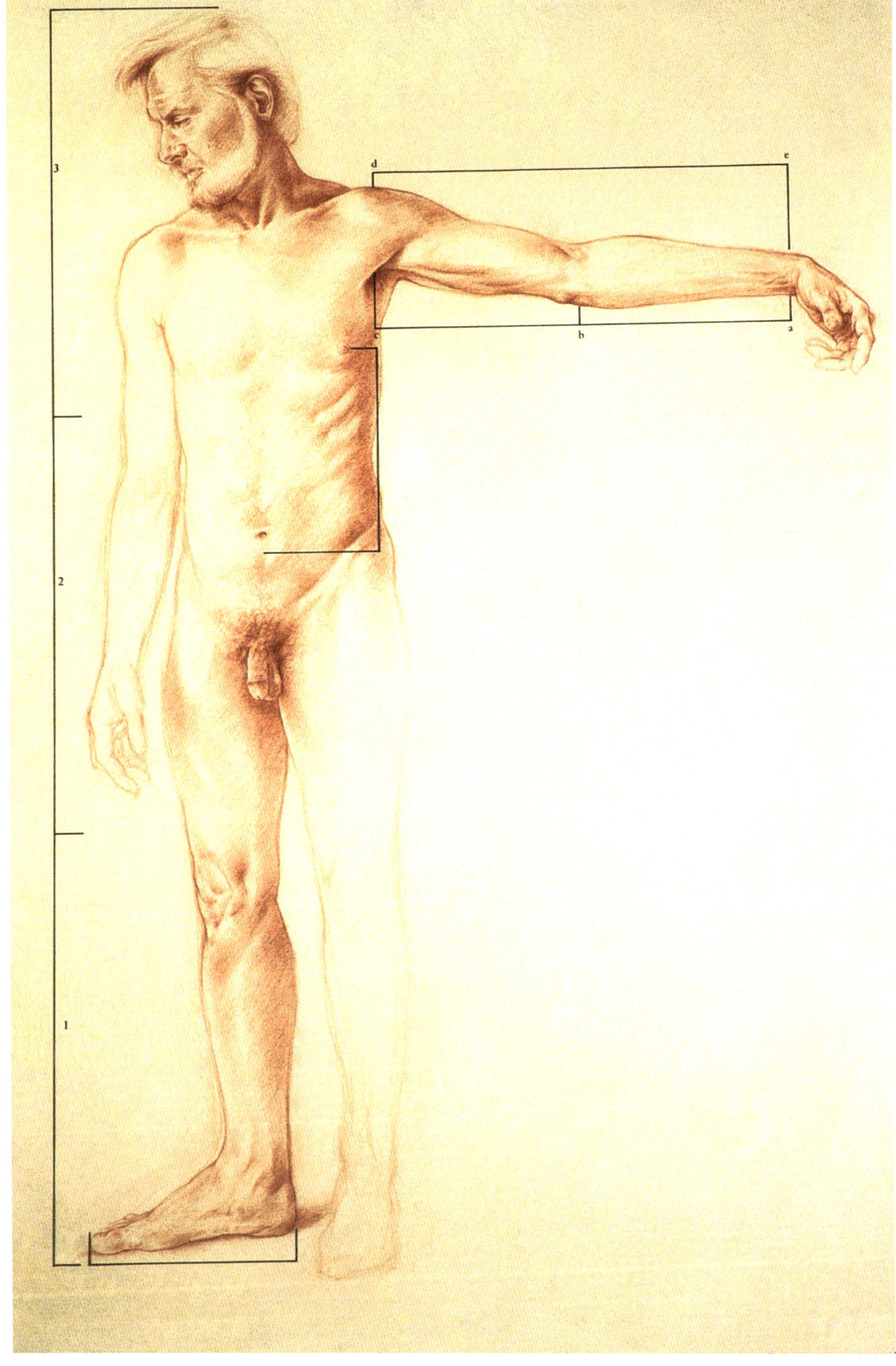

Cat. 57

AP 185

W. 19131a, Royal Library, Windsor **AP 185**
c. 1490 **R 347**
Folio 7 Recto I

a b c are equal to each other and to the foot and to the space which is from the nipple to the navel (mamolino); d e will be the third part of the whole man.

Leonardo draws three arms (Plate 21) on a modest-size sheet, 4⅞ x 8¼ inches (128 x 210 mm): one left arm pointing left and two right arms. His small drawing of a lateral view of an outstretched left arm illustrates this entry. Here he uses the full length of the arm to measure the height of the whole figure but shows us only the module and not the figure. Compare this entry to the following, AP 186, which is the sentence directly below the above Leonardo quote. I used each sentence to create separate drawings, each with its own full figure to illustrate the point.

The distance from a, the wrist, to b, the elbow, is equal to the distance from the elbow, b, to the armpit, c. Both are similar to the length of the foot and the space between the nipple and the navel. Robert Beverly Hale, the great anatomist, teacher, and draftsman of the Art Students League, used to say, "Never trust a nipple or a navel—like traveling salesmen they're all over the place." Leonardo, however, uses the nipple and the navel often throughout his notes as essential surface landmarks.

d e is the distance from the joint of the shoulder to the wrist. In the same drawing, Leonardo makes a distinction between the armpit and the shoulder joint, not lining one above the other. I have measured many men and am convinced that the armpit is directly under the conjuncture of the humerus, scapular, and clavicle where they all merge together, and I have therefore lined up the letter d directly above the letter c.

In addition, Leonardo simply states the reference to the length of the whole man but does not illustrate it, as he also fails to do in many other entries. I have included the whole figure and found that the arm, from the wrist to the shoulder joint, works as a canon of measurement and fits three times perfectly into the height of a man. One cannot help but wonder how Leonardo made his determination. Was it from another drawing or directly from a model, or did he measure himself? It is another of those interesting enigmas surrounding Leonardo.

Compare this entry to AP 183 and AP 186, and take careful note of his use of a different canon of measurement.

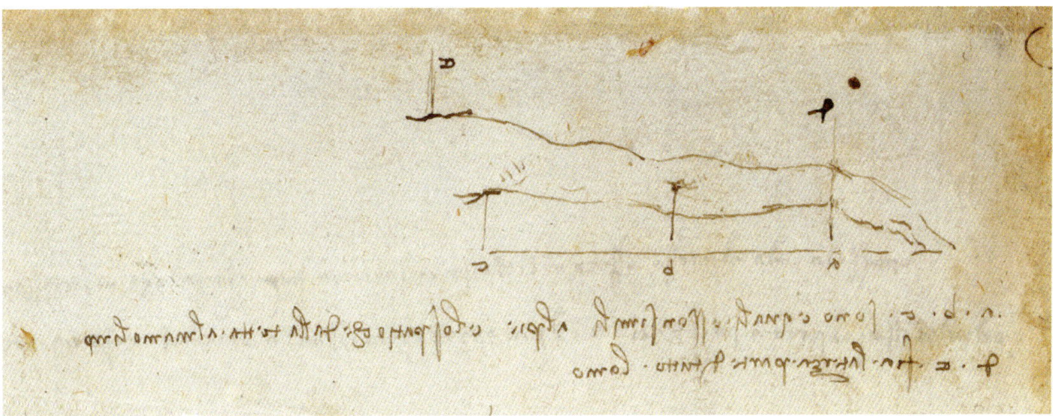

Detail, Plate 21, W. 19131a, Royal Collection, Windsor

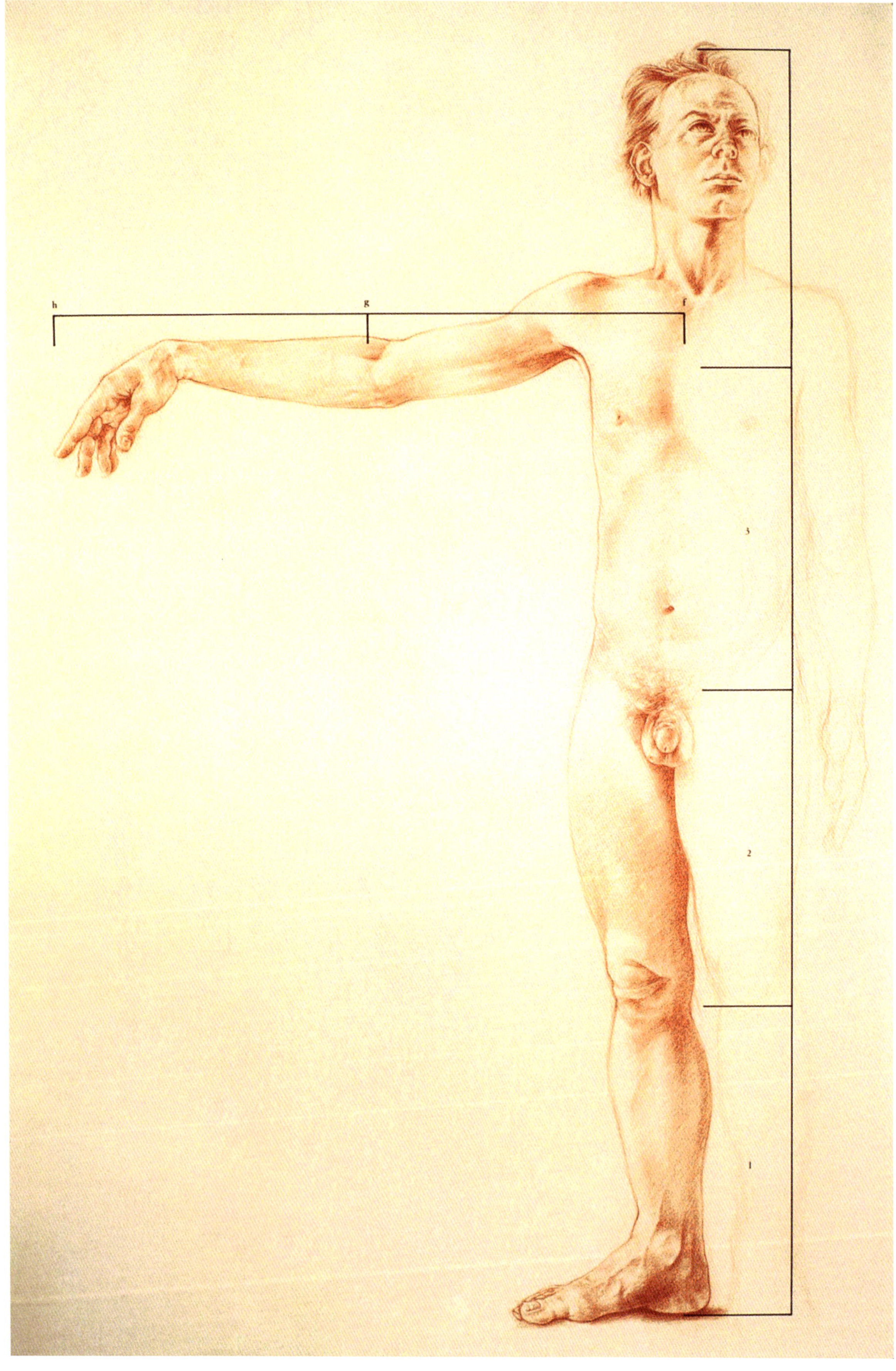

Cat. 58

AP 186

W. 19131a, Royal Library, Windsor **AP 186**
c. 1490 **R 347**
Folio 7 Recto II

f g is the fourth part of a man and is similar to g h and similar to the cubit.

Folio 7 (Plate 21) is a simple drawing of three outstretched arms. It is a rather small drawing, measuring about $4\frac{7}{8}$ x $8\frac{1}{4}$ inches (128 x 210 mm), yet it is one of the clearest of all Leonardo's observations. This sentence is directly below the sentence discussed in AP 185. He uses a different portion of the arm and the cubit as modules and again makes reference to the height of the whole man. But again he gives us no visual indication of how he arrived at that conclusion. I have incorporated this theory, and the theory in AP 185, into the visual context of the whole figure.

The distance from f, the center of the sternum, to g, the elbow, is the fourth part of a man and is equal to the distance from g, the elbow, to h, the tip of the longest finger of the hand, and also equal to the cubit. Take careful note of the different canons of measurement. In AP 185 Leonardo uses the entire length of the arm from the wrist to the shoulder joint. Here he uses only the distance from the elbow to the tip of the finger, or its equal, from the elbow to the center of the sternum, as a canon, a much smaller measurement than that used in AP 185. Therefore this module easily fits four times into the height of a man.

The cubit is an ancient length of measure. (See endnote to AP 141 for a more detailed definition of the cubit.) It is about 18 to 22 inches long and, according to *Webster's New World Dictionary,* originally indicated the length of the arm from the tip of the middle finger to the point of the elbow. Here, Leonardo, in starting with f, the middle of the chest, or the sternum, to g, the elbow, is emphasizing the similarity of f g to g h, the original cubit measurement. The cubit is used often as a convenient and common canon in Leonardo's theories of proportion, either directly or indirectly, and can be found in AP 141, AP 143, AP 144, and AP 161.

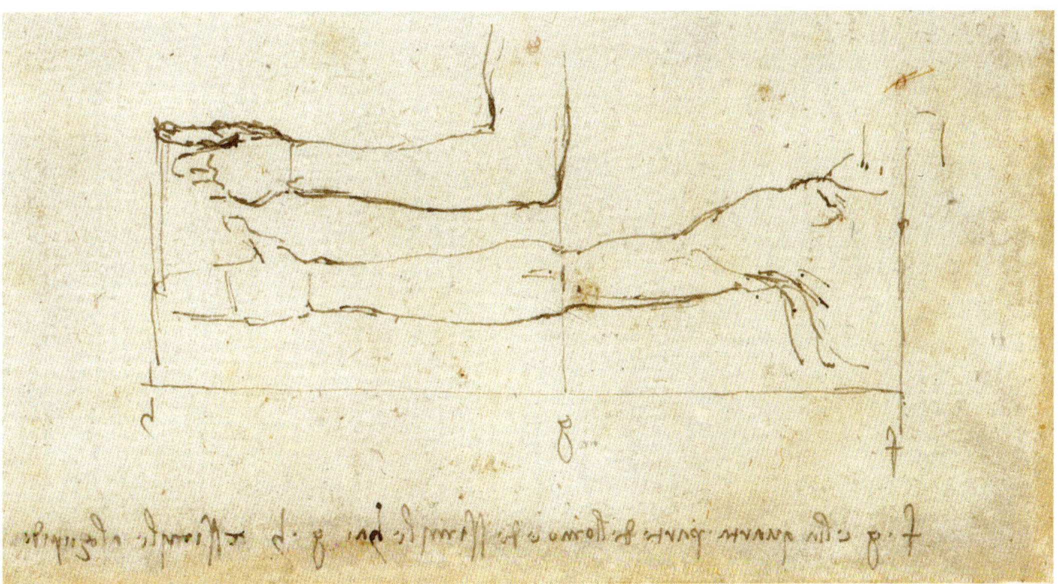

Detail, Plate 21, W. 19131a, Royal Collection, Windsor

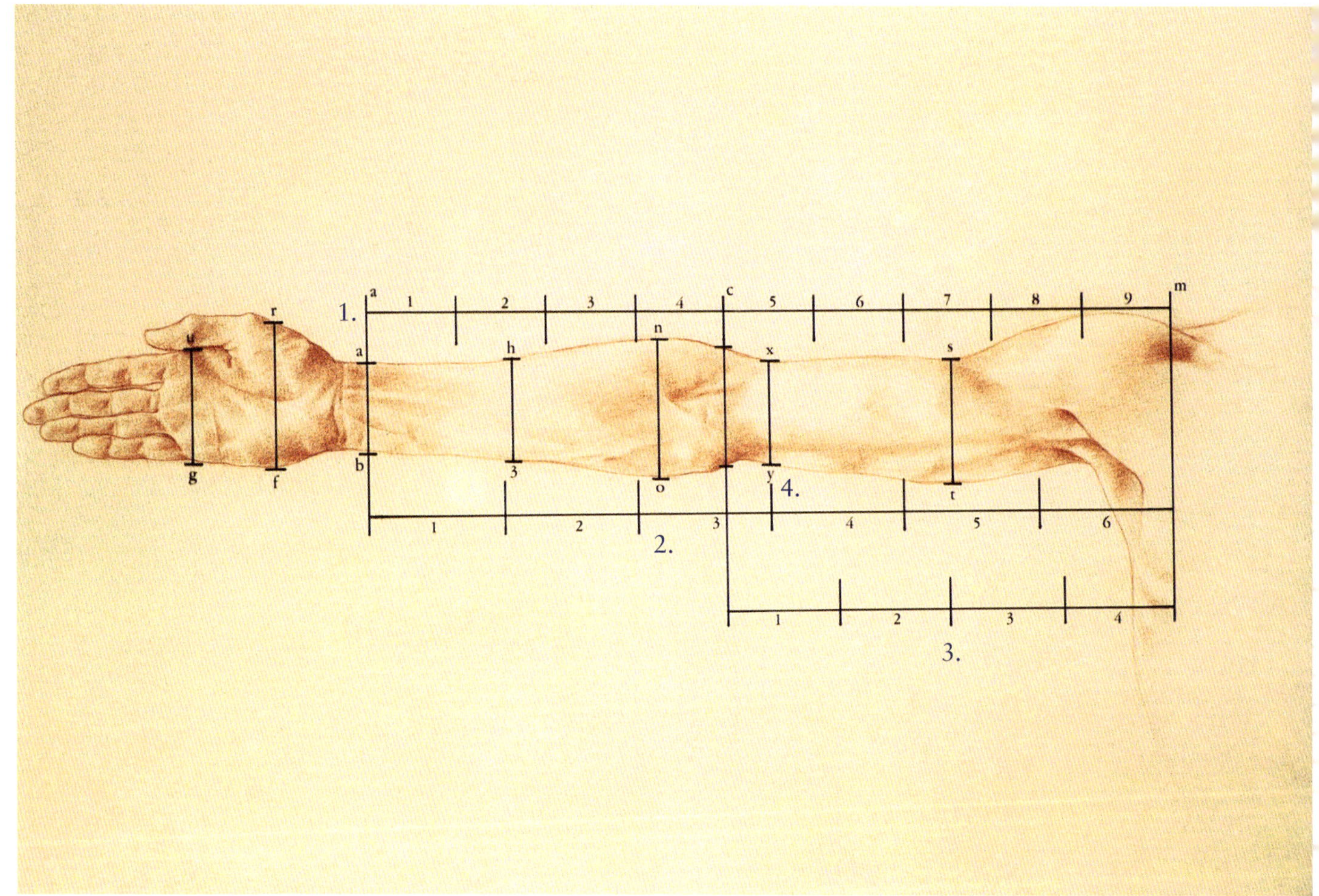

Cat. 59

AP 187

W. 19134–19135, Royal Library, Windsor **AP 187**
c. 1490 **R 348**
Folio 10 Recto XIV

1. *a b goes 4 times into a c and 9 into a m.*
2. *The greatest thickness of the arm between the elbow and the hand [n o] goes 6 times into a m and is similar to r f.*
3. *The greatest thickness of the arm between the shoulder and the elbow [s t] goes 4 times into c m and is equal to h n g.*
4. *The smallest thickness of the arm above the elbow x y is not the base of a square, but is equal to half the space [of] h 3 which is found between the inner joint of the arm and the wrist joint.*

This very complex, large sheet (Plate 27), measuring 12¼ x 16¾ inches (317 x 433 mm), is folded in half. Leonardo's entry, on the right half, is illustrated by an extended right arm with the palm side facing the viewer. It is surrounded by a number of entries referring mostly to the proportions of the arm and hand. This arm, with portions of the neck and chest visible, is drawn perpendicular to the bottom edge of the long side of the sheet, while the writing right under the arm is written parallel to the short edge of the page. It is a very confusing sheet. (See AP 184 for related proportional information found in this written entry.)

1. a b, the width of the wrist (as shown here), goes four times from a, the wrist, to c, the elbow, and a total of nine times from a to m, the top of the shoulder, or the insertion of the humerus.
2. The greatest thickness of the forearm, n o (Leonardo includes the letters in his drawing but omits them in his text), between the elbow and the hand, goes six times into a m, the wrist to the shoulder, and is similar to r f, the width of the palm of the hand, from r, the second joint of the first metacarpal bone of the thumb, to f, the thickest part of the palm of the hand.
3. The greatest thickness of the arm between the shoulder and the elbow, s t, the triceps and the biceps, goes four times into c m, the elbow to the shoulder, and is similar to n g, the width of the palm at the insertion of the fingers. This last comparison is translated by Richter as "equal to h n g." Leonardo actually writes "and similar has n g" (*ed simile ha n g*).
4. The thinnest portion of the arm above the elbow, x y, is not the base (*radice*) of a square but is equal to only about half the distance to h 3, which is a point on the arm found between the inner joint, or the crook of the arm, and the wrist joint, seen in the anterior aspect of the arm. If x y were the base of a square, the distance to h 3 would be the same width as x y and h 3, but in fact the distance between x y and h 3 is almost three times x y. This last phrase is unusual, because Leonardo seldom tells us what does not work but usually focuses on what does work. In any case there is little theoretical value in this obscure observation.

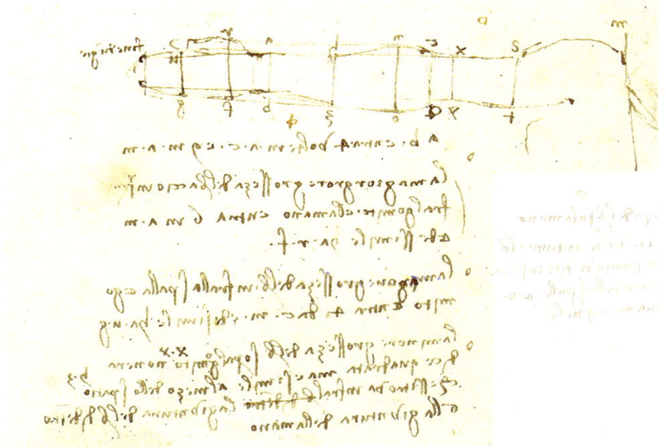

Detail, Plate 27, W. 19134–19135, Royal Collection, Windsor

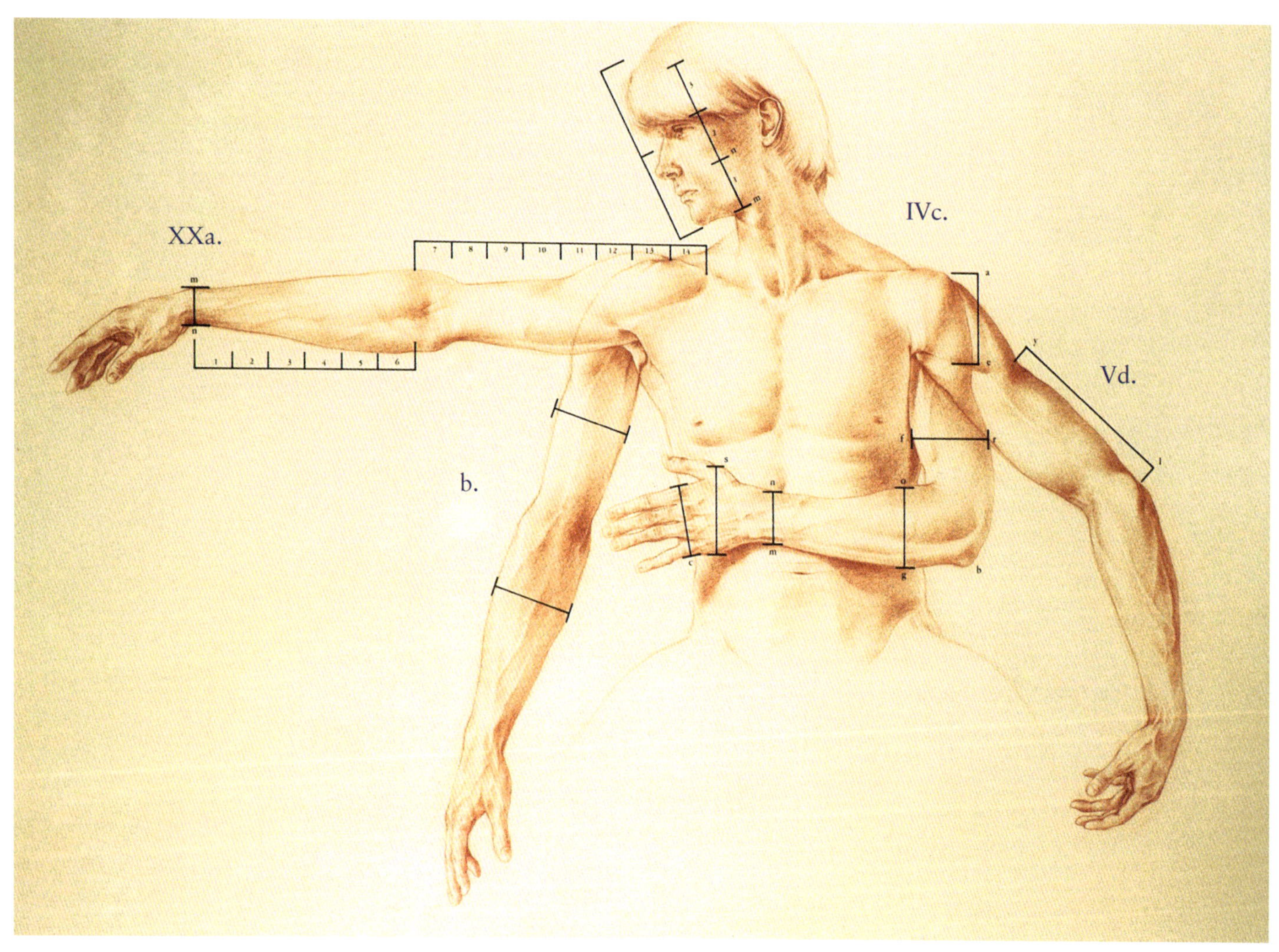

Cat. 60

AP 188

W. 19134–19135, Royal Library, Windsor AP 188
c. 1490 R 348
Folio 10 Recto XX

XX. a. *The smallest thickness of the arm in profile, m n, goes 6 times from the joint of the hand to the dimple of the elbow when extended, and 14 [times] into the whole arm, and 42 into the whole man.*

b. *The greatest thickness of the arm in profile is equal to the greatest thickness of the arm in front, but the first is placed at a third of the arm from the shoulder joint to the elbow, and the other at a third from the elbow joint towards the hand.*

W. 19136–19139a, Royal Library, Windsor R 349
c. 1490
Folio 11 Recto IV, V

IV. c. *a e is equal to the palm of the hand, r f and o g are equal to half a head and each goes 4 times into a b and b c. From c to m is* $^1/_2$ *a head; m n is* $^1/_3$ *of a head and goes 6 times into c b and into b a; a b loses* $^1/_7$ *of its length when the arm is extended; c b never alters; o will always be the middle point between a and s.*

V. d. *y l is the fleshy part of the arm and measures one head; and when the arm is bent this shrinks* $^2/_5$ *of its length; o a in bending loses* $^1/_6$ *and so does o r.*

XX. a. Leonardo says that the smallest thickness of the arm in profile [m n],[50] the width of the wrist in profile (the lateral view), goes six times from the joint of the hand and the wrist, specifically the head of the ulna, to the dimple of the elbow of the extended arm (Plate 27). The measurement is approximately correct. And that same module, the width of the wrist in profile, enters approximately fourteen times into the whole arm, again from the joint of the hand and the wrist to the top of the shoulder. Compare this to AP 181, 5. While this portion of the theory is only approximately accurate, the following, "42 [times] into the whole man," is rather cumbersome to be of use.

b. Here Leonardo is comparing the greatest thickness of the arm, the triceps and biceps, at their fullest, to the central muscle mass of the forearm, from the brachioradialis to the extensor carpi ulnaris. Each of these measurements can vary greatly from one person to another, and from one arm to the other in the same person. The key word here again is *similar.*

IV. c. a e, the length of the deltoid, is similar to the width of the palm of the hand, which includes the thickness of the thumb, here and in Leonardo's drawing (Plate 28). r f, the thickness of the arm at the biceps, and o g, the thickness of the muscle mass of the forearm, are similar to each other, and to half a head, which works nicely. However, each of these measurements does not go four times into the distance from a, the top of the shoulder, to b, the elbow, or from b to c, the width of the hand at the knuckles. At most it only goes three to three and a half times.

From c, where the knuckles attach to the hand, to m, the wrist joint, is half a head, and this works perfectly. The width of the wrist, m n, is in fact approximately one-third of the head, but that measurement only goes five to five and a half times into c b and b a, and not six times. I have, therefore, left out the next calculation, "a b, decreases by $^1/_7$ when the arm is extended…" because it is at best elusive and difficult to actually measure.

Lastly, in this section, Leonardo says that o, the crook of the elbow, will always be the middle point between a, the top of the shoulder, and s, the insertion of the thumb, the point just before c, the insertion of the fingers into the hand. This assessment works beautifully on both Leonardo's drawing and mine.

V. d. y l, the fleshy part of the arm, where the deltoid inserts into the humerus, to l, the elbow, is one head, and this is a perfectly reliable measurement. The last two parts of this entry have been left out because of the difficulty in proving the theory.

XX. a.

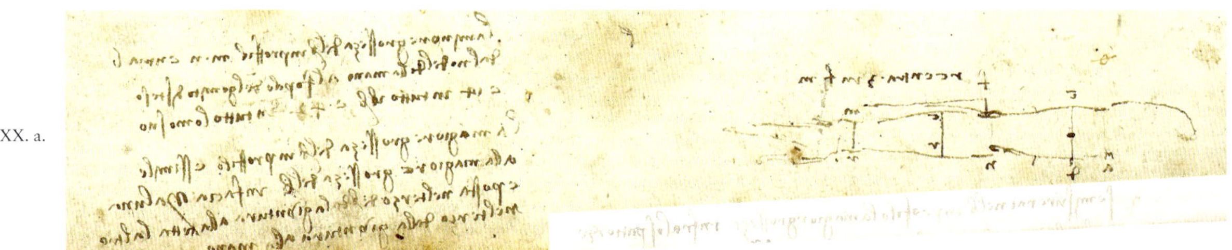

Detail, Plate 27, W. 19134–19135, Royal Collection, Windsor

IV. c.

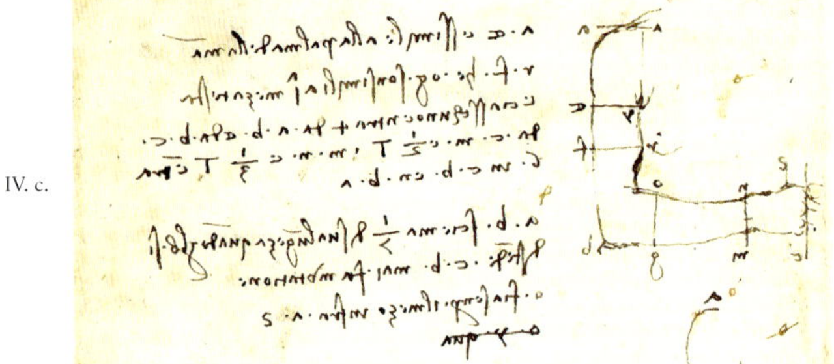

Detail, Plate 28, W. 19136–19139a, Royal Collection, Windsor

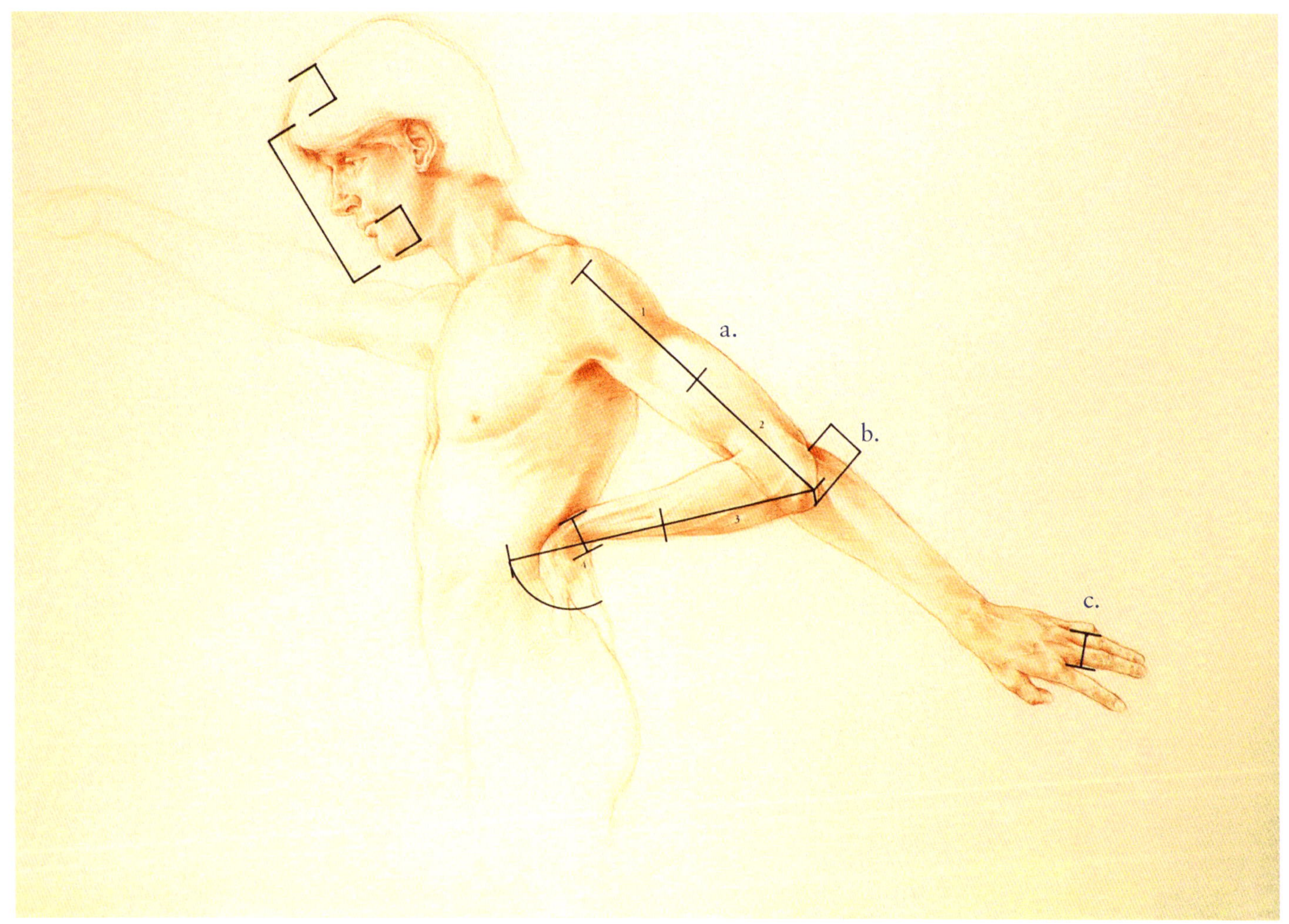

Cat. 61 AP 189

W. 19134–19135, Royal Library, Windsor **AP 189**
c. 1490 **R 348**
Folio 10 Recto V

a. *The arm when bent is 4 heads.*

b. *The arm from the shoulder to the elbow in bending increases in length, that is, in the length from the shoulder to the elbow; and this increasing is similar to the wrist when seen in profile.*

c. *And the space between the bottom of the chin and the parting of the lips is equal to the thickness of the 2 middle fingers, and to the width of the mouth and to the space between the roots of the hair on the forehead and the top of the head. All these distances are equal to each other, but they are not equal to the above-mentioned increase in the arm.*

This entry (Plate 27) is in the middle of the famous *Trezo* page (see note 52, AP 192). Isolated from the other entries on this page, it is part of a long series of statements dealing with the proportions of the arm and the head.

a. The arm when bent, from the top of the shoulder to the elbow and from the elbow to the hand, measures four heads. Leonardo again uses the word for heads, *teste* (actually just a capital T), when he means "faces." Compare this theory to AP 188 and AP 182.

b. The arm, from the top of the shoulder to the point of the elbow, in bending, increases in length that portion of the arm to a measurement equal to the width of the wrist as seen in profile.[51] Here we view the lateral aspect of the arm. As the arm bends, the olecranon of the ulna (a sharp prominent edge) projects out as it rotates on the epicondyle on the humerus and actually slides several inches away from where it was, thus making the arm appear longer. Although Leonardo refers to this several times, it is a very elusive calculation to make, and one I have avoided until this entry. If you compare the length of the arm in this drawing from the shoulder to the elbow, and then from the elbow to the tips of the fingers, you will find that it is longer than the bent arm. The increase is about the width of the wrist.

c. Leonardo goes on to describe the space between the bottom of the chin and the parting of the lips as equal to the thickness of the two middle fingers. This measurement is also equal to the width of the mouth (as this drawing is conceived as a profile, this view is not visible, but the measurement does hold true) and equal to the distance from the roots of the hair to the top of the head. (Compare this to AP 101.) However, all of these distances being similar, they are not equal to the width of the wrist, which is smaller. Interestingly, Leonardo goes over these same proportions, the number of heads in the bent arm, several times on the same sheet, in R 348 IX and in R 348 X.

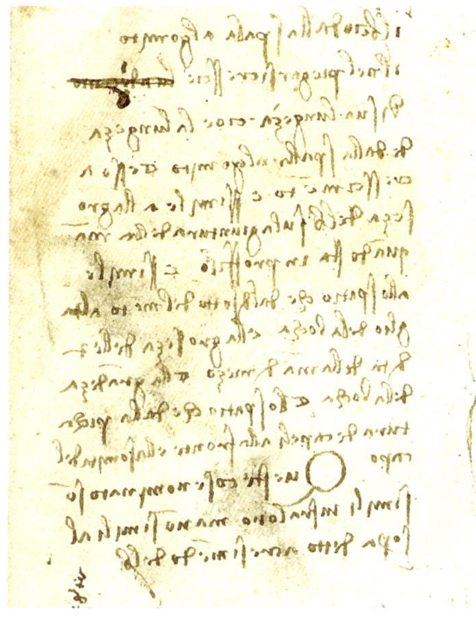

Detail, Plate 27, W. 19134–19135, Royal Collection, Windsor

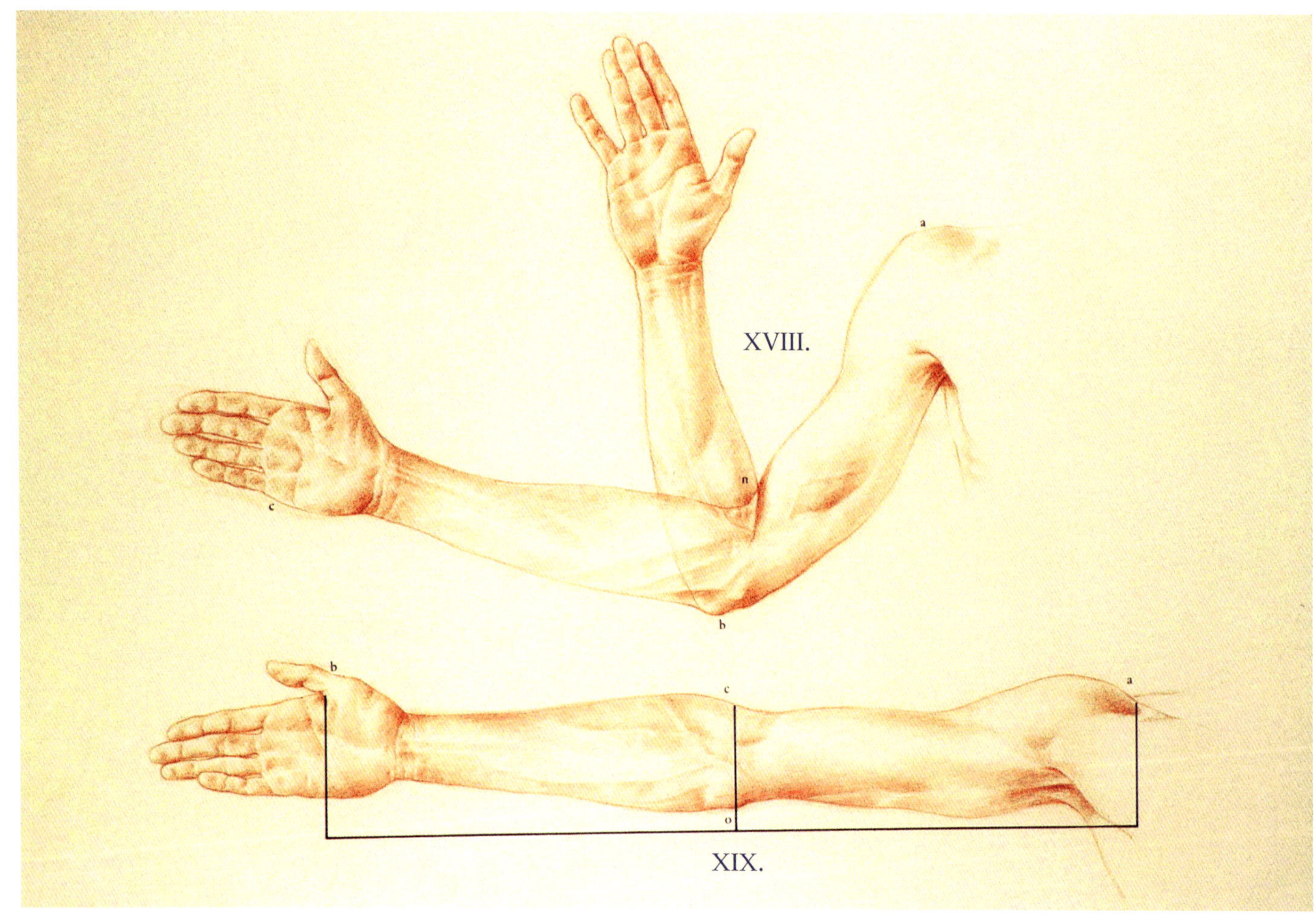

Cat. 62 **AP 190**

W. 19134–19135, Royal Library, Windsor — **AP 190**
c. 1490 — **R 348**
Folio 10 Recto XVIII, XIX

XVIII. *If the arm is extended it decreases by 1/3 of the length between b and n, and if—being extended—it is bent, it will increase half of o c.*

XIX. *The length from the shoulder to the elbow is the same as from the base of the thumb, inside, to the elbow, a b c.*

XVIII. This statement is accompanied by a tiny line drawing of both the bent and the extended arm (Plate 27). To put it simply, when the arm is extended, the muscle fibers elongate, and when the arm is bent the fibers contract and appear enlarged. The proportional increases and decreases are difficult to calculate and are best assessed visually.

XIX. The distance from the shoulder, a, to the elbow, c, is the same as the distance from the base of the thumb on the inside or palm side of the hand, b, to the elbow, c, or, as Leonardo phrases it, a b c. Compare this to AP 185, AP 186, AP 188, and AP 189, all of which have slightly different comparison points. It is the part, the specific module being used as the yardstick for the measurement, that determines the ratios. This, of course, is the basis of all Leonardo's theories on proportion.

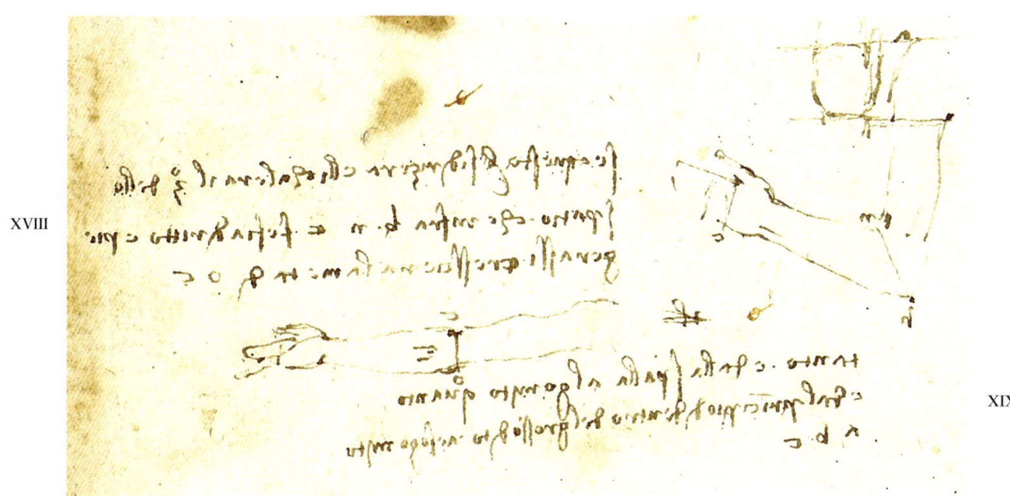

Detail, Plate 27, W. 19134–19135, Royal Collection, Windsor

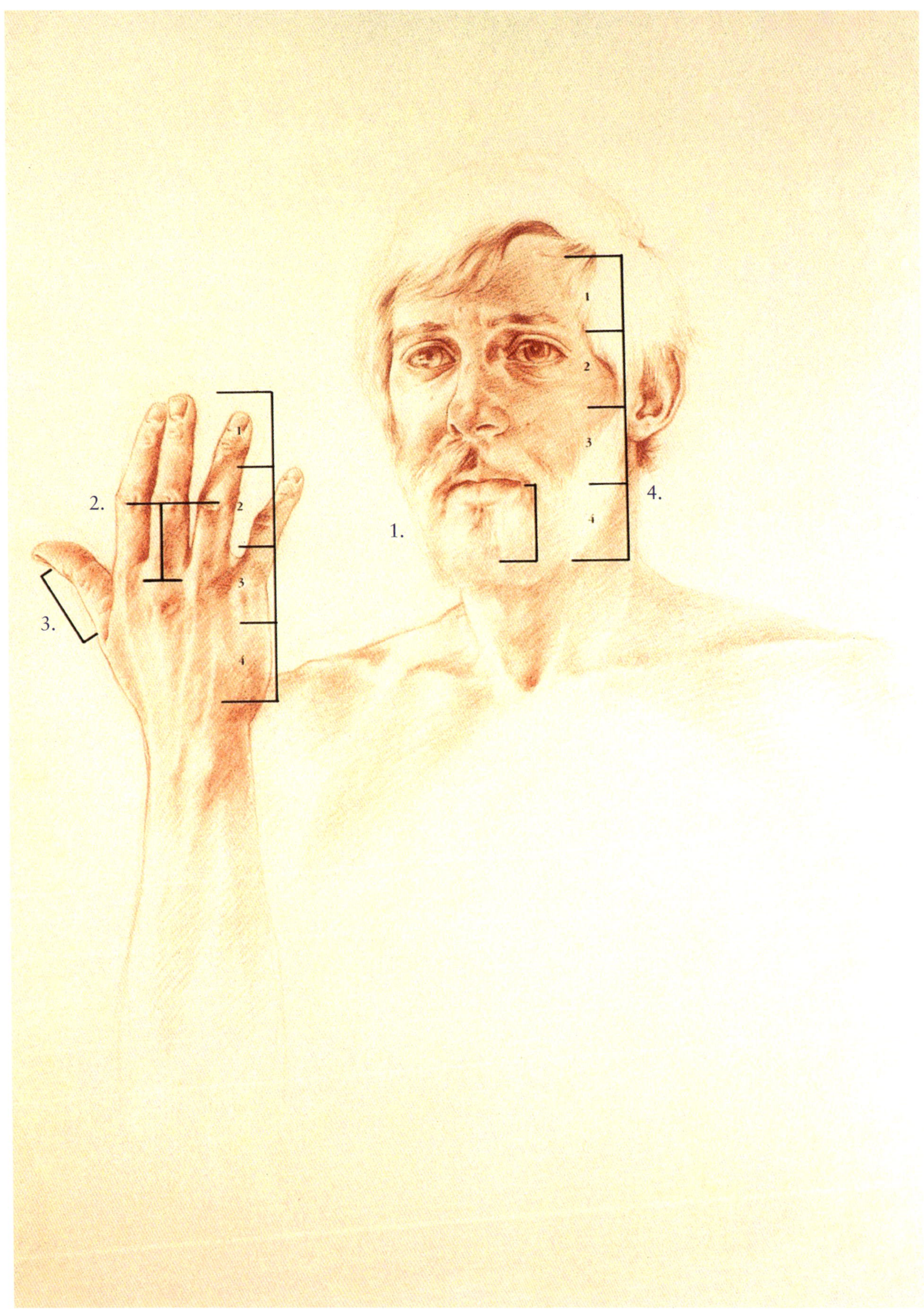

Cat. 63

AP 191

W. 19133a, Royal Library, Windsor **AP 191**
c. 1490 **R 324**
Folio 9 Recto X

1. *The distance between the mouth and the chin is equal to that of the knuckles of the 3 middle fingers*
2. *and to the length of their first joints if the hand is spread,*
3. *and equal to the distance from the joint of the thumb to the outset of the nails,*
4. *that is, the fourth part of the hand and of the face.*

I have divided this section, Folio 9 Recto X (Plate 25), into two parts, a and b, and I have separated one from the other and from their original context. Part a is discussed in AP 171; part b is discussed here. And because of its complexity and length, I have divided part b into four parts, numbered 1, 2, 3, and 4.

Leonardo uses as a module the distance between the mouth, that is, the parting of the lips, and the bottom of the chin in these examples:

1. the distance between the mouth and the chin is equal to the width of the three middle fingers at the knuckles,
2. and, that is equal to the length of the first joints of those fingers from the fifth metacarpal to the proximal phalanx,
3. and, the length of the thumb from the second joint to the beginning of the finger nail,
4. and, all of the above measure as the fourth part of the hand and the face from the chin to the hairline.

It works in Leonardo's drawing and in general.

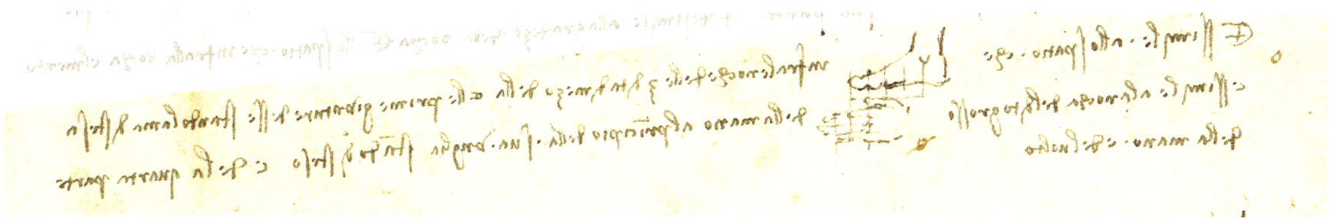

Detail, Plate 25, W. 19133a, Royal Collection, Windsor

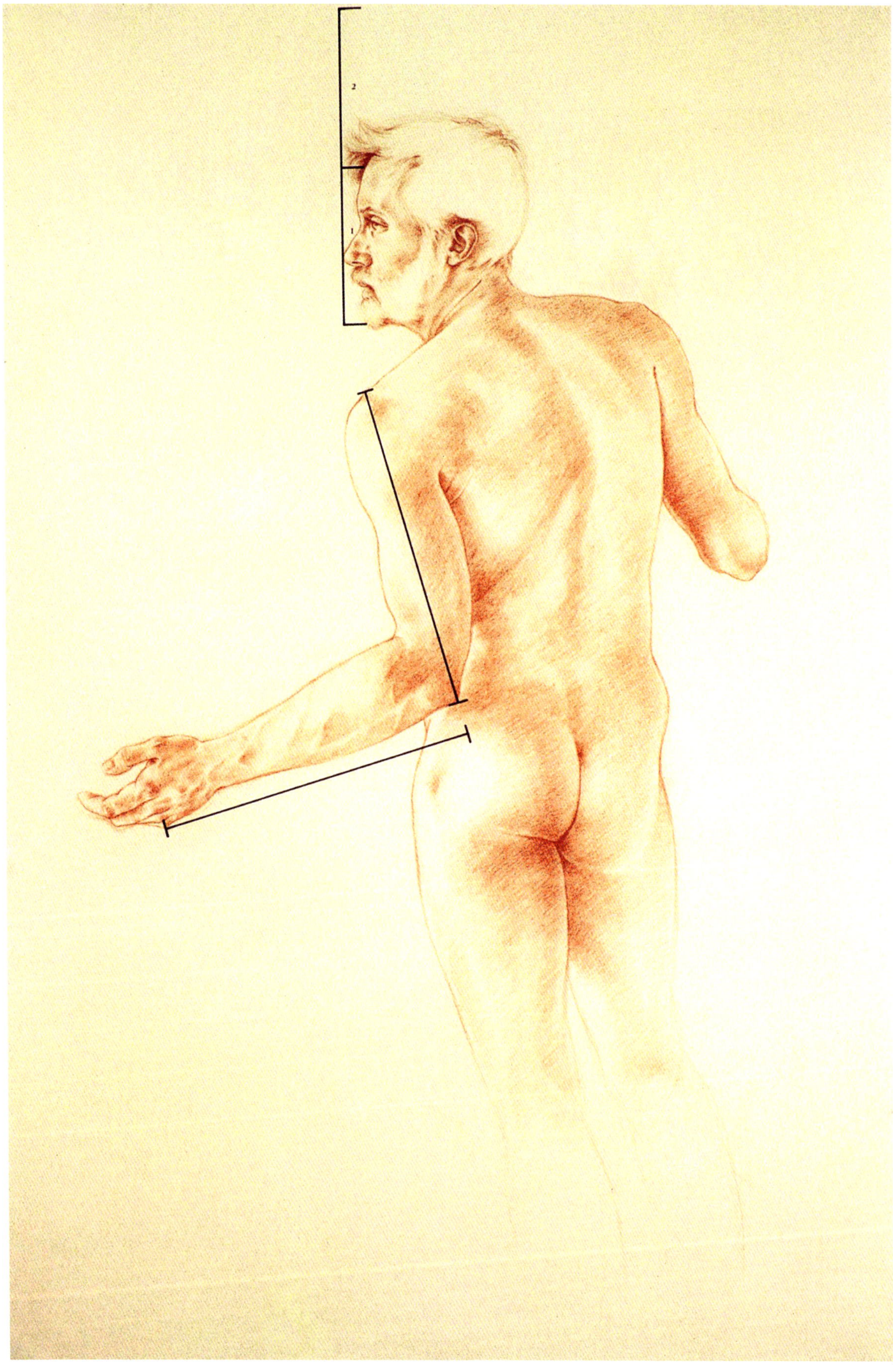

Cat. 64 AP 192

W. 19136 –19139a, Royal Library, Windsor **AP 192**
c. 1490 **R 349**
Folio 11 Recto IV

Trezo[52]

From the top of the shoulder to the point of the elbow is as far as from that point to the joints of the four fingers with the palm of the hand, and each is 2 faces [teste].

Leonardo again means faces here (Plate 28) and not heads, and Richter rightly transcribes "faces." However, the rest of Leonardo's words are explicit. The distance from the top of the shoulder to the elbow is equal to the distance from the elbow to the joints of the fingers of the hand. Compare this to AP 182. Here, he uses as a canon of measurement the length of the upper arm, and he confirms this by inserting the required number of faces or hands. In AP 182 Leonardo uses the hand or the face as a module, but at the very end he gives us the same comparison as here, simply by inserting the letters a b c at the proper points.

Trezo

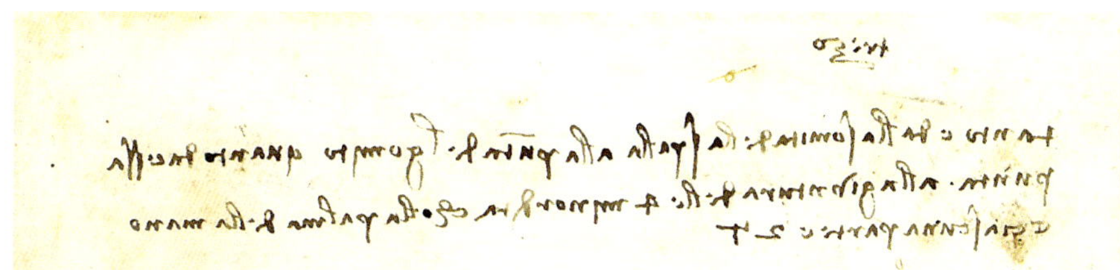

Detail, Plate 28, W. 19136–19139a, Royal Collection, Windsor

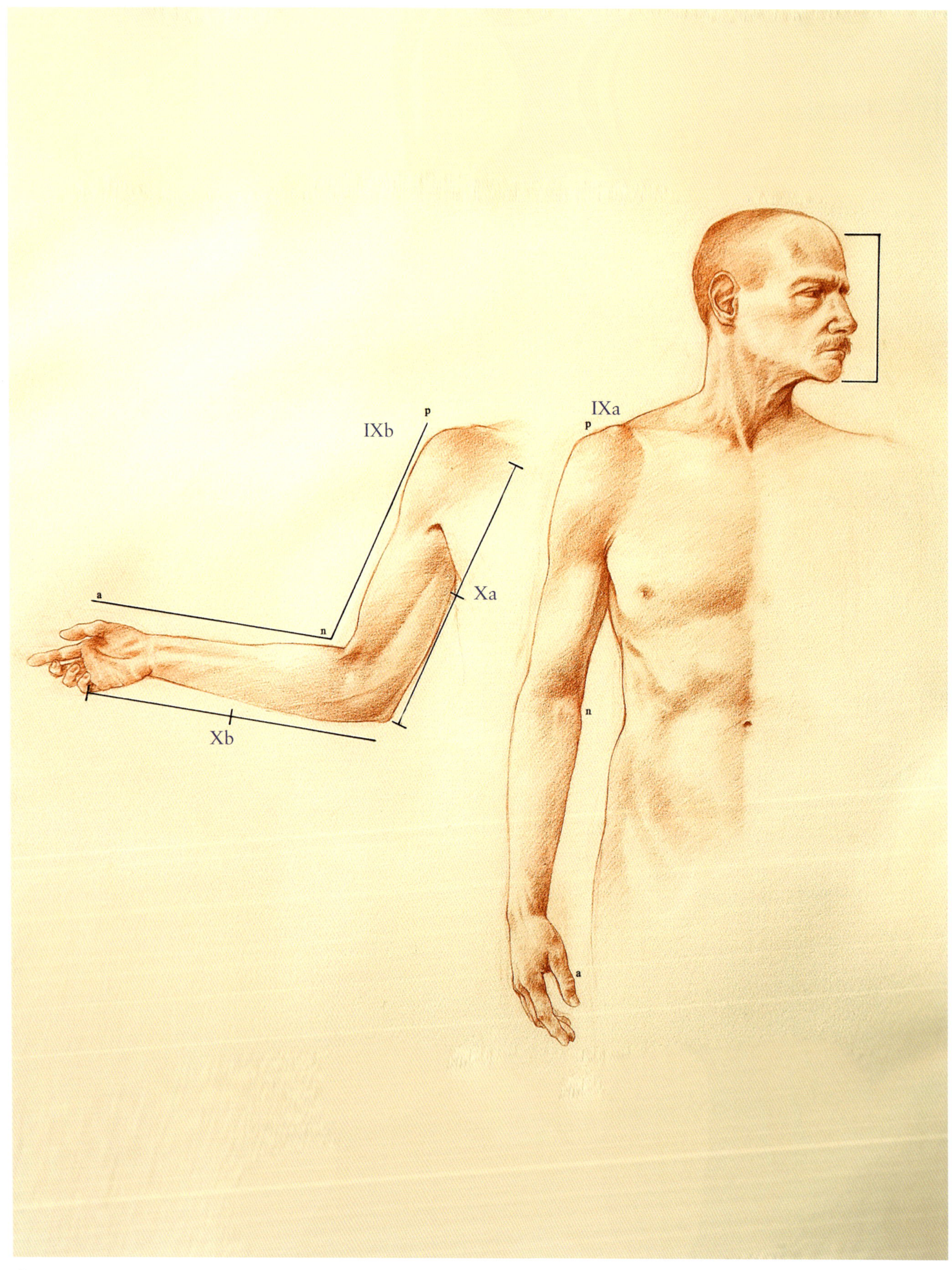

Cat. 65

AP 193

W. 19134–19135, Royal Library, Windsor **AP 193**
c. 1490 **R 348**
Folio 10 Recto IX, X

IX. a. ***When the arm is extended, p n is equal [similar] to n a.***

b. ***And when it is bent, n a diminishes 1/6 of its length, and p n does the same.***

c. ***The outer elbow joint increases 1/7 when bent; and thus by being bent it increases to the length of 2 heads [faces].***

X. a. ***The arm when folded will measure 2 faces [heads] up to the shoulder from the elbow and 2 from the insertion of the four fingers on the palm of the hand.***

b. ***The length from the base of the fingers to the elbow never alters in any position of the arm.***

This last entry (Plate 27) comes from the complicated and confusing *Trezo* sheet, Folio 10. It is found in the lower-right quadrant of the page in two columns with three very small pen-and-ink drawings of two bent arms and one straight arm. In my illustration for the text I have created only one drawing, with one arm bent and one arm straight, combining all of Leonardo's information.

Leonardo visits the proportions of the arm numerous times, using different modules, but in this little series he repeats himself more than usual. In AP 193, this entry, he uses the face as a module to measure the arm, and he uses it again, in exactly the same way, in AP 183, AP 189, and AP 192. He then comes to a slightly different conclusion about the length of the arm in AP 190, but in this case he does not use the face as a module. It is difficult to understand the repetition and the differences. One can only stress the importance of Leonardo's insistence on the empirical method, that every artist must take his own measurements from life and never use a theory as a fast, hard, and fail-proof rule for all.

IX. a. Leonardo's first drawing shows a frontal view of the extended arm on the right side of the figure with points marking the top of the shoulder, p, the inside hollow of the arm, or the elbow, n, and the knuckles of the hand at the inception of the fingers, a. Leonardo says these distances are similar to each other.

b. He then says that when the arm is bent, n a, the distance from the hollow of the elbow to the inception of the fingers is diminished by one-sixth of its length, and the same is true for p n. This theory holds true only if one measures the distance from the shoulder to the elbow on the inside angle of the bent arm and the distance from the hollow of the arm to the inception of the fingers of the hand. This delicate relationship is marked on my illustration as IX. b.

c. The small distinction in b (above) is reinforced by Leonardo's next phrase, "The outer elbow joint increases by 1/7 when bent…" While the fractions he uses might be a little difficult to prove, the general theory will work if you use a compass to compare the above distances, p n and n a, to each other and to the lengths of p n and n a on the extended arm at IX. a. The second part of c indicates that while the inside of the arm diminishes, the outer or elbow side increases and will measure two faces (not two heads, as Richter indicates). The last part of section c is very confusing and ambiguous and has therefore been left out of this analysis and my drawing.

X a. Leonardo takes up the issue of the bent arm again in this next section using the same module (*teste*), which Richter, rightly this time, translates as "faces." Thus, the arm, when folded, measures two faces up to the shoulder from the elbow and two faces from the elbow to the inception of the fingers, a confirmation of the statement above.

b. In the last part of this sentence, Leonardo states that the distance from the base of the fingers to the elbow never alters in any position of the arm, and this can easily be verified if you measure your own arm in both positions.

IX

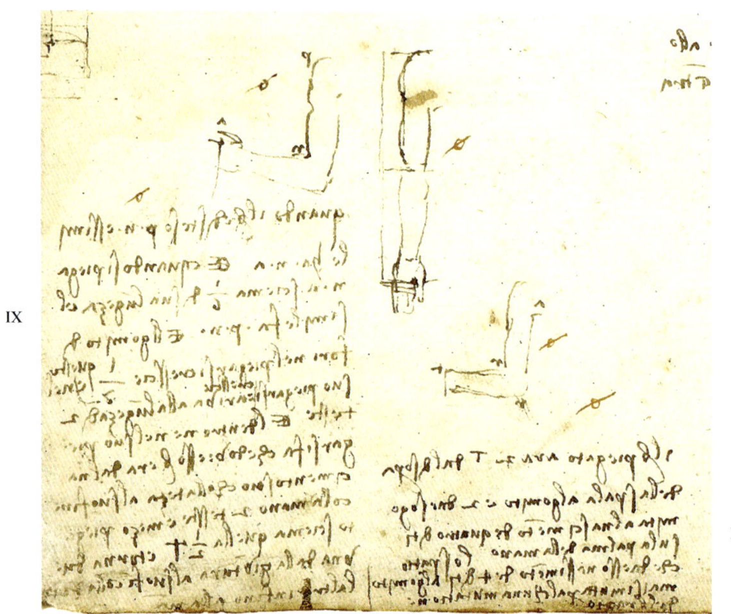

X

Detail, Plate 27, W. 19134–19135, Royal Library, Windsor

Notes
Chapter Seven.The Arm and Hand

[47] AP 182: "Profile of a young man turned to right, and two other studies of the eyes and nose in profile. Also a geometrical figure resembling a wheel with curved blades like a turbine, carefully incised on the paper and then carelessly gone over in ink. The profile, eyes and inking in of the geometrical figure were not by Leonardo."

Kenneth Clark and Carlo Pedretti, *The Drawings of Leonardo da Vinci In the Collection of Her Majesty the Queen, at Windsor Castle* 2nd edition, vol. III (London: Phaidon, 1968), 54.

[48] AP 182: The length of the hand from the wrist to the tip of the longest finger is exactly the length of the face from the chin to the hairline. If you place the beginning of your wrist at the chin and stretch the palm of your hand across your face, you will find that the tip of the longest finger will reach the hairline.

[49] AP 183: Charles Nicholl, *Leonardo da Vinci: Flights of the Mind* (New York: Viking Penguin, 2004), 569; and Jean Paul Richter, The Literary Works, vol. II, 405. These two citations explain that in about 1840 fifty pages from Ms. A and twelve pages from Ms. B were removed by Count Guglielmo Libri, and somehow the pages passed into the library of Lord Ashburnham. In 1875 the pages were returned to the Institut de France after having been restored and rebound. They are now a designated addition to Ms. B referred to as B.N. 2037 (Ash. I) 1875/1, and Ms. A as B.N. 2038 (Ash. II) 1875/2. Page 23b was one of the pages removed from the original binding in Ms. A and is now incorporated into Ms. B.N. 2038 (Ash. II).

[50] AP 188: Richter translates this section to read, "The smallest thickness of the arm in profile z c [instead of *m n*] goes 6 times between the knuckles of the hand and the dimple of the extended elbow." This phrase is written at the edge of the border on Folio 10, just to the left of a drawing of an extended arm in profile, which clearly indicates *m n* at the wrist. This confusing part becomes even more confusing when Richter, in his footnote to lines 62-64, page 258, says, "The arm sketch on the margin of the MS is identically the same as that given below on Plate XX, which may therefore be referred to in this place. In line 62 we read therefore z c for m n."

This Plate XX, cited by Richter in vol. I of *The Literary Works of Leonardo da Vinci*, is not from Folio 10 but from Folio 11, Recto VI. It shows a drawing of an arm not extended, but hanging straight down at the side of its owner. Why Richter would jump to another drawing, done at a different time, to explain a theory written on a different page is unclear. An explanation may be found, however, in Richter's translation of the phrase *...dal nodello [nodel] della mano...*, from the knuckles of the hand. The *Quaderni* translates *nodel*, or *nodello*, as "joint," the joint of the hand. The *Oxford Italian/English Dictionary* translates *nodello* as "a knot or node," and the word *nocella* as "the wrist bone," and the word *nocca* as "the knuckle." In the drawing that Richter refers to on Folio 11, there is the letter L placed at the knuckles of the hand. (See AP 181.) In using this drawing, Richter's translation makes sense, but the proportional theory falls apart. I have therefore used the *Quaderni's*, instead of Richter's, translation to interpret this passage. I think readers must find their own solutions through the empirical method, Leonardo's method, of experimentation and observation.

[51] AP 189: There is at this point a small detail illustration of the junction between the radius and the ulna and the humerus, pictured both straight and bent in an effort to justify the above statements.

[52] AP 192: An interesting observation. On Folio 10 Recto, at the top center, we find the words *il trezo*, and on Folio 11 Recto, on the top left, the word *trezo*. What Leonardo meant by this expression is not known, but it is worth quoting the speculation put forth in the *Quaderni d'Anatomia VI*, page IX:

"...Professor Lesca has informed us that in the neighbourhood [*sic*] of Milano there is a little village by [the] name Trezzo, from which he concludes that '*il trezzo*' might possibly mean: 'the man from Trezzo'. As this Trezzo d'Adda is close to Vaprio, a place where Leonardo is known to have often sojourned, the inference may be permissible that Leonardo here made measurements of a man in that village."

PART THREE

LEONARDO'S WORK ON PROPORTION: THIRTY SHEETS

But I believe that before I am at an end of this [task] I shall have to repeat the same things several times; for which, O reader!
do not blame me, for the subjects are many and memory cannot retain them [all] and say: "I will not write this because I wrote it before."
And if I wished to avoid falling into this fault, it would be necessary in every case when I wanted to copy a [passage] that, not to repeat myself, I should read over all that had gone before; and all the more since the intervals are long between
one time of writing and the next.

R 4b[53]

CHAPTER EIGHT THIRTY DRAWINGS AND PAGES FROM LEONARDO'S NOTEBOOKS

THIRTY NOTEBOOK PAGES AND DRAWINGS

Leonardo da Vinci's pages and drawings from his notebooks are identified here as Plate Numbers. They are arranged alphabetically by notebook letter and then by the collection and city in which they are housed. All dimensions are given in metrics, then in approximate equivalent inches, height followed by width.

We wish to gratefully thank the following institutions for their kind permission to reproduce these pages from their collections. Credits are provided for each entry below.

PLATE NUMBERS AND CREDITS

1. Ms. A, page 62b, c. 1490–1492, Bound Notebook marked A
   Pen and brown ink and sanguine chalk
   210 x 145 mm (8 1/4 x 5 3/4 inches)
   Contains drawings of two heads of horses, in profile and frontal views, and detailed proportions of the face.
   Bibliotheque de l'Institut de France, Paris
   Photo: Rene-Gabriel Ojeda, © RMN-Grand Palaise/Art Resource, NY
2. Ms. A, page 63a, c. 1490–1492, Bound Notebook marked A
   Pen and brown ink
   210 x 145mm (8 1/4 x 5 3/4 inches)
   Two drawings of profile heads and one frontal head. Contains proportional divisions and measurements.
   Bibliothéque de l'Institut de France, Paris
   Photo: Rene-Gabriel Ojeda, © RMN-Grand Palaise/Art Resource, NY
3. Ms. B, page 3b, c. 1490–1492, Bound Notebook marked B
   Pen and brown ink
   240 x 170 mm (9 1/2 x 6 3/4 inches)
   Two small line drawings at the very top of the page. On the left, a leg bended at the knee, on the right, a right arm in profile held straight, both with divisional marks, followed by notes on proportion.
   Bibliothéque de l'Institut de France, Paris
   Photo: Rene-Gabriel Ojeda, © RMN-Grand Palaise/Art Resource, NY
4. Ms. BN 2038 Ash. II, page 23b, c. 1490–1492, Bound Volume marked BN. 2038
   Pen and brown ink
   247 x 192 mm (9 3/4 x 7 1/2 inches)
   This sheet was one of sixty purloined pages eventually returned to France (see endnote 49). Small drawing of a right arm bent at the elbow to form a right angle.
   Bibliotheque de l'Institut de France, Paris
   Photo: Rene-Gabriel Ojeda, © RMN-Grand Palaise/Art Resource, NY
5. Ms. C.A. Inv. 160a (430a), c. 1490–1492 Bound Volume commonly called Codex Atlanticus, with 401 folios each containing one or more manuscript sheets
   Pen and brown ink
   247 x 192 mm (9 3/4 x 7 1/2 inches)
   The first paragraph is devoted to the proportions of the whole body using the hand and face as a module to measure.
   Biblioteca Ambrosiana, Milan
   © Dea/Veneranda Biblioteca Ambrosiana/Art Resource, NY
6. Ms. C.A. Inv. 358a (994a), c. 1487
   Bound Volume commonly called Codex Atlanticus, with 401 folios each containing one or more manuscript sheets
   Pen and brown ink
   380 x 275 mm (15 3/4 x 11 3/4 inches)
   A comprehensive list of proportions using different body parts to measure the whole figure.
   Biblioteca Ambrosiana, Milan
   © Dea/Veneranda Biblioteca Ambrosiana/Art Resource, NY
7. Ms. F, inside front cover, 1508, Bound Pocket Notebook 96 folios
   Pen and brown ink and sanguine chalk
   145 x 100 mm (5 3/4 x 4 inches)
   Bibliotheque de l'Institut de France, Paris
   Photo: Rene-Gabriel Ojeda, © RMN-Grand Palaise/Art Resource, NY
8. Ms. H1, page 31b, c. 1494, Bound Pocket Notebook
   Sanguine chalk
   13 x 9 mm (5 1/8 x 3 1/2 inches)
   Proportions of three-year-old boy.

PLATE NUMBERS AND CREDITS (continued)

Bibliotheque de l'Institut de France, Paris
Photo: Rene-Gabriel Ojeda, © RMN-Grand Palaise/Art Resource, NY

9. Trn. Inv. 15574 (right side), c. 1489–1490
Pen and brown ink over metalpoint on prepared paper
197 x 160 mm (7 3/4 x 6 1/4 inches)
Trn. Inv. 15576 (left side)
Pen and brown ink over metalpoint on prepared paper
144 x 116 mm (5 3/4 x 4 1/2 inches)
These two drawings were once separated but are now rejoined
197 x 276 mm (7 3/4 x 10 3/4 inches)
Proportional studies of the face and eyes with notes and measurements
Biblioteca Reale, Turin
Photo: Sergio Anelli; Photo Credit: Mondadori Portfolio/Electa/Art Resource, NY

10. V. Inv. 228 Frame 29, c. 1490
Pen and brown ink with touches of water color, silverpoint and stylus impressions
345 x 246 mm (13 1/2 x 9 3/4 inches)
Iconic study of the whole body known as the *Vitruvian Man.*
Gallerie dell'Accademia, Venice © 2014.
Photo SCALA, Florence, courtesy of the Ministero Beni e Att. Culturali

11. V. Inv. 236v Frame 33, c. 1489–1490
Pen and brown ink with metalpoint and stylus impressions
280 x 222 mm (11 x 8 3/4 inches)
Proportions of the head of a man.
Gallerie dell'Accademia, Venice ©2014.
Photo SCALA, Florence-courtesy of the Ministero Beni e Att. Culturali

12. V. Inv. 236r, Frame 33, c. 1489–1490 and 1503–1504
Pen and brown ink with metalpoint and stylus impressions
280 x 222 mm (11 x 8 3/4 inches)
Proportions of the head of a man with two horsemen.
Gallerie dell'Accademia, Venice © 2014.
Photo SCALA, Florence, courtesy of the Ministero Beni e Att. Culturali

13. W. 12304, c. 1489–1490
Pen and brown ink
264 x 215 mm (10 3/8 x 8 1/2 inches)
Studies of the proportions of the head, face, neck, and torso.
Royal Library, Windsor
Royal Collection Trust/
© Her Majesty Queen Elizabeth II 2014

14. W. 12601, c. 1489–1490
Pen and brown ink on prepared blue paper
213 x 153 mm (8 3/8 x 6 inches)
Study of proportions of the head and face.
Royal Library, Windsor
Royal Collection Trust/
© Her Majesty Queen Elizabeth II 2014

15. W. 12606, c. 1490–1492
Pen and brown ink
56 x 50 mm (2 1/4 x 2 inches)
Study of proportions of the head.
Royal Library, Windsor
Royal Collection Trust/
© Her Majesty Queen Elizabeth II 2014

16. W. 12607, c. 1487
Pen and brown ink
143 x 137 mm (5 5/8 x 5 3/8 inches)
Study of proportions of the head and chest.
Royal Library, Windsor
Royal Collection Trust/
© Her Majesty Queen Elizabeth II 2014

17. W. 12632, c. 1490
Pen and brown ink metal point
191 x 144 mm (7 1/2 x 5 5/8 inches)
Study of a robust, standing male nude in profile from chest to feet facing left.
Royal Library, Windsor
Royal Collection Trust/
© Her Majesty Queen Elizabeth II 2014

18. W. 19129, c. 1489–1490
Pen and brown ink
150 x 169 mm (5 7/8 x 6 5/8 inches)
Studies of the length of the foot as a module to measure the head and arm.
Royal Library, Windsor
Royal Collection Trust/
© Her Majesty Queen Elizabeth II 2014

19. W. 19130a, c. 1490
Pen and brown ink
146 x 218 mm (5 3/4 x 8 1/2 inches)
Study of the proportions of the head and torso.
Royal Library, Windsor
Royal Collection Trust/
© Her Majesty Queen Elizabeth II 2014

20. W. 19130b, c. 1490
Pen and brown ink
146 x 218 mm (5 3/4 x 8 1/2 inches)
Studies of the proportions of leg and torso in relation to each other.
Royal Library, Windsor
Royal Collection Trust/
© Her Majesty Queen Elizabeth II 2014

PLATE NUMBERS AND CREDITS (continued)

21. W. 19131a, c. 1490
    Pen and brown ink
    128 x 210 mm (5 x $8^{1}/_{4}$ inches)
    Study of the proportions of the length of the arm.
    Royal Library, Windsor
    Royal Collection Trust/
    © Her Majesty Queen Elizabeth II 2014
22. W. 19131b, c. 1490
    Pen and brown ink
    128 x 210 mm (5 x $8^{1}/_{4}$ inches)
    Study of the proportions of the foot to the face and head.
    Royal Library, Windsor
    Royal Collection Trust/
    © Her Majesty Queen Elizabeth II 2014
23. W. 19132a, c. 1490
    Pen and brown ink
    160 x 218 mm ($6^{1}/_{4}$ x $8^{1}/_{2}$ inches)
    Studies of the body sitting, standing, and kneeling.
    Royal Library, Windsor
    Royal Collection Trust/
    © H er Majesty Queen Elizabeth II 2014
24. W. 19132b, c. 1490
    Pen and brown ink
    160 x 218 mm ($6^{1}/_{4}$ x $8^{1}/_{2}$ inches)
    Proportions of the torso and whole body.
    Royal Library, Windsor
    Royal Collection Trust/
    © Her Majesty Queen Elizabeth II 2014
25. W. 19133a, c. 1490
    Pen and brown ink
    303 x 206 mm (12 x $8^{1}/_{4}$ inches)
    Studies of the proportions of the hand and the foot.
    Royal Library, Windsor
    Royal Collection Trust/
    © Her Majesty Queen Elizabeth II 2014
26. W. 19133b, c. 1490
    Pen and brown ink
    303 x 206 mm (12 x $8^{1}/_{4}$ inches)
    Studies of proportions of the foot.
    Royal Library, Windsor
    Royal Collection Trust/
    © Her Majesty Queen Elizabeth II 2014
27. W. 19134–19135, c. 1490
    Folded in half
    Pen and brown ink
    434 x 317 mm ($17^{1}/_{4}$ x $12^{1}/_{2}$ inches)
    Studies of proportions of the head, arm, hand, torso, and whole body.
    Royal Library, Windsor
    Royal Collection Trust/
    © Her Majesty Queen Elizabeth II 2014
28. W. 19136–19139a, c. 1490
    Folded in four
    Pen and brown ink
    405 x 281 mm (16 x 11 inches)
    Proportions of the arm, torso, and leg.
    Royal Library, Windsor
    Royal Collection Trust/
    © Her Majesty Queen Elizabeth II 2014
29. W. 19136–19139b, c. 1490
    Folded in four
    Pen and brown ink
    405 x 281 mm (16 x 11 inches)
    Proportions of the foot and the leg with a discussion of the force of man against a thousand pounds.
    Royal Collection Trust/
    © Her Majesty Queen Elizabeth II 2014
30. W. 19140, c. 1490
    Pen and brown ink with traces of stylus
    203 x 279 mm (8 x 11 inches)
    Studies of the proportions of the face, leg, arm, and foot.
    Royal Library, Windsor
    Royal Collection Trust/
    © Her Majesty Queen Elizabeth II 2014

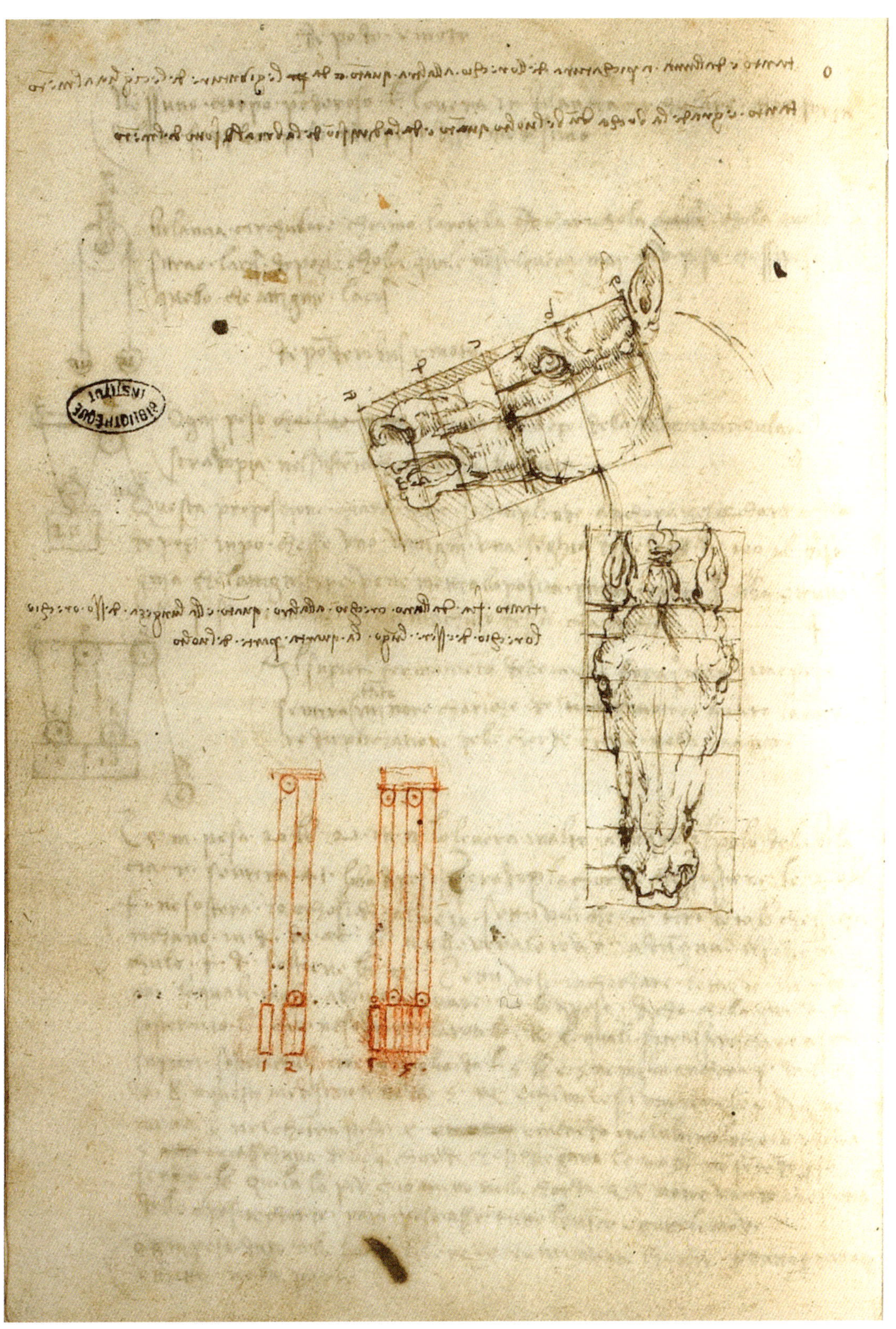

AP 109
(R 311)

Plate 1
Ms. A, page 62b, c. 1490–1492, Bound Notebook marked A, Pen and brown ink and sanguine chalk, 210 x 145 mm (8¼ x 5¾ inches). Contains drawings of two heads of horses, in profile and frontal views, and detailed proportions of the face. Bibliothéque de l'Institut de France, Paris. Photo: Rene-Gabriel Ojeda, © RMN-Grand Palaise/Art Resource, NY.

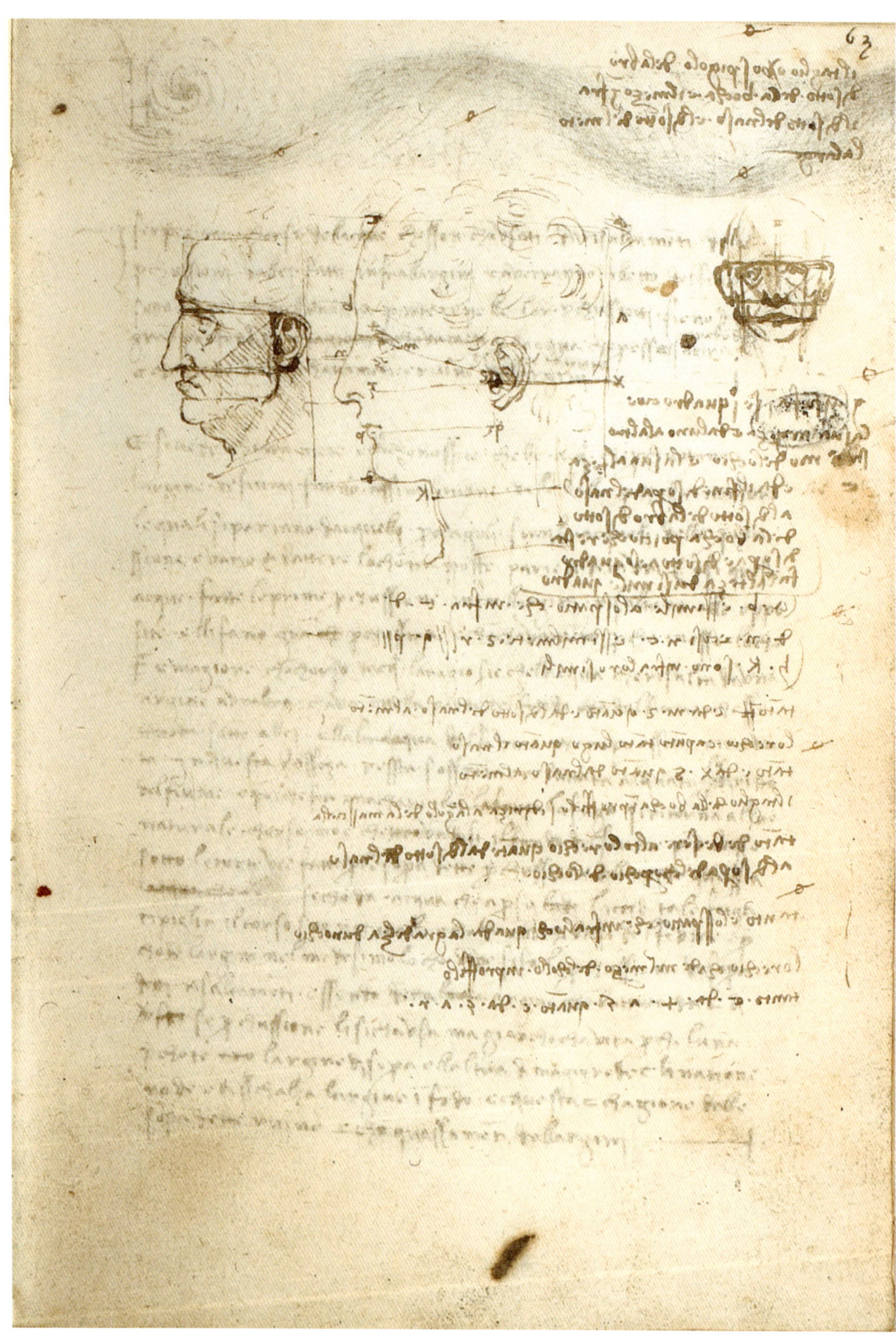

AP 105
(R 312)

Plate 2
Ms. A, page 63a, c. 1490–1492, Bound Notebook marked A, Pen and brown ink, 210 x 145mm (8¼ x 5¾ inches). Two drawings of profile heads and one frontal head, contains proportional divisions and measurements. Bibliothéque de l'Institut de France, Paris. Photo: Rene-Gabriel Ojeda, © RMN-Grand Palaise/ Art Resource, NY.

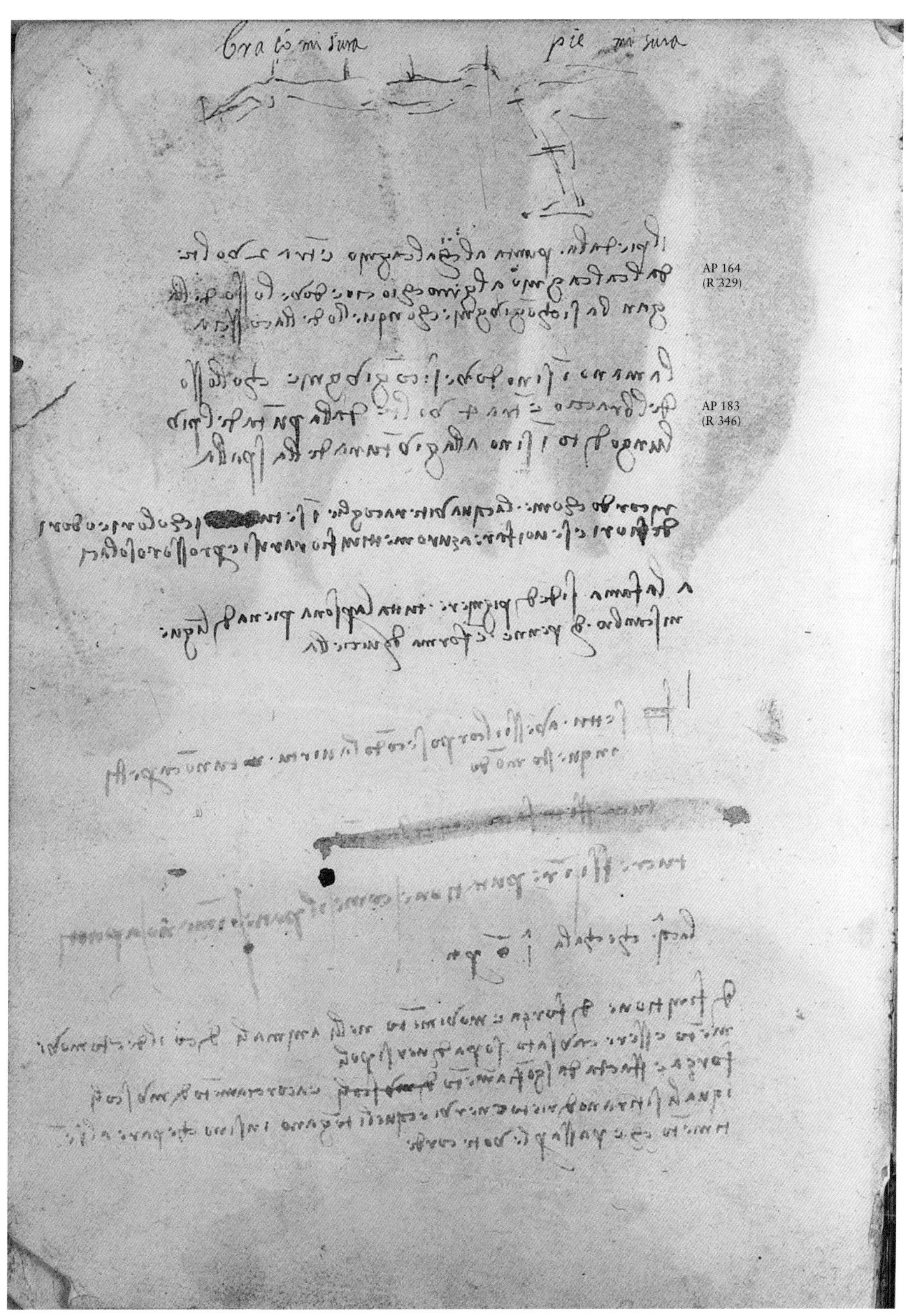

Plate 3
Ms. B, page 3b, c. 1490–1492, Bound Notebook marked B, Pen and brown ink, 240 x 170 mm (9½ x 6¾ inches). Two small line drawings at the very top of the page. On the left, a leg bended at the knee, on the right, a right arm in profile held straight, both with divisional marks, followed by notes on proportion. Bibliothéque de l'Institut de France, Paris. Photo: Rene-Gabriel Ojeda,© RMN-Grand Palaise/Art Resource, NY.

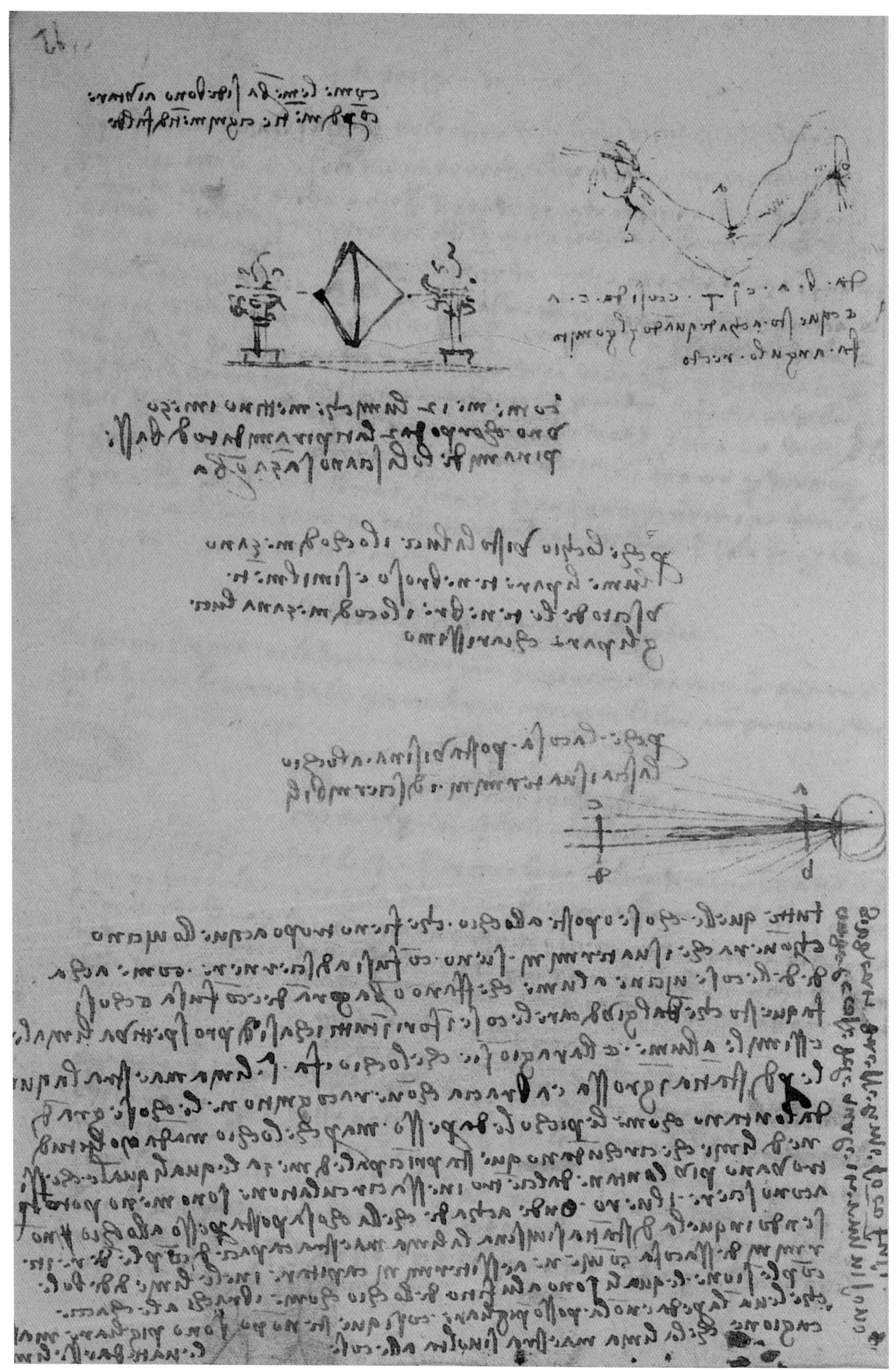

AP 183
(R 344)

Plate 4
Ms. BN 2038 Ash. II, page 23b, c. 1490–1492, Bound Volume marked BN. 2038, Pen and brown ink, 247 x 192 mm (9¾ x 7½ inches). This sheet was one of sixty purloined pages eventually returned to France (see endnote 49). Small drawing of a right arm bent at the elbow to form a right angle. Bibliothéque de l'Institut de France, Paris. Photo: Rene-Gabriel Ojeda, © RMN-Grand Palaise/Art Resource, NY.

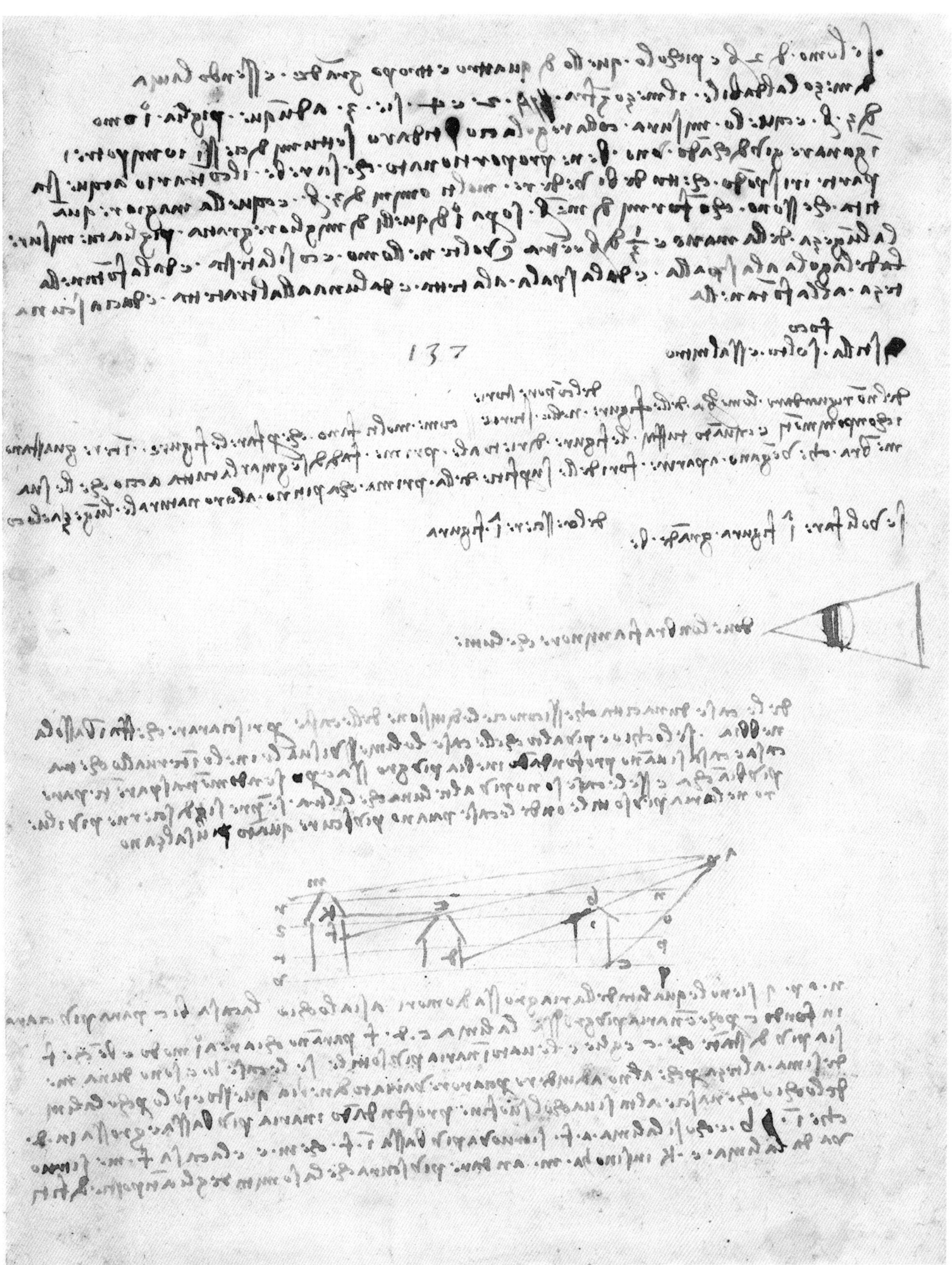

AP 146
(R 309)

Plate 5
Ms. C.A. Inv. 160a (430a), c. 1490–1492, Bound Volume commonly called Codex Atlanticus, with 401 folios each containing one or more manuscript sheets, Pen and brown ink, 247 x 192 mm ($9^{3}/_{4}$ x $7^{1}/_{2}$ inches). The first paragraph is devoted to the proportions of the whole body using the hand and face as a module to measure. Biblioteca Ambrosiana, Milan, © Dea/Veneranda Biblioteca Ambrosiana/Art Resource, NY.

AP 150
(R 340)

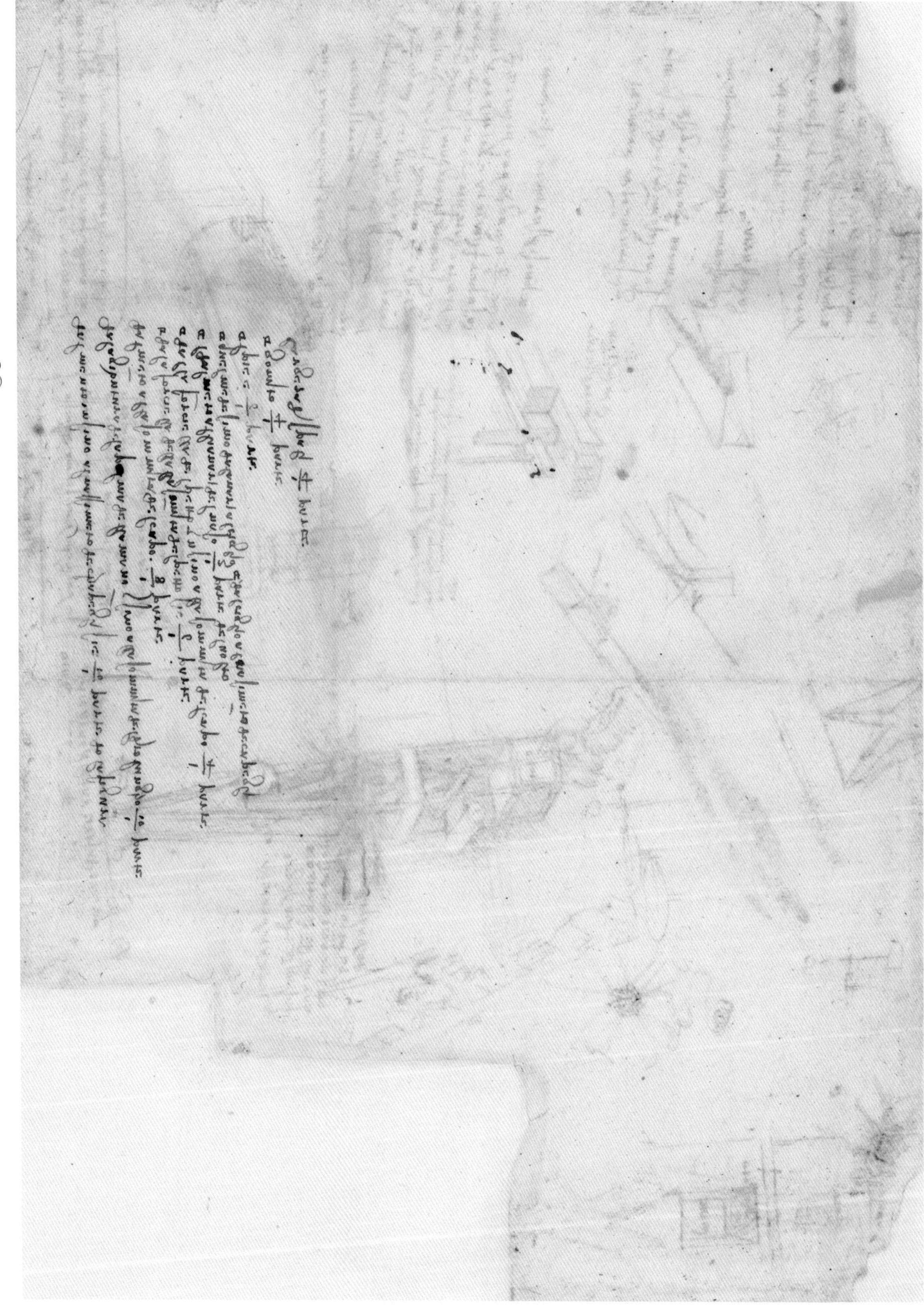

Plate 6
Ms. C.A. Inv. 358a (994a), c. 1487, Bound Volume commonly called Codex Atlanticus, with 401 folios each containing one or more manuscript sheets, Pen and brown ink, 380 x 275 mm (15¾ x 11¾ inches). A comprehensive list of proportions using different body parts to measure the whole figure. Biblioteca Ambrosiana, Milan, © Dea/Veneranda Biblioteca Ambrosiana/Art Resource, NY.

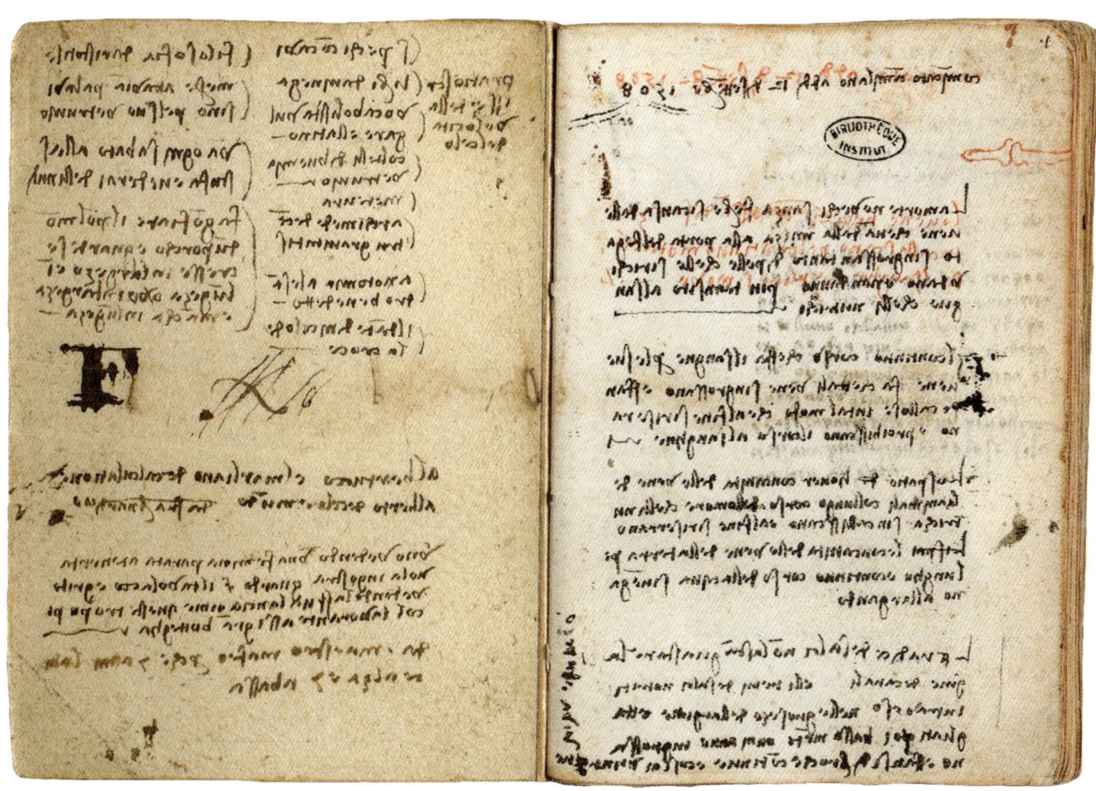

Plate 7
Ms. F, inside front cover, 1508, Bound Pocket Notebook 96 folios, Pen and brown ink and sanguine chalk, 145 x 100 mm (5¾ x 4 inches). Bibliothéque de l'Institut de France, Paris. Photo: Rene-Gabriel Ojeda, © RMN-Grand Palaise/Art Resource, NY.

AP 151
(R 308)

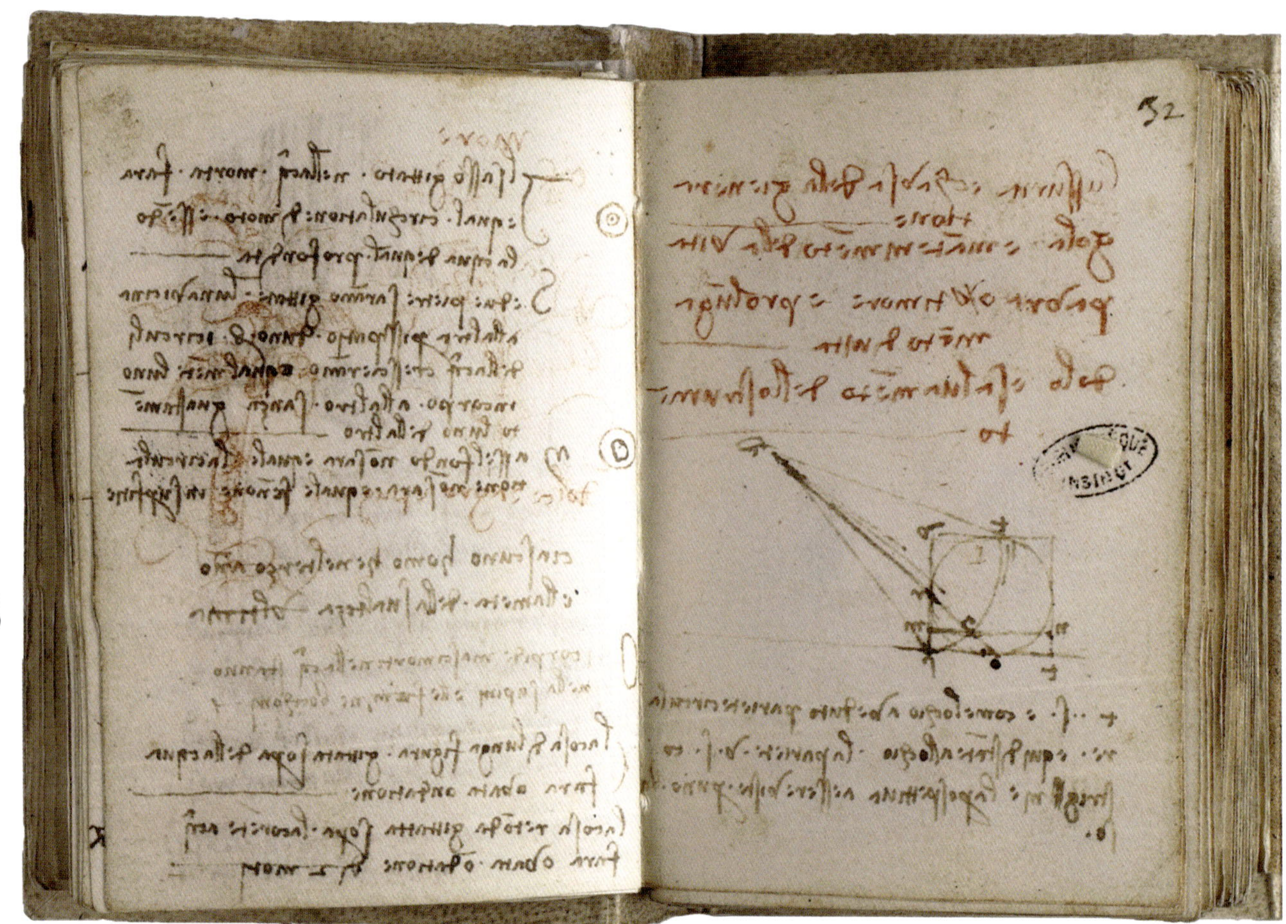

Plate 8
Ms. H1, page 31b, c. 1494, Bound Pocket Notebook, Sanguine chalk, 13 x 9 mm ($5^{1}/_{8}$ x $3^{1}/_{2}$ inches). Proportions of three-year-old boy. Bibliothéque de l'Institut de France, Paris. Photo: Rene-Gabriel Ojeda, © RMN-Grand Palaise/Art Resource, NY.

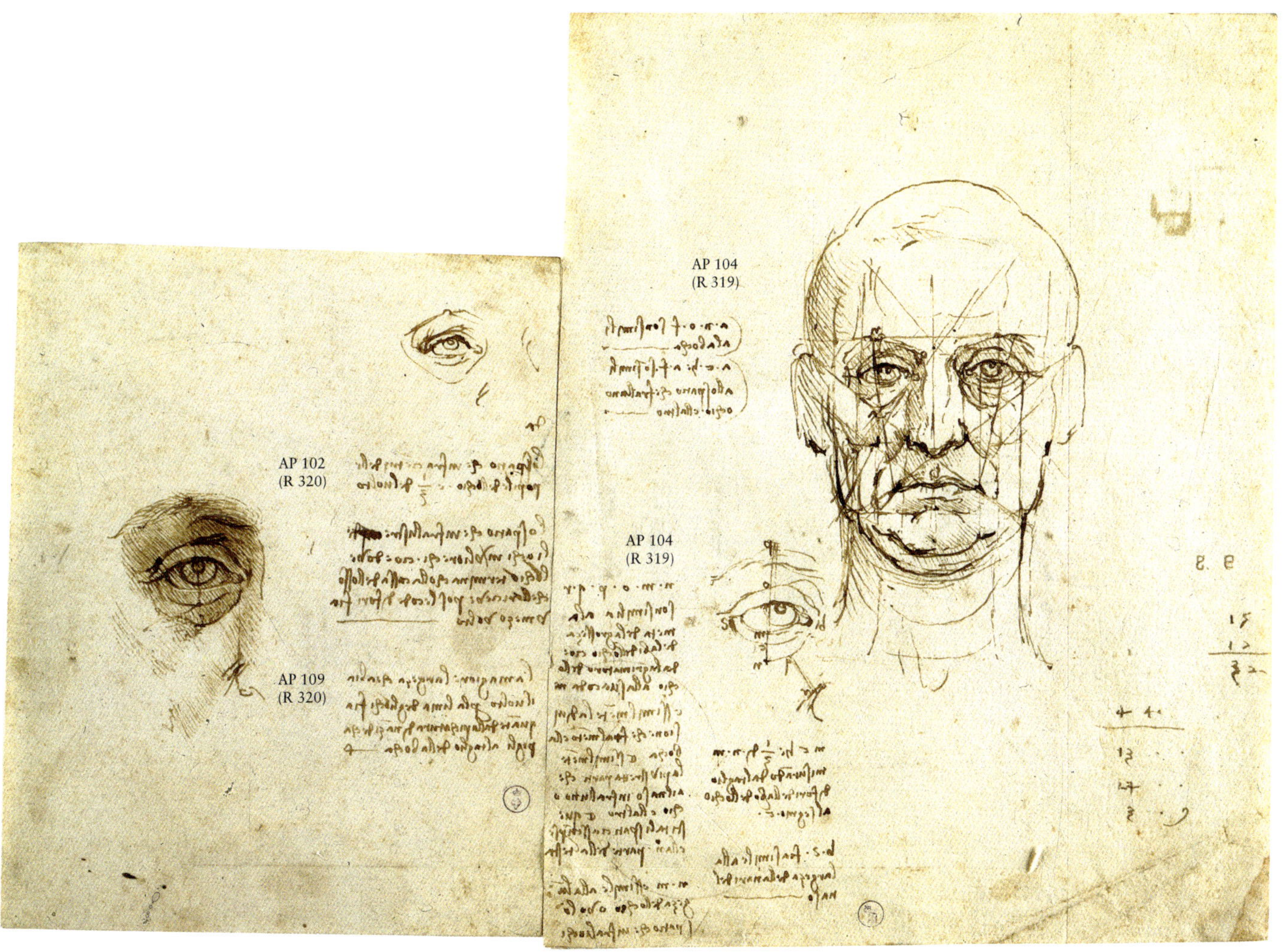

Plate 9
Trn. Inv. 15574 (right side), c. 1489–1490, Pen and brown ink over metalpoint on prepared paper, 197 x 160 mm (7¾ x 6¼ inches). Trn. Inv. 15576 (left side), Pen and brown ink over metalpoint on prepared paper, 144 x 116 mm (5¾ x 4½ inches). These two drawings were once separated but are now rejoined, 197 x 276 mm (7¾ x 10¾ inches). Proportional studies of the face and eyes with notes and measurements. Biblioteca Reale, Turin. Photo: Sergio Anelli, Photo Credit: Mondadori Portfolio/Electa/Art Resource, NY.

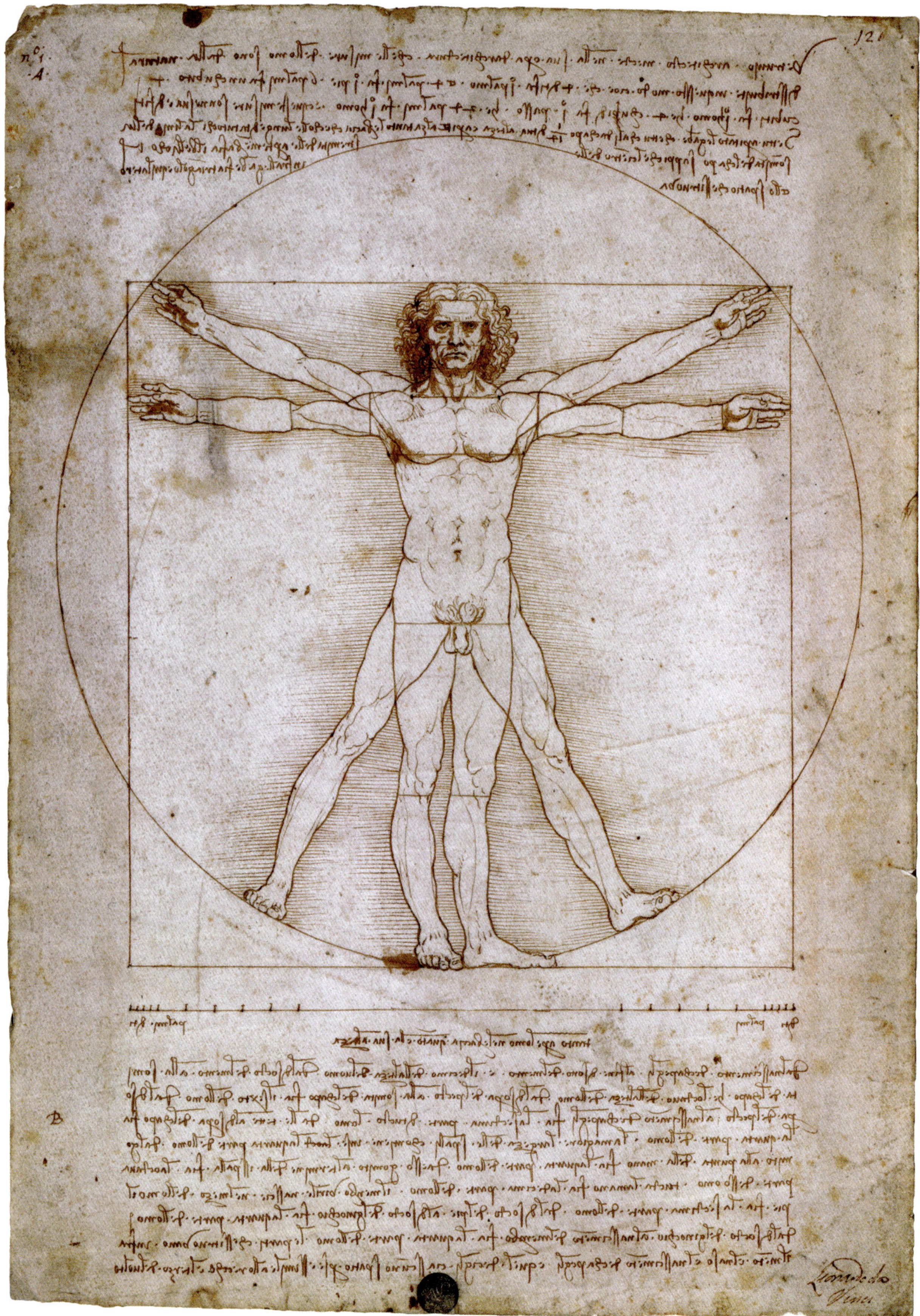

Plate 10
V. Inv. 228 Frame 29, c. 1490, Pen and brown ink with touches of water color, silverpoint, and stylus impressions, 345 x 246 mm (13½ x 9¾ inches). Iconic study of the whole body known as *The Vitruvian Man*. Gallerie dell'Accademia, Venice © 2014. Photo SCALA, Florence, courtesy of the Ministero Beni e Att. Culturali.

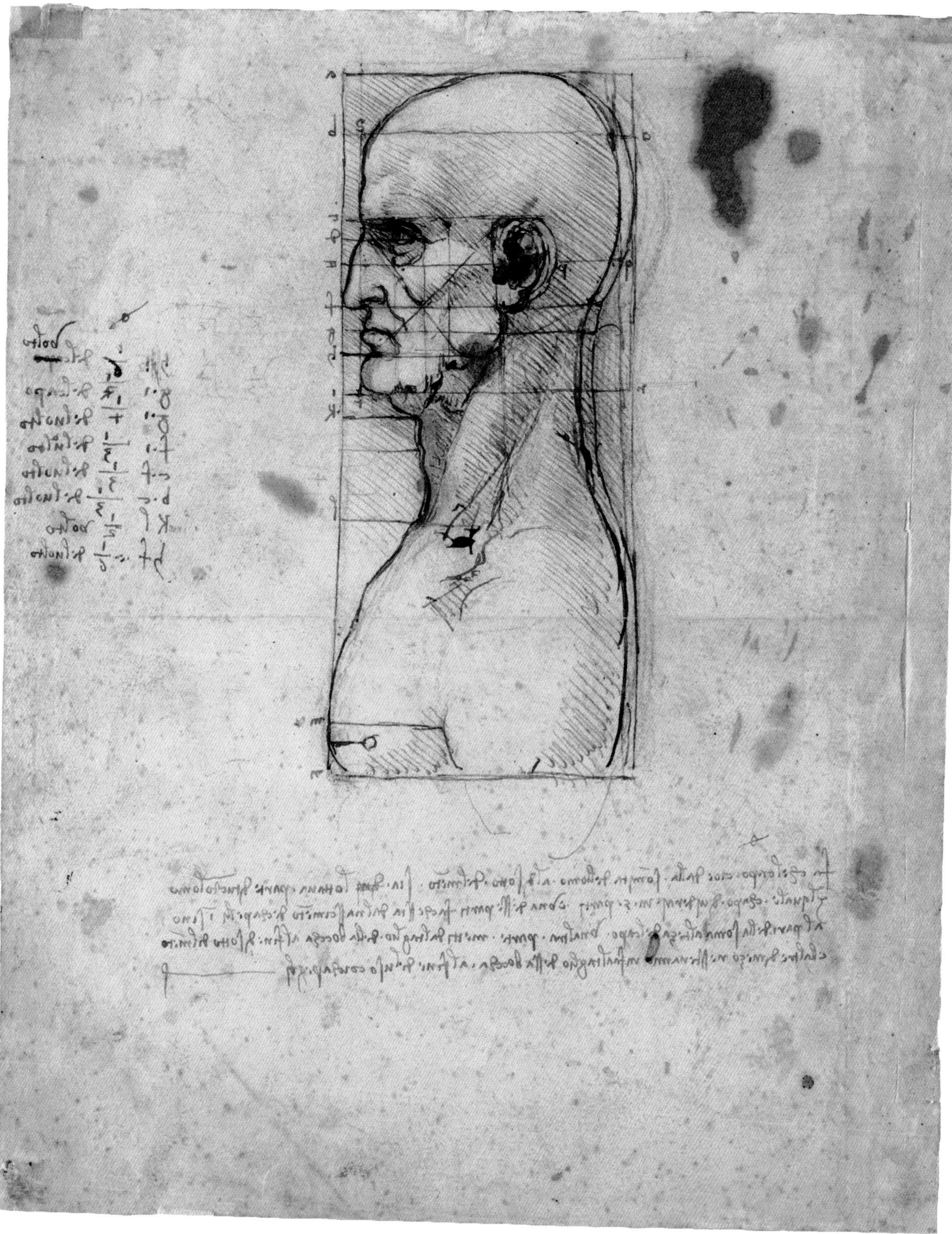

Plate 11
V. Inv. 236v Frame 33, c. 1489–1490, Pen and brown ink with metalpoint and stylus impressions, 280 x 222 mm (11 x 8¾ inches). Proportions of the head of a man. Gallerie dell'Accademia, Venice © 2014. Photo SCALA, Florence, courtesy of the Ministero Beni e Att. Culturali.

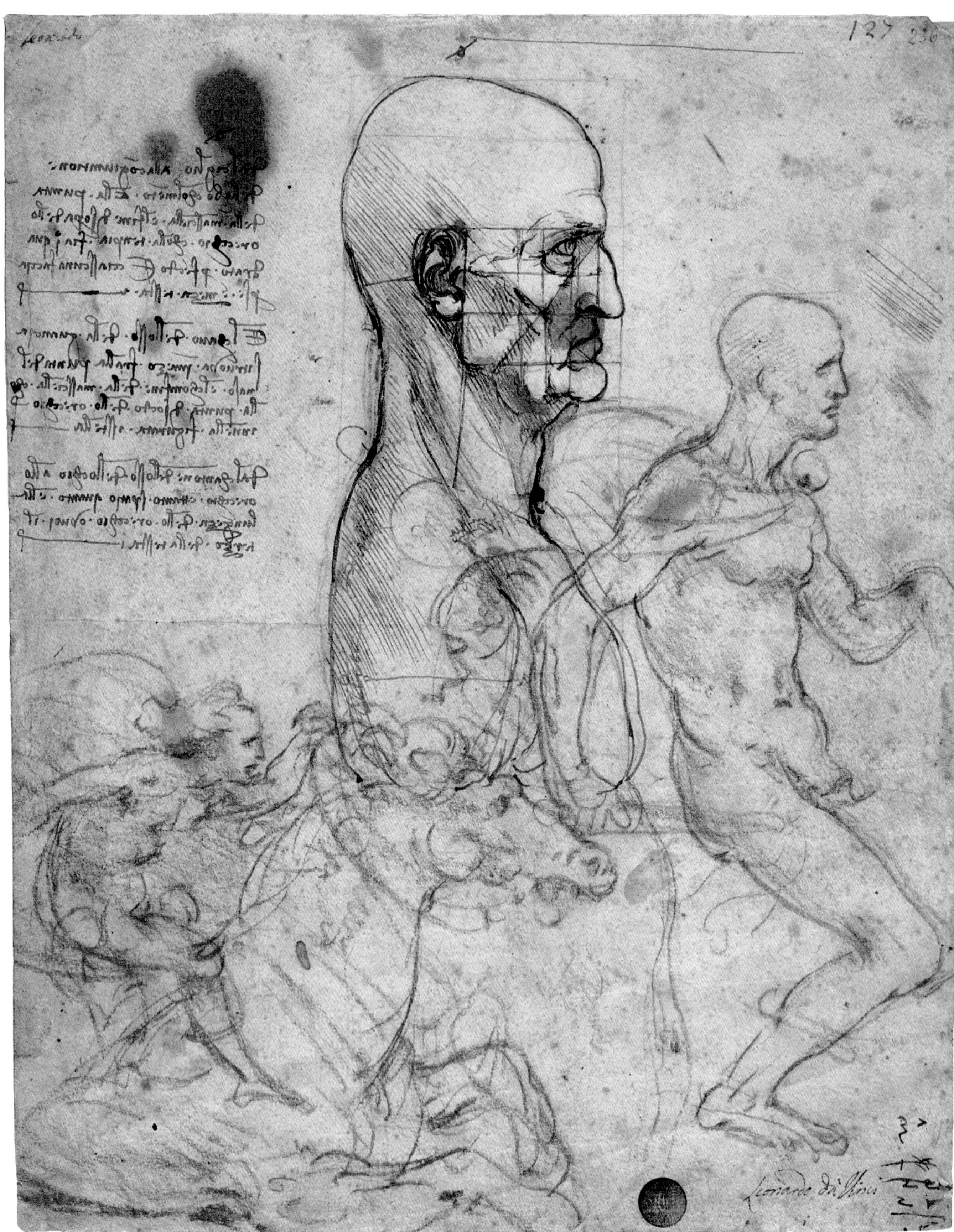

Plate 12
V. Inv. 236r, Frame 33, c. 1489–1490 and 1503–1504, Pen and brown ink with metalpoint and stylus impressions, 280 x 222 mm (11 x 8¾ inches). Proportions of the head of a man with two horsemen. Gallerie dell'Accademia, Venice © 2014. Photo SCALA, Florence, courtesy of the Ministero Beni e Att. Culturali.

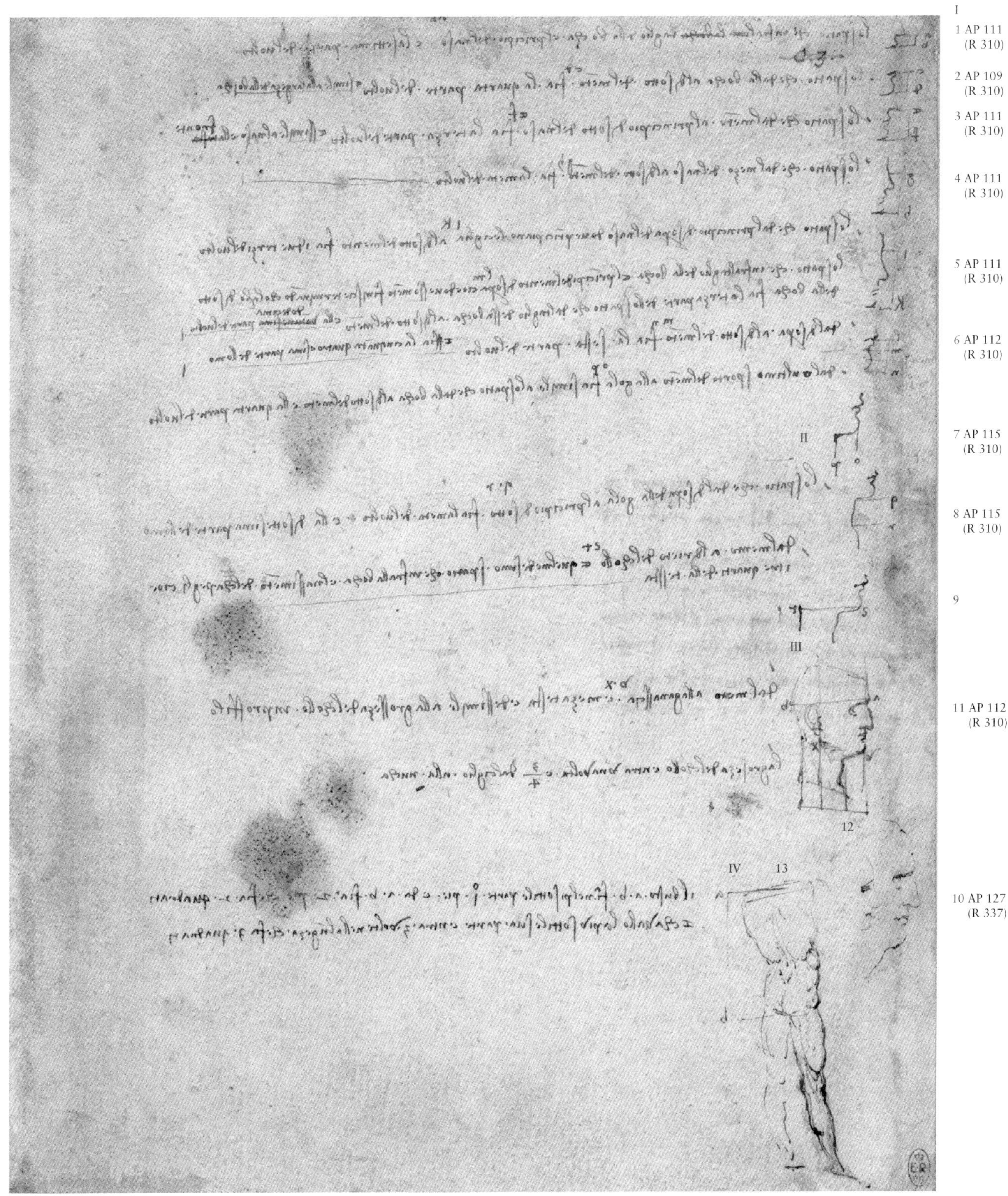

Plate 13
W. 12304, c. 1489–1490, Pen and brown ink, 264 x 215 mm (10 3/8 x 8 1/2 inches). Studies of the proportions of the head, face, neck, and torso. Royal Library, Windsor, Royal Collection Trust/ © Her Majesty Queen Elizabeth II 2014.

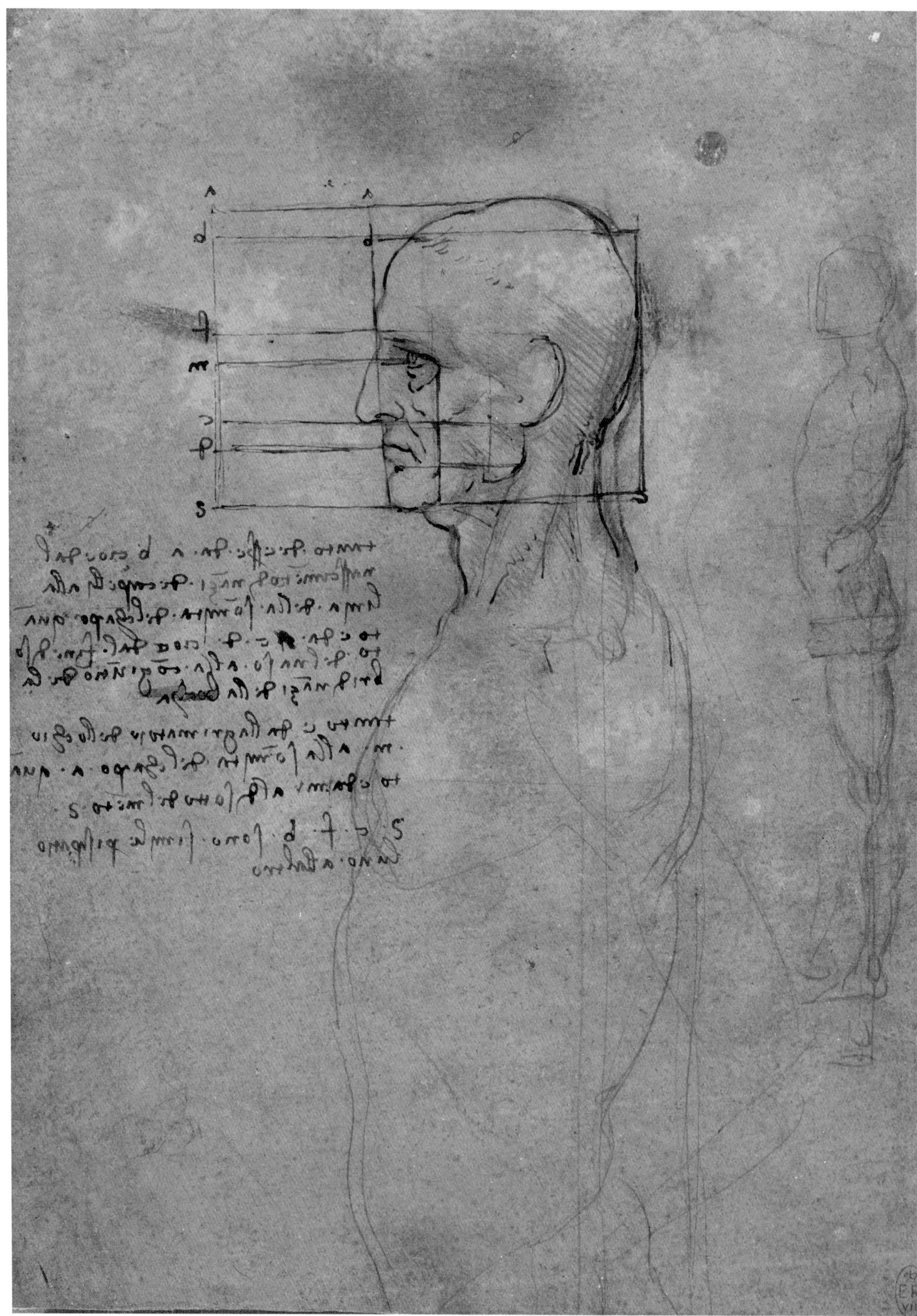

Plate 14
W. 12601, c. 1489–1490, Pen and brown ink on prepared blue paper, 213 x 153 mm (8⅜ x 6 inches). Study of proportions of the head and face. Royal Library, Windsor, Royal Collection Trust/ © Her Majesty Queen Elizabeth II 2014.

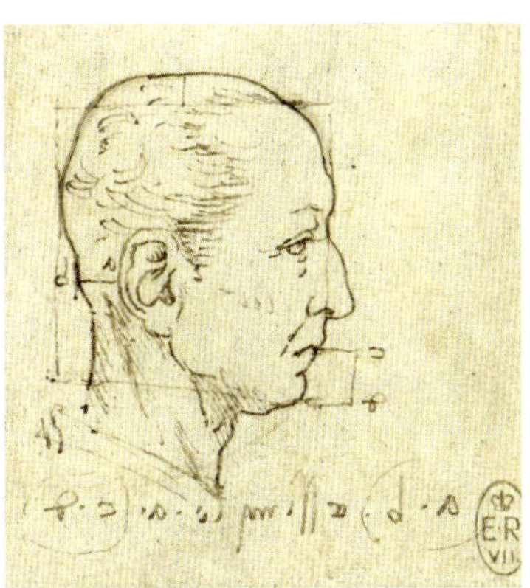

Plate 15
W. 12606, c. 1490–1492, Pen and brown ink, 56 x 50 mm (2¼ x 2 inches). Study of proportions of the head. Royal Library, Windsor, Royal Collection Trust/ © Her Majesty Queen Elizabeth II 2014.

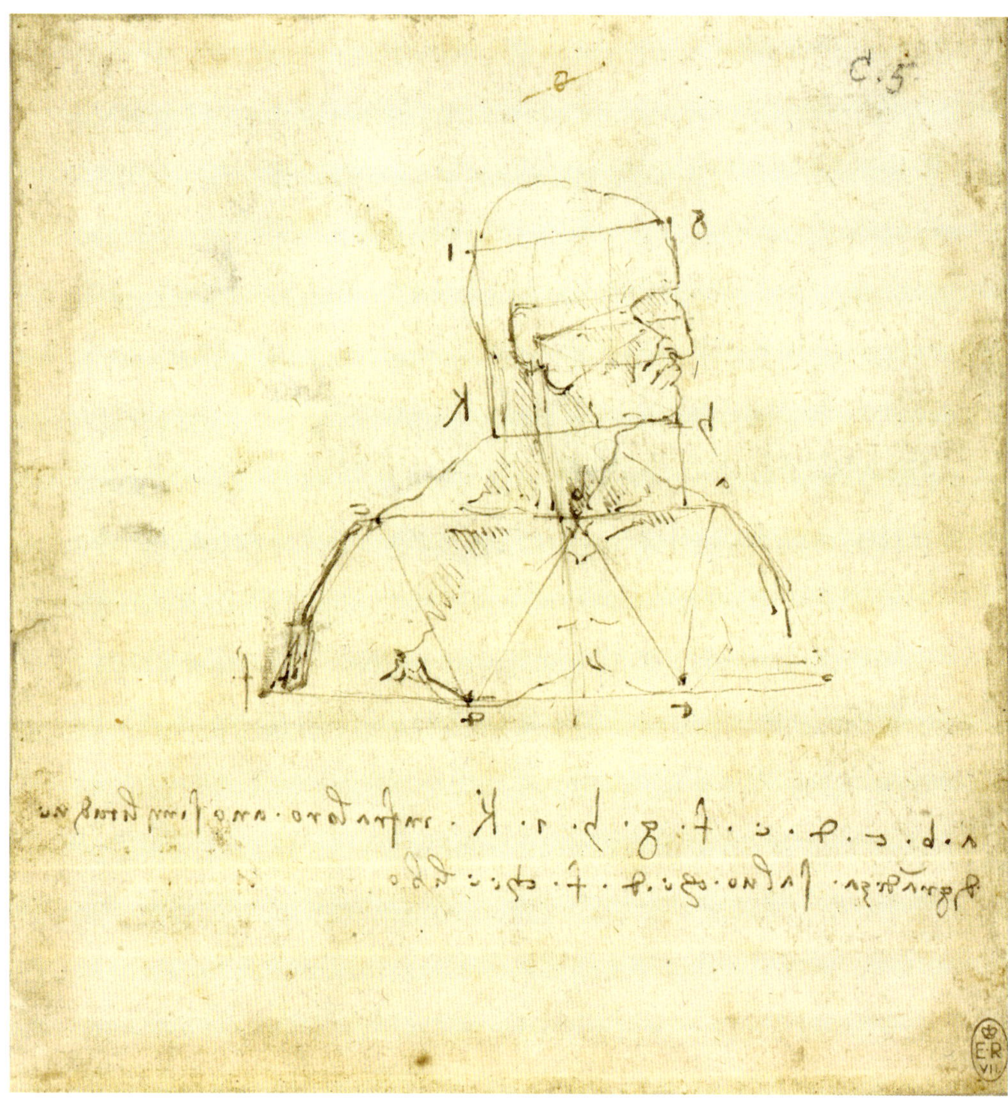

Plate 16
W. 12607, c. 1487, Pen and brown ink, 143 x 137 mm (5⅝ x 5⅜ inches). Study of proportions of the head and chest. Royal Library, Windsor, Royal Collection Trust/ © Her Majesty Queen Elizabeth II 2014.

AP 147

AP 148

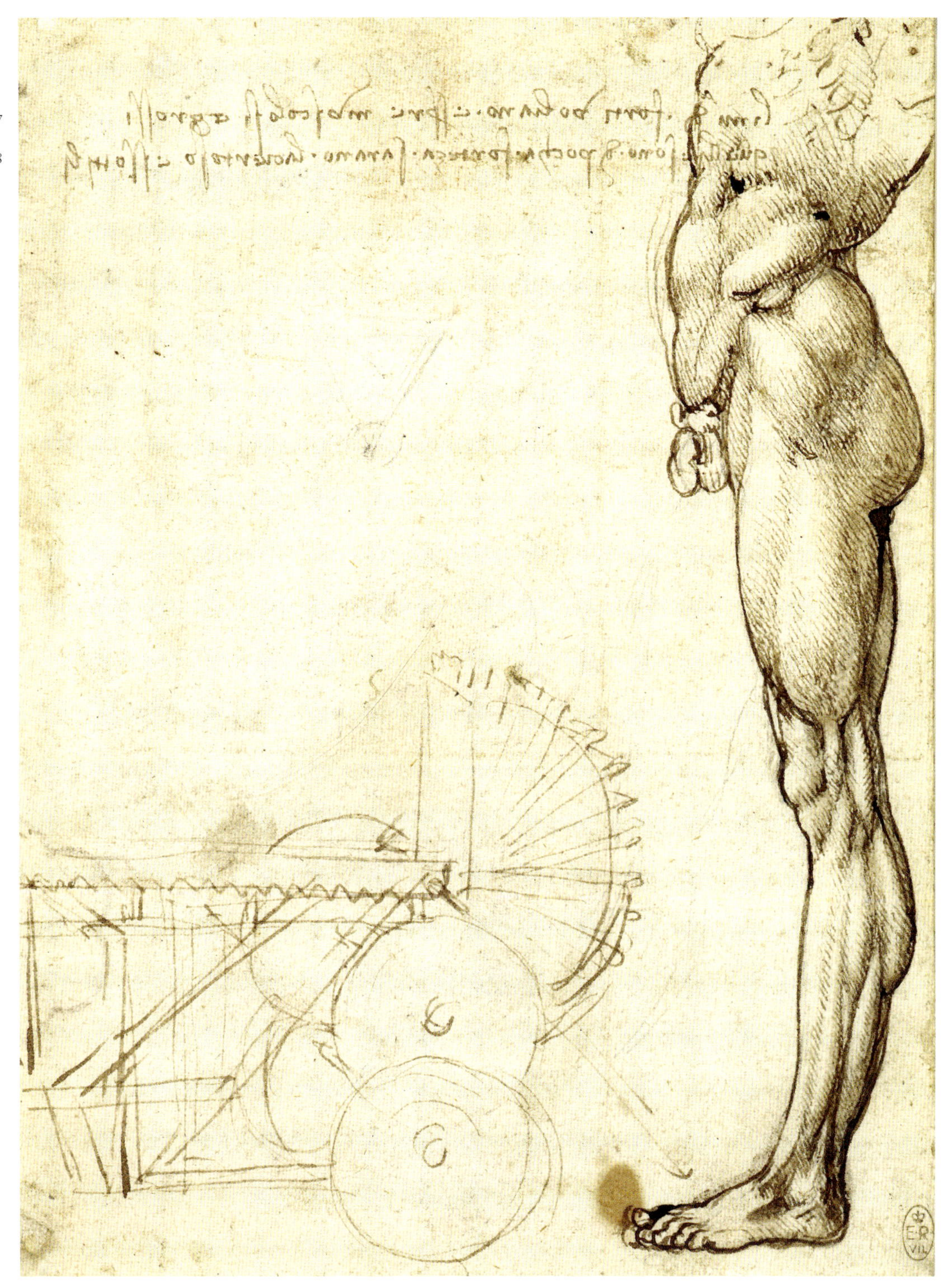

Plate 17

W. 12632, c. 1490, Pen and brown ink metal point, 191 x 144 mm (7½ x 5⅝ inches). Study of a robust, standing male nude in profile from chest to feet facing left. Royal Library, Windsor, Royal Collection Trust/ © Her Majesty Queen Elizabeth II 2014.

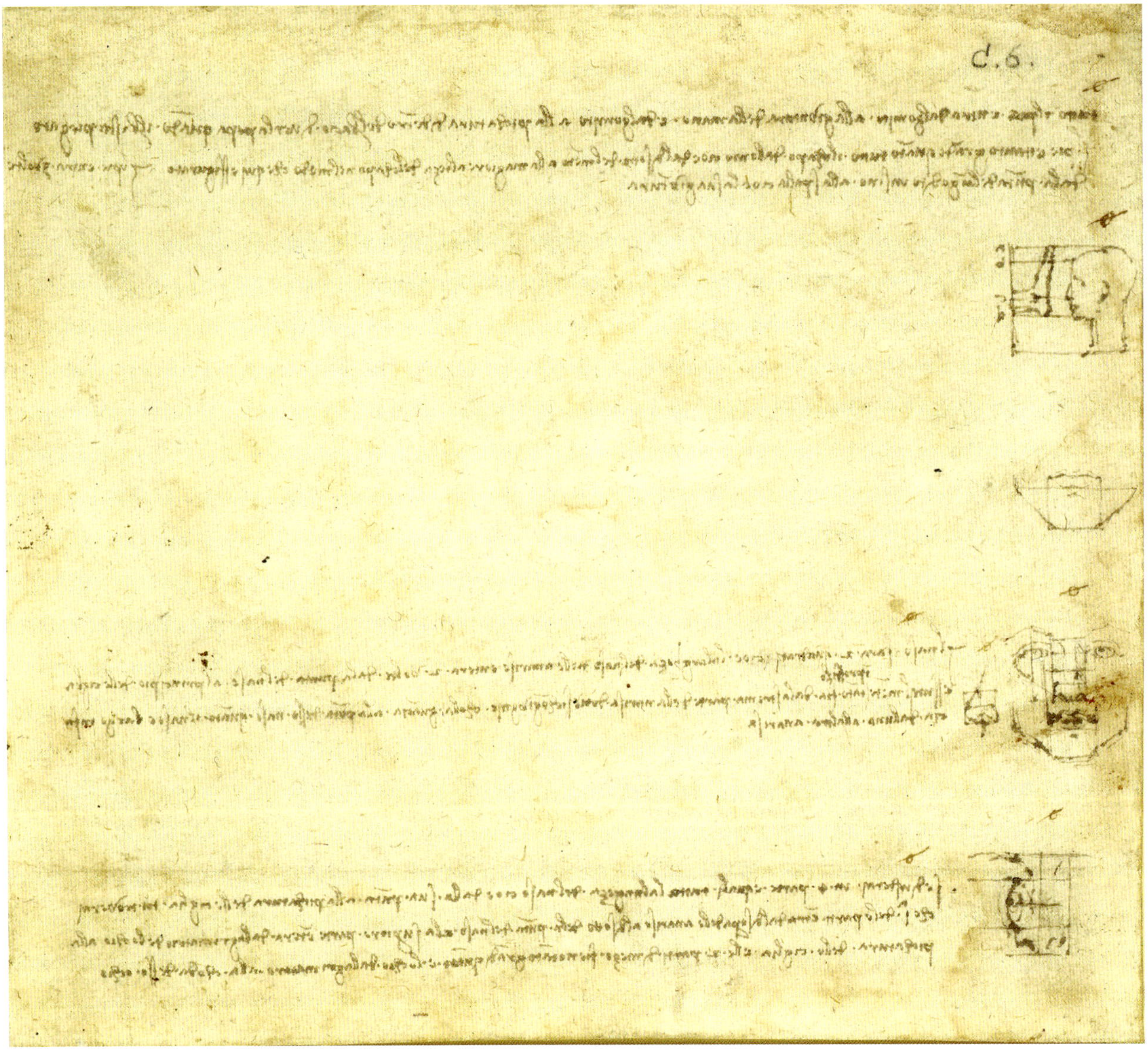

I AP 173
(R 327)

II AP 11
(R 321

III AP 11
(R 32

Plate 18
W. 19129, 1489–1490, Pen and brown ink, 150 x 169 mm (5⁷/₈ x 6⁵/₈ inches). Studies of the length of the foot as a module to measure the head and arm. Royal Library, Windsor, Royal Collection Trust/ © Her Majesty Queen Elizabeth II 2014.

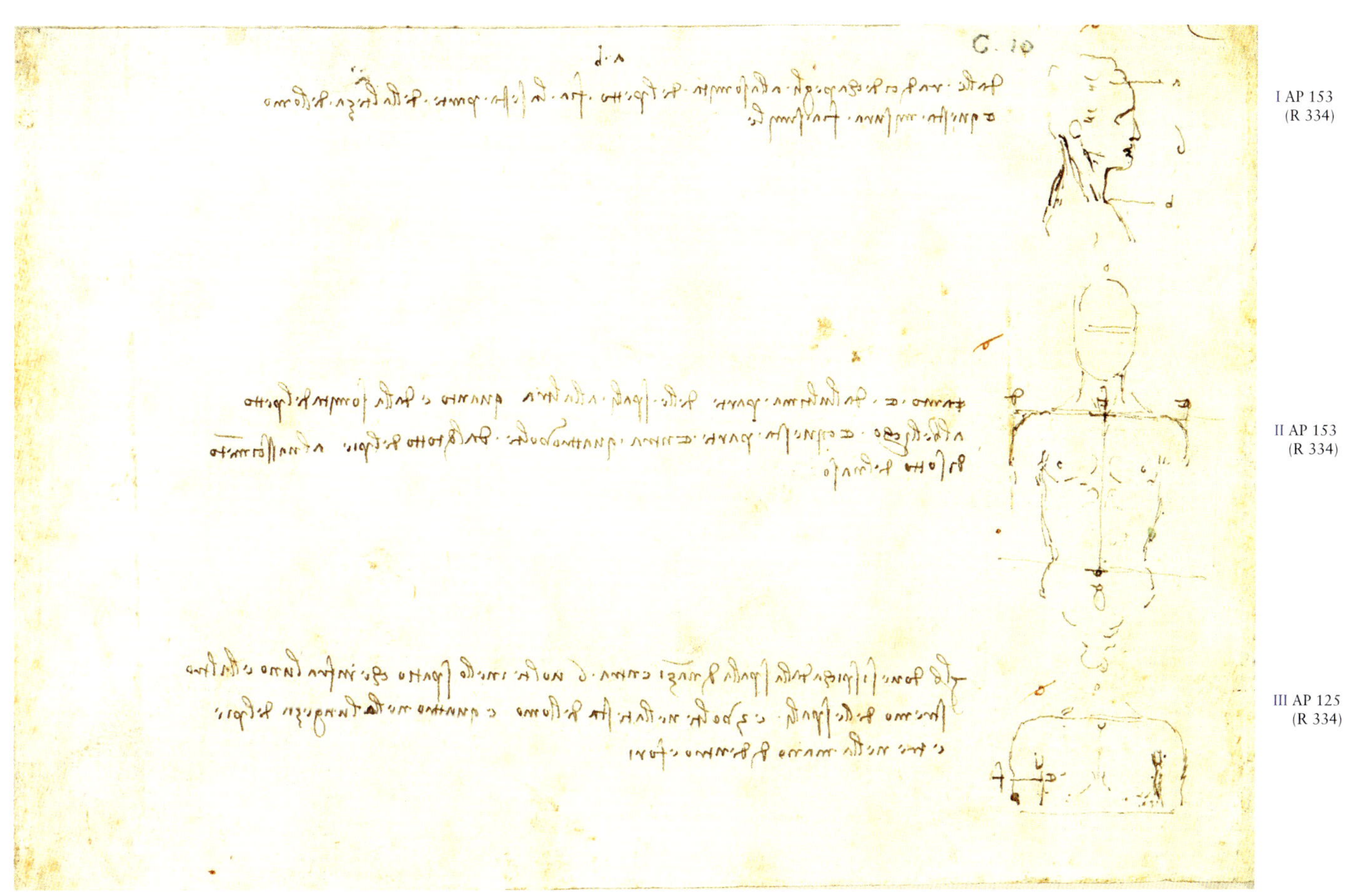

I AP 153 (R 334)

II AP 153 (R 334)

III AP 125 (R 334)

Plate 19
W. 19130a, c. 1490, Pen and brown ink, 146 x 218 mm (5¾ x 8½ inches). Study of the proportions of the head and torso. Royal Library, Windsor, Royal Collection Trust/ © Her Majesty Queen Elizabeth II 2014.

I AP 1
(R 3

AP 161 II
(R 335)

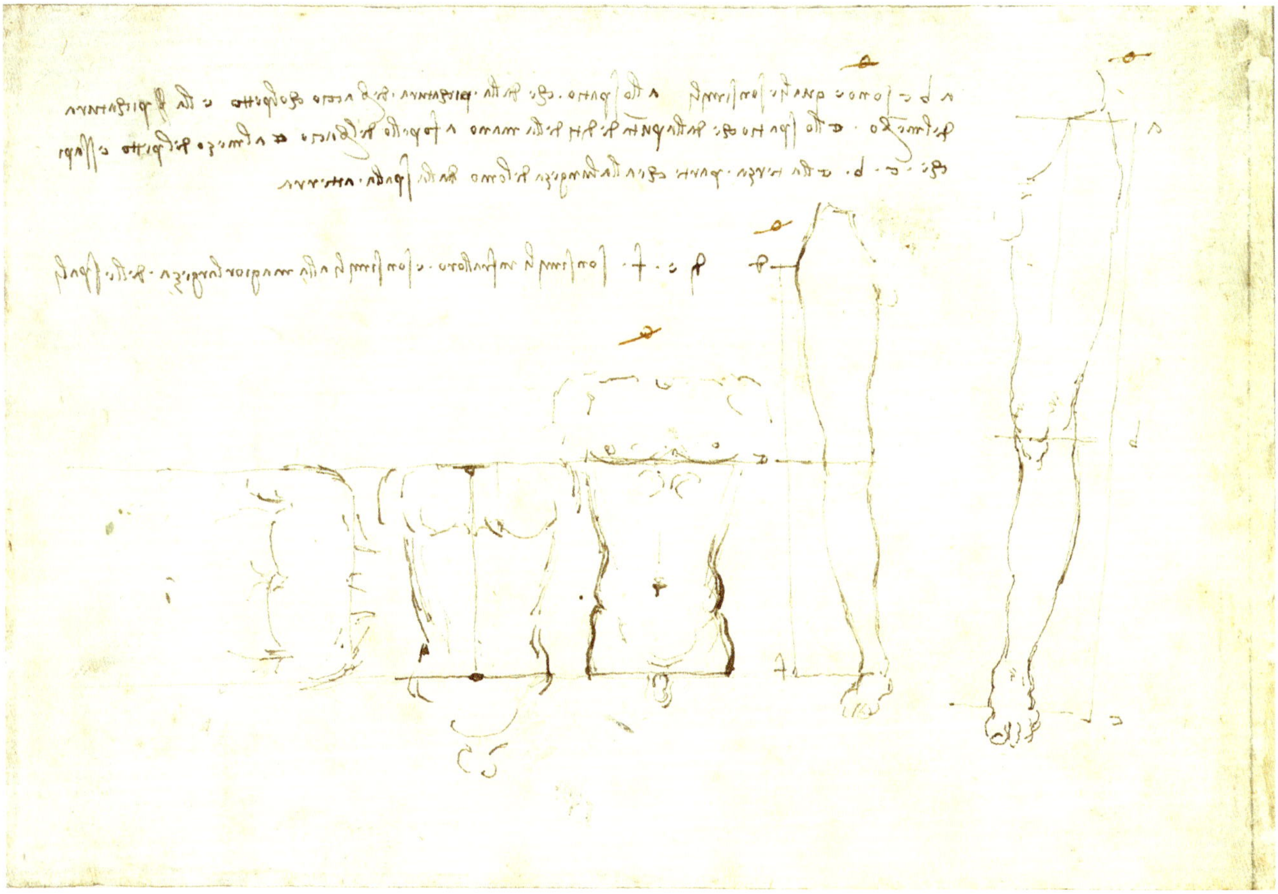

Plate 20
W. 19130b, c. 1490, Pen and brown ink, 146 x 218 mm ($5^{3}/_{4}$ x $8^{1}/_{2}$ inches). Studies of the proportions of the leg and torso in relation to each other. Royal Library, Windsor, Royal Collection Trust/ © Her Majesty Queen Elizabeth II 2014.

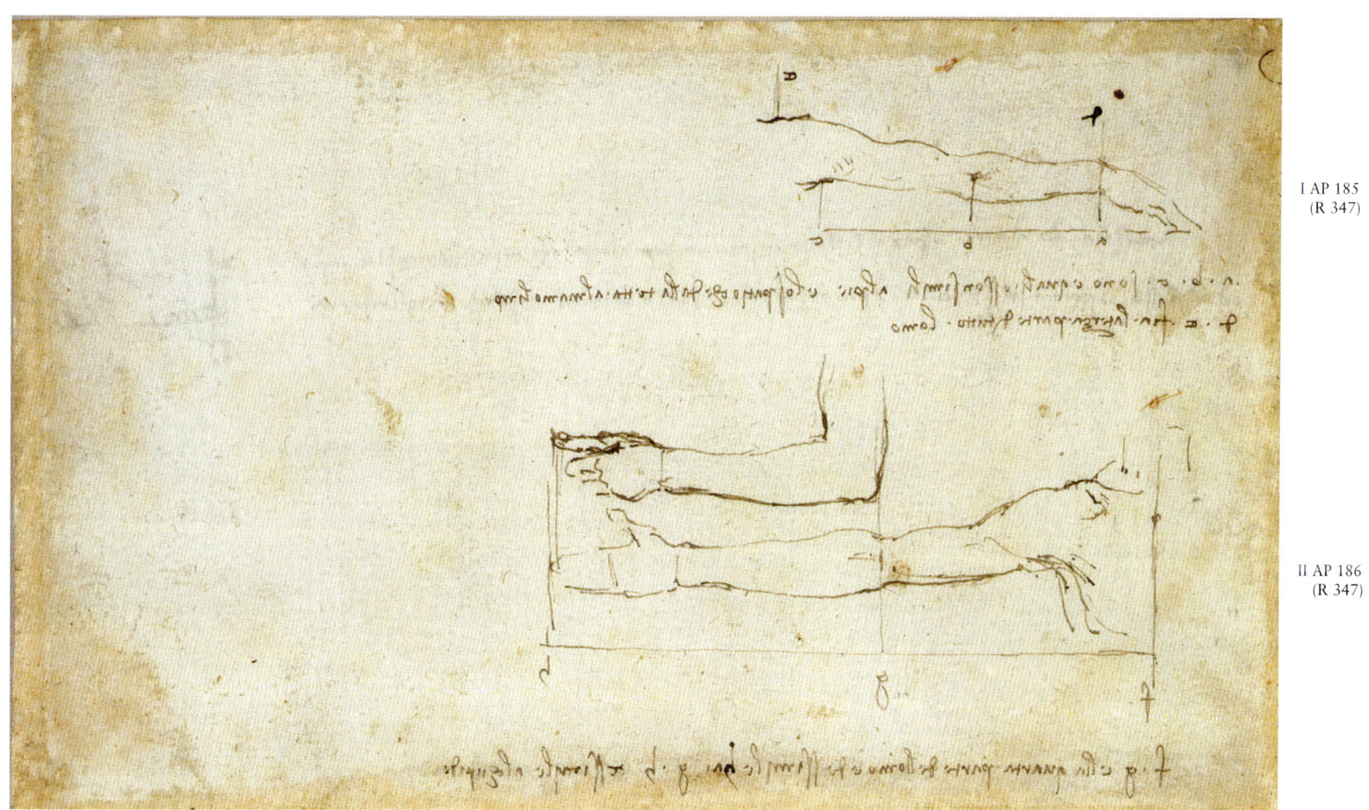

I AP 185
(R 347)

II AP 186
(R 347)

Plate 21
W. 19131a, c. 1490, Pen and brown ink, 128 x 210 mm (5 x 8¼ inches). Study of the proportions of the length of the arm. Royal Library, Windsor, Royal Collection Trust/ © Her Majesty Queen Elizabeth II 2014.

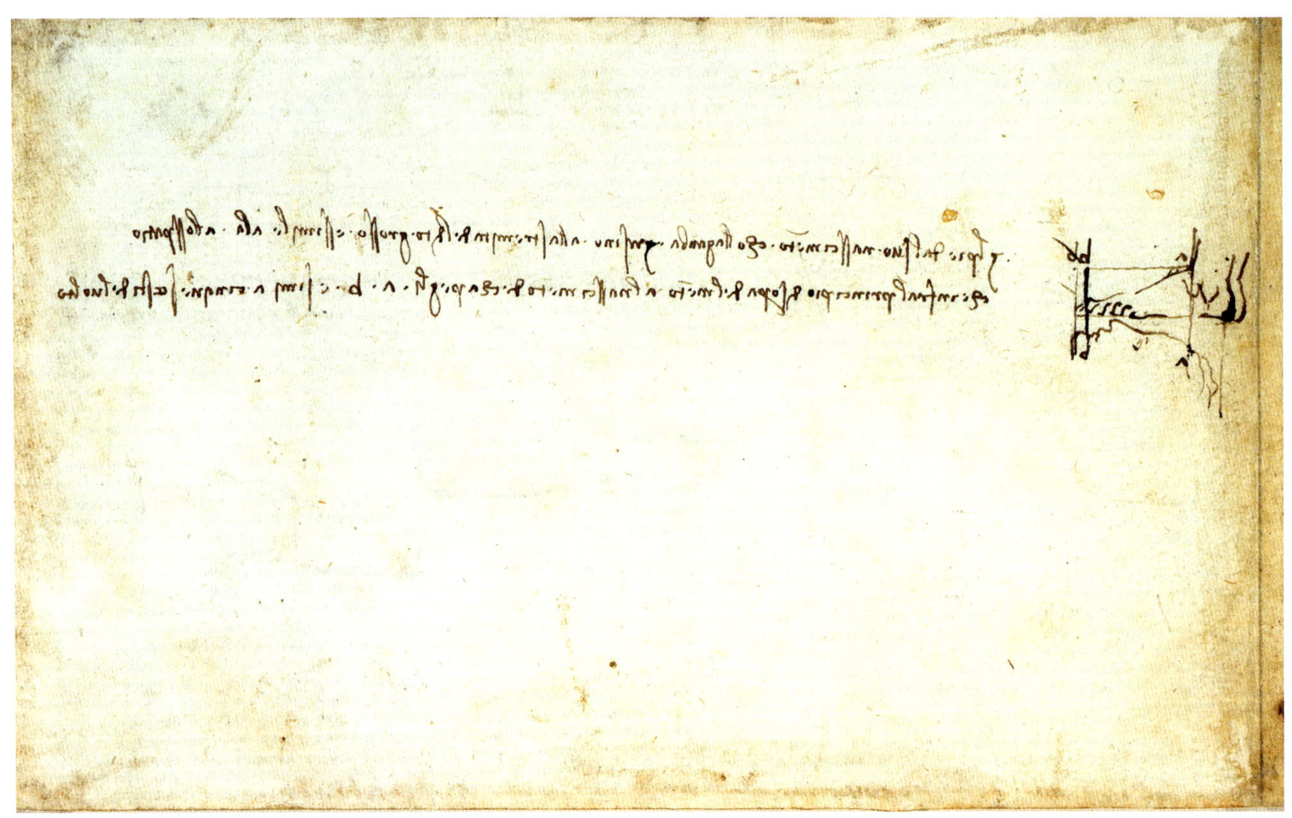

AP 11
(R 325

Plate 22
W. 19131b, c. 1490, Pen and brown ink, 128 x 210 mm (5 x 8$^{1}/_{4}$ inches). Study of the proportions of the foot to the face and head. Royal Library, Windsor, Royal Collection Trust/

I

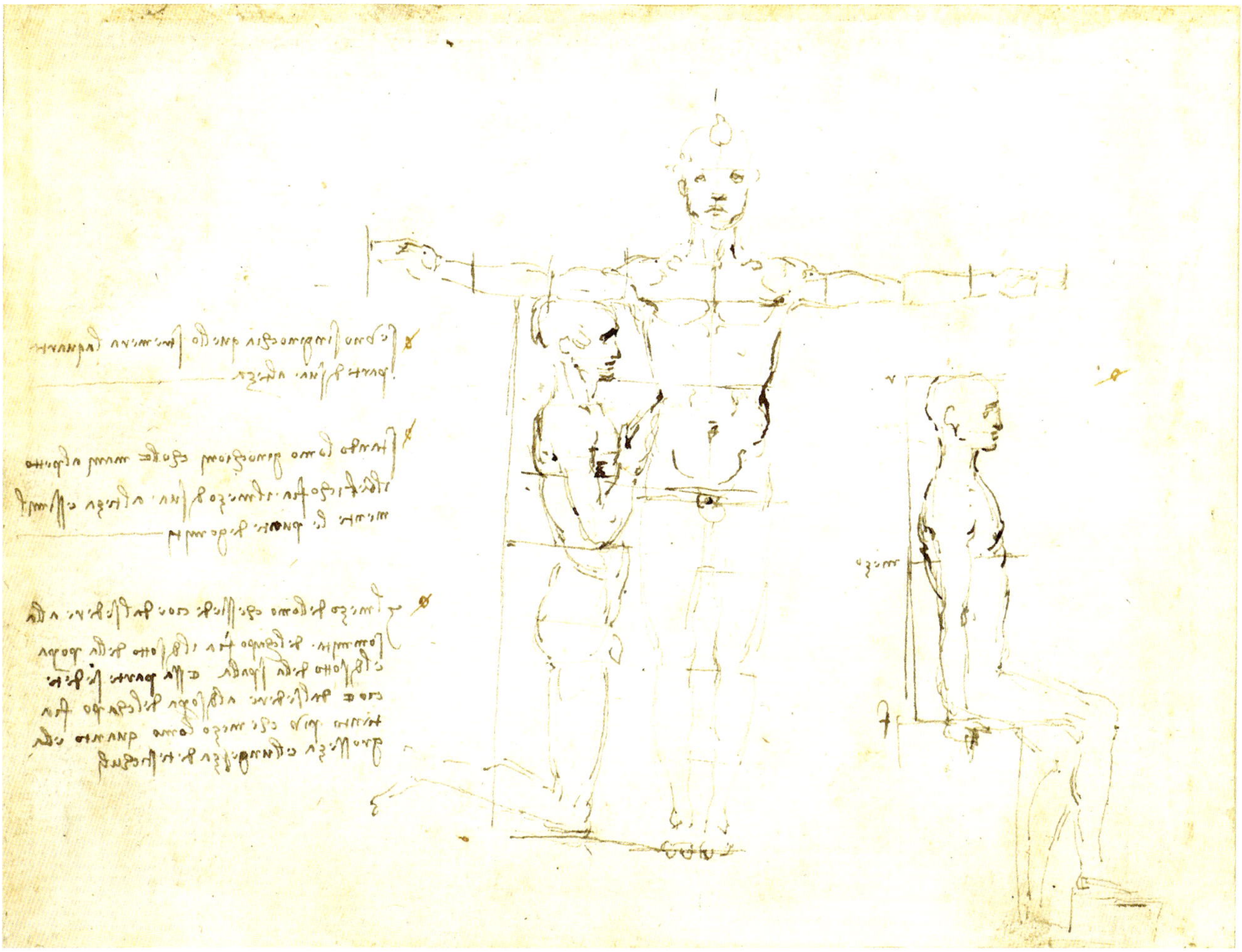

P 143
. 332)

II

P 144
. 332)

Plate 23
W. 19132a, c. 1490, Pen and brown ink, 160 x 218 mm (6¼ x 8½ inches). Studies of the body sitting, standing, and kneeling. Royal Library, Windsor, Royal Collection Trust/ © Her Majesty Queen Elizabeth II 2014.

I AP 1
(R 33

II AP
(R 3

Plate 24
W. 19132b, c. 1490, Pen and brown ink, 160 x 218 mm ($6^{1}/_{4}$ x $8^{1}/_{2}$ inches). Proportions of the torso and whole body. Royal Library, Windsor, Royal Collection Trust/ © Her Majesty Queen Elizabeth II 2014.

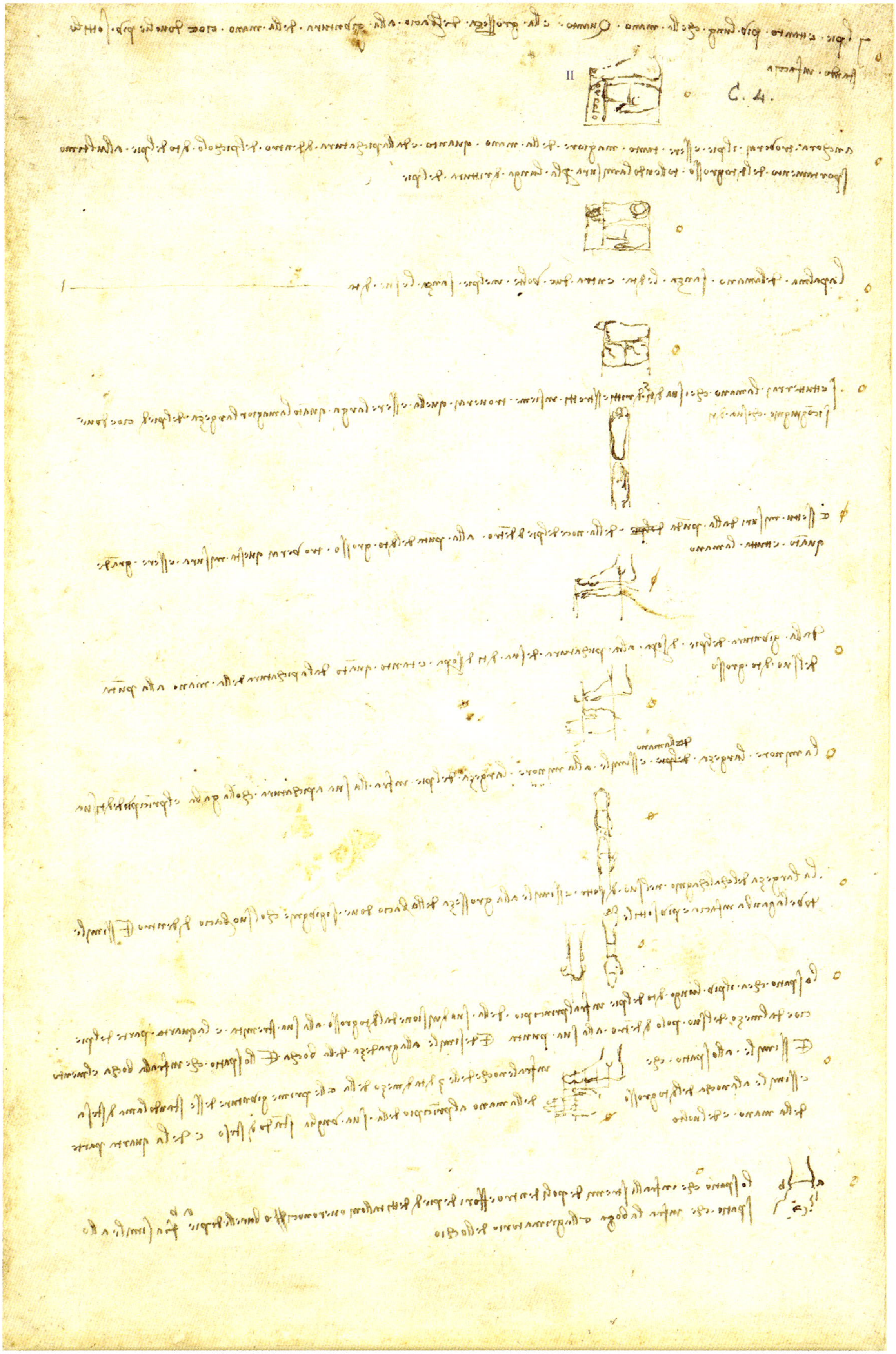

I AP 169 (R 324)

II

III AP 169 (R 324)

IV

V AP 169 (R 324)

VI AP 170 (R 324)

VII AP 170 (R 324)

VIII

IX AP 169 (R 324)

X AP 171 (R 324)

AP 191 (R 324)

XI AP 171 (R 324)

Plate 25
W. 19133a, c. 1490, Pen and brown ink, 303 x 206 mm (12 x 8¼ inches). Studies of the proportions of the hand and the foot. Royal Library, Windsor, Royal Collection Trust/ © Her Majesty Queen Elizabeth II 2014.

I AP 168
(R 322)

II AP 168
(R 322)

Plate 26
W. 19133b, c. 1490, Pen and brown ink, 303 x 206 mm (12 x 8¼ inches). Studies of proportions of the foot. Royal Library, Windsor, Royal Collection Trust/

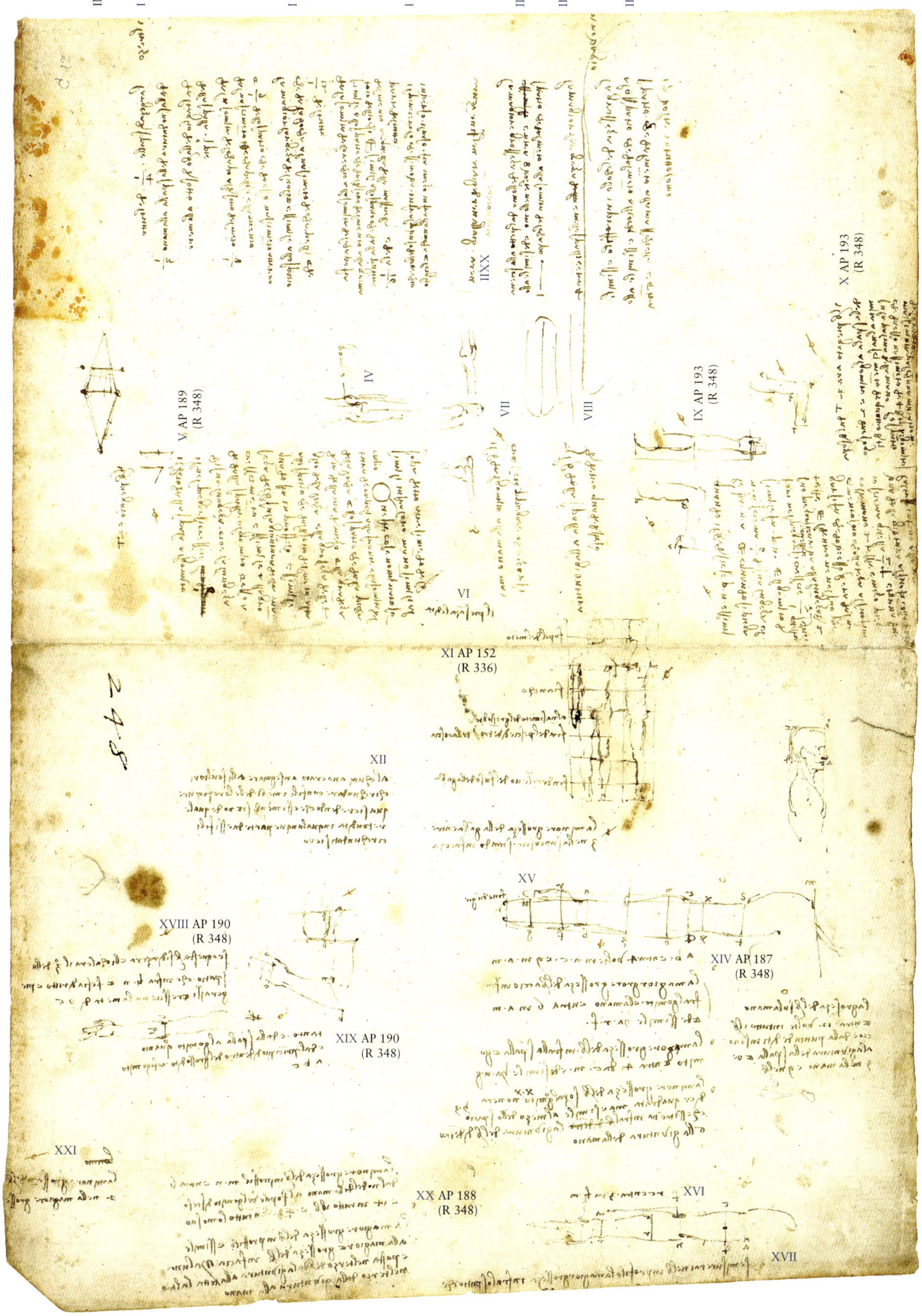

II Trezo
I AP 150 (R 340)
I AP 145 (R 317)
I AP 108 (R 317)
II AP 124 (R 341)
II AP 150 (R 341)
III AP 108 (R 317)
XXII
X AP 193 (R 348)
IV
VII
VIII
IX AP 193 (R 348)
V AP 189 (R 348)
VI
XI AP 152 (R 336)
XII
XV
XVIII AP 190 (R 348)
XIV AP 187 (R 348)
XIX AP 190 (R 348)
XIII AP 184 (R 348)
XXI
XX AP 188 (R 348)
XVI
XVII

Plate 27

W. 19134–19135, c. 1490, Folded in half, Pen and brown ink, 434 x 317 mm (17¹/₄ x 12¹/₂ inches). Studies of proportions of the head, arm, hand, torso, and whole body.

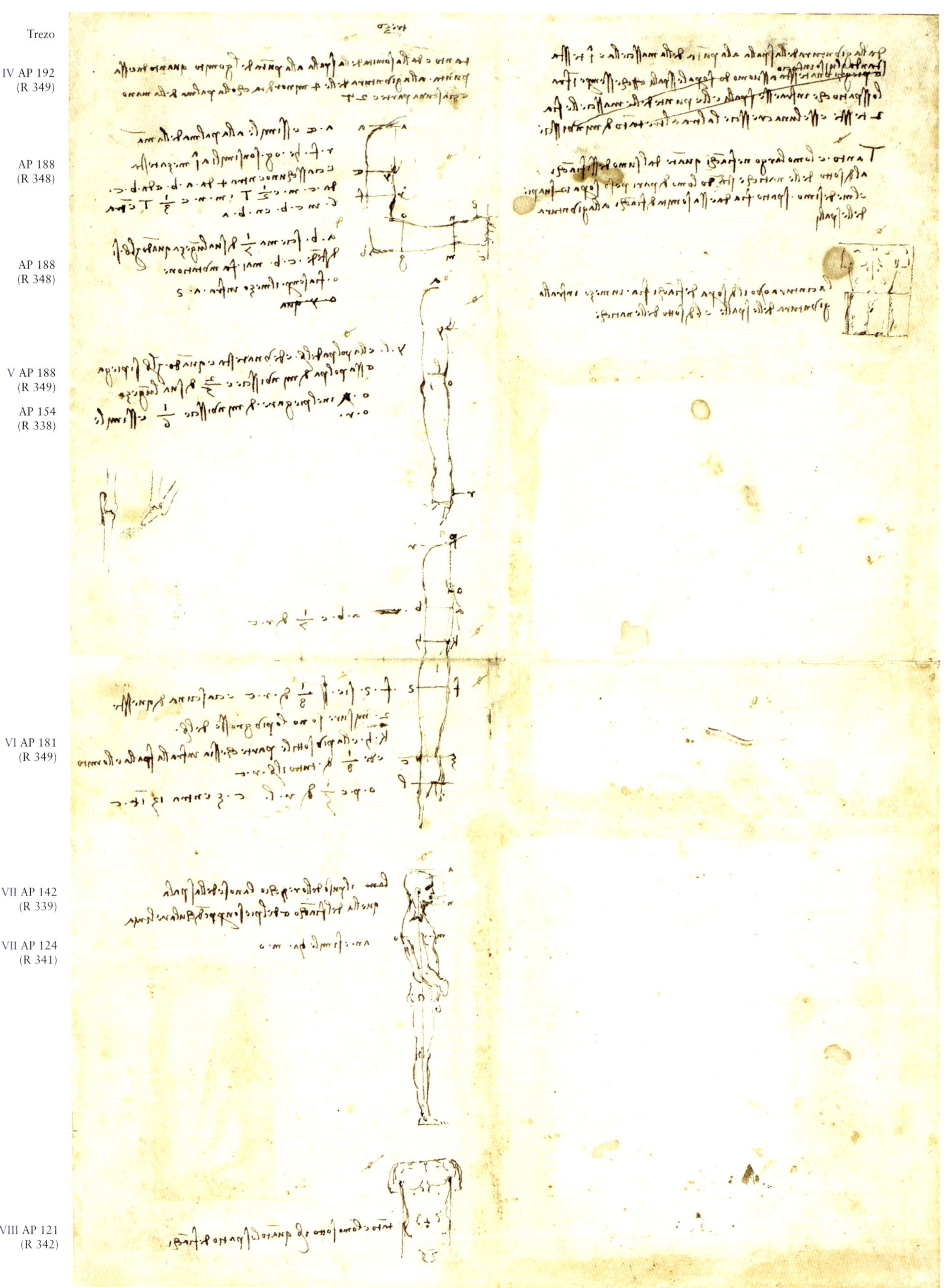

Plate 28

W. 19136–19139a, c. 1490, Folded in four, Pen and brown ink, 405 x 281 mm (16 x 11 inches). Proportions of the arm, torso, and leg. Royal Library, Windsor, Royal Collection Trust/ © Her Majesty Queen Elizabeth II 2014.

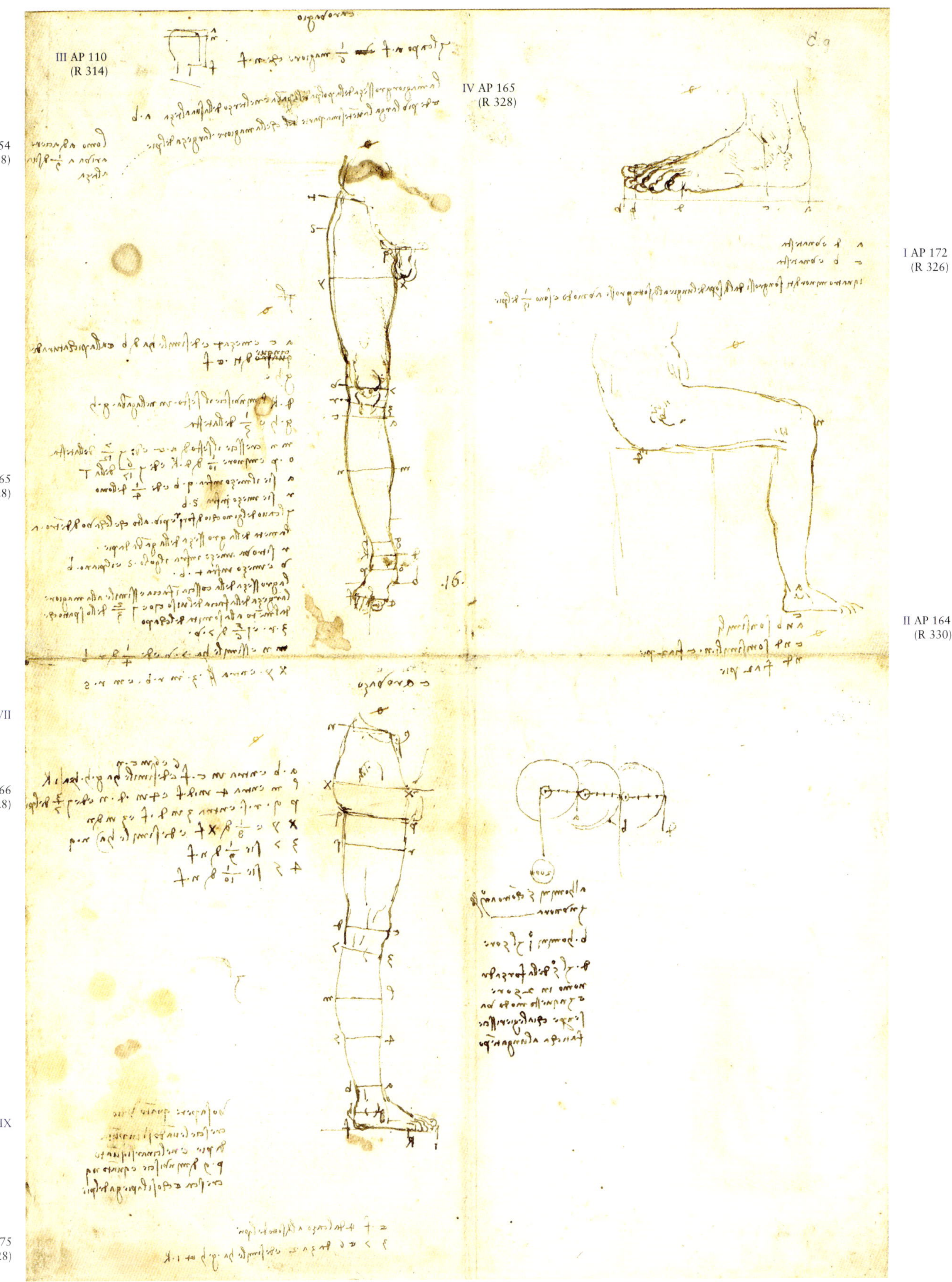

Plate 29
W. 19136–19139b, c. 1490, Folded in four, Pen and brown ink, 405 x 281 mm (16 x 11 inches). Proportions of the foot and the leg with a discussion of the force of man against a thousand pounds. Royal Collection Trust/ © Her Majesty Queen Elizabeth II 2014.

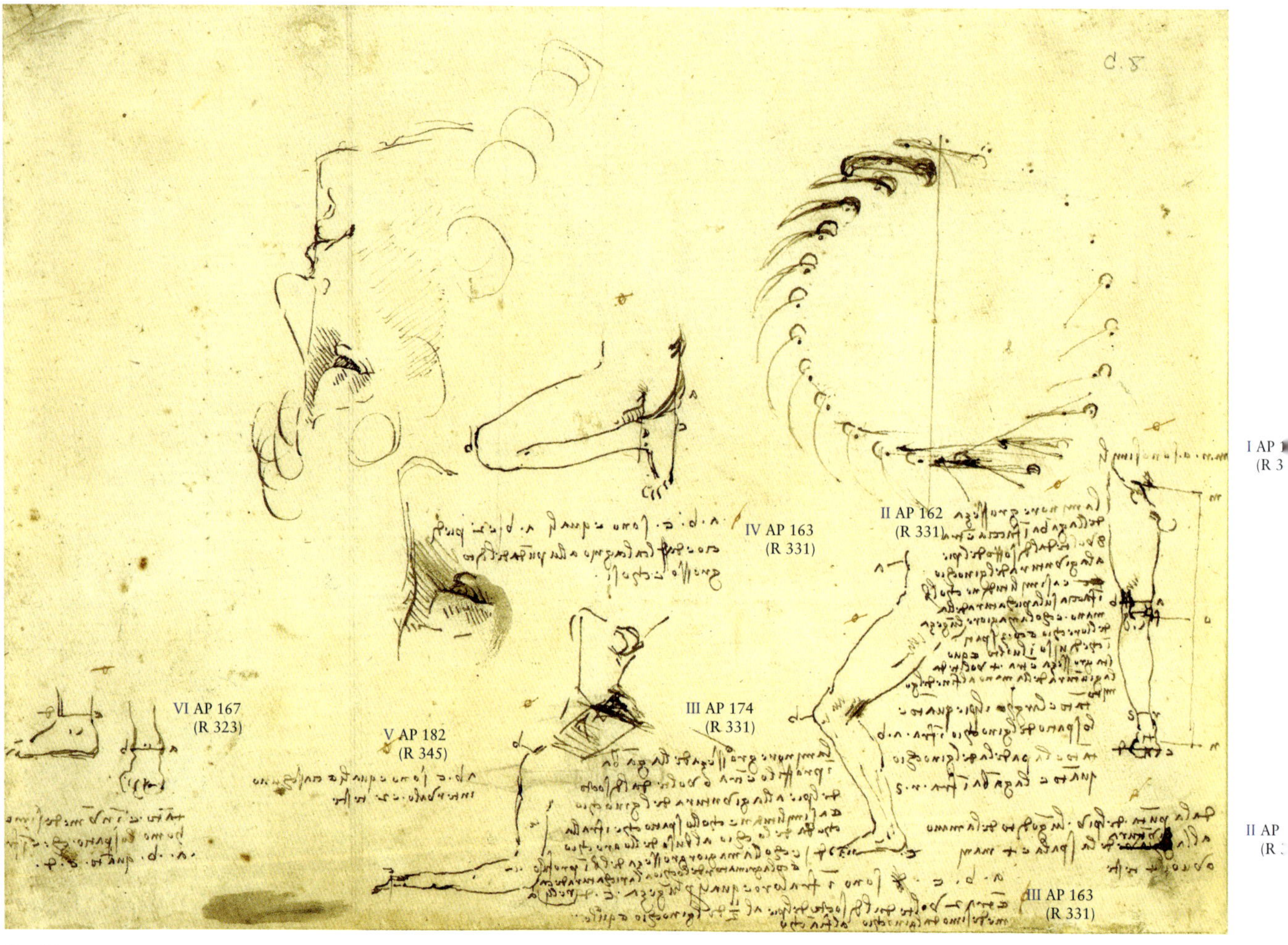

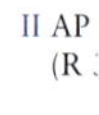

Plate 30
W. 19140, c. 1490, Pen and brown ink with traces of stylus, 203 x 279 mm (8 x 11 inches). Studies of the proportions of the face, leg, arm, and foot. Royal Library, Windsor, Royal Collection Trust/ © Her Majesty Queen Elizabeth II 2014.

Notes

Part Three. Thirty Drawings and Pages from Leonardo's Notebooks

[53] Richter, *The Literary Works of Leonardo da Vinci*, vol. I, R 4b, 112-113. As this quotation was quite long and both parts useful, I have divided it into two parts, R 4a and R 4b.

PART FOUR

A BRIEF HISTORY OF PROPORTIONAL STUDIES

Which is best, to draw from Nature or from the antique?

R 486

It is better to imitate [copy] the antique than modern work.

R 487[54]

CHAPTER NINE THE ANCIENT GREEKS AND THE IDEAL FORM

Throughout history, art has played an essential role in our understanding the past. Our knowledge of religious and cultural life and events of the past is based on literature and on visual records left by artists in the form of two- and three-dimensional works of art. These visual records inevitably reveal something of the human condition of those times, and until only recently, most of these images were based on the cultural representation of the human form. As visual ideas about the human condition evolved, artists' reliance on stylization gave way to a greater emphasis on reality in the human form, and along with this greater emphasis came standards of human proportion. Over the centuries, the pursuit to create a more realistic figure evolved into a desire to create the ideal human form.

Although we owe a great debt to the ancient Greeks in the development of human proportion, it was the Egyptians who, according to Dr. Paul Richer, developed the oldest text on record dealing with a system of proportion. They established a stylistically motivated canon for the human figure based on the length of the middle finger as a module, which constituted one-nineteenth of the total height of a man.[55] This system, however, was based less on proportional relationships and more on a grid of horizontal and vertical lines on which the parts of the figure were laid out from the soles of the feet to the hairline. For instance, the top of the knee could be found at horizontal grid line 6, the bottom of the buttocks at horizontal grid line 9, the hairline at grid line 19. Each square of the grid was equal to the length of the middle finger.

Bringing a greater naturalism to the human figure, while searching for the ideal human form, was the legacy left to us from the ancient Greeks. Influenced by the Greeks, artists in subsequent societies began to develop their own sets of standards to measure, and therefore render, the ideal human figure. In almost all Western art, these theories of human proportion were based on a mathematical relationship of parts of the body to the whole body.

Like the Egyptians, the early Greeks were motivated to develop ideas about proportion along stylistic and not naturalistic lines. Centuries of artistic evolution passed and numerous canons of proportional measurements were invented before the progression of naturalism unfolded. But it was not until the mid-fifth century BC that the sculptor Polycleitos developed the most famous, and the most lasting, of all of these canons. His treatise on proportion, entitled "Kanon," has survived only in a few fragmentary lines. One of them reads, "Perfection comes about little by little through many numbers."[56] The words reflect a mathematical relationship he devised using the parts of the body to construct the whole body. By themselves, the lines are insufficient evidence of a theory of proportion, until one sees the sculpture by Polycleitos, known as the *Doryphoros*, or Spear-Bearer. The bronze figure was created as a visual three-dimensional illustration for his written theory of proportion. Only fragments of the original figure remain, but there are numerous imitations reproducing both its proportions and posture. From many Roman copies of the *Doryphoros*, all of which rely heavily on the original sculpture, it is clear that Polycleitos's pedantic purpose had an enormous influence in antiquity. His sculpture and text were inextricably dependent on each other, and as Domenico Laurenza points out in his discussion of the influence of Polycleitos on Vitruvius, "in an age in which book illustration did not yet exist, the statue was the illustration of the treatise."[57] His achievement was of such magnitude that Pliny the Elder (first century AD) writes, "Polkleitos alone of men is deemed to have rendered art itself [that is, the theoretical basis of art] in a work of art."[58]

In the *Doryphoros*, Polycleitos set out to create the perfect statue based on the canon he formulated using numerical ratios laid out in his treatise. The second-century Roman physician Galen recognized this six centuries later and summarized the sculptor's theory by saying that beauty is found "in the commensurability of the parts, that is to say, of finger to finger, and all of the fingers to the palm and the wrist, and of these to the forearm to the upper arm, and of all the other parts to each other as set forth in the Canon of Polykleitos."[59]

One of the most perfect of these Roman copies of the *Doryphoros* is in the National Museum of Naples. The figure stands in a classic contrapuntal pose with the bulk of his weight on his right foot, the left foot slightly behind and lifted as if to take the next step. The head does not look straight ahead as in Archaic sculpture but is turned gently to the right in a three-quarter view. The right side of his pelvis is higher than the left side, while his right shoulder is lower than the left, a function of a perfectly articulated contrapuntal pose. His left hand is raised as if holding a spear upright or balancing it on his shoulder. In addition to these physical and character traits, the body is alive and in a state of transition. The posture of the figure is at once "intermediate between rest and movement, his physique and proportion between anorexia and corpulence, and his age between youth and manhood."[60] The *Doryphoros* is a paradigm of perfection not only because of its ideal proportions, but also because it defined the type of man the Greeks most admired, an athlete proficient in gymnastics, expert at handling weapons, and, most important, a man healthy and strong in both body and mind.

Vitruvius, the first-century-BC Roman architect and engineer, was surely familiar with the *Doryphoros* sculptural prototype and may have had access to the Polycleitos treatise. One thing is certain, Vitruvius relied heavily on Polycleitos when he outlined the proportions of the "well-formed" man in chapter 3 of his *Ten Books on Architecture*. While we don't know the exact order used by Polycleitos, whether he goes from the general to the specific or the specific to the general, we do know that he understood the finger as the smallest unit or module of proportion. Vitruvius understood this also, but he began his measurements with the overall proportions of the whole body and then moved on to the smaller ratios. He uses the face, the head, the foot, and other parts of the body as modules to immediately establish the height of a figure, eventually ending with mathematical theories in support of these proportional ratios. He progresses from the general to the specific. Leonardo's articulation of the individual parts of the body as units to comprehend the proportions of the whole body came directly from Vitruvius, just as Vitruvius received his information directly from Polycleitos. Unlike Vitruvius, Leonardo starts with the smaller units as simple building blocks within the figure, eventually leading up to the length of the entire figure. He progresses from the specific to the general. (See Appendix II, Texts, 2. Leonardo's reading of Vitruvius, and 3. Vitruvius's text.)

From Leonardo to modern times, the historic purpose underlying this compulsive artistic drive to comprehend the "rules" of proportion has been twofold. The first, the loftier of the two, is to make a human figure as realistic as possible, and in so doing to create an image filled with grace and elegance, an "ideal" figure of harmonic proportions. This idealization of beauty based on harmony and order is the ultimate aim of artists, designed to transcend the ordinary and bring the viewer one step closer to divinity. The secondary aim, while seemingly more practical and less exalted, is what enables the artist to achieve the first; it is to develop a complete understanding of the guidelines for the correct proportions of the figure. Thus, the artist learns the "rules" so they become second nature, freeing him to concentrate on other aspects of artistic creation. The concept of "freedom through discipline" was meant to allow the artist to attain the ultimate freedom while in the act of creation. Anyone who has ever attempted to draw the figure, and struggled to "get all of the parts right," will know exactly what is meant here. Having knowledge of the measurements of the figure provides the artist with a free hand and mind to develop and express his own sense of taste and humanity.

Notes

Chapter Nine. The Ancient Greeks and the Ideal Form

[54] Richter, *The Literary Works of Leonardo da Vinci*, vol. I, R 486, 303; R 487, 304.

[55] Dr. Paul Richer, *Artistic Anatomy* (New York: Watson-Guptill Publishers, 1971), 179.

[56] Thomas Gordon Smith, *Vitruvius on Architecture* (New York: Monacelli Press, 2003), 27.

[57] Domenico Laurenza, "The Vitruvian Man by Leonardo: Image and Text," *Quarderni d'italianistica*, XXVII, no. 2 (2006): 49.

[58] J.J. Pollitt, trans., *The Art of Ancient Greece: Sources and Documents* (New York: Cambridge University Press, 1990), 75.

[59] Helen Gardner, *Gardner's Art Through the Ages*, ed. Fred Kleiner, Christian Mamiya, Richard Tansey, Eleventh Edition (Belmont, Calif.: Thomson Wadsworth Publisher, 2001) 126.

[60] Thomas Gordon Smith, *Vitruvious on Architecture*, 27, footnote 68, citing Andrew Stewart, *Greek Sculpture: An Exploration* (New Haven: Yale University Press, 1990), 160–161.

Concave mirrors
the books from Venice
Italian and Latin Vocabulary
Bohemian knives
Vitruvius

philosophy of Aristotle
Messer Ottaviano Palavicino for his Vitruvius
go every Saturday to the hot bath where you will see naked men…

R 1421[61]

CHAPTER TEN
LEONARDO'S *VITRUVIAN MAN*

Leonardo was constantly making lists. The notes on the previous page are part of a larger list of things to buy, books to borrow, people to see, and events to remember. The items are neatly arranged in three columns on the inside cover of a small pocket book measuring 6 x 4¹/₈ inches, designated as MS. F, at the Institut de France, in Paris (Plate 7).

The writing is very small, some of it in sanguine pencil, written over in pen and brown ink to make it permanent. Vitruvius's name appears along with various other items in the far left corner and under it Leonardo writes, "Messer Ottaviano Pallavicino pel suo Vetruvius" ([see] Mr. Ottaviano Pallavicino for his [copy of] Vitruvius's [Ten Books on Architecture]). Leonardo's relationship to Ottaviano is unclear, but he must have known him well enough to borrow his copy of the Vitruvian manuscript. Opposite the list, to the right, on the first page of the book, is the inscription "Cominciato a Milano addi 12 di Setembre 1508" (Begun in Milan on September 12, 1508).

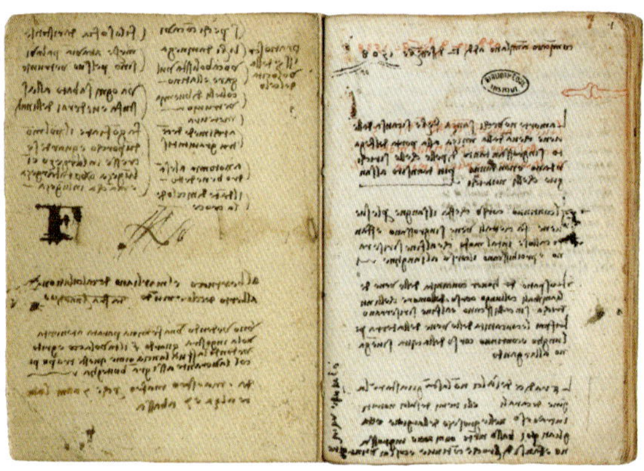

Detail, Plate 7, Ms F, Bibliothéque de l'Institut de France, Paris

It had to have been a rather valuable, hand-copied manuscript, because the first printed editions did not appear until 1511, and presumably, it was a manuscript copied in the vernacular (the "vulgar" Italian), because Leonardo could read neither Latin nor Greek. Why Leonardo would have wanted, or needed, to see a copy of the Vitruvius manuscript is unclear. He was already well acquainted with the book, or at least that portion of the book's teachings which inspired his drawing of the famous figure inscribed in a circle and a square, *The Vitruvian Man*. It established, in both word and image, the core of his theories on human proportion, as well as a visual analysis of the Vitruvian text. What is important here is how Leonardo first learned of Vitruvius's book before he asked to see Pallavicino's copy, because that iconic drawing, probably the most famous drawing in the world, was created by Leonardo in 1490, some eighteen years earlier.

Vitruvius's *Ten Books on Architecture*

Marcus Vitruvius Pollio, the famous architect and engineer, lived and worked in Rome in the last century before Christ, c. 90 to 20 BC.[62] Toward the end of his life, in about the mid-20s BC, he presented to Augustus Caesar ten written scrolls containing everything he knew and had learned from the ancient Greeks about architecture. Together with his own practical architectural experience, Vitruvius merges knowledge from various Greek treatises collected from his own extensive library to create the most informative and comprehensive set of ten books on architectural practice and design ever written in antiquity.[63] In the preface of Book VII, Vitruvius lists a bibliography of twenty-six Greek architectural treatises from which much of his information came.[64] Although his *Ten Books on Architecture* comes down to us without any illustrations (it is thought that there may have been ten illustrations in the original), it is still our most authoritative source on ancient architecture and the only such source to have survived from ancient times. The ten books cover a myriad of topics (not only architectural), beginning with the education of architects and ending with architectural contracts and descriptions of machines and tools with which to build.

The scrolls were intended as a guide to aid in the proper education and practice of young architects at a time when, Vitruvius felt, the lessons and knowledge learned from the ancients were being lost. He had hoped to revive the grandeur and stability of Hellenistic architecture by reestablishing the rules and ideals of the past. Vitruvius's book continues to be, in Thomas Gordon Smith's words, "the most complete and authentic source for cataloguing the elements, proportioning systems, and ideals underlying the classical architectural system."[65]

In defining the essence of sound architecture as "integrity, strength, function, and beauty,"[66] he stressed an understanding of building materials, the essential features and character of the three great architectural orders, the Doric, Ionic, and Corinthinian, and the elements of proportion. In his treatise, Vitruvius describes the six most important principles necessary in resolving issues of architectural design. They are listed in Latin as: *Ordinatio, Symmetria, Dispositio, Eurythmia, Decor,* and *Distributio.* (For a thorough and illuminating explanation of these six principles, see Thomas Gordon Smith's *Vitruvius on Architecture.*)[67]

For the purpose of our discussion, only the first two, *Ordinatio* and *Symmetria,* concern us. Each of these is a method used to determine numerical ratios to calculate the proportions of small-scale elements to large elements in the design of a building.[68] *Ordinatio,* Smith writes, "is...the basis for proportional relationships based on the module that serves as the common denominator for a complex whole."[69] *Symmetria* "is the relationship between the modular unit and the figure by which it is multiplied or divided to arrive at the dimensions of the whole."[70] Implied here is not the conventional meaning of symmetry, where one side is the exact and perfect duplicate of the other, but a secondary meaning: an ideal balance of form represented by the correspondence of its individual parts in proportion to all other parts, in the service and fulfillment of a greater sense of beauty.[71]

As Vitruvius explains (for Vitruvius's full text, see Appendix II, section 3):

> The design of a temple depends on symmetria, the principle of which must be most carefully observed by the architect. They are due to proportion, in Greek, analogia. Proportion is a correspondence among the measures of the members of an entire work, and of the whole to a certain part selected as standard. From this result the principles of symmetria. Without symmetria and proportion there can be no principles in the design of any temple; that is, if there is no precise relation between its members, as in the case of those of a well shaped man.[72]

While the main topic of Book III is the building of Ionic temples, Vitruvius begins with a definition of *symmetria* and how the concept may be used to derive the ideal proportions of the human form. In praising several of the great Greek artists of ancient times he mentions Polycleitos, on whose *Doryphoros* (Spear-Bearer) Vitruvius probably based his ratios of human proportion. His codification of these rules was the culmination of the "Greek aesthetic convention" of defining "the ideal proportions of the human body."[73] In establishing the relationship between architecture and the human form, he unknowingly laid the basis for humanism and the Renaissance centuries before they flourished.

The Supposed "Rediscovery" of Vitruvius's Text

What happens to the Vitruvian text is a complicated and interesting story and is somewhat beyond the scope of our purpose here. However, some illumination of its "rediscovery" and its profound influence during the fourteenth and fifteenth centuries will bring us closer to an understanding of Leonardo's drawing.

During the mid-twentieth century, modern architectural historians disproved the popular notion that the Vitruvian text was lost sometime after its delivery to Augustus Caesar. It was believed to have remained unknown until 1416, when Poggio Bracciolini,[74] while traveling with the Roman Curia, discovered a Vitruvian text in the library of the St. Gall monastery in Switzerland—a text that, it was thought, might even have been one of the Roman originals.[75] According to these contemporary scholars, however, Vitruvius was relatively well known to the Italian Humanists from the middle of the fourteenth century on.[76] There is also concrete evidence of knowledge of the Vitruvian text found in the tenth and eleventh centuries, and during the latter Middle Ages the text was known to intellectuals, clergy, and architects and even played a marginal role in a limited number of building programs. Copies of the manuscript were available in many centers of learning throughout Europe by the twelfth century, and by the mid-fifteenth century, the treatise was available throughout Europe, not only in Italy but also in England, Spain, and Poland. In a most illuminating article in the *Journal of the Warburg and Courtauld Institutes* by Carol Herselle Krinsky, a medieval scholar, we learn that no fewer than seventy-eight Vitruvian manuscripts have been accounted for and are held in libraries all over Europe.[77] And from these many other handwritten copies were made.

Indeed, although Bracciolini's copy, and subsequent copies of his copy, played a important role in disseminating Vitruvius's theories to a wider audience in the mid-fifteenth century, scholars now believe that as early as the mid-1300s the influence of Vitruvius began to play a pivotal role in architectural theory through others. For example, Francesco Petrarch (1304–1374), eminent poet, rhetorician, and humanist, owned his own manuscript copy of Vitruvius, which, now housed at Oxford, contains notes in the margin in Petrarch's hand.[78] And the humanist Giovanni Boccaccio (1313–1375), author of the *Decameron*, refers extensively to Vitruvius in his writings, also from his own personal copy. It was through writers such as these that Vitruvian theories began to spread and ignite not only other humanists, but also artists and architects, in a "common new interest in the architecture of classical antiquity, for which Vitruvius was the only literary source."[79]

It was not only the interest in architectural theory that inspired imaginations; it was Vitruvius's conception, based on ancient sources that the proportions of the human form were the source and foundation of architecture. The concept, however, had its roots even prior to the 1400s. As early as the eleventh century, the mystic Hildegard von Bingen (1098–1179) understood and knew of the human/architectural connection in Vitruvius, for she wrote, quoting Vitruvius, that "the height of a man is equal to his breadth when his arms and hands are extended on both sides from his chest," just as, she goes on to explain, "the human figure is...interpreted as a mirror of the cosmos..., 'for in like manner the firmament has its length equal to its breadth...'"[80] In essence, the human body is a microcosm of the divine universe as a macrocosm.

Further evidence of the human form as a basis for architectural proportions is found in another early author, Cennino Cennini. While it is uncertain if Cennini in his famous early fourteenth-century handbook for artists and craftsmen had ever seen a copy of Vitruvius, it is clear that he understood and was familiar with Vitruvius's theories on human proportion. His lists of proportional relationships, his use of the tripartite divisions of the face, and his description of a man's height being equal to the width of his outstretched arms and hands are all theories originating with Vitruvius. (See Appendix II.)

Thus, the beauty and genius of the early Italian Renaissance is that the human form was seen as the measure of all things. It became the visual framework for order and harmony in all art, while its proportions were rationalized into the ideal figures of the circle and the square and became the basis of architectural design in both religious and public buildings. "The faith in the human intellect and the joyous celebration of the figure were all understood as the best way of expressing divinity," explains art historian Eve Borsook, and it was this belief that "constituted the optimism of the Quattrocento.[81]

In fact, recent scholarship suggests that while the Vitruvian text was well known by scholars from at least the eighth century, and that its influence increased during the Middle Ages, its importance soared during the Renaissance "to a degree of fame that Vitruvius can hardly have dreamt of. The peculiar fate of Vitruvius's treatise has been aptly characterized as follows: 'In the history of art there is probably no other example of a systematic textbook aiming at a contemporary influence, missing its target, and yet achieving such overwhelming success centuries after its appearance.'"[82]

Leonardo and the Vitruvius Text

"In Leonardo's time, Vitruvius' treatise was at the center of humanists' attention,"[83] and to trace its journey from the obscure monastic libraries of Europe to Leonardo we return to Poggio Bracciolini and his "rediscovery" of the Vitruvian manuscript.

Gian Francesco Poggio Bracciolini (1380–1459) was born in a small town near Arezzo. He had a classical education, studying Greek and Latin under renowned tutors in Florence. He distinguished himself as a copyist of manuscripts and was eventually brought into the service of the Roman Curia in 1402 or 1403. In his position as secretary he traveled throughout Europe with the Church hierarchy. Through his early education and his love of learning he became one of Italy's leading humanists, and, as such, he scoured the libraries and monasteries of Europe. And so it was that in the year 1416, while in St. Gall in Switzerland, he found and copied a number of manuscripts of immeasurable value, including the Vitruvius treatise.

Was Bracciolini aware of the Vitruvian text before he found it at St. Gall, and was he actually looking for it? Probably so. This "rediscovery" of Vitruvius, his transcription of the entire text, and his return with the manuscript to Italy helped set in motion an even greater interest in, and further dissemination of, the text. Bracciolini married a young noblewoman in 1435 and eventually retired from the Roman Curia. Interestingly, in 1452, the same year Leonardo was born, he moved back to the city of Florence to live out the rest of his life.

By the mid-1400s, many more humanists, artists, and

intellectuals knew of or actually owned copies of the treatise. These are some of the individuals who transcribed, translated, or wrote commentaries on the Vitruvian text.

- 1427: The great goldsmith and sculptor Lorenzo Ghiberti (1378–1455), who designed and executed, among many other works, the famous bronze Doors of Paradise for the Baptistry in Florence, is known to have owned his own Latin copy of Vitruvius; he began, though never completed, his own translation of the text. It has also been demonstrated that Vitruvius's proportions were understood and used by Ghiberti in his bronze cast of Saint Stephen in 1427–28 for one of the niches of the Orsanmichele.[84]
- 1452: Leon Batista Alberti (1404–1472) wrote his own book on architecture, *De re aedificatoria,* inspired by and patterned directly on the Vitruvian manuscript. His book, as well as his architectural designs and his emphasis on the return to classical architecture, based on what he saw and experienced in Rome and what he learned from Vitruvius, exerted an enormous influence during and after his lifetime.
- 1464: Another treatise on architecture, showing a thorough understanding of Vitruvius, appears, by Antonio Averlino, known as Filarete (1400–?). Filarete was trained as a goldsmith and bronze founder in the studio of Lorenzo Ghiberti. What distinguishes Filarete from Vitruvius and Alberti is his use of the vernacular, as well as his use of architectural illustrations.[85] It can safely be assumed that Filarete's effort was in direct response to Alberti's treatise,[86] which was in Latin and, like Vitruvius's, had no illustrations.
- 1478: Francesco di Giorgio Martini (1439–1501), also known as Francesco di Giorgio, the Sienese artist, architect, and engineer, produced his first translated version of the Vitruvian text in 1478–81, but then followed with a second, more elaborate version, with illustrations for the text, c. 1487–1489. It was the first time an illustration was used to define the Vitruvian section on human proportion.
- 1486: Sulpico de'Veroli published the first printed edition of the treatise of Vitruvius in Latin and made clear, as did Alberti, that the text was extremely difficult to interpret.
- 1507: Albrecht Dürer (1471–1528), the great master from Northern Europe, who wrote and illustrated his own treatise on proportion, incorporated two drawings into the margin of his handwritten copy of the Vitruvian text, one with a figure in a square and one with a figure in a circle.[87]
- 1511: Fra Giovanni Giocondo (1433–1515), engineer, architect, and scholar, provided a series of 136 woodcuts with his version of the Vitruvian text. It included the *homo ad circulum* (man in a circle) and the *homo ad quadratum* (man in a square) for his translation of Vitruvius. This version was the first to attempt the circle in the square, and the first to be commercially printed.
- c. 1500s: Antonio da Sangallo (1453–1534), the illustrious architect, used the same format as Dürer for his own illustration of the Vitruvian text, now housed in the Uffizi Gallery, one with a figure in a circle and one with a figure in a square.
- 1521: Cesare Cesariano (1476–1543), architect, theorist, and painter, published his own version of Vitruvius in Latin. He, however, adopted Fra Giocondo's interpretation of the Vitruvian figure *ad circulum ad quadratum,* the figure inscribed in a circle within a square, with perhaps too great an emphasis on the male figure's prowess.

Leonardo's Drawing as Illustration of the Vitruvian Text

In the Florentine studios of the fifteenth century it was common for artists and apprentices to meet with each other, discuss new theories, and share new technical and evolving advances in art. Surely something as important as the Vitruvian text was, by the mid-fifteenth century, discussed and analyzed in various intellectual and artistic circles, not only all over Florence, but all over Italy as well. The manuscripts mentioned above, having been translated into the vernacular, must have spread like wildfire as copies were borrowed, shared, copied, and recopied.

In 1490, Francesco di Giorgio arrived in Milan at the invitation of Lodovico Sforza to advise on the construction of the "lantern" for the Milan Cathedral. In that same year he traveled to Pavia, and Leonardo, who submitted drawings in the competition for the Cathedral plan, traveled with him.[88] It is possible that by this time Leonardo may have known about Francesco di Giorgio's second translation of Vitruvius and his illustrations for it, and if not, he certainly learned of it on their trip together. Clearly the two had a great deal to discuss, as both men, at about the same time, were immersed in an attempt to understand and to illustrate the famous Vitruvian passage:

> [I]n the human body the central point is naturally the navel. For if a man be placed flat on his back, with his hands and feet extended, and a pair of compasses [centered] at his navel, the fingers and toes of his two hands and feet will touch the circumference of a circle therefrom. And just as the human body yields a circular outline, so too a square figure may be found from it. For if we measure the distance from the soles of the feet to the top of the head, then apply that measure to the outstretched arms, the breadth will be found to be the same height, as in the case of plane surfaces which are perfectly square.[89]

We also know that Leonardo intended to write a book on the human figure in 1489,[90] and it may be that some of his investigations could have started even earlier, as some of the pages exploring human proportions in the Codex Atlanticus may date to as early as c. 1483. In any case, Leonardo's interpretation of the Vitruvian passage goes far beyond that of Francesco di Giorgio,[91] and indeed, beyond all other illustrations that follow.

Francesco di Giorgio's version is accompanied by two drawings inscribing the male figure in a circle and a square. In one drawing, the circle is enclosed by the square and the figure stretches his arms and hands out beyond the circle to touch the sides of the square. In the second drawing, the figure stretches his arms and hands within the confines of the circle, but this time the circle projects beyond the sides of the square while meeting the top and bottom of the square. Francesco accomplishes this by making the height of the square greater than its width, thereby turning the square into a rectangle.[92]

Leonardo's drawing solves the problem with one image by establishing the figure within the confines of the square, then superimposing the circle over the square and using the male figure's umbilicus not as the center of the figure but as the center of the circle. He also adds a second set of arms and a second set of legs on the same figure. It is an entirely different interpretation of the Vitruvian text, and it solves the visual problems inherent in the text within the economy of a single drawing. Leonardo literally thought "outside the box."

The drawing by Leonardo measures 13½ x 9¾ inches (344 x 245 mm) and is executed in light-brown watered ink on a soft, warm-gray paper. It was done during his first Milanese period, around 1490. His text divides Vitruvius's information into three paragraphs, not entirely in the order established by Vitruvius. (See Appendix II, Section 2, for Leonardo's interpretation of the Vitruvian text, and also AP 149.) The writing was obviously added after the drawing was completed, because the paragraphs conform to the width of the square, and a portion of the first paragraph is written to conform to the top of the circle.

During my visit to the Venice Academy in the summer of 2007, I discovered two aspects of the drawing not observable in reproduction. It was a brilliant Venetian morning and the light was spectacular. As I held up the drawing, the raking light from the window revealed on both the recto and verso sides of the drawing incised lines made by a stylus. These incised lines cast delicate, but clearly observable, shadows that conformed perfectly to the outline of the figure as well as to the edges of some of the large muscle groups, particularly evident in the legs. In addition, tiny pinholes were in the drawing, at the essential points of intersection: where the circle intersected the square, at the corners of the square, and where the tips of the middle fingers of each of the four hands touched the square and the circle. Pinholes were also evident in the ledger line, below the drawing, on the lines indicating the widths of the fingers and the palms. There were other pinholes on the face, on the torso, and most important, in the center of the umbilicus.

Another drawing, or a least an original sketch, must have been made prior to the final drawing. The initial drawing had to have been laid over the final sheet and pierced with a pin to mark the essential points. Then the sketch was incised with a stylus around the outline of the figure and large muscle groups and the impression passed through the top sheet to the sheet below it. The inked lines were then added. They are so perfect and complete that there is a sense that the drawing was done only after thorough and careful preparation, the kind of preparation used for presentation or instructional purposes.

In the first paragraph above the *Vitruvian Man* drawing, Leonardo describes how Nature has determined the proportional measurements of the human body, using small parts of the body as modules to define larger parts of the body. Referring to the ledger, or measuring line, at the bottom of the drawing, he says that "4 fingers make 1 palm, and 4 palms make 1 foot, 6 palms make 1 cubit; 4 cubits make a man's height."[93] Below this text is his famous drawing.

The second paragraph, a single sentence, indicating the length of a man's outstretched arms is equal to his height, is written below the drawing and measuring line. Leonardo's *Vitruvian Man* depicts the height of the figure, from the soles of the feet to the top of the head, as equal to his horizontally outstretched arms and hands. This is defined by the sides of a perfect square.

In the third and final paragraph, Leonardo sums up all of the major variables of anatomical modules used to measure the whole figure, defining the height of the whole figure using a variety of parts of the body as modules. He describes how each module is used as a canon to discover the proportional ratio of that part in relation to the whole height of a man. (For a thorough analysis and practical application of the drawing, see AP 149.)

The genius of the drawing is that after establishing the height of a man as equal to the width of his outstretched arms in a perfect square, Leonardo then draws the circumference of the circle along the bottom edge of the square using the man's umbilicus as the compass point. The circle then passes outside the square and crosses over the square at the upper corners, and a second set of outstretched arms pivot up, without any distortion, until they reach the point where the tips of the fingers touch the intersection of the circle and the top line of the square at the exact height of the man. Leonardo does the same thing with the added second set of legs spread out on the circumference of the circle, thereby creating a perfect equilateral triangle.

Leonardo's ability to thoroughly understand and digest the deeper meaning of the Vitruvian text is evident in the clarity of the drawing. Using his language, the visual language of drawing,[94] he was able to do what others had failed to do. By visually combining in one drawing the figure in the square and the figure in the circle, he gave movement and meaning to Vitruvius's words. The poetic synthesis linking the combined figures of the circle and the square creates a harmony of such universal proportion that the visual image allows for instant recognition and clear comprehension of the meaning behind the words. In some ways the drawing represents the very beginning of Leonardo's investigations into human proportions, and in other ways it seems to represent their beautifully eloquent culmination.

Notes
Chapter Ten. Leonardo's *Vitruvian Man*

[61] Richter, *The Literary Works of Leonardo Da Vinci*, vol. II, R 1421, 355.

[62] Zollner, *Leonardo da Vinci 1452–1517, The Complete Paintings and Drawings*, 104.

[63] Smith, *Vitruvius on Architecture*, 9.

[64] Smith, 12, see note 17 for a complete list of the Greek Treatises.

[65] Smith, 9.

[66] Smith, 15.

[67] Smith, 15–25.

[68] Smith, 16.

[69] Smith, 17.

[70] Smith, 18.

[71] *Webster's New World Dictionary*, 1477.

[72] Marcus Vitruvius Pollio, *The Ten Books on Architecture*, trans. Morris Hicky Morgan, Book III, Chapter I, section 1, 72. This Dover edition is an unabridged and unaltered republication of the first edition of the English translation by Morris Hicky Morgan originally published by Harvard University Press in 1914. In quoting this paragraph from the Dover edition I have substituted the word *Symmetria* for symmetry in order to emphasize the more complex meaning of the concept.

[73] Smith, 27.

[74] Carol Herselle Krinsky, "Seventy-Eight Vitruvian Manuscripts," *Journal of the Warburg and Courtauld Institutes* 30 (1967): 36.

[75] Richard Krautheimer, "Alberti and Vitruvius," The Renaissance and Mannerism, Studies in Western Art, *Acts of the Twentieth International Congress of the History of Art*, New York, 1961, Princeton: Princeton University Press, (1963): 2. 42–52.

[76] Hanno-Walter Kruft, *A History of Architectural Theory from Vitruvius to the Present* (New York: Princeton Architectural Press, 1994), 39.

[77] Krinsky, 37.

[78] Kruft, 39.

[79] Kruft, 40.

[80] Kruft, 35; also Krinsky, 40.

[81] Eve Borsook, *The Companion Guide to Florence* (London: Fontana Collins, 1966), 281.

[82] Kruft, p. 30.

[83] Domenico Laurenza, "The Vitruvian Man by Leonardo: Image and Text," *Quaderni d'italianistica* XXVII, no. 2 (2006): 43.

[84] Piero Morselli, "The Proportions of Ghiberti's Saint Stephen: Vitruvius's De Architectura and Alberti's De Statua," *The Art Bulletin* 60, no 2 (June 1978): 235–241.

[85] Carlo Vecce in *Leonardo da Vinci, Master Draftsman*, Carmen Bambach, ed., exhibition catalog, the Metropolitan Museum of Art, (New Haven and London: Yale University Press, 2003), 69.

[86] Kruft, 51.

[87] Laurenza, 37–46.

[88] Bambach, 230.

[89] Vitruvius, 73.

[90] Richter, *The Literary Works of Leonardo da Vinci*, vol. I, R 370, 343, "On the 2nd of April 1489, book entitled 'Of the human figure.' "

[91] Laurenza, 46.

[92] Laurenza, 43, see figures 4 and 5.

[93] Richter, vol. I, R 343, 255.

[94] Laurenza, 48.

The youth should first learn perspective, then the proportions of objects.
Then he may copy from some good master, to accustom himself to fine forms.
Then from Nature, to confirm the rules he has learnt.
Then set a time for the works of various masters.
Then get the habit of putting his art into practice.

R 483[95]

CHAPTER ELEVEN
LEONARDO, DÜRER, LOMAZZO, AND THE ADVENT OF THE ACADEMIES

In Leonardo's words, in a structured program for artists, perspective is the first and most important theory to be taught, followed immediately by proportion. Leonardo was part of an ever-growing number of artists, and later academies, who focused their attention on developing theories of human proportion as an essential part of artistic training. Along with this more structured education of the artist, there developed a greater interest in the theory of art, an interest in raising the status of the artist above the medieval image of a manual laborer. Thus, the search for the "ideal" proportions of the human figure was an integral part of the growing emphasis on the education of the artist, and it evolved consistently over the next four centuries. Albrecht Dürer and Giovanni Paolo Lomazzo are just two prominent examples of what occurred between Leonardo and the advent of an academy.

Albrecht Dürer (1471–1528), Germany's preeminent painter, printmaker, and draftsman, was also, like Leonardo, a prolific writer. He completed a number of treatises on a variety of subjects and, most importantly, conducted extensive investigations on human proportion for his treatise *The Four Books on Human Proportion* (*Vier Buchen von menschlicher Proportion*). Unlike Leonardo, however, he completed his work on human proportion, and it was published shortly after his death in 1528.[96]

Dürer was among the first of the Northern European artists to travel to Italy and begin to incorporate Renaissance ideas in his work. He made two trips there, the first in 1494–1495 and the second in 1505–1506. Both trips were to Venice and the northern parts of Italy, and on his second trip he was on his way to visit the painter Mantegna, whom he greatly admired, when he died.[97] Dürer learned much on his Italian sojourns, including a working knowledge of Vitruvius.

In 1504 he completed his engraving of *Adam and Eve*, an enormously detailed wooded scene, richly ornamented with vegetation, symbolic figures and animals, and Adam and Eve, fully frontal in the altogether, feeding each other, and the snake, the forbidden fruit. In the engraving, Dürer attempted to synthesize his extensive knowledge of the human figure with his understanding of Vitruvius's theory of human proportion, which is based on mathematical relationships, to create the perfect male and female figures. However, Dürer modified his idealization with a devotion to observation and naturalism.[98] It became clear to him that to fully understand the outward appearance and proportions of the human figure, he would have to undertake extensive measurements and calculations on many men, women, and children. Like Leonardo, the empirical method proved to be the foundation of his work on human proportion.

Dürer's *Four Books* was clearly intended as a practical guide for artists and for students of art. Each section concentrates on a different method for understanding proportion.

Book I focuses on the distances between clearly defined points on the body measured in numbers that can only be divided evenly and leave no remainder. Dürer uses the 8-head system to establish the height of the figure.

Book II is based on a system described in Alberti's *De Statua*, in which Alberti's figure is based on the Vitruvian canon dividing the figure into six parts using the foot as a module: "The length of the foot is one-sixth of the height of the body..." (Vitruvius). This is known as the "exempeda [i.e., six-feet] method."[99]

Book III introduces a system devised by Dürer. The first two systems of measuring the human figure were based on specific human types, of white male and female figures, which Dürer felt inadequate for the working artist and student. He therefore devised a system concentrating on the construction of the head to determine the proportions of various racial types. Dürer closes this book with a reflection on the nature of art in relation to God.

Book IV explores a theory of movement in which the external appearance of the figure is based on posture, with a section especially devoted to bent and twisted poses. Yet there is no consideration of an anatomical explanation of movement.

Dürer's book is extensive and addresses the many situations an artist may encounter. While these practical considerations were a major concern, it was his interest in the theoretical foundations of Vitruvius that seemed to inspire him. As mentioned earlier in this chapter, there are examples of his early (1507) investigations into the construction of the figure in the circle and the square, taken directly from Vitruvius. In his *Dresden Sketchbook*, Dürer provides several examples of the proportions of the figure by using the circle and the square.[100] By comparing the height of the figure as equal to the width of the figure's outstretched arms, he composes the figure in a square, and by using the navel of the figure as the point of a compass, he inscribes a perfect circle with the foot and hand touching the diameter of the circle. But in each case, just as in all his predecessors, the figure in the square and the figure in the circle are treated quite separately. Only Leonardo effectively joins the two.

From Dürer we move forward to Lomazzo, born ten years after Dürer's death. Giovanni Paolo Lomazzo (1538–1600), the Milanese painter, draftsman, and writer, was born into a family of some social importance. Because of this he received a better-than-usual education and traveled in the intellectual and humanist circles of Milan.

Lomazzo had a modest career as a painter and spent his early years fulfilling small commissions for murals and altarpieces. His subsequent desire to write a treatise on painting was motivated by a strong conviction that the art of painting be elevated to the level of dignity enjoyed by poets and rhetoricians. He believed that the enormous advances made over the hundred years prior to his birth raised painting far above its present station and elevated the artist above the status of manual laborer. The advanced techniques of the time were tools intended to free the artist to achieve the noble ends behind the intellectual and spiritual themes of his subject matter. Gerald Ackerman, in his article on the treatise, points out that "against the background of Neo-Platonic cosmology," Lomazzo "demonstrated how the painter could form his ideas, through contemplation, in harmony with or directly from the world of forms. His manual activity, the painting of the picture, was simply the rationalized, technical execution of the mental idea."[101]

Prior to Lomazzo's time, the first half of the sixteenth century, information was disseminated during an apprenticeship period in the shop of a master artist. The apprenticeship with the master usually lasted anywhere from four to six years. The rules and techniques were loosely and casually passed on to the apprentice, who served as an aide in the production of a work of art. There were no formal lessons or instruction. The information passed from master to apprentice, from apprentice to apprentice, and from shop to shop. But as the advances in methods and techniques progressed, and as the amount of information grew, the need for demonstrations and explanations became greater, until the idea for a structured "curriculum," taught outside the shop, began to unfold. By this time the medieval model of the studio assistantship was beginning to break down, and while it would last for at least another century, it was in this newly controversial environment that Lomazzo began to write his treatise.

Lomazzo's treatise consists of the *Trattato della arte della pittore,* written in 1584, and the *Idea del tempio della pittore,* in 1590. The *Trattato* is mainly devoted to the practical aspects of painting, while the *Idea* is devoted to aspects of theory, such as perspective and proportion. Progress on the book was slow and further complicated by Lomazzo's progressive blindness. By the time he was thirty-three he was too blind to paint,[102] and the publisher, frustrated by the slow progress of the treatise, decided to print the work as two separate books, although they were always intended as a single entity.

The *Idea del tempio della pittura* was originally intended to precede the *Trattato.* Divided into five sections, it ran on for thirty-eight chapters beginning with a *proemio,* or brief introduction. The first section is in praise of painting; the second an analogy of painting as a temple with seven pillars (each representing a part of painting); the third section divides each of the seven pillars of painting into subcategories; the fourth is a discussion on the need for "discretion" by painters in order to accomplish their aims; and the fifth section is an incomplete theory of aesthetics, based on eurythmy, the art of various movements in rhythmic proportion characterized by harmony.[103] In this last section, Lomazzo uses examples of contemporary artists to bolster his arguments.

The heart of the treatise, the *Trattato della arte della pittore,* written before the *Idea,* is divided into seven books, each dealing with a different aspect of art. Each book begins with a rhetorical praise of art, but it is the first book, the Book on Proportion, that concerns us. Lomazzo begins with a definition of proportion, discusses the parts of the body, includes a section on the *Vitruvian Man,* and then proceeds with the proportions of a man of 10 heads, followed by the proportions of a woman of 10 heads. He follows with a discussion of the proportions of sickly men and sickly women, children, and horses, and lastly a discussion on architecture. Book II concentrates on motion, Book III on color, Book IV on light, Book V on perspective, and Book VI on practice; VII is the Book of Forms.

Because the book took so long to write, was enormously lengthy and cumbersome, and, due to the onset of his blindness, was so poorly edited, it never received the critical attention it might have. However, Lomazzo is to be remembered as "having written the first methodical manual...of painting,"[104] devoted to the education of the young artist. In so doing, he was one of those in the forefront of establishing an academic tradition.

Thus we see that the idea of a structured system of art education had its origins in three separate but related factors: the breakdown of the medieval system of workshops with a master craftsman and multiple assistants, the elevation of the status of the artist, and the birth of art academies devoted to a structured system. Following is a brief history of those factors.

The Decline of the Medieval Workshop

The workshop of the Renaissance, based on the medieval system, had a carefully defined set of rules and time requirements for its assistants and apprentices. The workshops were engaged in the production of artworks of all kinds, and at the same time were required to fulfill the very specific function of training young artists, a system clearly laid out in *The Craftsman's Handbook* by Cennino Cennini.[105] A young boy entered a master's studio as a "shop boy" at twelve to fourteen years of age. He usually lived with the master and the rest of the studio hands; his parents either paid for his apprenticeship or he was paid a minimal sum for his services, depending upon his age and experience. The shop boy spent his first year drawing, then moved to mixing and grinding colors, preparing panels, and learning gilding and stamping for five to six years as an "apprentice." He then moved into the position of "assistant," just below the master, gaining experience in painting, working on walls, learning to mix and work with formulas (and sharing in the profits with the master) for another five or six years more, "all the time drawing." If a shop boy entered a studio at the age of twelve, he might have earned his certification as an assistant by his early twenties and qualified to take the official tests set up by a committee of the guild. Upon passing the test, he would be certified as a master and be allowed to set up his own workshop.

The studio functioned like a well-run factory. Everyone had a hand in seeing to the completion of a commission. In the production of a commission, a young man learned all of the necessary skills to complete a project, with the master passing on information to the assistant and the assistant passing it on to the apprentice. There was little time for theoretical lessons or technical training. As new techniques and methods developed at such a rapid pace in the fifteenth century, it eventually became essential for the master to conduct some discussions and demonstrations to keep the entire workshop up to speed. At some point, however, the new techniques became so complex and difficult that only experienced practitioners could teach them.[106]

In-depth theoretical instruction, a major departure from the on-the-job training that was common to the medieval workshops of the thirteenth, fourteenth, and fifteenth centuries, was becoming necessary. In 1490, Lorenzo di Medici moved to create an intensive "school," appointing as its head Bertoldo di Giovanni, a former assistant to the aging master Donatello (1386–1466). The following account was written by Vasari more than half a century later:

> Lorenzo the Magnificent had at that time [about 1490] appointed the sculptor Bertoldo to a post in his garden at the Piazza San Marco, less as a superintendent of his many and beautiful antiques, than as a master and head of a school which he intended to set up for the education of outstanding painters and sculptors. For Lorenzo gravely complained of the lack in his time of famous and noteworthy sculptors, whereas there were so many great and prominent painters; and therefore he decided...to establish the school. For this he asked Domenico Ghirlandajo to send him to the garden any apprentices of his whose talents might point in that direction. He would have them instructed in such a way that it would do credit to himself and Ghirlandajo and the city of Florence.[107]

The master Ghirlandaio obliged and recommended several students, among them the fifteen-year-old Michelangelo Buonarroti (1475–1564).

In this setting, the young apprentices could study the sculptural work of the ancients, and even some of the Renaissance masters of the fifteenth century, at first hand. Lorenzo's school was totally independent of the rules and restrictions of the guilds, and with this new educational approach, there emerged a new brand of artist, intellectually freed from the standard apprenticeship program of the past.

At about exactly the same time, in Milan, Leonardo da Vinci, while at the court of Lodovico Sforza, had been collecting notes for a treatise on painting, his *Trattato della Pittura.* At the request of the Duke, Leonardo was commissioned to clarify for Lodovico which of the arts was the greatest, poetry, painting, music, or sculpture. This work culminated in the famous *Paragone* (The Comparison). In 1584, Lomazzo says, "In this way Leonardo da Vinci continues to discuss and reason in his book, which I read in recent years, and which he wrote with his left hand, on request of Lodovico Sforza, Duke of Milan, in order to decide the question whether painting or sculpture is more noble…"[108] In the process of doing so, he embarked on a thorough explanation on the education of the artist, as well as a philosophical discussion on the hierarchy of all the arts. In 1498, Luca Pacioli writes in an introductory letter to the Duke about his book, *Divina Proportione,* that "…Leonardo with all diligence has finished his praiseworthy Book on Painting and Human Motion."[109] That manuscript, now lost to us, was later reassembled from Leonardo's notebooks by his lifelong assistant, Franceso Melzi, who was also heir to the contents of Leonardo's studio, including his Notebooks.

We therefore know, from these Notebooks, much of what Leonardo theorized about art. He believed, and was probably one of the first to so believe, that the education of the young artist must begin with the acquisition of knowledge. By the acquisition of knowledge he did not mean the humanities, nor was he thinking of theoretical abstractions. He was specifically talking about practical visual theories that can be taught, learned, and practiced. The theory of perspective, because he believed it to be of primary importance, was the first to be taught. It was followed by the second most important theory, the theory of proportion, both human and architectural. Third came a system concentrating on drawing, beginning with copies of his master's drawings, then drawing from relief and three-dimensional sculpture; once the young artist became proficient in drawing from Nature, he might then, and only then, move forward to the material procedures of painting.[110] Theory over manual skills, that was Leonardo's edict, and that was how he trained and worked with his small circle of assistants in Milan.

The Elevation of the Artist

The rise and spread of humanism during the late fifteenth century was an essential factor in the change of the social standing of the artist. The humanists' commitment to the study of the liberal arts included an intensive investigation of and interest in antiquity. It was their belief that in the study of the ancient texts, as well as in the art of the ancient artists, a new and greater understanding of the human condition might unfold.

A growing intimacy between the humanist writers and Renaissance artists was based on an affinity of common goals. The new humanist focused on the individuality of human beings and their achievements. This individuality stressed personality, genius, and uniqueness and the capability to achieve one's complete potential. As the humanists stressed the dignity of man made in the image of God, the artists manifested those lofty precepts in works of art glorifying the image of man. The humanists, in celebration of these achievements, began to "praise the individual works of art and individual artists" in such a way that was totally incompatible with the medieval tradition, and "whereas the artists alone might not have been able to achieve their goal, success was secured" by the support of these humanist writers.[111] As the humanists were welcomed at the courts of Europe, so artists began to take their places at the courts of the nobles with the same social status as the humanists.

Leonardo was at the forefront of raising painting from a manual craft to the status of art. He praised painting in his writings, elevating it above all the arts, including sculpture, which he believed to be a manual, mechanical labor, and even above poetry. In the following passage from his famous *Paragone,* he makes perfectly clear the difference between painting and poetry.[112]

> Painting is poetry which is seen and not heard, and poetry is a painting which is heard and not seen. These two arts, you may call both either poetry or painting, have here interchanged the senses by which they penetrate to the intellect. Whatever is painted must pass by the eye, which is the nobler sense, and whatever is poetry must pass through a less nobler sense, namely the ear, to the understanding.[113]

Leonardo was passionate about his crusade to elevate painting. In his *Trattato della Pittura* he set out to reveal both "the principles of the science of painting" and praise the art of painting as a relative of God (*parente d'Iddio*).[114] So with the elevation of art, the artist found a new voice and individuality he could never have known under the old medieval guild system. The trust and esteem Lorenzo di Medici showed Bertoldo di Giovanni, and that Lodovico Sforza showered upon Leonardo, was a mark of the changing times. Michelangelo, one of the first to grow up outside the old guild system and its binding ties, eventually became the epitome of the favored, pampered, contentious artist and enjoyed unparalleled reverence and fame in his lifetime.

The Birth of the Art Academy

With the guilds collapsed and the artist elevated to a rank of new respect, the ground was prepared for the philosophical and social academies that grew up in the fifteenth century. In the first half of the fifteenth century, writes historian Nikolaus Pevsner, "a rebirth of Platonism was brought about by the influence of the Greek scholars" who arrived in Italy to participate in the negotiations of a reunion between the Greek and Roman Churches."[115] With their arrival and the stimulating atmosphere of religious and philosophical debates, the term *academy,* first associated with Plato and his community of followers, was revived.

The concept of the academy held great appeal for the humanists, and several small discussion groups were formed. Out of those, under the influence and protection of Lorenzo di Medici, grew the Academy of Neo-Platonists with Marsilio Ficino as its founder. By the end of the fifteenth century and the beginning of the sixteenth, philosophical academies were numerous. At first, they were the courts of kings and princes who surrounded themselves with intellectuals of all walks of life: poets, theologians, mathematicians, and scientists. This interest in a variety of subjects, and the desire to share and discuss this knowledge, brought together diverse groups of intellectuals. It was in the Italian academies of the 1500s that the true spirit of the High Renaissance manifested itself.

There was no end to the enormous variety of academies with diverse specialties. Indeed, they multiplied like wildfire throughout Italy. There were academies devoted to philological studies in Italian and in Greek. Groups formed to study problems in divinity, archeology, and medicine, and even social groups interested in fencing, riding, and dancing met to discuss their issues. (Nikolaus Pevsner gives an exhaustive scholarly account of European academies in his book *Academies of Art, Past and Present,* 1940.)

From here it is but a small jump to the formal academies of art that developed in the sixteenth century and later flourished during the seventeenth, eighteenth, and nineteenth centuries. In the same letter of 1498 to the Duke of Milan mentioned above, Luca Pacioli refers to a "laudable and scientific debate" (*laudibile e scientifico duello*) that took place at the castle of Lodovico. He says "that in the presence of numerous clerical and secular scholars, theologians, doctors, astrologers, lawyers, and above all [those], that most perceptive architect and engineer and assiduous inventor of all things new, [was] Leonardo da Vinci."[116] There are those who have argued that this singular quotation (along with a few engravings done by students) constitutes proof that an academy existed with Leonardo at its artistic and intellectual center.[117] This is theory only. What seems to have arisen in his Milanese studio in the early 1500s is an academy-like atmosphere among a small group of confederates (Melzi and Boltraffio) and a few young apprentices (Salai). We know from his Notebooks of his ambition to create a Painter's Handbook (*Trattato della Pittura*), much of which was written but little of which was organized until after his death, by Francesco Melzi. Most assuredly no formal school ever existed, but there is little doubt that Leonardo became "the founder of the first academy of art" by establishing the foundation for that academy in his theoretical writings "for all future systems of academic instruction up to the nineteenth century."[118]

During the second half of the sixteenth century, Vasari, Zuccaro, and the Carracci family took up the mantle and developed theories for organized academies, all based entirely on or derived from Leonardo's theories as stated in his Notebooks.

Giorgio Vasari's (1511–1574) proposal for a new system of art education was formulated in a manifesto or charter in 1563 that brought together a group of artists whose common interest was in *disegno*, drawing. The charter had a set of rules comprising forty-seven articles that outlined both the moral and the practical code of the new academy, the Accademia del Disegno. With the rules laid out and the most prominent painters, sculptors, and architects as members, Vasari petitioned the Grand Duke Cosimo I, under whose protection and patronage the group placed themselves. This gave the new academy legitimacy and moral support and legally freed its members from the obligation of membership in their respective guilds. All old ties, however, were not suspended; membership in the Compagnia di San Luca continued, and this organization, which dealt with festivals, religious functions, and funerals, became a subordinate body of the academy.

Michelangelo, by this time an older man and a respected, prominent figure, was titular head of the academy along with the Grand Duke, while Cosimo's representative, Vincenzo Broghini, was to officiate over the daily operations. The charter called for the education of young artists and drawing as the core of the academy's program. Lectures in theory, geometry, and anatomy were envisioned, and prominent artists were to be selected to make the rounds of the various Florentine studios, correcting drawings and offering advice. In addition, membership was opened to "amateurs and dilettantes," and young artists who showed promise, and who submitted drawings, were invited to apply for membership as well. However, it seems that the educational program never got off the ground with any degree of continuity or commitment, and the academy foundered.[119] Within a decade after its inception, Michelangelo died (1564), Vasari died (1574), and it was left to a new and younger generation to revitalize the idea of the academy.

The challenge was assumed by Federico Zuccaro (1540–1609), who was elected to the Accademia del Disegno in Florence in 1565. In 1574, after extensive travels to Rome, the Netherlands, France, and England, Zuccaro returned to Florence to complete the painting on the interior of the cupola of the Duomo, left incomplete at the death of Vasari.[120] It was at this point, sometime between 1575 and 1578, that Zuccaro wrote a letter to the members lamenting the static condition of the academy, pleading that if reforms are not undertaken, the "name of the Academy will return to us in vain."[121] He introduced a new curriculum in his letter intended to revitalize the institution. His proposals included the teaching of mathematics, regular classes in art theory, a room dedicated to life drawing once a week, and prizes offered for students. The program represented an expansion beyond Vasari's initial plans, with the life-drawing room and student prizes becoming an integral part of most academies thereafter.

Once again, though, the impetus and energy behind the academy wavered and the Accademia del Disegno of Florence quietly disappeared, not to reemerge until the mid-seventeenth century. Zuccaro left Florence and established himself in Rome but brought with him his ideas for revitalizing the academy. He turned his attention to the Accademia di San Luca in Rome, and, using his proposals from the Florence academy, hoped to revive its program. He was elected the first president of the newly reorganized Rome academy in 1593. Its new rules provided for regular discussions on art theoretical issues, as Zuccaro considered lectures and discussions to be "virtuous conversation"; as such, they were held as "the mother of all studies and the true fountain of every science."[122] In addition, twelve visiting artists were to be hired each year as teachers, one a month, to review students' work and decide who was to move from cast drawing to life drawing. But again, as its member artists found the lectures tedious and the debates repetitious, the teaching program stagnated, and Zuccaro seems to have lost interest in the venture.

These public academies, under the protection of either the Pope or members of the nobility, were but one form that art education took. In addition to these formal academies, it was common in the latter part of the sixteenth century to find artists gathering regularly to draw, sometimes from plaster casts and skeletons but particularly from the live model. These informal sessions took place either in someone's studio or in an atelier rented for the purpose. Out of just such an informal setting developed the famous Carracci Academy.

In about 1580, the Carracci family in Bologna banded together to form their own workshop to provide mutual support in the production of various commissions. Ludovico (1555–1619), as the eldest family member, was the titular head of the shop, and he was joined by his cousins, the brothers Agostino (1557–1602) and Annibale (1560–1609). They held informal drawing sessions in their studio. In about 1582, the idea to form their own academy arose, credited to Agostino, the most verbal and theoretical of the group. The academy was initially called the Accademia dei Desiderosi, explains Donald Posner in his definitive study of Annibale's life and work, because of "the desire of its members for learning and fame."[123]

As the Carracci academy became more popular and the three cousins established themselves more assuredly in the artistic circles of Bologna, their academy changed in nature and in name. The group became more organized, and the new name, Accademia degli Incamminati, as in "those who are making progress" or "those who are arriving," reflected a change in philosophy. Agostino, the leader thanks to his "verbal fluency," set the new intellectual tone of the academy as it gained in popularity and attracted new students. The new tone also reflected the wide range of cultural interests of Agostino, who was directly inspired by his understanding of the Florentine Accademia del Disegno.[124]

The Carracci academy was a school without a formal teaching program, and, Posner tells us, "one must assume that the lectures and competitions" were held only on an irregular basis. However, there was much discussion both on a formal and informal basis, on "mathematics, science, history, and literature," and there were even visits by a professional anatomist providing anatomical lessons and demonstrations.[125] A steady stream of scholars, scientists, literati, and aristocrats came through to meet with the young artists of the academy.

But the core of the academy was clear and consistent. Art professor Albert Boime sums up the Carracci model:

> As outlined in Leonardo, the Carracci began students copying from engravings—the "flat," as this exercise came to be known in Anglo-Saxon academies—passed them from there to casts, and finally, to the live model. The training of the Carracci, however, centered on the living human form, nude and studiously posed. This special attention given to life drawing distinguished their school from other contemporary institutions. By the 17th century, the Carracci-style academy, rather informal and providing a meeting place for communal discussion, provided a model for art schools. The new academies which spread throughout Europe assembled either in an artist's studio, a rented locale or the palace of a patron, and their members met primarily to draw from life.[126]

The growing influence and originality of the Carracci clan and their success eventually made the academy the most popular in Bologna. They drew together the principles of two worlds: the Florentine belief in the importance of drawing from Nature, as exemplified by Leonardo, and the Venetian influence on the importance of color, as emphasized by Correggio and Titian. Never before had these separate camps, Florentine drawing and Venetian color, seemed compatible. Each city had its artistic heroes, and they were separated by hundreds of miles and mountains. As independent city-states, they remained isolated enclaves unto themselves. So it was left to Bologna, the city in between, and the inseparable activities of the Carracci teaching and workshop to join these principles together. But it was the didactic nature of the academy inspired by the legacy of Leonardo da Vinci that shaped the structure of all future art academies to come.

Notes

Chapter Eleven. Leonardo, Dürer, Lomazzo, and the Advent of the Academies

[95] Richter, *The Literary Works of Leonardo da Vinci*, vol. I, R 483, 303.

[96] Helen Gardner, *Art Through the Ages*, ed., Frank Kleiner, Christian Mamiya, Richard Taney, 11th edition (Belmont, Calif.: Thomson Wadsworth, 2001), 698.

[97] Frederick Hartt, *Italian Art*, 396–397.

[98] Gardner, 698.

[99] Albrecht Dürer, *The Human Figure, The Complete Dresden Sketchbook*, introduction, translations, and commentary by Walter Strauss (New York: Dover Publications, 1972), 170.

[100] Durer, *The Human Figure*, plate numbers 45, 85, 86.

[101] Gerald M. Ackerman, "Lomazzo's Treatise on Painting," *The Art Bulletin* 49, no. 4 (Dec. 1967): 317.

[102] Ackerman, 317, footnote 5.

[103] The term *Eurythmy*, according to Vitruvius, is one of the six most important principles necessary in determining issues of architectural design, listed in his book, *The Ten Books on Architecture. See Thomas Gordon Smith, Vitruvius on Architecture*, 15–25, or, *The Ten Books on Architecture*, 13–17. For a brilliant visual interpretation of the term, see the painting by Ferdinand Hodler, *Eurythmy*, 1895, oil on canvas, Kunstmuseum, Bern, in the exhibition catalogue by Peter Selz, *Ferdinand Hodler* (Berkeley: University Art Museum, 1972), fig. 22, 37.

[104] Ackerman, 323.

[105] Cennini, *The Craftsman's Handbook*, 64–65.

[106] Ackerman, 317.

[107] Nikolaus Pevsner, *Academies of Art, Past and Present* (New York: Da Capo Press, 1973), 38, footnote 1; see also GiorgioVasari, *Lives of the Most Eminent Painters, Sculptors, and Architects*, abridged and edited by Robert N. Linscott (New York: The Modern Library, Random House, 1959), 311–312.

[108] Carlo Pedretti, *Leonardo da Vinci on Painting, A Lost Book (Libro A)*, (Berkeley and Los Angeles: University of California Press, 1964), 7–8, footnote 2.

[109] Kate Trauman Steinitz, *Leonardo da Vinci's Trattato della Pittura* (Copenhagen: Published by the University Library, 1958), 21–22.

[110] Pevsner, 35; see also Kemp, Martin, *Leonardo on Painting*, Edited by Martin Kemp, Selected by Martin Kemp and Margaret Walker (New Haven and London: Yale University Press, 1989), 197; see also Richter, 1970, vol. I, R 482, R 483, R 484, R 485, 303.

[111] Pevsner, 17.

[112] Pedretti, *Leonardo da Vinci on Painting*, 121–128, The *Paragone* (The Comparison) was the name given to the treatise written for Lodovico Sforza. It was compiled and included as an introduction to Leonardo's *Trattato della Pittura* by Francesco Melzi.

[113] Elizabeth Gilmore Holt, ed., *Literary Sources of Art History: An Anthology of Texts from Theophilus to Goethe* (Princeton: Princeton University Press, 1947), 172. Also, Richter, The Literary Works of Leonardo da Vinci, vol. I, R 24, 58.

[114] Pevsner, 30.

[115] Pevsner, 1.

[116] Pevsner, 27.

[117] Pevsner, 24–26.

[118] Pevsner, 37.

[119] Pevsner, 39–50.

[120] Carl Goldstein, "Vasari and the Florentine Accademia del Disegno," *Zeitschrift für Kunstgeschichte*, 38 Bd., H.2. (1975): 145–152.

[121] Pevsner, 51.

[122] Pevsner, 60.

[123] Donald Posner, *Annibale Carracci*, vol. I (New York: Phaidon, 1971), 62.

[124] Posner, 63.

[125] Posner, 64.

[126] Albert Boime, *Strictly Academic, Life Drawing in the Nineteenth Century*, exhibition organized by the University Art Gallery, State University of New York, Binghamton (Binghamton: University Gallery, 1974), 7.

PART FIVE
CHRONOLOGY

Be it known to all persons, present and to come, that at the court of our Lord the King at Amboise before ourselves in person, Messer Leonardo da Vinci, painter to the King, at present staying at the place known as Cloux near Amboise, duly considering the certainty of death and the uncertainty of time, has acknowledged and declared in the said court and before us that he has made, according to the tenor of these presents, his testament and the declaration of his last will, as follows. And first he commends his soul to our Lord, Almighty God, and to the Glorious Virgin Mary, and to our lord Saint Michael, and to all the blessed Angels and Saints male and female in paradise.

From the will of Leonardo da Vinci
R 1566[127]

Leonardo's Life in Brief, 1452–1519[128]

1452
Leonardo is born on April 15 in Vinci, west of Florence, to Ser Piero di Antonio da Vinci, a notary, and a young peasant woman named Caterina. The couple is not married.

Later in the year, Ser Piero, Leonardo's father, marries Albiera di Giovanni Amadori, the sixteen-year-old daughter of a wealthy Florentine.

1453
Leonardo's mother, Caterina, marries Accattabriga di Piero del Vacca.

1457
Leonardo, now five years old, is listed as a dependent in the tax declaration of Ser Antonio, his grandfather, who is living on the Piazzetta Guazzesi (now Via Roma) in Vinci.

1462
Leonardo's father, Ser Piero, works as a notary for Cosimo de' Medici, il Vecchio, in Florence.

1464
Leonardo's stepmother, Albiera, dies in childbirth.

1465
Leonardo's father marries his second wife, Francesca di Ser Giuliano Lanfredini.

1468
Leonardo's grandfather, Ser Antonio da Vinci, dies at the age of ninety-six.

1469
According to tax declarations filed by Leonardo's father, Ser Piero, and his uncle, Francesco, Leonardo at seventeen is living with his father, an established notary in Florence, employed by the Palazzo del Podesta (now the Bargello).

Leonardo begins an apprenticeship, arranged by his father, in the workshop of the painter and sculptor Andrea Verrocchio. During his time there, his fellow apprentices include Sandro Botticelli, Piero Perugino, and Lorenzo di Credi. While there, Leonardo assists with many pieces, including Verrocchio's *Baptism of Christ* (c. 1472), in which he paints the angel.

1470
Leonardo is registered on the tax declaration of his father.

1471
Pope Sixtus IV is elected. He will later commission the building of the Sistine Chapel in Rome.

1472
Leonardo's name is inscribed as an independent master in the account book of the confraternity of painters, the Compagnia di San Luca, in Florence.

1473
On August 5, Leonardo inscribes the date on his first recorded drawing, a landscape of the Arno valley.

Leonardo begins *The Annunciation* (c. 1473–1474), the first independent painting attributed to him.

Ser Piero's second wife, Francesca, dies.

1475
Leonardo begins the painting *Madonna and Child with a Carnation* (Alte Pinakothek, Munich) around this time.

Leonardo's father marries his third wife, Margherita di Francesco.

1476
Although by now an independent artist, Leonardo continues to work at Verrocchio's studio.

Leonardo's Times, 1452–1519

1452
Birth of Savonarola in Ferrara.

1453
Constantinople falls.

1454
Pinturicchio is born.

1455
Vittore Carpaccio is born.

1457
Filippino Lippi is born.

1470
Matthias Grünewald is born sometime in the 1400s.

1462
Piero di Cosimo is born.

1464
Cosimo de' Medici, Il Vecchio, dies. His son Piero assumes power.

1466
The Arno overflows its banks in Florence and its surroundings.

Donatello dies.

1469
Machiavelli is born.

Piero de' Medici, The Gouty, dies. Lorenzo Il Magnifico comes to power.

1471
Albrecht Dürer is born.

1472
Leon Batista Alberti, a humanist much admired by artists of the time for his treatise *On Painting*, dies.

Dante's *Divine Comedy* is published.

Lucas Cranach is born.

1473
Copernicus, the astronomer, is born.

1475
Michelangelo Buonarroti is born.

Cesare Borgia, the son of Rodrigo Borgia (who would become Pope Alexander VI), is born. Cesare would later employ Leonardo as military architect and engineer.

1476
Verrocchio completes his statue of *David*.

Leonardo's Notebooks

1473
On the upper left-hand corner of his pen and ink drawing, *Landscape of the Arno River and Valley*, housed in the Uffizi Gallery's collection, Leonardo da Vinci inscribed: "On the Day of Santa Maria delle Neve (Saint Mary of the Snow), 5 August 1473." Most scholars believe it is his earliest known dated work.

In April, Leonardo is among those charged with sodomy with Jacopo Saltarelli, a seventeen-year-old apprentice in a goldsmith's workshop. The charge is eventually dismissed.

Leonardo begins the painting *Ginevra de' Benci* (c. 1476–78) around this time.

Antonio, Ser Piero's first legitimate child and Leonardo's half-brother, is born on February 26.

1478
Leonardo wins a commission for an altarpiece in the San Bernardo Chapel in the Palazzo della Signoria in Florence. He never completes the painting.

1479
Leonardo begins painting the *Benois Madonna* (Hermitage, St. Petersburg) around this time.

1480
Leonardo begins his *St. Jerome* (Vatican Museums, Rome), circa 1480. It is never completed.

1481
Leonardo is commissioned by an order of monks to paint the *Adoration of the Magi* (Uffizi, Florence) for the main altar in San Donato a Scopeto, near Florence. He does not complete the work.

The Pope calls several Florentine painters, Botticelli, Perugino, Roselli, and Ghirlandaio, to Rome to decorate the walls of the Sistine Chapel. Leonardo is not among them.

Leonardo begins work on the design of the *Madonna Litta* (Hermitage, St. Petersburg), circa 1481 to 1497. Although based on his drawings, some scholars believe it may have been painted by his student Giovanni Antonio Boltraffio.

1482
Leonardo moves to Milan, after offering his services to Lodovico Sforza, il Moro. He stays in Milan under his patronage through 1499.

1483
In April, Leonardo receives a commission for the first version of *Madonna of the Rocks* (Louvre, Paris) from the order of the Confraternity of the Immaculate Conception. He is to collaborate with the brothers Evangelista and Giovan Ambrogio da Predis in decorating a chapel in the church of San Francesco Grande in Milan. A dispute wages for years over the unfinished work. Some scholars believe the second version of the painting (completed with the help of assistants and now in London) was hung here in 1508 as settlement.

1487
Leonardo begins the Codex Forster I around this time.

Leonardo enters a competitive project to design a domed crossing tower or *tiburio* for Santa Maria Nascente, the cathedral in Milan. He hires an assistant to build a model in wood.

1489
In July, Lodovico Sforza (il Moro) asks Leonardo to work on a model for the equestrian statue of Francesco Sforza.

1490
Leonardo, engaged with directing feasts and pageants at the court of Lodovico Sforza, designs the stage set for Bernardo Bellincioni's *La Festa del Paradiso* to mark the January nuptials of Gian Galeazzo Sforza and Isabella of Aragon.

In April, Leonardo indicates he is continuing work on the Sforza horse.

Leonardo paints (c. 1489–1490) the *Lady with the Ermine* (Cecilia Gallerani), a portrait of Lodovico Sforza's young mistress. The painting is in the Czartoryski Museum, Crakow.

On June 21, Leonardo and Francesco di Giorgio travel to Pavia on the rebuilding of the Milan cathedral.

Some historians speculate that Leonardo is the model.

Lorenzo de' Medici sets up the Platonist Academy.

1477
Girogione is born.

1478
Botticelli paints his *Primavera.*

Florence experiences the Pazzi conspiracy, terrible floods, and an outbreak of the plague.

The Spanish Inquisition is founded by the Catholic Church to destroy heresy.

1480
Lorenzo de' Medici takes Naples as an ally and makes peace with the Pope.

Lodovico Sforza, il Moro (who is to become Leonardo's greatest patron), becomes Regent of Milan and takes control of the city-state.

1481
Verrocchio works on the model for his statue *Il Colleone* around this time.

Savonarola, the Dominican zealot and reformer, is sent by his superiors to Florence, where he gives his first sermons. They are a failure and he is recalled to the monastery.

1483
Raphael is born in Urbino.

Charles VIII becomes king of France.

1484
Botticelli paints *The Birth of Venus.*

Pope Innocent VIII is elected.

1485
The plague ravages Milan.

Titian is born.

1486
Vitruvius's *De Architectura* is published by Sulpico de Veroli in its first printed edition.

Andrea del Sarto, the Florentine painter, is born.

1488
Verrocchio dies in Venice.

1489
Correggio is born.

1490
Savonarola, back in Florence, delivers sermons from the pulpit of San Marco

---

1478
Codex Atlanticus (c. 1478–1518), Biblioteca Ambrosiana, Milan
This is the largest collection of the Notebook pages. It consists of twelve leather-bound volumes, which originally housed 401 folios; now after years of conservation it consists of 1,119 folios. There are notes on hydraulics, mathematics, geometry, astronomy, botany, zoology, painting, perspective, light and shade, and studies for the commissions of the Sforza and Trivulziano equestrian monuments.

Windsor Castle Collection (c. 1478–1518), Royal Library, Windsor Castle
Comprising some 600 unbound drawings, most of which are anatomical and proportional studies.

1487
Codex Trivulzianus (c. 1487–1490), Trivulziana Library, Sforza Castle, Milan
This collection consists of fifty-five sheets containing notes on literary efforts, including vocabulary lists and how to standardize the Italian language.

Codexes Forster I (c. 1487—1490), **Forster II** (c. 1495–1497), and **Forster III** (c. 1493–1496), The Victoria and Albert Museum, London.
Three parchment-bound volumes house five small notebooks, which include studies of geometry, notes on physics and drawings of horses for the Sforza monument.

1488
Paris Manuscript B (c. 1488–1489), Institut de France, Paris
The manuscript contains notes and drawings of mechanical inventions, architectural studies of churches, and engines of war. It also includes some pages removed from the original manuscript, and later returned, now designated as B.N. 2037 (Ash. I) 1875/1.

Trattato della Pittura, also known as **Codex Urbinas Latinas 1270** (c. 1488–1519), The Vatican Library, Rome
Leonardo made notes on the subject of painting in several notebooks from the late 1480s to the early 1500s but never compiled them. Francesco Melzi, Leonardo's heir and friend, gathered the notes and compiled them over a period of decades. The treatise

Leonardo's Life in Brief, 1452–1519[128]

In late June, Leonardo learns he has not won the commission for the *tiburio* in Milan's cathedral. It is given to Giovanni Antonio Amadeo and Giovanni Giacomo Dolcebono.

Leonardo executes his drawing *The Vitruvian Man* (Galleria dell'Accademia), based on Vitruvius's book on architecture.

The ten-year-old Gian Giacomo Caprotti di Oreno comes to work in Leonardo's workshop in July. Leonardo nicknames him Salai (little devil) because he is always in trouble.

1491
Leonardo prepares a festival to celebrate the wedding of Lodovico Sforza and Beatrice d'Este in the house of Galeazzo da Sanseverino.

1492
Leonardo travels to Lombardy and visits Valtellina, Valsassina, Bellagio, and Ivrea.

1493
Leonardo's full-scale model for the equestrian statue of Francesco Sforza is displayed in Milan at the November wedding of Bianca Maria Sforza to the Emperor Maximilian I of Hapsburg.

Leonardo takes a woman named Caterina (perhaps his mother) into his home in July.

In December, Leonardo decides to cast the ill-fated Sforza horse in bronze on its side and without a tail.

1495
Leonardo begins *The Last Supper* in the refectory of the Santa Maria delle Grazie monastery in Milan.

Leonardo travels to Florence to consult in the building of the Sala del Gran Consiglio in the Palazzo Vecchio.

Around this time, Leonardo and assistants begin the second version of the *Madonna of the Rocks,* perhaps for the altarpiece in San Francesco Grande. It is completed in 1508.

1496
Leonardo works on the painting *La Belle Ferronière* (Louvre, Paris), perhaps a portrait of Lucrezia Crivelli, a mistress of Lodovico Sforza.

1498
Early in the year, Fra Luca Pacioli publishes *De Divina Proportione* and dedicates it to Lodovico Sforza. In the book's preface, Pacioli notes that Leonardo designed the geometric drawings.

In April, Leonardo and assistants work on a decorative mural in the Sala delle Asse in the Castello Sforzesco in Milan.

1499
In April, Lodovico Sforza gives Leonardo a vineyard adjacent to the monastery of San Vittore, near Santa Marie delle Grazie in Milan.

Leonardo sends money to his bank account in Florence in preparation for his return to that city with Luca Pacioli.

1500
Leonardo and Fra Luca Pacioli leave for Mantua, where they are the guests of Prince Francesco Gonzaga and his wife, Isabelle d'Este, a musician and art collector. There, Leonardo draws the *Portrait in Profile of Isabelle d'Este.*

Leonardo and Pacioli go on to Venice, where Leonardo prepares a proposal for a defense system against a Turkish invasion of the area.

Leonardo returns to Florence in April and spends time with the Servite monks at the church of Santissima Annunziata. He draws a cartoon for the *Virgin and Child with Saint Anne.*

1501
In Florence, Leonardo paints, with his pupils, the *Madonna with the Yarnwinder* (collection of the Duke of Buccleuch) for Florimond Robertet, Secretary of State for King Louis XII. Leonardo and his pupils create a second, very similar version of the

Leonardo's Times, 1452–1519

calling for reform. His zealous delivery, honed in Brescia, now garners support and some hail him as a prophet.

1492
Piero della Francesca dies (born in 1420). His treatises on solids and perspective most likely influenced Leonardo.

Bramante begins the choir of Santa Maria delle Grazie in Milan.

Christopher Columbus sails to the new world.

Lorenzo de' Medici, Il Magnifico, dies. His son Piero II assumes control of Florence.

Rodrigo Borgia is elected Pope Alexander VI by a very slim margin.

1493
Maximilian I becomes Holy Roman Emperor.

1494
The Italian wars begin. Charles VIII of France, an ally of Lodovico il Moro, invades Italy and takes control of Naples.

Charles VIII takes control of Florence and Piero de' Medici is deposed.

Savonarola, renouncing the humanism of the Medicis and calling for a republic devoted to God and a strict moral code, becomes a leading figure in Florence.

Pisa asserts its independence.

The mathematician Fra Luca Pacioli publishes his *Summa de Arithmetica*

Lodovico Sforza (il Moro) sends the bronze for the Sforza equestrian monument to his father-in-law, Ercole d'Este, Duke of Ferrara, to make a cannon.

Domenico Ghirlandaio dies.

1495
Albrecht Dürer is in Italy.

1496
Piero Pollaiuolo dies.

1497
Hans Holbein the Younger is born.

1498
Beatrice d'Este dies.

In Florence, Savonarola is burned at the stake.

In France, Louis XII succeeds Charles VIII.

Antonio Pollaiuolo dies.

Michelangelo begins the *Pieta.*

Leonardo's Notebooks

contains notes on perspective, elements of composition, human form, and the effect of light and shadow. Emphasis is on the need for consistent study and practice of the craft.

1489
Winsor, Royal Library, 19059a, Richter 1370. Leonardo, while working on a drawing of a skull, writes, "A di 2 Aprile 1489 titolato de figure umano [On the 2nd of April 1489, book entitled 'Of the human figure']."

1490
Paris Manuscript C (c. 1490–1491),
Institut de France, Paris
This collection contains notes and drawings on Leonardo's theories on the study of light and shade. It also includes observations on landscape and hydraulic works.

1492
Paris Manuscript A (c. 1492),
Institut de France, Paris
The basis of the *Trattato della Pittura*, these pages include theoretical notes and drawings on painting, perspective, water, and mechanics. It also includes pages removed from the original, but later returned, and now designated as B.N. 2038 (Ash. II) 1875/2.

Codex Arundel (c. 1492–1516),
British Library, London
Comprising 238 sheets, this collection includes studies of weights, balance, friction, light, sound, mirrors, optics; and hydraulics, as well as diving equipment, drawings of war machines and an armored car, lists of allegories and proverbs, and plans for the royal residence of King Francis in Romorantin.

1493
Paris Manuscript H (c. 1493–1494),
Institut de France, Paris
This consists of three pocket notebooks relating to Euclidean geometry, including notes and drawings of polyhedrons, presumably drawn for Luca Pacioli's *De Divina Proportione.*

Codexes Madrid I (c. 1493–1497) and **Madrid II** (c. 1503–1505),
National Library, Madrid
Seven hundred pages include drawings and notes on a mechanical robot, hydraulics, geometry, birds, canals, and plans for diverting water from the Arno River.

Madonna of the Yarnwinder, called *The Lansdowne Madonna* (private collection). Scholars are not certain which of the paintings went to his patron Robertet.

1502
In May, Cesare Borgia, Captain General of the Papal Armies (who is also the Pope's son), appoints Leonardo architect and military engineer of the Marche and Romagna regions. In the line of duty, Leonardo inspects fortresses, witnesses the Romagna campaign, engages in cartography, travels to Urbino, Cesena, Porto Cesenatico, Pesaro, and Rimini and meets Machiavelli.

1503
Leonardo returns to Florence at the beginning of the year.

Florence is at war with Pisa. Leonardo sketches designs for military machines and fortifications for the Signoria. He and others work on plans, originated by Machiavelli, to divert the Arno River. The scheme fails.

In July, Leonardo's name is reentered into the account book of the Florentine painter's guild.

Leonardo works on the cartoon for *The Battle of Anghiari* in his workshop in the great cloister of Santa Maria Novella.

Leonardo begins the painting of *Mona Lisa* (Louvre, Paris), seemingly a portrait of Lisa Gherardini, the wife of a prominent Florentine, Francesco del Giocondo. The painting is completed much later, around 1516.

1504
In January, a committee of some twenty-nine artists, including Leonardo, decides on the site for Michelangelo's completed *David.*

In February, Leonardo designs a movable scaffold for the huge *Battle of Anghiari.*

A May contract with the Signori of Florence confirms Leonardo's monthly stipend of fifteen florins for his work on the *Battle of Anghiari.*

In July, Ser Piero di Antonio da Vinci, Leonardo's father, dies in Florence. Settling his estate causes disputes for years between Leonardo and his seven legitimate half-brothers.

Leonardo's uncle, Francesco, makes him his heir.

Leonardo records in November that he thinks he has the solution to squaring the circle.

Leonardo begins drawings for *Leda and the Swan,* circa 1504 to 1508, at this time.

1505
In June, Leonardo writes that he began to paint *The Battle of Anghiari* in the Palazzo Vecchio in Florence. He had three assistants, Raffaello d'Antonio di Biagio, Spagnolo, and Tomaso di Giovanni, a color grinder.

1506
Leonardo stops work on *The Battle of Anghiari* and goes to Milan with Salai in early September at the request of Charles d'Amboise, the city's French governor. He is to design a villa and gardens. D'Amboise notes his satisfaction with the work.

Leonardo begins his drawings for *Leda and the Swan* around this time, most likely in preparation for a painting. He never paints one, but one of his students creates one from his drawings.

1507
Still in Milan serving the French, Leonardo recovers the San Vittore vineyard in Milan (given to him by Lodovico Sforza) by decree. The French had confiscated the property during the fall of Milan in 1499.

Leonardo is involved in a legal dispute against his brothers regarding his father's will.

Leonardo's uncle, Francesco, dies, leaving him sole heir.

1499
The second Italian war begins. On September 9 and 10, French troops led by Gian Giacomo Trivulzio, a mercenary general, storm the city of Milan. King Louis XII himself enters Milan about a month later. Milan falls to the French in December and Lodovico Sforza is expelled. Cesare Borgia, the son of Pope Alexander VI, aligns himself with Louis XII. He is named Duke of Valentinois.

The Turks threaten Venice.

Luca Signorelli paints the *Last Judgment* frescoes in the cathedral of Orvieto.

1500
Lodovico Sforza, il Moro, is taken prisoner by the French.

Pope Alexander VI proclaims a crusade against the Turks while his son, Cesare Borgia, conquers much of central Italy on his behalf.

1501
The French occupy Rome.

Michelangelo begins the *David* in Florence.

1502
Piero Soderini is named *gonfaloniere* (chief magistrate) of Florence for life.

Francesco di Giorgio Martini dies.

1503
Cesare Borgia falls ill and Alexander VI dies. With the death of his father, Borgia loses power and flees to Spain.

Giuliano delle Rovere, an enemy of Alexander VI, is elected Pope Julius II.

Pope Julius engages the architect Bramante to plan a new Saint Peter's Basilica. He would also ask Michelangelo to paint the Sistine ceiling and Raphael to decorate the papal apartments.

France suffers defeat throughout Italy.

1504
Michelangelo executes the cartoon for *The Battle of Cascina* as a pendant to Leonardo's *Battle of Anghiari.*

Filippino Lippi dies.

1505
Michelangelo goes to Rome to work for Pope Julius II and is commissioned to create his tomb.

1497
Paris Manuscript I (c. 1497–1505), Institut de France, Paris
Two pocket-size books in their original bindings include studies on Euclidean geometric theory, architecture, perspective, heating water, and Latin.

Paris Manuscripts L (c. 1497–1503), Institut de France, Paris
A small, intact notebook, seemingly created when Leonardo was military architect and engineer for Cesare Borgia, includes notes and drawings related to defense fortifications and maps. It also references his *Last Supper.*

Paris Manuscript M (c. late 1490s to 1500), Institut de France, Paris
The smallest of Leonardo's manuscripts, it includes observations and drawings on Euclidean geometric theory, Bramante's architectural theories, and botany.

1503
Paris Manuscript K, including **K1**, **K2**, and K3 (c. 1503–1508), Institut de France, Paris
Three pocket-size notebooks in their original bindings are filled with more observations on geometric theory and optics.

1505
Codice del Volo degli Uccelli (c. 1505), Biblioteca Reale, Turin
Notes and sketches on the flight of birds.

1506
During the year, Leonardo most likely began what is now the third part of Manuscript K, 1506–1508 (Institut de France, Paris)

1508
Codex Leicester, previously **Codex Hammer** (c. 1508–1512), now Collection of Bill and Melinda Gates, Seattle, Washington
Eighteen leather-bound sheets, folded into seventy-two pages, are primarily devoted to scientific notes on hydraulics, including studies on the engineering of dams and the nature of water in rivers and seas; there are also notes on astronomy, geology, nature, and travel in Tuscany and Lombardy, as well as a record of work on the Sforza monument. There are some 300 small illustrations in the margins of the folios.

Leonardo's Life in Brief, 1452–1519[128]

In September, Leonardo meets a young nobleman, Francesco Melzi, in Milan, who will become his devoted pupil, companion, and major heir.

Leonardo most likely begins the cartoon for the *Virgin and Child with Saint Anne* (c. 1507–1508).

1508
Leonardo, now fifty-six, divides his time between Florence and Milan.

In the winter, he dissects the body of an old man at the Hospital of Santa Maria Nuova in Florence.

Staying at the Florentine home of Piero Baccio Martelli in March, Leonardo begins his Codex Arundel, "a collection without order, composed of many pages which I have copied, hoping then to put them in their appropriate place, according to the topics that they treat" (Ar. Fol. 11, R 4).

Leonardo returns to Milan in April to serve King Louis XII. He lives in the church of San Babila.

Leonardo arranges for the removal of the *Virgin of the Rocks* altarpiece (newly installed in San Francesco Grande in Milan) so Giovan Ambrogio can copy it under his supervision. Some scholars speculate that this second version of the painting is the one hung at the National Gallery, London.

Leonardo begins work on a funerary equestrian monument to Gian Giacomo Trivulzio, intended for the church of San Nazaro.

Leonardo may have begun his painting *Saint John the Baptist* (Louvre, Paris), circa 1508 to 1516, at this time.

Leonardo begins to paint the *Virgin and Child with Saint Anne* (Louvre, Paris), circa 1508 to 1517, most probably his final painting.

1509
Leonardo prepares triumphal festivities for Louis XII to celebrate his defeat of the Venetians.

1510
Still in Milan serving the French, Leonardo earns a yearly salary of 104 *livres*, paid by the French state under Louis XII.

In October, Leonardo is asked to advise on the choir stall design for the Milan Cathedral.

Leonardo is granted permission to build a wall separating his vineyard from the garden of the monks at San Vittore in Milan.

Leonardo works with Marcantonio della Torre, a professor of anatomy at the University of Pavia, on his anatomical investigations. It results in the notes and drawings in what is now the Windsor Anatomical Manuscript A (R 1376).

1511
Leonardo writes that invading Swiss soldiers have set fire to Milan, marking the end of French domination. Leonardo leaves the city with his retinue and stays at the Melzi villa in the Vaprio d'Adda.

1513
By December, Leonardo is in Rome in the house of Giuliano de' Medici, Il Magnifico, the brother of Pope Leo X. Giuliano's patronage provides Leonardo with a workshop in the Belvedere wing of the Vatican Palace.

1514
Around September, Leonardo goes to Civitavecchia to study the harbor and archaeological ruins. For Leo X he produces a map illustrating a project to drain the Pontine marshes.

1515
Leonardo writes that Giuliano de' Medici left for Rome on January 9 for his marriage in Savoy (Paris Ms. G, verso of cover, R 1377).

Leonardo's Times, 1452–1519

1506
In Florence, Raphael makes sketches based on the *Mona Lisa* and, circa 1506, the *Leda and the Swan* around this time.

Bramante is in Rome to begin work on the commission granted by Pope Julius II to create a new Saint Peter's.

The painter Mantegna dies.

Dürer on his second trip to Italy.

1507
Michelangelo's statue of Pope Julius II is installed in Bologna around this time.

Pope Julius II begins to sell indulgences to pay for the building of Saint Peter's Basilica.

1508
Leonardo's most important patron, Lodovico Sforza, dies in France, having been imprisoned by the French for ten years.

Michelangelo begins work on the Sistine Chapel ceiling in Rome.

The League of Cambrai is formed against Venice as it seeks to expand its territories. Pope Julius II, the Holy Roman Emperor Maximillian I, King Louis XII, King Ferdinand V of Aragon, and several Italian city-states join ranks to keep the Venetians at bay.

1509
The French defeat the Venetians at Agnadello.

Raphael is commissioned by Pope Julius II to fresco the Vatican *Stanze* (papal apartments).

Henry VIII becomes king of England.

1510
Melzi draws a man in profile in one of Leonardo's notebooks, dated 15 August.

Botticelli, the Florentine painter, dies.

The Venetian painter Giorgione dies.

1511
Charles d'Amboise dies.

Swiss troops reach the outskirts of Milan, and Pope Julius II forms the Holy League against the French, who withdraw their troops from Milan after the battle of Ravenna. The Holy League alliance is created by Julius II to get the French out of

Leonardo's Notebooks

Paris Manuscript D (1508–1509), Institut de France, Paris
This treatise explores theories on vision related to light, shadow, and color.

Paris Manuscript F (1508–1513), Institut de France, Paris
This notebook, in its original binding, investigates the science of optics, geology, and astronomy and studies of water dynamics.

1509
In April, Leonardo notes that he has solved the geometric problem of squaring two outlines (Windsor, RL 19145).

On May 3, Leonardo records the making of the canal of San Cristoforo in Milan (Codex Atlanticus, fol. 1097r; R 1009).

1510
Paris Manuscript G (c. 1510–1515), Institut de France, Paris

In July, a mechanical lion by Leonardo is given to King Francis I, in Lyons, on a gift from Lorenzo de' Medici, to mark the King's return from Italy.

Pope Leo X makes his triumphal entry into Florence in November with Leonardo and Giuliano de' Medici as part of his papal entourage.

Leonardo plans a new palace for Lorenzo di Piero de' Medici opposite Michelozzo's Palazzo Medici.

In December, Leonardo leaves Florence for Bologna, where Pope Leo X is to have peace talks with King Francis I. Giuliano pays Leonardo forty *ducati* for the trip. They return to Rome.

1516
Giuliano de' Medici dies in March, prompting Leonardo to write, "The Medici made me and destroyed me" (C.A., fol. 429r; R 1368a).

1517
Leonardo, now sixty-five, goes to France as the guest of Francis I. As "peintre du Roy," he is granted a house at the chateau of Cloux, near the royal court at Amboise. Francesco Melzi and Salai accompany him.

Leonardo receives Cardinal Luigi d'Aragona and his secretary, Antonio de Beatis, in October. De Beatis records the event—and the works of Leonardo's that he views—in his diary. He also indicates that Leonardo is partially paralyzed, perhaps by a stroke.

By the end of the year, Leonardo is in Romorantin working on plans to build a palace for King Francis I.

1518
Leonardo receives a generous stipend of 2,000 *ecus soleil* from the King for two years. Melzi receives 800 *ecus* for the same period, and Salai gets 100 *ecus*.

Leonardo stays in Romorantin and continues work on King Francis's palace and related canals.

Leonardo designs a ring with the emblems of the Medici.

Leonardo writes on June 24 that he has left Romorantin for the castle of Cloux.

At the June wedding of Lorenzo de' Medici and Maddalena de la Tour d'Auvergne, the niece of King Francis I, *The Feast of Paradise* (first staged by Leonardo in 1490 at the Castello Sforza) is performed in Cloux.

1519
On April 23, Leonardo, now sixty-seven and ill, goes before the court at Amboise to record his will. Francesco Melzi is the executor of his estate and inherits all drawings, manuscripts, tools, and works of the painter, which Melzi will bring back to his family's villa in 1520. Salai and Battista de Vilanis, his servants, as well as his half-brothers and half-sister are among the other heirs. Salai inherits the vineyard in Milan, where he builds a house; he is also bequeathed some of his Master's major paintings (those still in his studio): *Leda and the Swan, Virgin and Child with Saint Anne, Mona Lisa, Saint John the Baptist,* and *Saint Jerome.*

Leonardo dies on May 2 in the castle of Cloux. In accordance with his wishes, he is buried in the cloister of Saint-Florentin at Amboise. The church is later destroyed.

His companion, friend, and heir, Francesco Melzi, writes to notify Leonardo's half-brother Ser Giuliano da Vinci of his death.

Italy so he can extend his papal properties. Major participants include Maximilian I, Venice, the Swiss cantons, Ferdinand II of Aragon, and Henry VIII of England.

Erasmus, the humanist, prints his *Praise of Folly,* a satire on the abuses of the Catholic Church.

Raphael completes the *Camera della Segnatura* in the Vatican.

Vasari is born.

1512
The Florentine Republic falls and the Medici regain power.

In Milan, the Sforza are reinstated.

1513
Pope Julius II dies. Giovanni de' Medici is elected Pope Leo X, reigning until December 1521.

Machiavelli writes *The Prince* (based on the ruling tactics of Cesare Borgia) and works on his *Discourses.*

The French withdraw from Italy.

Pinturricchio dies.

1514
Bramante dies in Rome on April 11.

Raphael begins his frescoes at the Villa Farnesina in Rome.

1515
In January, Louis XII, Leonardo's patron, dies. Francis I becomes king of France. Francis reconquers the Milanese region at the battle of Marignano and the French reoccupy Milan.

1516
In October, Giuliano da Sangallo, Leonardo's colleague and friend, dies in Rome.

Charles V becomes king of Spain.

Ariosto publishes *Orlando Furioso.*

Sir Thomas More's *Utopia* is published.

Erasmus translates the New Testament.

1517
Luther writes his ninety-five theses against indulgences sold in the Catholic Church.

1519
Charles V is crowned emperor.

Cortez lands in Mexico.

1512
Leonardo continues to work on and document his landscape and canal studies in the Lombardy region.

1513
Paris Manuscript E (c. 1513–1514), Institut de France, Paris
A study of weight and gravity, with reference to the draining of the malarial Pontine marshes south of Rome. Leonardo writes that he and his household, including Melzi and Salai, left on September 24 for Rome (R 1465).

1514
Leonardo writes, "Finished today July 7th an hour before midnight at his Belvedere studio ..."
(Codex Atlanticus, fol. 244v; R 1376).

Throughout the year, he continues to work on notes for the *Libro di pittura,* his treatise on painting, which is eventually published by Francesco Melzi as the *Trattato della Pittura.*

Notes

Part Five. Chronology

[127] The opening paragraph of Leonardo's original will was written on April 23, 1519. He died on May 2, 1519 at the age of 67. Richter, 1970, vol. II, R 1566, 388–389.

[128] The timeline relies mainly on the following sources:
Carmen C. Bambach, ed., *Leonardo da Vinci, Master Draftsman*, 2003, 227–241.

Serge Bramly, *Leonardo: Discovering the Life of Leonardo da Vinci*, 1988.

Andre Chastel, *The Genius of Leonardo*, 1961.

Martin, Kemp, *Leonardo da Vinci: Experience, Experiment and Design*, 2006, 199–206.

PART SIX
APPENDICES

As a day well spent brings happy sleep,
so a life well used brings happy death.

R 1173[129]

APPENDIX I
DEFINITIONS

Braccio. The Italian word for arm, *braccio,* was also a standard unit of measurement in Italy from the Middle Ages until only recently. As a measurement it varied in size from city to city. The unit *braccio* is the not the length of an arm. Rather, it was merely the name of a unit of measure. Pedretti in his *Commentaries* provides us with no fewer than four different units from three different cities and calculates the height of a man in each unit by multiplying each *braccio* by three. One of the Florentine units of measure, *the braccio Fiorentino da panno,* is equal to 0.5836 m. or 22.9768 in. Because Leonardo does not specify which unit he used, Richter specifically suggests that is was the *braccio Fiorentino da panno,* since other types of *braccia* would have resulted in a figure with unacceptable proportions. (Richter, 1970, vol. I, 245, footnote to R 309; see also Pedretti, vol. I, 232.)

Cubit. An ancient measure of length about 18 to 22 inches; originally, the length of the arm from the end of the middle finger to the elbow. (*Webster's New World Dictionary,* New York: World Publishing Company, 1959, 357.)

Pace. 1. A stretching out of the leg in walking, running, etc.; stride. 2. A conventional measure of length, approximately the distance covered in a step or a stride; it is generally estimated at 2½ feet, or sometimes in measuring, 3 feet or 3.3 feet (⅕ of a rod). The regulation pace of the United States Army is 30 inches, or 36 inches for double time. The Roman pace, measured from the heel of one foot to the heel of the same foot in the next stride, was 5 Roman feet, or 58.1 inches; it is now know as the *geometric pace,* about 5 feet (*Webster's,* 1048).

APPENDIX II TEXTS

The Medieval Apprenticeship Process

Cennini, Cennino d'Andrea. *The Craftsman's Handbook: 'Il Libro dell' Arte'*. Trans. Daniel V. Thompson, Jr. New York: Dover Publications, 1960, 64–65.

THE SYSTEM BY WHICH YOU SHOULD PREPARE TO ACQUIRE THE SKILL TO WORK ON PANEL

Know that there ought not to be less time spent in learning than this: to begin as a shopboy studying for one year, to get practice drawing on the little panel; next, to serve in a shop under some master to learn how to work in all the branches which pertain to our profession; and to stay and begin the working up of colors; and to learn to boil the sizes, and grind the gesso; and to get experience in gessoing anconas, and modeling and scraping them; gilding and stamping; for the space of a good six years. Then to get experience in painting, embellishing with mordants, making cloths of gold, getting practice in working on the wall, for six more years; drawing all the time, never leaving off, either on holidays or on workdays. And in this way your talent, through much practice, will develop into a real ability. Otherwise, if you follow other systems, you need never hope that they will reach any high degree of perfection. For there are many who say that they have mastered the profession without having served under masters. Do not believe it, for I give you the example of this book: even if you study it by day and by night, if you do not see some practice under some master you will never amount to anything, nor will you ever be able to hold your head up in the company of masters.

Beginning to work on panel, in the name of the Most Holy Trinity: always invoking that name and that of the Glorious Virgin Mary.

Leonardo's Interpretation of the Vitruvian Text

Richter, J. P., and Irma A. Richter, enlarged and rev. *The Literary Works of Leonardo da Vinci.* 2nd ed. London: Oxford U P, 1939. 3rd ed. New York: Phaidon, 1970, 255–256.

Vitruvius, the architect, says in his work on architecture that the measurements of the human body are distributed by Nature as follows: that is, that 4 fingers make 1 palm, and four palms make one foot, 6 palms make one cubit; 4 cubits make a man's height. And 4 cubits make one pace and 24 palms make a man; and these measures he used in his buildings. If you open your legs so much as to decrease your height $^{1}/_{14}$ and spread and raise your arms till your middle fingers touch the level of the top of your head you must know that the center of the outspread limbs will be in the navel and the space between the legs will be an equilateral triangle.

The length of a man's outspread arms is equal to his height.

From the roots of the hair to the bottom of the chin is the tenth of a man's height; from the bottom of the chin to the top of his head is one-eighth of his height; from the top of the breast to the top of his head will be one-sixth of a man. From the top of the breast to the roots of the hair will be the seventh part of the whole man. From the nipples to the top of the head will be the fourth part of the man. The greatest width of the shoulders contains in itself the fourth part of the man. From the elbow to the tip of the hand will be the fifth part of a man; and from the elbow to the angle of the armpit will be the eighth part of the man. The whole hand will be the tenth part of the man; the beginning of the genitals marks the middle of the man. The foot is the seventh part of the man. From the sole of the foot to below the knee will be the fourth part of the man. From below the knee to the beginning of the genitals will be the fourth part of the man. The distance from the bottom of the chin to the nose and from the roots of the hair to the eyebrows is in each case the same, and like the ear, a third of the face.

Vitruvius Book III, Chapter 1

Smith, Thomas Gordon. *Vitruvius on Architecture.* Translation/Emendation of Morris Hicky Morgan's original translation by Stephen Kellogg. New York: Monacelli Press, 2003, 86–88. Reprinted here by permission.

Chapter 1

1. The design of a temple depends on *symmetria,* the concept of which architects must diligently maintain. *Symmetria* is born from proportion, in Greek *[analogia]*. Proportion is the correspondence of measure between the members of a work and the whole work to a certain part selected as standard. From this the principle of *symmetria* is brought about. Without *symmetria* and proportion there can be neither rhyme nor reason in the composition of a temple—that is, unless there is a precise correspondence of measure like that found in the parts of the well-formed human being (fig. 137).
2. The human body is so designed by nature that the face, from the chin to the top of the forehead and the lower roots of the hair, is a tenth part of the whole height (fig. 138). The open hand from the wrist to the tip of the middle finger is exactly the same. The head from the chin to the crown is one-eighth, and from the top of the breast with the neck and shoulder to the lowest roots of the hair is one-sixth. From the middle of the breast to the summit of the crown is one-fourth. If we take the height of the face, the distance from the bottom of the chin to the underside of the nostrils is one-third of it; the nose from the underside of the nostrils to a line between the eyebrows is the same; and further, from there to the lowest roots of the hair is also a third, this comprising the forehead. The length of the foot is one-sixth of the height of the body; the forearm is one-fourth; and the breadth of the breast is also one-fourth. The other members, too, have their own proportions of relative measurements. By employing these, the famous painters and sculptors of antiquity attained great and everlasting renown.
3. Similarly, the members of a temple must have a perfect correspondence of measure of individual parts to the whole. Then again, in the human body the central point is naturally the navel. If a person lies flat with hands and feet extended, the fingers and toes of each hand and foot would touch the circumference of a circle described by placing a pair of compasses centered on the navel. Just as the human body yields this circular outline, a square figure can also be found from it. If we measure the distance from the soles of the feet to the top of the head, and apply that measure to the outstretched arms, the breadth will be the same as the height—as in the case of plane surfaces that are perfectly square.

4. Therefore, since nature has designed the human body so that there is a proportional correspondence between the members and the whole, it seems that the ancients were right when they established the idea that measures of individual members in the construction of buildings should also have an exact relation to the whole composition. While transmitting the proper arrangements for all sorts of buildings to us, then, they were careful to do so, especially in the case of temples of the gods, buildings in which merits and flaws generally last forever.

5. Further, it was from the members of the body that they derived ratios of measurements that seemed to be necessary in all works, namely the finger, palm, foot, and cubit (fig. 139). They apportioned these to form the perfect number, which the Greeks called [*teleon*], and the ancients fixed this as ten. The palm is found from the number of the fingers of the hand and the foot from the palm. Again, while ten is naturally perfect because it is made up by the fingers of the two palms, Plato also held that this number was perfect because ten was composed of the individual units, called by the Greeks [*monades*]. But as soon as eleven or twelve is reached, the numbers become excessive and cannot be perfect until they come to ten for the second time. This is because the component parts of the number are the individual units.

6. The mathematicians, however, maintain a different view, saying that the perfect number is six because this number is composed of integral parts that correspond in their ratios to the number six. Thus, one is one-sixth; two is one-third; three is one-half; four is two-thirds, or in Greek [*dimoeros*]. Five is five-sixths, in Greek [*pentemoeros*], and six is the perfect number. As the number grows larger, the addition of the unit above six is in Greek [*ephektos*]. Eight, formed by the addition of a one-third part of six, is the integer and a third, in Greek [*hemiolios*]. The addition of two-thirds makes the number ten, the integer and two-thirds, which in Greek is [*epidemoeros*]. In the number eleven, where five are added, we have the five-sixths, in Greek [*epipemptos*]. Finally, twelve, being composed of the two simple integers, is called in Greek [*diplasios*].

7. Further, as the foot is one-sixth of a man's height, the height of the body as expressed in the number of feet being limited to six, the ancients held that this was the perfect number. They observed that the cubit consisted of six palms or of twenty-four fingers. This principal seems to have been followed by the states of Greece, and as the cubit consisted of six palms, they made the *drachma,* which they used as their monetary unit, consist in the same way of six bronze coins, like our *asses,* which they called *oboli.* To correspond to the fingers they divided the *drachma* into twenty-four quarter-*obolos*, which some called *dichalca* and others *trichalca.*

8. But our countrymen at first fixed upon the ancient number and made ten bronze pieces go to the *denarius,* and this is the origin of the name applied to the *denarius* to this day. One-fourth part of it, consisting of two *asses,* they called *sesterce.* But later, observing that six and ten were both perfect numbers, they combined the two and made the most perfect number, sixteen. They found the foot to be the basis of this. For if we take two palms from the cubit, there remains the foot of four palms, but the palm contains four fingers. Hence, the foot contains sixteen fingers and the *denarius* the same number of bronze *asses.*

9. Therefore, if it is agreed that number was derived from the human fingers and that there is a correspondence of measurement between the members separately and the entire form of the body in accordance of a certain part selected as standard, we can have nothing but respect for those who, in constructing temples to the immortal gods, have arranged their elements so that the separate parts and the whole design may harmonize in their proportions and *symmetriae.*

APPENDIX III
CONCORDANCES

1. INDEX OF MANUSCRIPTS

Mark of Manuscript	Description of Manuscript	Place/Location	Date
A.	Fragment of manuscript, treating on various matters.	Institut de France, Paris	c. 1490–1492
B.	Bound volume, marked B.	Institut de France, Paris	c. 1488–1490
B.N. 2038. (Ash. I) B.N. 2037. (Ash. II)	Treatise on Painting marked 1875/2, and 1875/1	Institut de France, Paris	c. 1490–1492
C.A.	Bound volume, commonly called Codex Atlanticus, 401 folios, each containing one or more manuscript sheets.	Biblioteca Ambrosiana, Milan	c. 1478–1518
H.	Notebook, forming the first portion of a bound volume, marked H.	Institut de France, Paris	1494
Trn.	Volume in original binding, treating on flights of birds, geometry, etc., and thirteen drawings.	Biblioteca Reale, Turin	c. 1487–1505
V.	Five loose sheets.	Accademia, Venice	c. 1490–1511
W.	Sheets from Leoni's collection: originally one volume bound; some six hundred drawings.	Royal Library, Windsor	1489–1516

2. CONCORDANCE OF AP NUMBERS

Anthony Panzera AP #	Richter R #	Notebook/Page Catalogue #	*Quaderni d'Anatomia* Folio #
101	316	W. 12601	Folio 1 R
102	320	Trn. 15576a, b	
103	315	V. Inv. 236r, 236v frame 33	
104	319	Trn. 15574	
105	312	A. 63a	
106	318	W. 12607	Folio 2 R
107	313	W. 12606	Folio 3 R
108	317	W. 19134–19135	Folio 10 R I, III
109	320	Trn. 15576	
109	310	W. 12304	Folio 4 R 2
109	311	A. 62b	
110	314	W. 19136–19139b	Folio 11 V III
111	310	W. 12304	Folio 4 R 1, 4, 3, 5
112	310	W. 12304	Folio 4 R 6, 12, 6, 11
113	325	W. 19131b	Folio 7 V
114	No R#	W. 19136–19139a	Folio 11 R I
115	310	W. 12304	Folio 4 R 7,8
116	321	W. 19129	Folio 5 R II, III
121	342	W. 19136–19139a	Folio 11 R VIII
122	342	W. 19136–19139a	Folio 11 R II, III
123	333	W. 19132b	Folio 8 V II
124	341	W. 19134–19135	Folio 10 R II
124	339	W. 19136–19139a	Folio 11 R VII
125	334	W. 19130a	Folio 6 R III
126	335	W. 19130b	Folio 6 V I
127	337	W. 12304	Folio 4 R 13
141	333	W. 19132b	Folio 8 V I
142	339	W. 19136–19139a	Folio 11 R VII
143	332	W. 19132a	Folio 8 R I
144	332	W. 19132a	Folio 8 R II
145	317	W. 19134-19135	Folio 10 R I
146	309	C.A. 160a (430a)	
147	No R#	W. 12632	Folio 14 R
148	No R#	W. 12632	Folio 14 R
149	343	V. Inv. 228 frame 29	
150	340	C.A. 358a (994a)	

2. CONCORDANCE OF AP NUMBERS (CONTINUED)

Anthony Panzera AP #	Richter R #	Notebook/Page Catalogue #	*Quaderni d'Anatomia* Folio #
150	341	W. 19134–19135	Folio 10 R I, II
151	308	H. 31b	
152	336	W. 19134–19135	Folio 10 R XI
153	334	W. 19130a	Folio 6 R I, II
154	338	W. 19136–19139b	Folio 11 V V
161	335	W. 19130b	Folio 6 V II
162	331	W. 19140	Folio 12 R I, II
163	331	W. 19140	Folio 12 R III, IV
164	329	B. 3b	
164	330	W. 19136–19139b	Folio 11 V II
165	328	W. 19136–19139b	Folio 11 V IV, VI
166	328	W. 19136–19139b	Folio 11 V VIII
167	323	W. 19140	Folio 12 R VI
168	322	W. 19133b	Folio 9, V I, II
169	324	W. 19133a	Folio 9 R I, III, IX, V
170	324	W. 19133a	Folio 9 R VI, VII
171	324	W. 19133a	Folio 9 R X, XI
172	326	W. 19136–19139b	Folio 11 V I
173	327	W. 19129	Folio 5 R I
174	331	W. 19140	Folio 12 R III
175	328	W. 19136–19139b	Folio 11 V X
181	349	W. 19136–19139a	Folio 11 R VI
182	345	W. 19140	Folio 12 R II, V
183	344	B.N. 2038. 23b Ash. II	
183	346	B. 3b	
184	348	W. 19134–19135	Folio 10 R XIII
185	347	W. 19131a	Folio 7 R I
186	347	W. 19131a	Folio 7 R II
187	348	W. 19134–19135	Folio 10 R XIV
188	348	W. 19134–19135	Folio 10 R XX
188	349	W. 19136–19139a	Folio 11 R IV, V
189	348	W. 19134–19135	Folio 10 R V
190	348	W. 19134–19135	Folio 10 R XVIII, XIX
191	324	W. 19133a	Folio 9 R X
192	349	W. 19136–19139a	Folio 11 R IV
193	348	W. 19134–19135	Folio 10 R IX, X

3. CONCORDANCE OF RICHTER NUMBERS

Anthony Panzera AP #	Richter R #	Notebook/Page Catalogue #	*Quaderni d'Anatomia* Folio #
151	308	H. 31b	
146	309	C.A. 160a (430a)	
109	310	W. 12304	Folio 4 R 2
111	310	W. 12304	Folio 4 R 1, 4, 3, 5
112	310	W. 12304	Folio 4 R 6, 12, 6, 11
115	310	W. 12304	Folio 4 R 7, 8
109	311	A. 62b	
105	312	A. 63a	
107	313	W. 12606	Folio 3 R
110	314	W. 19136–19139b	Folio 11 V III
103	315	V. Inv. 236r, 236v frame 33	
101	316	W. 12601	Folio 1 R
108	317	W. 19134–19135	Folio 10 R I, III
145	317	W. 19134–19135	Folio 10 R I
106	318	W. 12607	Folio 2 R
104	319	Trn. 15574	
109	320	Trn. 15576	
102	320	Trn. 15576a, b	
116	321	W. 19129	Folio 5 R II, III
168	322	W. 19133b	Folio 9 V I, II
167	323	W. 19140	Folio 12 R VI
169	324	W. 19133a	Folio 9 R I, III, IX, V
170	324	W. 19133a	Folio 9 R VI, VII
171	324	W. 19133a	Folio 9 R X, XI
191	324	W. 19133a	Folio 9 R X
113	325	W. 19131b	Folio 7 V
172	326	W. 19136–19139b	Folio 11 V I
173	327	W. 19129	Folio 5 R I
175	328	W. 19136–19139b	Folio 11 V X
165	328	W. 19136–19139b	Folio 11 V IV, VI
166	328	W. 19136–19139b	Folio 11 V VIII
164	329	B. 3b	
164	330	W. 19136–19139b	Folio 11 V II
174	331	W. 19140	Folio 12 R III
162	331	W. 19140	Folio 12 R I, II
163	331	W. 19140	Folio 12 R III, IV

3. CONCORDANCE OF RICHTER NUMBERS (CONTINUED)

Anthony Panzera AP #	Richter R #	Notebook/Page Catalogue #	*Quaderni d'Anatomia* Folio #
143	332	W. 19132a	Folio 8 R I
144	332	W. 19132a	Folio 8 R II
141	333	W. 19132b	Folio 8 V I
123	333	W. 19132b	Folio 8 V II
153	334	W. 19130a	Folio 6 R I, II
125	334	W. 19130a	Folio 6 R III
126	335	W. 19130b	Folio 6 V I
161	335	W. 19130b	Folio 6 V II
152	336	W. 19134-19135	Folio 10 R XI
127	337	W. 12304	Folio 4 R 13
154	338	W. 19136-19139b	Folio 11 V V
124	339	W. 19136-19139a	Folio 11 R VII
142	339	W. 19136-19139a	Folio 11 R VII
150	340	C.A. 358a (994a)	
124	341	W. 19134-19135	Folio 10 R II
150	341	W. 19134-19135	Folio 10 R I, II
121	342	W. 19136-19139a	Folio 11 R VIII
122	342	W. 19136-19139a	Folio 11 R II, III
149	343	V. Inv. 228 frame 29	
183	344	B.N. 2038. 23b Ash. II	
182	345	W. 19140	Folio 12 R II, V
183	346	B. 3b	
185	347	W. 19131a	Folio 7 R I
186	347	W. 19131a	Folio 7 R II
184	348	W. 19134-19135	Folio 10 R XIII
187	348	W. 19134-19135	Folio 10 R XIV
188	348	W. 19134-19135	Folio 10 R XX
189	348	W. 19134-19135	Folio 10 R V
190	348	W. 19134-19135	Folio 10 R XVIII, XIX
193	348	W. 19134-19135a	Folio 10 Recto IX, X
181	349	W. 19136-19139a	Folio 11 R VI
188	349	W. 19136-19139a	Folio 11 R IV, V
192	349	W. 19136-19139a	Folio 11 R IV
114	No R#	W. 19136-19139a	Folio 11 R I
147	No R#	W. 12632	Folio 14 R
148	No R#	W. 12632	Folio 14 R

4. CONCORDANCE OF NOTEBOOK NUMBERS

Anthony Panzera AP #	Richter R #	Notebook/Page Catalogue #	*Quaderni d'Anatomia* Folio #
109	311	A. 62b	
105	312	A. 63a	
164	329	B. 3b	
183	346	B. 3b	
183	344	B.N. 2038. 23b Ash. II	
146	309	C.A. 160a (430a)	
150	340	C.A. 358a (994a)	
151	308	H. 31b	
104	319	Trn. 15574	
109	320	Trn. 15576	
102	320	Trn. 15576a, b	
149	343	V. Inv. 228 frame 29	
103	315	V. Inv. 236r, 236v frame 33	
109	310	W. 12304	Folio 4 R 2
111	310	W. 12304	Folio 4 R 1, 4, 3, 5
112	310	W. 12304	Folio 4 R 6, 12, 6, 11
115	310	W. 12304	Folio 4 R 7, 8
127	337	W. 12304	Folio 4 R 13
101	316	W. 12601	Folio 1 R
107	313	W. 12606	Folio 3 R
106	318	W. 12607	Folio 2 R
147	No R#	W. 12632	Folio 14 R
148	No R#	W. 12632	Folio 14 R
116	321	W. 19129	Folio 5 R II, III
173	327	W. 19129	Folio 5 R I
153	334	W. 19130a	Folio 6 R I, II
125	334	W. 19130a	Folio 6 R III
126	335	W. 19130b	Folio 6 V I
161	335	W. 19130b	Folio 6 V II
185	347	W. 19131a	Folio 7 R I
186	347	W. 19131a	Folio 7 R II
113	325	W. 19131b	Folio 7 V
143	332	W. 19132a	Folio 8 R I
144	332	W. 19132a	Folio 8 R II
141	333	W. 19132b	Folio 8 V I
123	333	W. 19132b	Folio 8 V II

4. CONCORDANCE OF NOTEBOOK NUMBERS (CONTINUED)

Anthony Panzera AP #	Richter R #	Notebook/Page Catalogue #	*Quaderni d'Anatomia* Folio #
169	324	W. 19133a	Folio 9 R I, III, IX, V
170	324	W. 19133a	Folio 9 R VI, VII
171	324	W. 19133a	Folio 9 R X, XI
191	324	W. 19133a	Folio 9 R X
168	322	W. 19133b	Folio 9 V I, II
108	317	W. 19134–19135	Folio 10 R I, III
145	317	W. 19134–19135	Folio 10 R I
152	336	W. 19134–19135	Folio 10 R XI
124	341	W. 19134–19135	Folio 10 R II
150	341	W. 19134–19135	Folio 10 R I, II
184	348	W. 19134–19135	Folio 10 R XIII
187	348	W. 19134–19135	Folio 10 R XIV
188	348	W. 19134–19135	Folio 10 R XX
189	348	W. 19134–19135	Folio 10 R V
190	348	W. 19134–19135	Folio 10 R XVIII, XIX
193	348	W. 19134–19135	Folio 10 R IX, X
181	349	W. 19136–19139a	Folio 11 R VI
188	349	W. 19136–19139a	Folio 11 R IV, V
192	349	W. 19136–19139a	Folio 11 R IV
124	339	W. 19136–19139a	Folio 11 R VII
142	339	W. 19136–19139a	Folio 11 R VII
121	342	W. 19136–19139a	Folio 11 R VIII
122	342	W. 19136–19139a	Folio 11 R II, III
114	No R#	W. 19136–19139a	Folio 11 R I
172	326	W. 19136–19139b	Folio 11 V I
175	328	W. 19136–19139b	Folio 11 V X
165	328	W. 19136–19139b	Folio 11 V IV, VI
166	328	W. 19136–19139b	Folio 11 V VIII
164	330	W. 19136–19139b	Folio 11 V II
110	314	W. 19136–19139b	Folio 11 V III
154	338	W. 19136–19139b	Folio 11 V V
174	331	W. 19140	Folio 12 R III
162	331	W. 19140	Folio 12 R I, II
163	331	W. 19140	Folio 12 R III, IV
182	345	W. 19140	Folio 12 R II, V
167	323	W. 19140	Folio 12 R VI

5. CONCORDANCE OF *QUADERNI* NUMBERS

Anthony Panzera AP #	Richter R #	Notebook/Page Catalogue #	*Quaderni d'Anatomia* Folio #
109	311	A. 62b	
105	312	A. 63a	
164	329	B. 3b	
183	346	B. 3b	
183	344	B.N. 2038. 23b Ash. II	
146	309	C.A. 160a (430a)	
150	340	C.A. 358a (994a)	
151	308	H. 31b	
104	319	Trn. 15574	
109	320	Trn. 15576	
102	320	Trn. 15576a, b	
149	343	V. Inv. 228 frame 29	
103	315	V. Inv. 236r, 236v frame 33	
101	316	W. 12601	Folio 1 R
106	318	W. 12607	Folio 2 R
107	313	W. 12606	Folio 3 R
109	310	W. 12304	Folio 4 R 2
111	310	W. 12304	Folio 4 R 1, 4, 3, 5
112	310	W. 12304	Folio 4 R 6, 12, 6, 11
115	310	W. 12304	Folio 4 R 7, 8
127	337	W. 12304	Folio 4 R 13
173	327	W. 19129	Folio 5 R I
116	321	W. 19129	Folio 5 R II, III
153	334	W. 19130a	Folio 6 R I, II
125	334	W. 19130a	Folio 6 R III
126	335	W. 19130b	Folio 6 V I
161	335	W. 19130b	Folio 6 V II
185	347	W. 19131a	Folio 7 R I
186	347	W. 19131a	Folio 7 R II
113	325	W. 19131b	Folio 7 V
143	332	W. 19132a	Folio 8 R I
144	332	W. 19132a	Folio 8 R II
141	333	W. 19132b	Folio 8 V I
123	333	W. 19132b	Folio 8 V II
169	324	W. 19133a	Folio 9 R I, III, IX, V
170	324	W. 19133a	Folio 9 R VI, VII

5. CONCORDANCE OF *QUADERNI* NUMBERS (CONTINUED)

Anthony Panzera AP #	Richter R #	Notebook/Page Catalogue #	*Quaderni d'Anatomia* Folio #
171	324	W. 19133a	Folio 9 R X, XI
191	324	W. 19133a	Folio 9 R X
168	322	W. 19133b	Folio 9 V I, II
108	317	W. 19134–19135	Folio 10 R I, III
145	317	W. 19134–19135	Folio 10 R I
152	336	W. 19134–19135	Folio 10 R XI
124	341	W. 19134–19135	Folio 10 R II
150	341	W. 19134–19135	Folio 10 R I, II
184	348	W. 19134–19135	Folio 10 R XIII
187	348	W. 19134–19135	Folio 10 R XIV
188	348	W. 19134–19135	Folio 10 R XX
189	348	W. 19134–19135	Folio 10 R V
190	348	W. 19134–19135	Folio 10 R XVIII, XIX
193	348	W. 19134–19135	Folio 10 R IX, X
114	No R#	W. 19136–19139a	Folio 11 R I
122	342	W. 19136–19139a	Folio 11 R II, III
192	349	W. 19136–19139a	Folio 11 R IV
181	349	W. 19136–19139a	Folio 11 R VI
188	349	W. 19136–19139a	Folio 11 R IV, V
124	339	W. 19136–19139a	Folio 11 R VII
142	339	W. 19136–19139a	Folio 11 R VII
121	342	W. 19136–19139a	Folio 11 R VIII
172	326	W. 19136–19139b	Folio 11 V I
164	330	W. 19136–19139b	Folio 11 V II
110	314	W. 19136–19139b	Folio 11 V III
165	328	W. 19136 19139b	Folio 11 V IV, VI
154	338	W. 19136–19139b	Folio 11 V V
166	328	W. 19136–19139b	Folio 11 V VIII
175	328	W. 19136–19139b	Folio 11 V X
162	331	W. 19140	Folio 12 R I, II
182	345	W. 19140	Folio 12 R II, V
174	331	W. 19140	Folio 12 R III
163	331	W. 19140	Folio 12 R III, IV
167	323	W. 19140	Folio 12 R VI
147	No R#	W. 12632	Folio 14 R
148	No R#	W. 12632	Folio 14 R

BIBLIOGRAPHY

Ackerman, Gerald M. "Lomazzo's Treatise On Painting." *The Art Bulletin* 49 (1967): 317–327.

Alberti, Leon Battista. *On the Art of Building in Ten Books.* Trans. Joseph Rykwert, Neil Leach, Robert Tavernor. Cambridge: The MIT Press, 1988.

Andres, Glenn, John M. Hunisak, and A. Richard Turner. *The Art of Florence.* 2 vols. New York: Abbeville Press, 1988.

Arano, Luisa Cogiati. *Leonardo: Disegni di Leonardo e Della Sua Cerchia Alle Gallerie dell' Academia.* Venezia, Galleie dell'Academia. Exhibition catalogue. Milan: Electra Editrice, 1980.

Bambach, Carmen C., ed. *Leonardo da Vinci Master Draftsman.* Exhibition catalogue. The Metropolitan Museum of Art, New Haven and London: Yale University Press, 2003.

Barcsay, Jeno. *Anatomy for the Artist.* London: Octopus Books, 1973.

Baxandall, Michael. *Painting and Experience in Fifteenth-Century Italy.* 2nd ed. New York: Oxford University Press, 1972.

Baxandall, Michael. *Shadows and Enlightenment.* New Haven: Yale University Press, 1995.

Beck, James. *Leonardo's Rules of Painting: An Unconventional Approach to Modern Art.* New York: The Viking Press, 1979.

Boime, Albert. *Strictly Academic: Life Drawing in the Nineteenth Century.* Exhibition catalogue. Binghamton: University Art Gallery, 1974.

Borsook, Eve. *The Companion Guide to Florence.* London: Fontana Collins, 1973.

Bramly, Serge. *Leonardo: Discovering the Life of Leonardo da Vinci. Biography.* Translated by Sian Reynolds. New York: Edward Burlingame Books, Imprint of Harper Collins, 1991

Cennini, Cennino d'Andrea. *The Craftsman's Handbook: 'Il Libro dell' Arte.'* Trans. Daniel V. Thompson, Jr. New York: Dover Publications, 1960.

Chastel, Andre. *Studios and Styles of the Italian Renaissance.* Translated by Jonathan Griffin. New York: Odyssey Books, 1966.

Chastel, Andre. *The Genius of Leonardo da Vinci.* New York: Orian Press, 1961.

Clark, Kenneth. *Leonardo da Vinci: An Account of His Development as an Artist.* New York: Penguin Books, 1982.

Clark, Kenneth. *The Nude: A Study in Ideal Form.* Bollingen Series XXXV. 2. Princeton: Princeton University Press, 1990.

Clayton, Martin. *Leonardo da Vinci: One Hundred Drawings from the Collection of Her Majesty the Queen.* Exhibition catalogue. London: Merrell Holberton Publishers, 1996.

Clayton, Martin. *Leonardo da Vinci: The Anatomy of Man.* Commentary by Ron Philo. Houston: Bulfinch P, 1992.

Conant, Kenneth J. "The After-Life of Vitruvius in the Middle Ages." *Journal of the Society of Architectural Historians* 27, no. 1 (March 1968): 33–38.

Da Vinci, Leonardo. *Quaderni d'Anatomia. Twenty-three Sheets From the Royal Library at Windsor Castle.* Vol. VI, Compiled by Ove C. L. Vangensten, A. Fonahn, and H. Hoptock. Christiania: Casa Editrice Jacob Dybwad, 1916.

Da Vinci, Leonardo. *I Manoscritti dell'Institut de France / Leonardo da Vinci.* Edizione in fascimilie sotto gli auspice della Commissione Nazionale Vincianna e dell'Institut de France. Trascrizione diplomatic e critica di Augusto Marinoni. Firenze: Giunti Barbera, 1986–1990, Ms. A., 62b, 63a; Ms. B, 3a, 3b; Ms. B N 2038, 23b (Ash. I).

Da Vinci, Leonardo. *Il Codice Atlantico della Biblioteca Ambrosiana di Milano.* Trascrizione diplomatica e critica di Augusto Marinoni. Firenze: Giunti Barbera, 1975–1980, C.A., 403r (160a), and C.A., 994r (358a).

Da Vinci, Leonardo. *The Codex Atlanticus of Leonardo da Vinci: A Catalogue of Its Newly Restored Sheets.* Carlo Pedretti. Firenze: Giunti Barbera, Johnson Reprint Corporation, 1973–1975, 12 volumes numbered codex leaves transcribed in each volume correspond to the numbered plates in each of the respective facsimile volumes.

Dürer, Albrecht. *The Human Figure: The Complete Dresden Sketchbook.* Edited and translated by Walter L. Strauss. New York: Dover Publications, 1972.

Fahy, Everett. *The Legacy of Leonardo: Italian Renaissance Paintings from Leningrad.* New York: M. Knoedler & Co., 1979.

Farago, Claire. *Leonardo da Vinci: Codex Leicester, a Masterpiece of Science.* Introduction by Martin Kemp, Owen Gingerich, Carlo Pedretti. New York: American Museum of Natural History, 1996.

Freud, Sigmund. *Leonardo da Vinci and a Memory of His Childhood.* Trans. Alan Tyson. New York: W.W. Norton and Co., 1964.

Gardner, Helen. *Art Through the Ages.* Edited by Frank Kleiner, Christian Mamiya, Richard Tansey. 11th ed. Belmont, Calif.: Thomson Wadsworth, 2001.

Goldstein, Carl. "Vasari and the Florentine Accademia del Disegno." *Zeitschrift für Kunstgeschichte* 38 Bd., H. 2. (1975): 145–152.

Gould, Cecil. *Leonardo: The Artist and the Non-Artist.* Boston: New York Graphic Society, 1975.

Hale, Robert Beverly, and Terence Coyle. *Anatomy Lessons from the Great Masters.* New York: Watson-Guptill Publications, 1977.

Hartt, Frederick. *History of Italian Renaissance Art.* 3rd ed. New York: Harry N. Abrams, 1987.

Holt, Elizabeth Gilmore, ed. *Literary Sources of Art History: An Anthology of Texts from Theophilus to Goethe.* Princeton: Princeton University Press, 1947.

Janson, H.W. *History of Art.* New York: Harry N. Abrams, 1966.

Keele, Kenneth D. *Leonardo da Vinci: Anatomical Drawings from the Royal Collection, Windsor Castle.* Exhibition catalogue. Introduction by Carlo Pedretti. Firenze: Casa Editrice Giunti Barbera, 1979.

Kelen, Emery, ed. *Leonardo da Vinci's Advice to Artists.* Philadelphia: Running Press, 1990.

Kemp, Martin. *Leonardo.* New York: Oxford University Press, 2004.

Kemp, Martin, ed. *Leonardo on Painting*. Translated by Martin Kemp and Margaret Walker. New Haven: Yale University Press, 1989.

Kemp, Martin, Jane Roberts, and Philip Steadman. *Leonardo da Vinci*. London: Yale University Press with the South Bank Center, 1989.

Kemp, Martin. *Leonardo da Vinci: Experience, Experiment and Design*. Exhibition catalogue. London: V&A Publications, 2006.

Krautheimer, Richard. "Alberti and Vitruvius." *The Renaissance and Mannerism, Studies in Western Art, Acts of the Twentieth International Congress of the History of Art 2.* (1963): 42–52.

Krinsky, Carol Herselle. "Seventy-Eight Vitruvian Manuscripts." *Journal of the Warburg and Courtauld Institutes* 30 (1967): 36–70.

Kruft, Hanns-Walter. *A History of Archifectual Theory from Vitruvius to the Present*. Princeton: Architectural Press, 1994.

Laurenza, Domenico. "The Vitruvian Man by Leonardo: Image and Text." *Quaderni d' Italianistica* XXVII, no. 2 (2006): 37–56.

Livio, Mario. *The Golden Ratio: The Story of Phi, the World's Most Astonishing Number*. New York: Broadway Books, 2002.

MacCurdy, Edward, ed. *The Notebooks of Leonardo da Vinci*. 2 vols. New York: Reynal and Hitchcock, 1938.

Mayor, A. Hyatt. *Artists and Anatomists*. New York: The Artist's Limited Edition in Association with the Metropolitan Museum of Art, 1984.

Morselli, Piero. *"The Proportions of Ghiberti's Saint Stephen: Vitruvius' De Architectura and Alberti's De Statua."* The Art Bulletin 60, no. 2 (June 1978): 235–241.

Mundy, E. James. *Renaissance into Baroque: Italian Master Drawings by the Zuccari 1550–1600*. Exhibition catalogue. Milwaukee: Bulfin Printers,1989.

Nicholl, Charles. *Leonardo da Vinci: Flights of the Mind*. New York: Penguin Group, 2004.

O'Malley, Charles D., and J. B. de C. M. Saunders, eds. *Leonardo da Vinci on The Human Body*. New York: Crown Publishers, 1982.

O'Neill, John P., and Polly Cone, eds. *Leonardo da Vinci: Anatomical Drawings, from the Royal Library Windsor Castle*. Exhibition catalogue. New York: The Metropolitan Museum of Art, 1983.

Orlandi, Enzo, ed. *The Life, Times and Art of Leonardo*. Translated by C.J. Richards. New York: Crescent Books, 1965.

Ottino della Chiesa, Angela. *The Complete Paintings of Leonardo da Vinci*. Introduction by L.D. Ettlinger. 1969. Harmondsworth: Penguin Books, 1985.

Pedretti, Carlo. *Leonardo da Vinci on Painting, a Lost Book (Libro A)*. Reassembled from the Codex Vaticanus Urbinas 1270 and from the Codex Leicester. Foreword by Sir Kenneth Clark. Berkeley and Los Angeles: University of California Press, 1964.

Pedretti, Carlo. *The Literary Works of Leonardo da Vinci*. Compiled and Edited from the Original Manuscripts by John Paul Richter. Commentary by Carlo Pedretti. Two volumes. Berkeley and Los Angeles: University of California Press, 1977.

Pedretti, Carlo. *Leonardo da Vinci: Nature Studies from the Royal Library at Windsor Castle*. Catalogue. Introduction by Kenneth Clark. Florence, Italy: Giunti Barbera, Johnson Reprint, 1980.

Pedretti, Carlo. *Leonardo: A Study in Chronology and Style*. New York: Johnson Reprint, 1982.

Pedretti, Carlo. *Leonardo's Horses: Studies of Horses and Other Animals by Leonardo da Vinci from the Royal Library at Windsor Castle*. Introduction by Jane Roberts. Exhibition catalogue. Giunti Barbera Editore. New York: Harcourt Brace Jovanovich, 1984.

Pevsner, Nikolaus. *Academies of Art, Past and Present*. New York: Da Capo Press, 1973.

Pomilio, Mario, ed. *L'opera Completa di Leonardo Pittore*. Milano: Rizzoli Editore, 1967.

Popham, A. E. Introduction and Notes. *The Drawings of Leonardo da Vinci*. New York: Reynal and Hitchcock, 1945.

Posner, Donald. *Annibale Carracci*. vol. 1. New York: Phaidon, 1971.

Richer, Dr. Paul. *Artistic Anatomy*. Translated by Robert Beverly Hale. New York: Watson-Guptill Publications, 1971.

Richter, J. P. *The Literary Works of Leonardo da Vinci: Compiled and Edited from the Original Manuscripts*. 2 vols. London: Low, Marsten, Seale, and Rivington, 1883.

Richter, J. P. *The Literary Works of Leonardo da Vinci*. Two Volumes. (Unabridged edition first published in London, 1883). New York: Dover Edition, 1970.

Richter, J. P., and Irma A. Richter, enlarged and revised. *The Literary Works of Leonardo da Vinci*. Two Volumes. 3rd ed. New York: Phaidon, 1970.

Schaar, Eckhard. "A Newly Discovered Proportional Study by Dürer in Hamburg." *Master Drawings* 36, no. 1. (Spring 1998): 59–66.

Smith, Thomas Gordon. *Vitruvius on Architecture*. New York: Monacelli Press, 2003.

Starnazzi, Carlo. *Codices and Machines*. Foreward by Carlo Pedretti. Florence: Cartei & Bianchi Editors, 2005.

Steinberg, Leo. *Leonardo's Incessant Last Supper*. New York: Zone Books, 2001.

Steinitz, Kate Trauman. *Leonardo da Vinci's Trattato della Pittura, Treatise on Painting*. Copenhagen: Munksgaard, 1958.

Strauss, Monica. *Leonardo da Vinci*. New York: The Artist's Limited Edition, 1984.

Vasari, Giorgio. *The Lives of the Artists*. Translated by George Bull. Baltimore: Penguin Books, 1965.

Vasari, Giorgio. *Vasari on Technique*. Translated by G. Baldwin Brown. London: J. M. Dent & Company, 1907.

Marcus Vitruvius Pollio. *The Ten Books on Architecture*. Translated by Morris Hicky Morgan, PH.D., Ll.D. New York: Dover Publications, 1960.

Wallace, Robert. *The World of Leonardo: 1452–1519*. New York: Time-Life Books, 1966.

Wehlte, Kurt. *The Materials and Techniques of Painting*. Translated by Ursus Dix. New York: Van Nostrand Reinhold, 1982.

Winternitz, Emanuel. *Leonardo da Vinci as a Musician*. New Haven: Yale U P, 1982.

Wittkower, R. "Brunelleschi and 'Proportion in Perspective.'" *Journal of the Warburg and Courtauld Institutes* 16, no. 3/4 (1953): 275–291.

Wolf, Alice. "Jacopo de'Barbari's Apollo and Durer's Early Male Proportion Figures." *The Art Bulletin* 25, no. 4 (Dec. 1943): 363–365.

Zollner, Frank. *Leonardo da Vinci 1452–1519: The Complete Paintings and Drawings*. London: Taschen, 2005.

Notes
Part Six. Appendices

[129] Richter, *The Literary Works of Leonardo da Vinci*, vol. II, R 1173, 244.